"How can psychoanalysis be a researc
generalizing one, but a particularizing (
and convey complexity? Michael Ru
learned answers to this question. He shows how psychoanalysis does
generate knowledge and should respect its own methods of doing so.
Read him and learn!"

—**Anne Alvarez, PhD, MACP**, Consultant Child and
Adolescent Psychotherapist

"Michael Rustin is an outstanding contributor to the development of
psychoanalytic studies, and author of several works of seminal importance in British sociology. In this lucid and rational book, he distils his
thinking from many years of teaching and scholarship to offer a persuasive defence of psychoanalysis as a rational and progressive social
science of huge cultural significance. The book is crucial reading for everyone interested in the standing of psychoanalysis as a human science."

—**Stephen Frosh**, Department of Psychosocial Studies,
Birkbeck, University of London, UK

"This is an impressive work. Rustin is uniquely equipped to show
how methods of research consistent with psychoanalytic approaches
can produce an objective body of knowledge. His book continues the
remarkable tradition of Jaspers and Ricoeur. It provides a great deal
of what researchers and mental health therapists will need to meet the
challenges of the future."

—**David Taylor**, psychoanalyst and Visiting Professor,
UCL Psychoanalysis Unit, UK

RESEARCHING THE UNCONSCIOUS

Researching the Unconscious provides an exposition of key issues in the philosophy and methods of the social sciences that are relevant to psychoanalysis, both as a clinical practice and as a human science.

These include the debates initiated by Thomas Kuhn's theory of scientific revolutions, the "actor-network theory" of Bruno Latour, the ideas of philosophical realism, distinctions between "meaningful" and "causal explanation", and the relevance of complexity theory and "part–whole analysis" to psychoanalysis. The book goes on to discuss specific forms and methods of psychoanalytic research, including the role of case studies, of outcome research, and of "grounded theory" as a key methodological resource, of which it provides a detailed example. The book concludes by outlining principles and methods for psychoanalytic research in the wider contexts of infant observational studies, society, and culture.

Michael Rustin provides a unifying account of the methodological principles that underlie the generation of knowledge in psychoanalysis, in the light of recent developments in the philosophy and sociology of science. In doing so, it provides a coherent rationale for psychoanalytic investigation, which will be of value to those pursuing research in this field.

Researching the Unconscious is unusual in its being based both on a deep understanding of and respect for psychoanalytic clinical practice and on its author's wider knowledge of the philosophy and sociology of science. It is unique in its comprehensive approach to the principles of psychoanalytic research.

Michael Rustin is a Professor of Sociology at the University of East London, UK. He has been a significant contributor to psychoanalytic debate over many years and is the author and editor of many books, including *The Good Society and the Inner World* (1991), *Reason and Unreason* (2001), and, with Margaret Rustin, *Mirror to Nature* (2002) and *Reading Klein* (2017). He has played a major role in the development of postgraduate and doctoral research at the Tavistock Clinic. He is an Associate of the British Psychoanalytical Society.

Tavistock Clinic Series

Margot Waddell, Jocelyn Catty, & Kate Stratton (Series Editors)

Recent titles in the Tavistock Clinic Series

RESEARCHING THE UNCONSCIOUS

Principles of Psychoanalytic Method

Michael Rustin

Routledge
Taylor & Francis Group

LONDON AND NEW YORK

First published 2019
by Routledge
2 Park Square, Milton Park, Abingdon, Oxon OX14 4RN

and by Routledge
52 Vanderbilt Avenue, New York, NY 10017

Routledge is an imprint of the Taylor & Francis Group, an informa business

© 2019 Michael Rustin

British Library Cataloguing in Publication Data
A catalogue record for this book is available from the British Library

Library of Congress Cataloging in Publication Data
Names: Rustin, Michael, author.
Title: Researching the unconscious : principles of psychoanalytic
    method / Michael Rustin.
Description: New York City : Routledge, 2019. |
Series: Tavistock clinic series | Includes bibliographical references and
    index.
Identifiers: LCCN 2018042267 (print) | LCCN 2018043194 (ebook) |
    ISBN 9780429020339 (Master) | ISBN 9780429671982 (Pdf) | ISBN
    9780429670497 (ePub) | ISBN 9780429669002 (Mobipocket) | ISBN
    9781138389199 (hardback : alk. paper) | ISBN 9781782204374 (pbk. :
    alk. paper) | ISBN 9780429020339 (ebk)
Subjects: LCSH: Psychoanalysis. | Subconsciousness. | Research—
    Methodology.
Classification: LCC BF175 (ebook) | LCC BF175 .R87 2019 (print) |
    DDC 150.19/5—dc23
LC record available at https://lccn.loc.gov/2018042267

ISBN: 978-1-138-38919-9 (hbk)
ISBN: 978-1-78220-437-4 (pbk)
ISBN: 978-0-429-02033-9 (ebk)

Typeset in Palatino
by Swales & Willis Ltd, Exeter, Devon, UK

In memory of my friends
Stuart Hall, Doreen Massey, and
Robin Murray

CONTENTS

SERIES EDITORS' PREFACE

Margot Waddell, Jocelyn Catty, and Kate Stratton

Since it was founded in 1920, the Tavistock Clinic—now the Tavistock and Portman NHS Foundation Trust—has developed a wide range of developmental approaches to mental health which have been strongly influenced by the ideas of psychoanalysis. It has also adopted systemic family therapy as a theoretical model and a clinical approach to family problems. The Tavistock is now one of the largest mental health training institutions in Britain. It teaches up to 600 students a year on postgraduate, doctoral, and qualifying courses in social work, systemic psychotherapy, psychology, psychiatry, nursing, and child, adolescent, and adult psychotherapy, along with 2,000 multidisciplinary clinicians, social workers, and teachers attending Continuing Professional Development courses and conferences on psychoanalytic observation, psychoanalytic thinking and management, and leadership in a range of clinical and community settings.

The Tavistock's philosophy aims at promoting therapeutic methods in mental health. Its work is based on the clinical expertise that is also the basis of its consultancy and research activities. The aim of this Series is to make available to the reading public the clinical, theoretical, and research work that is most influential at the Tavistock. The Series sets out new approaches in the understanding and treatment of psychological disturbance in children, adolescents, and adults, both as individuals and in families.

In *Researching the Unconscious: Principles of Psychoanalytic Method*, Michael Rustin draws on decades of experience as a sociologist, as a teacher and supervisor of psychoanalytic research, and as a passionate advocate of the psychoanalytic method. A central thread of his argument is that "psychoanalysis has constituted itself as a research programme from its beginnings in Freud's early work". As such, he states that it has developed "one of the most substantial paradigms of knowledge to have been created in the human sciences during the last 100 or more years". Professor Rustin traces the development of psychoanalysis as a method of scientific enquiry, examining and drawing on the philosophy and sociology of science to underpin his position: that "none of this development would have happened, nor would psychoanalysis have achieved its large influence in Western culture, if it had not always been a theoretically coherent and empirically grounded form of knowledge".

Making the case that it constitutes a distinctive field of knowledge, Rustin draws attention to the ways in which psychoanalysis, in examining the unconscious and the subjective, shares with other branches of science a recognition of "deep structures and their causal powers", along with subjective meanings. In so doing, he highlights the humanity in the debate: "it seems to be only when experiences compel individuals to recognize that they have states of mind that are deeply troubling to themselves and others, and that cannot be readily understood, that the idea of an unconscious mind is likely to gain acceptance" (chapter 4).

Turning to the particularities of psychoanalytic method, Rustin robustly defends the case study and its methodology against the charges of scientific inferiority by which it has been for so long beset. He returns to the notion of the "clinical fact", examined so productively by David Tuckett, Edna O'Shaughnessy, and others. Here he highlights the contribution of child psychotherapists to this scholarship, arguing that clinical facts "have their principal location in the transference–countertransference relationship of psychoanalytic practice".

Researching the Unconscious is a very significant contribution to debate about psychoanalytic research methodology and practice, one that continues to thrive despite the rise of so-called evidence-based practice, and defends it in the face of attacks from more positivist quarters. It does so graciously but firmly. Rather than launch a counter-attack, Rustin closely and fairly explores the merits and disadvantages of quantitative methods, such as the randomized controlled trial, examining three trials in particular in which the Tavistock has been closely involved. Yet he also gives a very clear exposition of observational methods in general and of grounded theory in particular, the latter being enlivened by examples of its practical use in relation to clinical

material. Finally, he turns to literature and art, posing questions about whether the psychoanalytic study of culture and its methods is "similar to or different from the psychoanalytic study of other phenomena or forms of life" (chapter 16).

The clinical encounter itself is never far from the surface of this book. Psychoanalysis and child psychotherapy as endeavours rooted in the human experience do not vanish, here, under the weight of methodological debate. Rustin argues, for instance, that the relationship between grounded theory and psychoanalysis has been facilitated by "the early commitment of psychoanalysts to the need for an open-ended responsiveness to clinical experience" (chapter 11). Rustin's contribution to psychoanalytic thinking—hitherto expressed in his extensive academic output, in his dual role as Professor of Sociology at the University of East London and Visiting Professor at the Tavistock and Portman NHS Trust, and in his role as the initiator of the Tavistock child psychotherapy doctoral programme—is developed and consolidated in this important new work.

ACKNOWLEDGEMENTS

I am grateful to the Tavistock's Child Psychotherapy programme for having allowed me to work with its students over this long period, and to its students for their interest in and contribution to this work. I would particularly thank the many students whose doctoral research theses I have supervised (not only in child psychotherapy, but also in social work and organizational consultancy). They have stimulated me to clarify and communicate the issues in question. I have been made to feel welcome by child psychotherapists in many contexts of their work, and also in recent years by Members of the British Psychoanalytical Society, who have given unusual opportunities to a non-clinician like me to attend and participate in their discussions.

I would like to thank Margot Waddell, Kate Stratton, and Jocelyn Catty, the editors of the admirable Tavistock Clinic Book Series (until recently jointly published with Karnac, now with Routledge), for their encouragement and help in the production of this book. My thanks are also due to Eric and Klara King, of Communication Crafts, and to Natalie Clark, of Swales & Willis, for their excellent editorial contribution.

Most of all, I must thank Margaret for her help, advice, and support in undertaking work in this field, in its several varieties and guises, over most of our adult lives. Without her involvement and love, none of this would have been possible at all.

PREFACE

This book has two principal origins. The first lies in my encounter, while I was working mainly in the field of sociology, with psychoanalysis as a field of knowledge and clinical practice. I was immensely impressed with the scope and power of the psychoanalytic paradigm, especially in the Kleinian variant to which I was most exposed. I came to believe that this model of understanding was comparable in its explanatory capabilities with the perspectives of sociology, to which I remain strongly committed. The fact that this psychoanalytic paradigm had sometimes been extended to the explanation of social phenomena (for example, in Freud's writing, and in the Tavistock Institute tradition of social science research) was an additional reason for my interest in it.

I also became close at this time to the clinical practice of child psychotherapy at the Tavistock Clinic, where Margaret Rustin (my wife) first trained and has since worked for the whole of her professional career. Although I have never trained as a clinician, I have been able to have an unusual degree of contact with the clinical work of child psychotherapists. My personal analysis gave another much-needed dimension to my understanding of this field, though this was different from an intellectual kind of engagement with it.

During the late 1980s, the Tavistock Clinic became interested in the idea of providing an academic accreditation, at postgraduate level, for its many educational programmes, in the field of psychoanalytic and systemic therapy, social work, and consultancy. The Faculty of Social Sciences at the University of East London, of which I was Dean for ten years, became a significant participant in this accreditation process, and this became an additional context for developing my understanding of the theory and practice of psychoanalysis. We developed, for example, a Master's course in Psychoanalytic Studies in which psychoanalytic infant observation, psychoanalytic theory, and many social and cultural applications of psychoanalytic ideas could be pursued: I have taught on this programme for more than 25 years since its inception. At a later stage I was fortunate to be made an Associate (academic) of the British Psychoanalytical Society and was for five years Chair of its Applied Section. This associate membership gave me invaluable access to the larger field of psychoanalysis.

However, more specific interests and concerns were also part of the origin of this book. It was decided in the context of the academic accreditation of Tavistock programmes to develop the long (2 + 4 years) clinical training of child psychotherapists as a professional doctorate, to include the preparation of a substantial research thesis. This programme (and others adjacent to it at the Tavistock) were unusual among professional doctorate programmes in then being configured as "research doctorates", framed to conform in many respects to the format and procedures of a PhD.

As a basis for this doctoral programme, it had to be determined how its field of research was to be defined. It was decided that the trainees' research should be integrated closely with their clinical learning and practice. The belief was that the programme was adding a dimension of systematic method and accountability to a clinical process that already had many of the attributes of research. The aim was to develop and extend the kinds of knowledge on which psychoanalytic child psychotherapy was firmly based. Child psychotherapists who had qualified in this programme were permitted (indeed encouraged) to undertake this research programme as a "top up" to their completed training, and this gave further substance to our model of the "clinical researcher".

I had responsibility for ten years for teaching the Philosophy and Methods of Psychoanalytic Research to students on the programme. I believed that understanding the nature of psychoanalytic knowledge and situating its knowledge-claims within the current field of debate in the philosophy and sociology of science were critical to their learning. The aim was to develop and enhance what I believed to be a long-standing and successful (although informal) "research programme" in psychoanalysis and child psychotherapy. Although many kinds of development of research methods were necessary and desirable—for example, in data analysis and in the measurement of treatment effectiveness—I believed that it was essential to this clinically based research programme that students should have an understanding of the fertility and validity of their own field of knowledge. Approximately 70 doctoral theses have been so far completed in this programme, many of which are accessible on-line. Findings from a selection of them will soon be published as a book in this series (M. E. Rustin & Rustin, forthcoming). This was the context in which this work evolved and is one of the purposes it aims to fulfil.

CHAPTER ONE

Introduction

The central presupposition of this book is that psychoanalysis has constituted itself as a research programme from its beginnings in Freud's early work, and as such has, during its history, achieved a remarkable development of theories, clinical techniques, and applications. These make up one of the most substantial paradigms of knowledge to have been created in the human sciences during the last 100 or more years.

The argument will be made that none of this development would have happened, nor would psychoanalysis have achieved its large influence in Western culture, if it had not always been a theoretically coherent and empirically grounded form of knowledge. Its methods of research have enabled new discoveries to be made, significant theoretical developments to take place, and valid and productive hypotheses to be distinguished from invalid and unproductive ones. The purpose of this book is to explicate and justify the methods of research on which psychoanalytic knowledge is based and to clarify its principles in order to further research in this field.

The advance of psychoanalytic knowledge and understanding has not been of a unified and linear kind, parallel to the triumphal progress that some attribute to the natural sciences. From the very beginning, in the work of Freud and his immediate circle, differences of approach were apparent, some of them leading to the enrichment of the central tendency of Freudian work, others to divergence and the development of separate schools of thought. Psychoanalytic work, since it is based on the study of and interaction with human subjects, has always been located in particular historical and social contexts. The different tendencies of psychoanalytic thought—for example, the Freudian, Object-Relations, Relational, and Lacanian schools—have been specifically shaped by their cultural and national locations. But such a diversity of theoretical approaches, values, and methods is also to be found in other fields of human knowledge—for example, in historiography, philosophy, sociology, and anthropology. By contrast, economics and psychology, in their dominant contemporary forms, are exceptional in the social sciences in the claims they make for the universal scope and applicability of their explanatory schema, which they sustain by excluding social particularities and differences from their modelling. The universalization and homogenization of their fields of study, as constituted by their rational, interest-seeking ideal-typical individuals, is perhaps more the prosecution of an ideological world view than a genuinely universal human science that is truly universal in its scope. This does not, of course, deny the power of neoclassical economists' and cognitive psychologists' theories and methods to explain the particular fields of phenomena that their models capture.

During most of its existence, psychoanalysis has been under attack as non-scientific, as "pseudo-scientific", or as largely out of touch with the mainstream of the social sciences. It has developed as a field largely outside the academic and university system, within the context of its practising professions. These have evolved their own systems of training, international conferences, and publication in scientific journals and books, which follow many of the norms and protocols of other scientific disciplines. It is through this substantial knowledge infrastructure that psychoanalysis has developed. Nevertheless, there is no doubt that the relative detachment of the psychoanalytic field from other fields in the academic human sciences has had its costs. Psychoanalysis has been unable to learn sufficiently from research in the psychological, biological, and social sciences, and these human sciences have found it difficult to take account of the reality and significance of unconscious phenomena for the mental lives of individuals and groups.

In recent years there has been some increased dialogue between some "mainstream" human sciences and psychoanalysis. One such bridge lies in the field of "attachment theory" developed by John Bowlby and his successors (Holmes, 2014), which, while absorbing some of the central insights of the psychoanalytic theory of infant development, nevertheless developed laboratory-based procedures to test and validate its hypotheses. It seems clear that the split that developed at one stage between attachment theory and psychoanalysis had limiting effects on the development of both fields. Its consequence was that psychoanalysts became further removed from empirical scientific procedures, and the attachment tradition lost contact with the subtleties of psychoanalytic theories and techniques and their relevance to clinical practice.

Advances in neuroscience have proved to be another source of interdisciplinary connection. They are bringing new kinds of evidence to support psychoanalytic conjectures derived from clinical inference—for example, regarding the functions of the affective centres of the brain and of dreams in shaping mental life. The demands of "evidence-based medicine", now widely imposed by public health systems on psychoanalytic practitioners, although often putting unduly restrictive pressures on the provision of good clinical services, have had positive as well as negative effects. They have required psychoanalysts and psychotherapists to provide empirically accountable answers to the crucial question, does psychoanalytic psychotherapy work? And if so, for whom, and at what cost, compared with other forms of treatment? Valuable work has followed from this, in empirical trials of psychoanalytic therapies, although it should be noted that the outcomes of these have often given quantitative validation to what psychoanalysts believed they already knew qualitatively from their clinical experience. Many researchers—philosophers, psychologists, psychoanalysts, and neuroscientists (for example, Antonio Damasio, 2000; Gerald Edelman, 1992; Peter Fonagy, 2001; Peter Fonagy & Mary Target, 2002; James Hopkins, 2004; Jaak Panksepp, 1998; Mark Solms, 2015; Allen Schore, 1994; Daniel Stern, 1985)—have contributed to this bridge-building, which greatly enhances the possibilities for psychoanalysis to take up its justified place within a more inclusive scientific discourse.

Nevertheless, this more active interchange between "mainstream" human science, with its accredited methods of research, and psychoanalytic practice is not without its risks. It could be that psychoanalytic practitioners and researchers will, in their pursuit of conventional scientific legitimation (and of authorization of their services by health commissioners), lose sight of the distinctive kinds of knowledge that their own psychoanalytic research tradition can produce. Psychoanalysts need a systemic understanding of their own established methods of knowledge-generation, and of its particular criteria of sense and validity, if their relationship with other human sciences is to take the form of dialogue and not become a mere surrender to positivism. The risk in the embrace of the conventional measures of empirical measures characteristic of mainstream psychology is that they will find themselves measuring something other than the essential objects of psychoanalytic study.

Plan of the book

Psychoanalysis as a distinctive form of knowledge

The argument of chapters 2 and 3 draws upon seminal works in the recent literature of the philosophy and sociology of science to establish the view that psychoanalysis constitutes a distinctive field of knowledge, with its own research methods and its own means of representing its findings. The developments in these fields that have been most essential in establishing the ontological and epistemological foundations of psychoanalysis are those of the historian and philosopher of science, Thomas Kuhn, and the anthropologist and sociologist of science, Bruno Latour: their relevance for the understanding of the psychoanalytic field is examined. Crucial in Kuhn's work (chapter 2) is his recognition of the diversity of scientific paradigms and the research methods on which their development is based. The misconception that there is but one scientific method, exemplified by physics, has provided influential but mistaken grounds for the rejection of psychoanalysis as a valid scientific practice. The significance of Bruno Latour's research (chapter 3) is his demonstration of the central importance of the laboratory as the location of transformative discoveries. When one recognizes that the clinical consulting room has some of the attributes of the scientific laboratory, one understands why this setting has been so productive of psychoanalytic knowledge.

Realism and social science

The science of the unconscious is, more or less by definition, a study of phenomena that lie beneath the surface of everyday perception and understanding. It is argued in chapter 4 that psychoanalysis is by no means unique as a form of knowledge in postulating underlying depths of phenomena that must be understood if the life-world of everyday experience is to be understood. This chapter draws on the "realist" theories of knowledge developed by Rom Harré, Roy Bhaskar, Russell Keat, and John Urry to locate psychoanalysis in a conception of scientific knowledge that recognizes the need for the understanding of deep structures and their causal powers, including those located in the unconscious mind.

Cause, meaning, and interpretation

The project, still influential, to assimilate the psychological and social sciences to the methods of the natural sciences has struggled with the fact that human experience is constituted through "subjective meanings"— that is, through the meanings assigned to phenomena by human persons. The natural sciences do not need to be concerned with dimensions of consciousness or "subjective" explanation in investigating their objects of study. A problem for the social sciences is to reconcile the idea that social phenomena must be conceived not only as entities in causal relations to the material world and to each other, but also as agents who interpret the world and act through their own understandings of it. If social behaviour is understood only in its "objective" aspects, the essence of human subjectivity and consciousness is lost. If, on the other hand, human life is understood only in the dimension of subjective meanings and intentions, causal relations and their determinations vanish from sight. Progress has been made in the social sciences in bringing together these two necessary forms of understanding—the "nomothetic" and "idiographic"—for example, in sociology, through the duality of structure and agency (Archer, 2003; Giddens, 1979, 1984).

Psychoanalysis brings an additional dimension to problems of causal and interpretative explanation of mental life. Central is the idea of unconscious meanings and intentions. These are states of mind and feeling that are influential in shaping human consciousness and action, but which cannot readily be recognized by their subjects. Unconscious meanings in the psychoanalytic sense do not go unrecognized merely because people have too little cognitive capacity to keep everything in mind. Implicit beliefs and rules of behaviour of this "ordinary" kind are the frequent field of study of historians and anthropologists. The psychoanalytic meaning of the unconscious—the "dynamic unconscious"—refers to states of mind understanding of which is resisted, through the operation of processes such as repression, splitting, and projective identification, as Freud, Klein and Bion described these. The problem for psychoanalysis has been to show how these unconscious dimensions of meaning can be captured, through observation and in transference–countertransference interactions, and theoretical inferences from these shown to be valid. Chapter 5 examines these issues.

Classifications and kinds

Psychoanalytic approaches are sometimes differentiated from those of medicine and psychiatry by their avoidance of schematic diagnostic categories, conventionally arrived at through clinical assessments that take place prior to treatments designed by reference to the problems they define. Psychiatric classification commonly takes the form of diagnostic categories, schematic differentiations of kinds of psychopathology, formulated in manuals intended to guide their practice, such as the *Diagnostic and Statistical Manual of Mental Disorders–5* (*DSM–5*) published by the American Psychiatric Association (APA, 2013), or the *ICD–10: Classification of Mental and Behavioural Disorders*, produced by the World Health Organization (WHO, 2016). By contrast, psychoanalytic therapy is usually particularistic and individual-centred in its approach. Psychoanalysts and psychotherapists often believe that useful diagnoses emerges mainly from what is learned during therapeutic practice itself, and that its agendas cannot be set in advance of its actual experience.

However, as chapter 6 shows, psychoanalysis has evolved elaborate forms of classification of its own, different from—though overlapping with—the diagnostic models of psychiatry. The structure of psychoanalytic theory depends on the classifications that it has itself evolved, which identify, for example, "kinds" of mental function, personality organization, developmental pathways, and psychopathology. The *DSM* diagnostic categories are largely a typology of symptoms, with little theoretical or explanatory rationale. The classifications of psychoanalysis, by contrast, derive from, and condense, the theoretical findings of its field. Clinical psychoanalytic practice involves a constant interchange between the meanings and patterns that are discerned in flows of clinical material, in their specificity, and in the concepts that locate such particulars within the frames of psychoanalytic theories. The specific nature and function of classification in psychoanalysis is considered.

Cases and case-study methods

The clinical case studies, which have been the most common form in which psychoanalysts have obtained and presented their findings, are sometimes dismissed as an inferior kind of research. There is a conventional hierarchy of scientific methods, in which the "double-blind randomized controlled trial" is positioned at the summit and the single clinical case study is relegated to the base. The argument of this book is that research methods need to be appropriate to their objects of study, and in this domain "one size does not fit all". Randomized controlled trials of the treatment outcomes have an essential value. But researches have more than one purpose. The principal objects of psychoanalytic investigation have been, for example, personality structures, psychopathologies, and therapeutic techniques, accomplished through the study of phenomena revealed principally in the context of the transference relationship. This constitutes a form of fundamental scientific research and is more than the study of the effects of specified treatment interventions, or "technologies".

Human minds have the attributes of both complexity and variety. For most purposes, they cannot be reduced to interactions between small numbers of uniform "variables", if one is to grasp the attributes of the individuals who are the centre of psychoanalytic inquiry. Case-study methods, discussed in chapter 7, have evolved to investigate entities that possess high degrees of both idiosyncrasy and complexity, such as the objects of inquiry of psychoanalysis.

Parts and wholes

What do we do when we seek an explanation in psychoanalysis? What is it to understand an aspect of behaviour? One common-sense idea is that what we do is to identify a phenomenon as the effect of a cause. Thus it is often appropriate, for example, to causally link the difficulties of patients with disturbances in their early life. But although such causal connections are well established and provide the context for the treatment of, for example, deprived children, they are insufficient to guide psychoanalytic practice.

Psychoanalysts understand specific states of mind in their patients by identifying patterns that give them meaning. Particular aspects of thought and behaviour are understood psychoanalytically with reference to a larger holistic structure of patients' minds. For sufficient understanding to be achieved, "parts" (e.g., symptomatic behaviours) need to be located in the context of relevant "wholes", which may well be the configuration of a patient's internal world. The psychoanalytic idea of "parts of the self" involves such states of intrinsic connectedness. There is a theory of part–whole relations in the human sciences (Capra, 1997; Scheff, 1997) that is relevant to understanding these psychoanalytic perspectives. The relevance of this model of explanation is explored in chapter 8.

Complexity

The emergence of the field of "complexity theory", discussed in chapter 9, has suggested new ways of understanding the mind and the psychoanalytic work of doing so. The central idea that has been found relevant to many objects of study in the natural and social sciences is that of self-organizing systems. The human mind is a prime example of a self-organizing structure, which has innate capacities for development and change but also depends on essential attributes of constancy. Different ideas developed within this perspective can enhance psychoanalytic understanding. For example, that a structure may reproduce itself at different scales (as "fractals"); that it may maintain continuity and coherence because of the existence of an attractive internal force ("strange attractors"); and that development may take the form of oscillating or bifurcating patterns set off by apparently insignificant or contingent events. It has been shown that each of these ideas, as well as the broader conception of complexity, can illuminate the understanding of persons, the unconscious mind, and clinical processes.

What is a clinical fact?

Arising from uncertainties and disputes about the nature of evidence in psychoanalysis, a symposium was published in the *International Journal of Psychoanalysis* (Tuckett, 1994a) to investigate whether psychoanalytic explanation could be established on a more solid empirical foundation. (These ideas are further developed in Tuckett, 2008.) The question was to see whether there was a kind of "fact", specific to psychoanalysis and its practice, by reference to which the validity of explanations could be tested. Were there "clinical facts" with a function in psychoanalysis parallel to the kinds of facts that are key points of reference in other scientific fields? The argument proposed in chapter 10, following the contributions of O'Shaughnessy and Quinodoz in the symposium, is that there are such clinical facts, and they have their principal location in the transference–countertransference relationship of psychoanalytic practice.

Grounded theory

The concerns about the adequacy of psychoanalytic methods of knowledge-generation, both within and outside the psychoanalytic field, that gave rise to the debate about "clinical facts", also gave rise to a search for procedures of data analysis that might enable these concerns to be addressed. The academic accreditation of psychoanalytic and psychotherapeutic training programmes at Masters and Doctoral level gave rise, in any case, to a need for the specification and justification of research methods comparable to those employed in other human sciences.

The methods of grounded theory originally devised in the field of sociology (Glaser & Strauss, 1967) and widely followed in the social sciences since then have proved to be well adapted to qualitative psychoanalytic research. (Interpretative Phenomenological Analysis [IPA]—whose origins lie in psychology—has served a similar purpose.) Grounded theory methods were designed to generate and analyse data of relatively unstructured kinds. Rather than conceiving research as the testing of hypotheses whose origin lay in systematic bodies of preconceived theory (which was the dominant sociological research paradigm of the time), the grounded theorists proposed that theories should emerge by "induction" (or in a more adequate formulation "abduction") from the data of observation and description itself, such as anthropologists often acquire in their field of study.

This conception that theoretical understanding best emerges from observations and interactions with subjects and environments, rather than mainly by theoretical deduction, has been found to have an exceptional correspondence with the practice of psychoanalysts. Especially in the clinically oriented British School of psychoanalysis, the idea that theoretical understanding should follow, not precede, experience has had great resonance. It has been shown that the procedures of clinical supervision in this tradition have a considerable affinity with the methods of data analysis of grounded theory. Both insist on the importance of grounding every theoretical conjecture or inference in relation to specific facts, such as the "clinical facts" discussed in chapter 10.

Chapter 11 describes the origins and development of the grounded theory method and its relevance to psychoanalytic research.

Grounded theory in practice

Chapter 12 follows the previous chapter's expositions of the principles and justifications of grounded theory with a detailed example of a grounded theory analysis of a clinical record of the kind commonly produced in child psychotherapy practice. The material in question is from a three-session psychoanalytic assessment of two children. The fact that this reports a complete clinical interaction, rather than being a segment of a longer treatment, may add to the transparency of the analysis. The tabular arrangement of the material, in rows and columns that display both the detailed narrative of the session itself (as recorded in process notes by the therapist) and successive levels of abstraction in its analysis, is intended to show how inferences regarding the unconscious meaning of the children's communications and enactments can be precisely grounded in particular moments and sequences of the assessment sessions.

Psychoanalytic observational methods

In recent decades, methods of systematic observation have been added to clinical practice as a context for psychoanalytic learning. The psychoanalytic observation of infants and children under five has been the main setting for this work. In addition, a form of psychoanalytic reflection on the workplace known as "work discussion" has been developed, in which the observer is, through his or her normal employment, an active participant in as well as an observer of relationships in a social situation. These observational methods have been devised primarily for purposes of training, education, and professional development. However, it has been found that the observational data generated through these practices can be a source of psychoanalytic knowledge. Chapter 13 describes these extensions to established methods of psychoanalytic research and disagreements that these have provoked.

Outcome studies in psychoanalysis

In the current climate of "evidence-based medicine", the demonstration of the effectiveness of psychoanalytic treatments has become a necessity for psychotherapists and psychoanalysts, especially within the public sector. Chapter 14 discusses what can and what cannot be learned from investigations of this kind, while acknowledging their significance, not only in regard to their primary evaluative purpose, but also because the data they generate is also of potential value for fundamental psychoanalytic research of qualitative kinds.

This chapter describes three major outcome studies in which the Tavistock and partner institutions have been involved—the Childhood Depression Study, the IMPACT Study of Severe Adolescent Depression, and the Tavistock Adult Depression Study (TADS). It demonstrates how significant these studies are both with regard to the recognition of psychoanalytic therapies within the National Health Service and because of the intrinsic interest of their findings.

Psychoanalytic research in wider social contexts

The final two chapters of this book consider the methods appropriate for psychoanalytic research, both in society and its institutions beyond the clinical setting, and in the fields of literature and the arts. Because of its boundaries and consistent setting, the consulting room has constituted, as we have said, the principal "laboratory" for research throughout the history of psychoanalysis. Society at large has provided few comparably structured locations for psychoanalytic study. In fact, few codified methods exist for the study of the unconscious in society. (A forthcoming volume, *Methods of Research: Applying Psychoanalytic Ideas to the Social Sciences*, edited by Kalina Stamenova and Robert Hinshelwood, explores these problems and proposes solutions to them.) Nevertheless, from Freud's writing onwards, such wider studies have been made, generating indispensable insights. How this has been accomplished is considered in chapter 15, focusing on the way in which instances of disturbing irrationality in society have been the principal occasion for psychoanalytic social analysis. Some broad principles of method are outlined to suggest how such psychoanalytic social research can be undertaken.

The psychoanalytic study of literature and art

The psychoanalytic study of literature and art shares with psychoanalytic social research, but to an even greater degree, a combination of remarkable interpretative achievements by many psychoanalysts and psychoanalytic writers from Freud onwards, with an absence of established methods of researching its field. In the academy and elsewhere, many different theoretical perspectives have been brought to bear on the interpretation of cultural artefacts. Some have proposed radical revisions of the established canons of cultural value—for example, from Marxist, post-colonial, or feminist points of view. The Lacanian psychoanalytic tradition, for instance through its idea of a repressive symbolic order, has been a resource for cultural critics who have sought to challenge dominant forms of representation from the position of subordinate or marginalized groups. Psychoanalytic criticism within the British object-relations tradition has been from a different position. Rather than seeking to challenge the criteria of evaluation of traditionally valued works of art and literature, its purpose and practice has, rather, been to deepen the understanding of their unconscious levels of meaning.

Works of literature and art that psychoanalytic writers seek to understand are already interpretations of reality, rather than, as is sometimes mistakenly assumed, unmediated reality itself.[1] Such works represent the intentions of artists and authors, expressed through conventions and genres that may themselves be the bearers of meaning. Only limited understanding of such works can be achieved if this level of complexity is unrecognized. Those who engage in the psychoanalytic interpretation of a cultural artefact are thus unavoidably (if sometimes unknowingly) engaged in a process of "double mediation": they are, interpreting what is already an artist's representation of an object or an experience.

Valuable insights into unconscious dimensions of reality have, however, been achieved through such interpretations, in particular where works already embody their creator's own implicit understanding of unconscious states of mind. In chapter 16, different kinds of psychoanalytic interpretation of literature and art are considered, and examples of such work and the insights that can emerge from are given.

These final chapters identify the difficulties and complications of the psychoanalytic study of society and culture, more than they propose precise rules and procedures to prescribe how this should be done.

Note

1. On this distinction, see Eagleton (2014).

CHAPTER TWO

Psychoanalysis as a scientific paradigm

If one types the words "psychoanalysis and "paradigm" into Google, more than 2 million "results" come up. The Psychoanalytic Electronic Publishing Website (PEP-Web) lists over a thousand publications with these words in their title. These figures testify to the fact that the term "paradigm", introduced into the field of the sciences by Thomas Kuhn in 1962, has achieved an extremely wide currency among psychoanalysts and is widely used by them when they write about their field. This chapter sets out to explain why this idea has been, and remains, such an influential one, and how it has made it easier for psychoanalysts to recognize their field as one in which authentic and productive scientific research can be done.

To understand this, it is necessary to understand an earlier context in which the claims of psychoanalysis to constitute a valid area of knowledge were strongly disputed, and that, as a consequence, the field was largely excluded from the broader field of science and the academy, not least in Britain. The principal object of study for psychoanalysis is, of course, unconscious mental life. This is where the main problem in the recognition of psychoanalysis has arisen. The idea that the unconscious mind even exists and is a proper field for investigation was, from the beginning when Freud began his revolutionary work, and is in many circles even today, a highly contested one. A long-standing scepticism about the validity of the theories and methods of psychoanalysis pervades the mainstream human sciences and contributes to its marginal position within them even now.

Among the most influential philosophical critics of psychoanalysis was the philosopher of science, Karl Popper, and his many followers. Popper's *Logic of Scientific Discovery* (1934) and his subsequent writings on political philosophy (*The Open Society and Its Enemies*, 1945; *The Poverty of Historicism*, 1957) outlined a model of scientific investigation in which it was held that science had advanced in a cumulative process, through combining theoretical conjectures with rigorous procedures of empirical trial, undertaken through observation and experiment. Popper rejected the inductive approach, and thus the positivism, of David Hume and many subsequent empiricists and positivists, in which scientific laws were understood to be mere inferences from the constant correlations of observed facts. The crucial connection between theories and facts was, in Popper's view, achieved through a procedure of "falsification". Scientific hypotheses proposed law-like relationships between specified variables—for example, between mass, velocity and distance in the laws of gravitation—and were validated not by accumulated instances of their predictive powers, but by the fact that their predictions and explanations could survive disconfirmation by empirical tests (such as scientific experiments) of their validity.

Popper's idea of science was a highly prescriptive and indeed political one, designed to invalidate and exclude what he deemed to be false claimants to the status of science, as well as to explain the nature of scientific achievement. The false claimants were those "pseudo-sciences" that claimed to have discovered scientific laws, but whose propositions failed his critical test of falsifiability. Among these rejected theoretical systems were those of Marx and Marxism, and of Freud and psychoanalysis. In the political sphere, Popper (1945) held that false claims to the justifications of reason, such as those of Plato, Hegel, and Marx, were liable to become legitimations of tyranny. His philosophy (Popper, 1957) contrasted "piecemeal" (based on trial and error—that is, empirical evidence) with "utopian" or "holistic" social engineering. Popper's model of science as a competition between rival systems of ideas whose resolution should depend only on the rigorous recourse to empirical evidence made an influential contribution to the liberal critique of totalitarian rule of both Fascist and Communist varieties, which dominated political debate during much of his working life.

Popper's specific critique of psychoanalysis was very briefly stated (Popper, 1963, pp. 34–38), but despite this, the broad influence of his "falsificationist" position on the critical reception of psychoanalysis was immense.[1] Popper believed Freud to be dismissive of the requirement that scientific hypotheses needed to be able to survive empirical tests of their validity. He held that Freudian "predictions" about the thoughts and actions of human beings were inherently ambiguous, such that if one expectation derived from them was shown to be inconsistent with observed facts, then grounds could be advanced why even its opposite might be true, thus "saving" the original hypothesis. (The idea of a "reaction formation" could be an instance of this, where love may be manifested as hatred, or the reverse.) There is confusion in this argument between the disregard of reason and logic, which Freud did indeed assign to the unconscious mind, and Freud's project to find rational law-like explanations, respectful of evidence, of how the unconscious mind actually functioned. The essence of Freud's scientific project was to bring the irrational into the domain of rational explanation.

Popper's most intellectually rigorous disciple, Adolf Grünbaum (1974, 1993) gave much more detailed attention to Freud's writing than Popper had done, in an industrious lifetime of scholarly work. He disagreed with Popper that Freud was indifferent to issues of scientific validity, recognizing that he was, indeed, committed to establishing the scientific claims of his new field. However, Grünbaum, applying Popper's criterion of "falsifiability" to Freud's ideas, argued that despite his scientific intentions, they nevertheless failed to survive this crucial test. It was untenable to believe, Grünbaum argued, that the validity of psychoanalytic hypotheses, presented to analysands as interpretations of their unconscious wishes or states of mind, could be validated by their acceptance of them. What Grünbaum termed the "tally principle" (accepted interpretations confirming the existence of unconscious facts) could provide neither evidence nor proof, because of the "suggestibility" of the analytic patient, who, Grünbaum held, would be all too likely, because of his or her relationship with the analyst, to agree with whatever the analyst proposed.[2]

Popper's theory of scientific knowledge has subsequently been shown, even by philosophers of science basically sympathetic to him, to have many flaws. Grünbaum has mainly conducted detailed critical exegeses of Freud's writings and has paid little attention to the subsequent development of psychoanalytic knowledge. Many of Freud's critics[3] have been excessively—even obsessively—fascinated by him and by his often misrepresented personal and professional history, at the expense of giving much attention either to his actual writings or to the large body of later psychoanalytic writing. Nevertheless, although many technical objections could be, and have been, made to the Popperian theory of scientific knowledge, a broad conception derived from it has continued to dominate the mainstream of the human sciences—especially the field of psychology, whose object of study might seem to be the closest to that of psychoanalysis. It is part of psychological, and even sociological, "common sense" that, although the ideas of psychoanalysis may be interesting and provoking, there is, after all, insufficient empirical evidence for them to be taken seriously.[4] The argument of this book, however, is that psychoanalysis in its intellectual development and practice has followed procedures, albeit often in an implicit way, that are consistent with Popper's most fundamental principle (more important than "falsificationism" per se), which is that the validity of scientific theories depends on their consistency with empirical evidence.

An interesting addition to Popper's critique of Freud was provided by the sociologist, Ernest Gellner. In *The Psychoanalytic Movement* (1985) Gellner attacked the cult-like character of the following and influence of psychoanalysis, arguing that while it had correctly recognized the problems brought about by irrationality in mental life, it failed (largely for the reasons suggested by Popper) to provide valid explanations of them. But ten years later Gellner (1995) saluted the way in which Freudian ideas had, after all, contributed greatly to human freedom and satisfaction by enabling burdens of sexual repression and religious superstition to be lifted. Thus Freud was recognized by Gellner as a significant contributor to the "Open Society".

From the 1960s onwards, there were major challenges to the philosophy or metatheory of science, which had rejected the claims of psychoanalysis as a form of scientific knowledge. These challenges have altered the environment of reception of psychoanalysis and make possible a new understanding of its actual and potential place within the human sciences.

Thomas Kuhn and scientific revolutions

The first of these challenges was Thomas Kuhn's *The Structure of Scientific Revolutions* (1962). This book initiated a new approach to the philosophy of science and to scientific method. Kuhn was a historian of science, as well as a philosophical analyst of its assumptions and procedures. His purpose was to describe and explain how the sciences had developed, not to define and prescribe universal and absolute criteria that could demarcate true from false sciences.[5]

Kuhn rejected the idea that science had developed as the linear advance of a unified corpus of knowledge of universal scope, taking place through a process of competition in which true theories about the phenomena of nature successively defeated and replaced false ones. Kuhn argued that what had taken place in the course of the history of science was, rather, that significant changes of perspective had taken place at certain moments, and that these had given rise to quite new ways of understanding the world. Kuhn described these new ways of seeing as "scientific revolutions", or "paradigm shifts", which he also referred to in psychological terms as "gestalt switches". The change from the Ptolemaic astronomical world-view (according to which the sun and the planets revolved round the earth) to the Copernican system (in which the earth and the other planets revolved round the sun) was one such paradigm shift. The changes from Aristotelian dynamics to Newtonian physics, from corpuscular optics to wave optics, and from a creationist to an evolutionary theory of the origin of species were others.

A scientific paradigm, for Kuhn, is an all-encompassing totality. He came to describe it (Kuhn, 1970, pp. 182–187) as a "disciplinary matrix", which is more than a specific theory. It defines its field of study, its key objects and entities, and its appropriate methods of research. It includes "law, theory, application, and instrumentation". Kuhn believed that a paradigm constructed a frame of investigation and, in doing so, constituted its particular domain of reality. Kuhn's model gave much more weight to the social construction of investigations by scientists, within their broader cultural environment, than was the case for standard empiricist models of science, in which the role of the scientist was to represent, with as little distortion as possible, the reality that existed "out there", independent of human understandings of it. Kuhn's world view was a sociologically informed, implicitly relativist one, although Kuhn was uncomfortable with and resisted a relativist definition of his position.

How, then, did the sciences advance, in Kuhn's view? He differentiated between moments of "revolutionary science", in which new paradigms would emerge, substantially redefining a field of investigation or changing its subject, and what he called "normal science". The latter were the routine scientific practices in which the descriptive and explanatory problems that had been identified in the construction and definition of a new paradigm were sequentially solved, through laboratory work, experimentation, systematic observation, and other investigative methods. Scientists, Kuhn noted from his historical study, did not, for the most part, spend their time in questioning or challenging the fundamental assumptions of their disciplines and their constitutive ideas. What they did he described as "puzzle-solving". Each of the major paradigms that have constituted Western science has thus given rise to an immensity of particular "puzzles"— phenomena that have invited description, conceptualization, and causal explanation within a broad paradigmatic frame. Most routine scientific practice is of this puzzle-solving kind, argued Kuhn. Darwinian theory provides a compelling and accessible example of a "normal science" whose work has been proceeding at least since the publication of *On the Origin of Species* in 1859. The "normal science" that has taken place within this paradigm has encompassed the investigation of enormous numbers of species and their relation their ecological environment, the understanding of the mechanisms of the inheritance of characteristics by Mendel in the 1860s, and the emergence of the field of molecular biology in the twentieth century, which explained the biochemical attributes of genes and their sequencing and "expression"—that is, their effect on the structures and processes of organisms. A parallel description could be given of the evolution of every major paradigmatic field: for example, gravitation, electromagnetism, or the structure and properties of the chemical elements.

Kuhn's theory needed to account for scientific development and, in particular, to explain how the largest changes in scientific understanding—what he called "paradigm shifts"—took place. Was it the case, as the Popperian falsifiability model and a broader triumphalist account of scientific progress suggested, that theories that captured a larger part of reality simply came to replace those that captured a smaller part? Kuhn believed that within paradigms, once these were established, this was the way in which knowledge routinely advanced. "Normal science" was, indeed, a practice that selected between more and less valid explanations. But shifts *between* paradigms were of a different order, since what was involved here involved a change of perspective and the choice of an at least partially different object of study. The concept of paradigm shifts replaced the view of science as a linear process of advance within which those understandings achieved within one frame of reference were fully captured and incorporated within the theory that supplanted it.

Within a paradigm, Kuhn noted, anomalies would accumulate, leading eventually to a loss of confidence in its continued explanatory powers. There were generational issues involved. Those who had risen professionally through their work within a paradigm during their scientific careers would be inclined to defend it, as embodying their own "human capital". But a new generation of scientists might see the old paradigm as an obstruction both to thinking and to their professional advancement, compared with fresh and different frames of inquiry. All this was sociologically perceptive and gave rise to a substantial work in the sociology of science, which investigated how scientists actually did work in their laboratories and journals and what sociological factors did, indeed, contribute to the outcome of scientific arguments. It became clear that wider factors in a social environment had considerable influence on scientific development—for example, funnelling resources into some fields of study while denying them to others. Popper's conception of scientists and their work was a heroic one—perhaps it reflected the brilliant innovations achieved by physics at the beginning of the twentieth century, with the emergence of the theory of relativity and quantum physics. Scientists were seen to be either making bold imaginative leaps and discovering new theories—like Einstein—or subjecting these theories to decisive tests, as in the Michelson–Morley experimental observations. Kuhn and his sociologist successors put forward a more mundane and collegiate view of scientific work, much of it seen as a more modest kind of problem-solving in contexts in which the broad theoretical assumptions that underlay specific investigations were not questioned.

Kuhn's account of the development of science was in many ways persuasive—his work itself constituted a "scientific revolution" in the study of science, parallel to that which it described in the fields of the sciences themselves. But it was also highly contentious in certain respects. This was in part because it seemed to suggest that the advances of the sciences were the outcome not merely of scientists' capacity to discover the truths of nature through their rational and objective procedures of investigation, but in part were the result of contingent social processes. Kuhn held on to a view of the sciences as having fundamentally advanced the knowledge of nature, while at the same time defending an approach that was realistic about scientific practices and avoided their idealization. An idea of triumphal progress, albeit against fierce enemies, with the advance of science central to it was implicit in Popper's world view. Kuhn wrote at the beginning of a period of scepticism in which there was greater interest in cultural differences.

His account of the development of science was implicitly pluralist, in comparison with the previous orthodoxy. Each successive paradigm, in his view, might capture some slice of reality. The relation to one scientific paradigm to another was, in part, one of difference, rather than of conquest, replacement, and total absorption. He later wrote of scientific development in evolutionary terms, as a process of "speciation" (Kuhn, 2000). One can, in these terms and within the frame of complexity theory, see the competitive success of paradigms as taking place within "fitness landscapes", these being defined by the specific fields within which knowledge is gained (Kauffman, 1995).

Various cultural affinities and correspondences with developments in the 1960s and 1970s help to explain why Kuhn's approach achieved such prominence. Its challenge to the idea of a single dominant ideology of science reflected a broader challenge to Western hegemony in the post-war period and the emergence of plural centres of power.

The idea of contests between different world views and approaches to nature echoes the wider rejection that became current later in the 1960s of "one-dimensional" rationalist ways of thinking. The very idea of a "revolution" also caught something that was in the air in the decade in which Kuhn's seminal book was written. The idea that scientific advances might be determined as much through the changing power relationships between social groups as by their innate rationality and truthfulness also reflected an emerging spirit of "relativism"—the idea that the interests of the advocates of any viewpoint needed to be taken into account if one were to fully understand it. This was a period in which sociological ways of thinking became influential in Western countries, as part of a broader questioning of established norms and authorities.

Kuhn's ideas contributed to the development of a "strong programme" (Bloor, 1976) in the sociology of science, in which scientific advances were wholly explained as the outcome of social processes—a position that brought fierce arguments about the rational basis of science: the "science wars". (These were attacks during the 1990s by advocates of the natural sciences on the emerging field of the Sociology of Scientific Knowledge.[6]) However, Kuhn did not subscribe to a thoroughgoing sociological determinism. His view was that scientists operated rationally, with respect to logical consistency and fidelity to observed facts, within their own paradigmatic conceptual frames, but that different frames might be incommensurable with each other. Differences between scientific perspectives might be unresolved and unresolvable simply because they were describing different "objects".

Kuhn and Popper

Kuhn's rejection of Popper's model of scientific discovery and his historically grounded account of scientific practice was both cogent and influential. It gave rise to a substantial defensive response from philosophers of science close to Popper's position. One of the major weaknesses of Popper's model was the significance he attached to the decisive empirical trials that he held scientific theories had to withstand if they were not to be rejected and displaced by rival theories. Even though significant examples could be cited of experiments and observations that had proved decisive in the history of science, it became clear that Popper's was an idealized and over-dramatized view of how scientific ideas actually came to be accepted. Kuhn had shown that well-established scientific paradigms were highly complex and durable structures, which normally rest on many pillars of theoretical implication and empirical evidence. The substantial bodies of theory and evidence that constitute a paradigm are not simply abandoned because one or more specific hypotheses derived from them are disproved in a single failed experiment. Too much is invested in research programmes for them to be given up just because some of their constituent fields of investigation encounter anomalies and counter-instances. In such circumstances, anomalies are usually put to one side, to be dealt with later, perhaps when better instruments for experimentation have been developed or when some other corroborative theoretical development has taken place. In other words, the sciences are complex organizational or networked systems and do not simply embody the outcomes of sequences of tests designed to test hypotheses by empirical falsification, developed by heroic theoretical and experimental scientists.

The most important revisionist defence of Popper's ideas was advanced by Imre Lakatos (1970), one of his associates. He argued that the sciences were, indeed, constructed, as Kuhn had shown, as more or less organized research programmes, and that they could and did survive failed experiments and instances of disconfirmation by evidence. He displaced Popper's criterion of falsifiability from the specific context of a discrete theory to the larger frame of an entire research programme. What mattered, so far as the advance of scientific truth was concerned, was whether the "problem shift" that took place as a scientific programme was pursued was a "progressive problem shift"— that is, one that enabled new phenomena to be incorporated within the terms of a theoretical system, perhaps through its selective revision— or a "degenerative problem shift" where the empirical refutation of a specific hypothesis led to the mere re-labelling and re-conceptualizing of "resistant" phenomena so as to avoid challenge to the ruling theory. This is indeed a valuable description of the different outcomes that are possible when advocates of theoretical perspectives find themselves struggling to account for empirical realities that appear to be inconsistent with their theoretical model. In such situations, theories can evolve to enhance their explanatory capacities through new conceptual development or improved techniques of empirical investigation. Or, they can adopt a defensive solution of denying the significance of contrary evidence while modifying their substantive theoretical model not at all.

Lakatos's aim was to reconcile Popper's crucial contention that scientific theories depended ultimately on the demonstration of their correspondence with observed facts with Kuhn's description of the complexity of actual scientific practice. Lakatos's "research programmes", which are analogous to Kuhn's scientific paradigms, succeed and survive because they are able to explain and encompass a larger number and range of phenomena and fail and are supplanted when they fail to do so. Certainly Lakatos's model describes the process of evolution of scientific programmes more adequately than Popper's had done. What remains questionable, however, is whether objective grounds in reality can be found for discriminating between "progressive" and "degenerative" revisions of scientific theories.

An analogue of Popper's model of falsifiability is the economic theory of perfect competition, in which suppliers of products in markets have no influence on the decisions of buyers about their relative merits. Lakatos's theory corresponds better to the economic models of imperfect and oligopolistic competition, in which suppliers have some power to influence the outcomes of market decisions—for example, through their ability to exclude rivals and through the accumulated advantages of earlier successes. Scientific programmes may, indeed, have acquired more corporate and oligopolistic attributes during a period in which the sciences, too, have become institutionalized.

Toulmin and the competitive evolution of disciplines

A third contribution from this period to debates about scientific method is relevant to the understanding of the research programme of psychoanalysis. Stephen Toulmin's (1972) major work, *Human Understanding*, both disagreed in significant respects from Kuhn's view of scientific development and yet in important respects endorsed it. His disagreement was with the idea of "scientific revolutions", and in particular with Kuhn's view that these gave rise to and constructed "incommensurable" objects of inquiry. Toulmin's term for theoretical systems was "disciplines", not paradigms, or research programmes. He rejected Kuhn's somewhat apocalyptic idea of revolutions, with their implied suddenness. He noted that arguments between such contending theoretical systems had often continued for many decades, rather than taking the form of sudden overthrows and supercessions of one "paradigm" by another. This was the case for three of Kuhn's major instances of "revolution"—for example, the development from Ptolemaic to Copernican astronomy, from Newtonian physics to relativity theory (within which Newtonian physics remains "locally" valid), and from wave to particle theories of light. Nor, Toulmin wrote, did the scientists involved in these controversies seem to believe that they had changed their basic object of inquiry, something that, Kuhn had suggested, was the usual outcome of a paradigm shift. Rather, in the above cases, they believed that they had merely revised and reformulated their field of study in light of new theoretical ideas and empirical findings. Toulmin's conception was of a competitive evolution of disciplines, each with long-term persisting cores of assumptions and methods and with many differences being disputed and negotiated within these frames.

Within a discipline, Toulmin argued, methods of evaluation and selection between ideas remained logical and respectful of evidence, since a basic frame of inquiry was shared within it. But Toulmin acknowledged that between disciplines, once these have evolved into distinctive fields of knowledge, there are often few common terms, or criteria of evaluation. Almost by definition, different disciplines are not investigating, describing, or explaining the same kinds of objects. Toulmin's model, like Kuhn's in his later writings, is Darwinian— that is, just as biological species evolve in such a way that they can no longer interbreed, so disciplines subdivide so they no longer occupy the same conceptual space.

While Toulmin disputed that major theoretical disagreements in fields such as astronomy or physics were best understood by reference to scientific revolutions or paradigm shifts, his account of the evolution of different disciplines seems to lead to rather similar conclusions so far as the diversity and incommensurability of fields of knowledge are concerned. However, he offers an explanation of how this differentiation comes about that diverges from that of Kuhn. In his view, it derives from different human interests, arising from practices.

Toulmin was critical of the assumptions of Western rationalist philosophy, with its idea of unitary, universal rational order whose ultimate correspondence to nature can be discovered and revealed by science. Ancient geometry was one version of this perspective, Russell's and Frege's symbolic logic, and Wittgenstein's early philosophical position were others. Toulmin believed that the development of the sciences had been driven not by a single template of universal rationality but, rather, in response to evolving human interests and desires.

The sciences normally look backwards in time, in order to maintain consistency with their own already established ideas. It is this "organic" and institutional attribute that explains the absence or infrequency of the "scientific revolutions" cited by Kuhn—parallel to this was the idea of the "epistemological break" formulated by the French philosophers Gaston Bachelard and Georges Canguilhem (Lecourt, 1975). But scientists also look forward in time, to locate and investigate new subjects and problems, which correspond to what at a given time a scientific community and the cultures that surround it find interesting. This openness to the present and future leads to the continuing differentiation of fields of knowledge, and to new theories and methods that are selected because of their usefulness and novelty, even when their adoption requires new criteria of evaluation. (For example, within evolutionary theory, testing hypotheses about the biochemistry of genes requires methods different from the observing and recording the behaviour of migratory birds.)

Toulmin's approach stressed the role of practices and usefulness to humankind in shaping the development of scientific knowledge. Many examples of such interdependence can be given. For example, Darwin's theory of natural selection was influenced by practices of horticultural plant selection known to him. The development of mechanical sciences, whose theoretical basis was physics, was pushed forward by practical human interests, both military and industrial. The science of medicine evolved because of the compelling desire for health and aversion to disease, with many related fields of interest developing from that starting point. Medical scientists became interested in the self-reproduction of bacteria or viruses as a distinct field of study, but a main reason for this was to find means through which human organisms could resist them more effectively. Toulmin's evolutionary view of scientific disciplines shaped by practical human interests is, in many respects, compatible with Kuhn's, even though it challenges some of his assumptions.

Psychoanalysis as a revolutionary science

Why are arguments such as these significant for psychoanalytic research? One reason for this is that the Popperian philosophy of science, which held sway prior to the challenges to it initiated by Kuhn's *Structure of Scientific Revolutions,* had sought to disqualify psychoanalysis from recognition as a human science and had marginalized it in the field of psychology, to a degree that often amounted to exclusion. The recognition that sciences were different in respect of their chosen and defined fields of study, and that such differences extended to their primary concepts, their methods of investigation, and the means by which their findings were represented created space for kinds of investigation that had hitherto struggled for recognition. The hypothetico-deductive method and the criterion of falsifiability prescribed by Popper had as its goal the discovery of universal laws, such as those revealed by the great discoveries and theoretical constructions of physics. It dismissed those fields in which particulars and differences were of significance to investigators. It held that those in which description and classification were crucial sources of knowledge were not properly scientific. Thus biology and the human sciences were assigned a second-class status and were put under great pressure to adopt methods close to those of the physical sciences. The more pluralist approach to scientific study that followed from Kuhn's intervention, his idea of differentiated "paradigms", and the subsequent development of the sociology of scientific knowledge liberated the social sciences in particular. It freed them to recognize the distinctive attributes, bound up especially with the idea of subjective meaning and cultural norms, that characterized their subject-matter. Recognition of the place of subjective meanings in the understanding of social phenomena, and of the significant array of differences between them, led to a significant broadening of research methodologies in the human sciences. It became acceptable, to some social scientists at least, to assert the necessity for qualitative, interpretative methods of research and the value of the study of particular forms of life, against the hegemony of quantitative research methods and the commitment to universal generalization. This wider acceptance in the field of sociology, anthropology, and even psychology that "meanings" and "cultures" were intrinsic to individual and collective life led to a broadening of their fields of study. As we see further on, recognition of the significance of meanings by no means entails acceptance of the idea of unconscious meanings, in psychoanalytic terms. But still, this "liberalization" of social scientific method to take account of "conscious" meanings opened up a methodological path to the study of unconscious meanings, as we note in a later chapter.

Toulmin's emphasis on the role of practice in defining the objects of scientific inquiry enables us to recognize the implications of the origins of psychoanalysis in the domain of medicine and psychiatry, to which it has remained fairly close. In fact, there was serious interest in what we would now term unconscious phenomena in European philosophy and culture long before Freud (Ffytche, 2011). Furthermore, as he himself noted, Freud's discoveries about the unconscious were often anticipated by centuries in the work of imaginative artists and writers (Trilling, 1951). Freud's achievement was to bring these intuitions and insights concerning the unconscious elements in mental life within the sphere of a scientific theory and method, in order to address the malfunctions of the mind in which he was interested, both in his own person and as a doctor.

Kuhn's theory of paradigms and paradigm shifts has been of great importance to the understanding and recognition of psychoanalysis as a field of science. Freud's discovery of the unconscious mind, and the complex ideas he set out to understand its nature and functions, can be understood as a classic example of a "scientific revolution". It identified an essentially new object of study, it devised new concepts and theories to classify its "regions" and to explain its functions and effects, and it proposed distinctive methods of investigation of this new sphere. Freud set out the key terms of this new paradigm, which included: the unconscious, located in a structural model of the mind, which he later revised; repression; the Oedipus complex; various psychopathologies (such as hysteria and obsessional neurosis), which were its effects; the unconscious meanings contained in dreams; the transference. What can in Kuhn's terms be described as a "normal science" developed from these foundational ideas, which have continued to be fundamental to psychoanalysis. The problems this set out to solve were of two kinds, which are in some ways parallel to those of medical science. The first were the practical problems of understanding the particulars of individual patients' illnesses. The second were the research problems that could be typified from these cases, the identification of the different kinds of dysfunctions that could be recognized. As in medical and other practical science, most routine professional work has made use of existing knowledge to understand individual cases. But arising from this has been the development of a field of distinctive psychoanalytic concepts, theories, and techniques. These have developed as innovations and as revisions of existing ideas, in response to problems and anomalies encountered in clinical practice, which needed to be understood and resolved. By no means every clinician in psychoanalysis is a researcher in this sense of being interested in or capable of adding to the body of knowledge of the field. However, there has been rather little psychoanalytic research that has not been based on clinical practice.

Through these two linked kinds of "puzzle-solving"—practical and theoretical—the scope of the original theoretical paradigm of psychoanalysis has been tested out, refined, and extended to explain many new phenomena. These developments include, for example, the theory of infantile development, and in particular how the earliest relationships of infants and their mothers were to be understood, at a phase prior to that at which Freud had located oedipal desires and the internal conflicts that arose from them. Another is in the field of clinical technique. The understanding of the functions of the transference in illuminating the nature of unconscious phantasies was deepened and clarified in an important paper by James Strachey (1934). Subsequently, it became recognized (Heimann, 1950) that the "countertransference" experiences of the psychoanalyst were also of great significance as a means of understanding the unconscious mental life of the patient. This is because they could be understood as the outcome of processes originating in the analysand, by which he projected into the analyst states of mind and feeling that were intolerable to him, but which sought use of the analyst to bear or to "contain" through understanding. This development of psychoanalytic theory and technique was closely connected to another sphere of investigation—that of the processes of projection, introjection, and containment that were believed by Klein, Bick, and Bion to characterize the relationships between mothers and babies in the earliest weeks. A problem that was encountered and solved in that field of work was one of investigative technique. How could the mental states of pre-verbal infants be observed and understood? Two linked solutions were proposed to this problem. One of these was the invention by Bick (1964) of the method of psychoanalytic infant observation. And the other was Bion's (1967b) demonstration that one could, from the evidence of the consulting room, make inferences from the states of mind of psychotic patients whose minds had virtually disintegrated, to an understanding of the mental states of infants whose minds were still in the process of being formed. The similarity between these phenomena lay, in Bion's view, in the mechanisms of projection and projective identification. Bion saw the psychoanalyst's role in giving these meaning for the patient as analogous to the earliest functions of the mother's mind in containing and processing the turbulent states of mind of her baby.

Another crucial "puzzle" that had to be solved lay in the psychoanalytic treatment of children. The crucial development here was by Melanie Klein, in her invention or discovery of her "play technique". This consisted of providing child patients with a small set of toys and materials for drawing and encouraging them to use these in the clinical setting in whatever ways they chose. Observation of the children in this situation, in the context of the transference relationship with the analyst that usually developed, enabled patients to make visible and to communicate what was in their minds, including its unconscious dimensions. Klein showed[7] that the free expression of children's play, within the developing context of a transference relationship with the analyst, was an effective substitute for the interpretation of dreams and associations which Freud (1900a, p. 608) had described as the royal road to the unconscious. From this beginning, the psychoanalysis of children was able to develop as a flourishing sub-specialism of psychoanalysis, at one stage, in the work of Anna Freud, Klein, Winnicott, and their colleagues, giving rise to some of the most important discoveries in the field.

The field of child analysis evolved further, as various additional puzzles within its "normal science" were addressed and solutions found to them. The development of therapeutic technique—underpinned by the understanding of the mechanisms of projective identification, the countertransference, and the container–contained relationship—enabled psychotherapy from the 1970s onwards to be effectively conducted with "severely deprived children"—that is, children who were far more disruptive and resistant to treatment than the less disturbed child patients who had previously been the majority of children referred for psychoanalysis (Boston & Szur, 1983). Another of the many sub-specialisms that developed in the field of child analysis was that concerned with children on the autistic spectrum.

Kuhn has characterized the development of scientific paradigms, from their revolutionary instigation through their programmes of "normal science", as a kind of "speciation" in which sub-fields of investigation evolve to fill available niches within the field of phenomena that are amenable to explanation within the source paradigm. The evolution of the psychoanalytic paradigm since Freud is well described by this metaphor.

Psychoanalysts have taken up the idea of the paradigm, and the idea of a legitimate field of inquiry that it seems to legitimate, with relief. It may be useful to understand why Kuhn's theory of the evolution of scientific knowledge is so liberating for the psychoanalytic field. The explanation lies in the way in which Kuhn's interpretation of the development of the sciences as a "revolutionary" process, and Toulmin's evolutionary revision of this idea, recognize the diversity of investigative spaces that the sciences have always filled, and the differences in the theoretical frames and investigative methods through which they have filled them. Equally important is the recognition that this conception makes possible of psychoanalysis as a "normal science", with a clinical practice of routine "puzzle-solving" based on its core postulates.[8] Psychoanalysis has become able to recognize itself as one among many such fields, each able to claim its own legitimacy as a form of knowledge. The idea of a plurality of fields of scientific inquiry, connecting with one another in various ways, has come to replace the binary demarcation between those fields of inquiry that can claim the legitimacy of science, and those that are deemed to fail in making this claim. It is easier for psychoanalysis to find an accepted place in a scientific environment that is less intolerant of diversity.

Notes

1. Among critics of psychoanalysis who were influenced by him were Hans Eysenck (1973, 2002), Frank Cioffi (1970, 1998), Adolf Grünbaum (1974, 1993), Frederick Crews (2017; Crews et al., 1997), Peter Medawar (1972), and Ernest Gellner (1985).

2. Richard Wollheim (1993a) has pointed out that psychoanalysts do not commonly find that their patients simply agree with their interpretations, and they do not use such agreement as a primary test of their validity. Analysts' interpretations and patients' responses to them are, indeed, important in analysts coming to understand a patient's unconscious mind, but this is a complex process, not matter of simple agreement or disagreement. Understanding of these issues has become deeper as the complexity of the transference relationship has become better understood by analysts

after Freud. The influence of the transference on analysands' (and analysts') states of mind has long been central topic for investigation by analysts (e.g. Heimann, 1950; Joseph, 1989; Strachey, 1934) and is not something that they have somehow managed to overlook, as Grünbaum seems to believe. One of the limitations of Grünbaum's critique of psychoanalysis is that he has given so little attention to the later development of the field.

3. Among many examples are Jeffrey Masson (1984) and Frederick Crews (1997, 2017).

4. Robert Hinshelwood (2013) has sought to show how clinical research methods in psychoanalysis can reliably validate psychoanalytic theories in a way that satisfies Popperian criteria. For reflections on his argument see Rustin (2014).

5. For a useful summary of Kuhn's ideas, see *Stanford Encyclopedia of Philosophy* (2011).

6. I once gave a paper in which I defended the rationality of psychoanalysis by reference to its distinctive object of study, the unconscious mind, contrasting its scientificity with that of astrology, for whose propositions I believed there to be no equivalent evidence. One response I received from adherents of the "strong programme" who took part in the seminar was that I was being unreasonably dismissive of astrology.

7. Demonstration of what could be learned about child patients using this technique was crucial in the contribution of Klein and her colleagues to the "Controversial Discussions" of 1940 (King & Steiner, 1991), since it gave grounds for recognizing that her conjectures about the inner world of young children might be supported by clinical evidence.

8. In an essay "Logic of Discovery or Psychology of Research" (1977), Kuhn formulated his principal disagreement with Popper as concerned with the importance of normal in contrast to revolutionary science. He suggests that Popper habitually conflates the two, thus overlooking the practicality of routine scientific work, which rarely questions a field's fundamental assumptions.

CHAPTER THREE

The consulting room as the psychoanalytic laboratory

The purpose of this chapter is to explore the primary context of discovery of psychoanalytic knowledge, the clinical consulting room, and to demonstrate affinities between the production of knowledge in the laboratories of the natural sciences, and its development in this equivalent laboratory of psychoanalysis. I argued above that Kuhn's recognition of the diversity of the objects of study of the sciences, and the idea that psychoanalysis constitutes a distinct "paradigm" of scientific knowledge, has been a liberating one, as it comparably was for other areas of the human sciences.

Whereas an earlier debate, following Kuhn, focused on the historical development of scientific ideas and on philosophical issues concerning their validity, the new sociologists of science and technology (SST) investigated its routine practices ("the normal science" described by Kuhn) by observing scientists at work in their laboratories and in the organization of the production and dissemination of scientific knowledge. For the most part, their work upheld and developed Kuhn's understanding of the sciences as diverse in their objects and methods—a view set out, for example, in *The Disunity of Science*, edited by Peter Galison and David Stump (1996), and in Karen Knorr-Cetina's (1999) comparison of the methodologies of the physical and the biological sciences. This recognition of scientific diversity was, as we have pointed out, significant in its implications for the field of psychoanalysis.

This chapter is mainly concerned with the application to psychoanalysis of the ideas of the French sociologist and anthropologist of science, Bruno Latour (1983, 1987, 1988, 1993; Latour & Woolgar, 1979), whose work has given rise to the field of "Actor-Network Theory" (ANT) in science studies. Latour's contribution to this debate makes it possible to understand psychoanalytic methods of research as comparable to those of other sciences, while avoiding a retreat into "relativism" or the idea that in regard to truth-claims "anything goes", as long as people hold certain coherent beliefs and can develop rationales for them.

The "strong programme" in the sociology of science (Barnes, Bloor, & Henry, 1996) had argued that the outcomes of scientific investigation should be understood as the outcome of social processes—the institutional practices of the scientists themselves. From this perspective, "scientific truth" was merely a legitimation accorded to those whose ideas and findings had happened to prevail.

This view contested the classical, rationalist view of science, which held that it was the properties of nature itself that determined its representations as scientific knowledge. Scientists believed themselves to be the bearers of truths. Their authority was challenged by the idea that the outcomes of their investigations depended not on their special access to nature and its attributes, but on social contingencies, such as power struggles within scientific institutions. Controversies, known as the "science wars" (Labinger & Collins, 2001), erupted between scientists and their advocates and the sociologists of science. This rejection of the idea that the scientists were the discoverers of universal laws of nature contributed to the "relativist" and "postmodern" climate of ideas that was influential during this period of the 1970s and 1980s. Kuhn had been apprehensive about this "relativist" interpretation of his own approach, but, despite his explicit repudiation of it, he found some difficulty in differentiating his position from it (Kuhn, 1970, 2000).

Latour rejected the sociologists' "strong programme" for the understanding of science. He thought that both sides in this controversy—the sociologists and the advocates of an "unmediated" scientific approach—were wrong. He asserted that, far from repudiating the idea of absolute truth, as they had claimed to do, the sociologists had merely substituted the truth-claims of sociological explanations for those of the scientists they studied. Latour held that while the sociologists (and Kuhn) had been correct to recognize the active role of scientists in the discoveries of scientific truths, what they had discovered were real properties of nature, and not the mere constructions of their own minds. Scientific knowledge was created by scientists, but only through their interactions with, and subject to the constraints imposed by, the qualities of nature itself. They were thus mediators in the apprehension of the properties of nature, and neither its passive witnesses nor its creators.

There is an affinity between Latour's conception and the famous formulation from Marx's *11th Brumaire of Louis Bonaparte*, "Men make their own history, but they do not make it as they please; they do not make it under self-selected circumstances, but under circumstances existing already, given and transmitted from the past." In the case of the sciences, the analogous "circumstances" are the constraints imposed on experimental or observational practices by nature.

Latour's view of the scientist as a kind of "mediator" between the natural world and the human societies that inhabit it (and are increasingly acquiring power to change it, to their own peril), has resonance for psychoanalysis. Psychoanalysts are also mediators, in so far as through their work they facilitate their analysands' greater access to and understanding of unconscious parts of their minds.

Latour's position was influenced by Kuhn's work, in so far as it identified the role of the creative imagination of scientists in making possible the development of knowledge. Latour rejected the idea that scientists were merely the neutral and objective recorders of the properties of nature, justified in claiming their authority principally because of the literal correspondence between nature itself and their descriptions of it. The scientists' role in the investigation of nature was in Latour's view a dynamic and interactive one. What they discovered was the result of their deliberate interventions and actions, not merely of their passive observations.

Latour elaborated his view through his study of the experimental sciences and of their applications in their associated technologies. Scientists have created specialized settings, called laboratories, in which selected entities can be identified and experimentally manipulated and their causal relations with other entities thereby made the object of systematic observation. The investigation of many phenomena of nature—for example, the physical properties of air, light, sound, or electricity, or the chemical properties of the elements—became possible and cumulative because of the design of experimental environments in which the causal powers of these selected entities could be put to work and their effects observed. It was the relative isolation of these entities in laboratory settings that made their investigation feasible.[1] Latour's argument was that hitherto unknown kinds of phenomena—in effect, new entities or "objects"—were identified through these experimental interactions. The causal powers of these discovered entities could then be understood and put to practical or technological use. Examples of such "discovered" entities are electromagnetism, chemical acids and alkalis, proteins, and genes. The human and, indeed, now the natural world has been transformed through the understanding of the causal powers of such entities. Even the "force of gravity", always a fundamental and taken-for-granted fact in human lives, became recognizable and capable of exploitation as a law-governed element of nature once its specific properties came to be understood and measured. This happened both through systematic observation of phenomena occurring in nature, such as the movement of the moon, the tides, and the planets, and through experimental design— for example, in the study of falling bodies, pendulums, and the like. These understandings were then put to use in many technologies—for example, those of ballistics and architecture.

Latour regarded the discovery of new entities of this kind as the primary achievement of the sciences. He terms them "actants" since, in his opinion, it was their recognition that gave rise to the transformations for which science has been responsible—for example, in many forms of engineering. Electrons, genes, and chemical elements are according to Latour, "hybrid" entities, in so far as they are real phenomena of nature and yet are discovered to possess causal powers that can be put to human use. Scientists are significant as the mediators—we might say, midwives—of these discoveries. These discoveries identify, often in precise and measurable ways, powers that are real attributes of nature but only become visible when they are "isolated", through experiment or observation. But once identified and their causal powers understood, in the laboratories and observatories of science, they become available for deployment in the constructed interventions and interactions of technologies. Latour's idea was that scientific discoveries were the products of interactions between human actors and specific attributes of nature. His concept of "hybridity" and of "actants" (neither human actors nor things) has both a scientific and a technological dimension. It is within the ideal-typical theoretical models that scientists construct that the entities that they contain can be understood to exercise their powers. The gravitational force that explains the physical ordering of the solar system can be understood as an "actant" because its power becomes recognizable within this invented framework of explanation. "Realists" would contend, however, that its causal powers are wholly independent of the human discovery of them. More important in Latour's use of the idea of "actant" is its "technological" dimension. This is the conversion of entities seen to possess causal powers, such as gravity, electromagnetism, and information, into means for acting upon nature in order to achieve specific purposes, such as those realized through the invention of weapons, machines, computers, or drugs. Classically, scientists used to see themselves as discoverers and observers of a nature that was largely unaffected by their presence and their activity. Astronomy, whose objects used to be beyond the scope of any human intervention, was a canonical example of such a perspective. Latour's perspective of the science and technologist as active mediators within an environment whose properties they learn about and modify through their interactions with it reflects a changing reality in which, indeed, much of the earthly environment is being greatly transformed by its human inhabitants.

The extent of "hybridity" (between man and nature) of the entities discovered by science is variable. A wild grass is less potent as an "actant" in its ecological environment than are purposefully selected strains of wheat, which, through human intervention, have been enabled to dominate large swathes of the earth's surface. Yet the properties of grass species had to be understood before their selective breeding became feasible. Genetic modification is adding a further dimension of causal potency, the gene and the alterable genetic code having become another "actant". Although this view of science is highly respectful of its transformative role, and that of scientists, Latour's argument was nevertheless resented by some advocates of science. Because Latour saw the scientists' role as an active one, always conducted within specific institutions and social contexts of application, he was accused of impugning the "objectivity" of science, conceived in traditional terms as an activity of "pure" discovery. Some wished to retain a view of science as the exact representation of nature, as if it were witnessed by scientists through a translucent window. In other words, Latour's ideas were misunderstood as proposing that scientific theories were wholly social constructions, whose validity was merely relative to the scientists' own perspectives, in contrast to the idea of science as the objective bearer of universal truths.

One of the most striking examples Latour gave to demonstrate his thesis was the discovery of the disease-causing bacillus, in the first instance anthrax, by the great French scientist, Louis Pasteur, and the feasibility of immunization against its effects. Latour (1983, 1988) described how Pasteur took anthrax bacilli from infected cattle and then cultivated them in the pure and uncontaminated environment of his laboratory. He then staged a famous demonstration in 1881 in the outside environment of the farms where the disease was killing cattle. A sample of cattle was injected with the cultivated bacteria, other animals (a "control group") were not. The infected cattle sickened and some of them died. The non-infected cattle remained healthy. Pasteur further discovered that the infective properties of these bacilli diminished as the bacilli aged and died. Cattle injected with dead bacilli did not become infected and, indeed, became immune from further infection with live bacilli. Pasteur had thus shown that the bacilli taken from animals and cultivated in his laboratory caused disease, and those dead bacilli if injected into animals could make them immune from it. Once this had been was demonstrated in the case of anthrax in cattle, it became possible to extend this understanding to other bacterial diseases in animals and in people. A controversy has recently been taking place in Britain regarding how infections of tuberculosis in cattle spread by badgers are best dealt with—for example, by culling or immunizing badgers that live in the vicinity of the cattle.

In effect, in his bacteriological research, the farm environment in which Pasteur constructed his trials was made into an extension of his laboratory, with the selected cattle (numbered, classified as infected or non-infected, immunized or not immunized) serving as the objects of his "outdoor" laboratory experiment. The outside "farm" environment needed to be controlled, in the respects relevant to his experiment of visibility and enumeration, infection or non-infection, as tightly as the cultivation of the bacteria in the lab. If Pasteur had chosen to use white mice instead of cattle, the experimental operations could have been conducted within the physical confines of his laboratory, but there were many advantages, in terms of public demonstration and practical relevance, in experimenting on ordinary cattle in a farming environment instead.

Pasteur's discovery had enormous transformative effects in regard to the control of diseases. Once it was recognized that diseases were carried by bacteria as their infectious agents, it became understood that providing a population with a supply of clean drinking water and separating the water supply from the sewage system could have major beneficial effects on public health. Immunization against common diseases became a routine practice, nearly all children in countries with advanced economies eventually receiving early inoculations against diseases (smallpox, diphtheria, etc.) that had previously been responsible for much loss of life. In medical practice, ensuring bacteria-free environments and avoiding contamination of wounds became routine. The serious problem of puerperal fever, causing many deaths of mothers in childbirth, was substantially reduced simply through the practice of doctors disinfecting their hands before delivering babies.[2] These developments provided a powerful example of how science worked—of "Science in Action", as the title of one of Latour's books puts it.

Latour's central argument was this. The constructed, purified, artificial condition of the laboratory was the means by which scientists were able to identify an element of nature, which, once identified and isolated, could be shown to be an agent with significant causal powers. For Latour, both the discovery of the newly recognized entity (bacteria, in the above case), and the demonstration of its effectivity in the world outside the laboratory were crucial in the understanding of science and its powers to transform the world. Latour noted that links between the "inside" of the laboratory and the "outside" of the world had to be created. To make such links, which were needed to obtain the resources for the work in the laboratories—required gaining external support. Pasteur enlisted the press and governmental agencies in staging his "trials" to attract the attention his findings needed if they were to be put to practical use. Pasteur's discoveries were widely recognized and acted upon, giving rise to huge investments in many fields and the changes to which these give rise.

Latour's argument is that scientific discoveries are achieved as a consequence of scientists acting on nature, or on selected and deliberately isolated elements of it. Laboratory experiments are examples of such actions. Where experiments are not possible, such as in most forms of astronomy, approximations to them are achieved through controlled observations of interactions between naturally occurring phenomena, which serve as if they were experiments. We can't make the moon vary in its distance from the earth in a giant laboratory experiment, but we can observe what happens when it does so naturally—for example, in the effects of the moon's proximity on the oceans and their tides, through what we ascribe to gravitational attraction. Sometimes the causal powers of the discovered entities are manifested without human intervention, as in the case of some effects of gravity. But with other entities, such as bacteria or genes, or processes, such as nuclear fission or nuclear radiation, gravitational or electromagnetic energy, significant changes have to be effected in nature and society—for example, through designing machines or bombs—in order for these causal powers to be demonstrated and put to human use, for good or ill.

Latour is describing a complex ecology, in which the entities discovered by scientists come to have a transformative role. This perspective on science has come to be called "Actor-Network Theory". Its principal actors are the hybrid entities that Latour calls "actants". These are not the human actors who do the discovering, the scientists, nor the human actors who "apply" them in society—the engineers, inventors, soldiers manufacturers, farmers, doctors, government officials, ordinary citizens—who render these "actants" effective by exploiting their causal powers. The primary causal agents are, in Latour's view, the discovered entities themselves, operating in a network of relations, which change the world once they are discovered and set free to do so, with the aid of human powers. Human agents become effective through the discoveries that scientists have made.

The networks that link up the laboratory and the environments external to it are both material and conceptual. On the material side, funds flow to resource research and its technological applications, and political decisions are made to regulate human activities in the light of scientific discoveries. But transmissions also take place in terms of the recognition of conceptual equivalences. These may be recognized through metaphors, in which some of the attributes of one field of phenomena are seen to correspond to those of another, which may be quite different in its other aspects. An example is the idea of a virus, which is a self-replicating organism that infects and damages human and other bodies. Its properties of self-replication, infection, and bodily damage are similar to those of certain "malicious" computer programmes that can inflect, self-replicate, and cause damage when they are transferred from one computer to another. Procedures of detection, hygiene, and (with difficulty in both organisms and computers) destruction are adopted to deal with both kinds of "infection". The explanatory power of this metaphorical equivalence[3] depends on the "deep structures" of both biological and computer viruses. Both are essentially constituted by units of information, programmes, or codes, which they carry and transmit to their hosts. The idea that the effective transmission of scientific ideas can take place through the discovery of conceptual or metaphorical equivalences, as well as through accumulations and comparisons of empirical findings, of observed facts, figures largely in Latour's account of the development of scientific knowledge. It shows the indebtedness of his approach to idealist traditions of thought that are stronger in French than in Anglo-Saxon philosophy.

The relevance of actor-network theory to psychoanalysis

What, one may ask, has all this to do with psychoanalysis and its own methods of research? The answer to this question is that Latour's model of scientific discovery is valuable in understanding the contexts of discovery and transmission of psychoanalytic ideas. The central object of inquiry in psychoanalytic investigation is unconscious mental life. The clinical consulting room and the transference relationships that are brought into existence within it are the primary contexts for its investigation. What makes psychoanalytic investigation more feasible and productive within the psychoanalytic consulting than outside it are the "controlled" conditions of the consulting room. The consulting room can be understood as the laboratory for psychoanalytic research, and the clinical practices of psychoanalysis are its "experimental" interventions.

What is "laboratory-like" about the clinical consulting room? In what follows, I describe the relatively strict conventions of analytic technique that are normative within the "British School" of psychoanalysis. According to this model of work, the consulting room has prescribed boundaries of time, space, and certain kinds of co-presence and interaction that are promoted between its principal actors—the analyst and the analysand. The aim is to create and maintain a setting in which, it is hoped, certain kinds of mental phenomena, derivative of the "inner world" or the unconscious of the patient and nowadays of the analyst too, will evolve and became accessible to understanding. The phenomena of these consulting-room interactions constitute the empirical albeit semantic material that is available for psychoanalytic investigation, usually in the form of written-up clinical reports.

Such reports are the equivalent of what Latour terms "inscription devices", which are the means of reporting the findings from investigations. Just as maps are a principal inscription device of geographers and numerical tables of statistical data those of demographers and epidemiologists, so clinical case studies have been those of psychoanalysts. The description of dreams and their associations, and the interpretations made of them by analysts, has always been a highly valued element in such reports. Descriptions and interpretations of children's play have an equivalent place in child analysis. Since psychoanalysis is an interactive process, the interpretations of analysts are as important a part of the data record as the words and actions of their patients, even though interpretations may subsequently be reworked as elements in an analyst's subsequent investigation of the meaning of a clinical session. A complication of psychoanalytic research is that the analyst is an active participant in the process of analysis, not its passive observer. He is not, as in a scientific laboratory, a passive observer of the interaction between certain elements, but is himself both an observer and one of the principal elements in the interaction being observed. This is also the case for some kinds of participative sociological and anthropological research and calls for a high degree of reflexive self-awareness if a necessary objectivity of understanding is to be achieved.

This reflexive dimension of psychoanalytic work has become more prominent since the entire field of conscious and unconscious interactions between analyst and patient in the consulting room became understood to be significant. The idea that the interactions of the transference and countertransference relationship provide the main means of access to unconscious states of mind has further given rise to the idea, in Betty Joseph's terms (1985, 1989), of the "total transference situation" as an object of investigation.

The "isolation" of unconscious transference phenomena so that they become "observable" (or understandable by inference) is in practice, of course, difficult. However, this is also the case for many of the phenomena that natural scientists investigate. Physicists study radiation from distant galaxies and seek to interpret the information it bears only with the aid of industrial-scale technologies—space rockets and platforms, giant radio telescopes, and the like. The Hadron Collider—an underground laboratory tunnel situated at a location on the French–Swiss border—was designed in part to detect a subatomic particle whose existence was theoretically conjectured, but which had never been empirically observed. If one thinks of laboratories and objects of study of those kinds, the idea that the investigation of transference and countertransference phenomena in the clinical consulting room might, nevertheless, be feasible does not seem anomalous.

Bion (1957) wrote about the "bizarre objects" of unconscious phantasy, suggesting that these could be understood only through an analyst's conjectures following the close observation of psychotic states in patients and perhaps through acts of unconscious projective identification recognized in an analyst's countertransference. Many "secondary" assumptions have to be made for such ideas to have credibility. But many secondary assumptions (regarding subatomic and cosmological theory, and about the functioning of many kinds of measuring instrument) are also necessary, if the investigation of hitherto unseen atomic particles is to be a plausible undertaking.

Psychoanalysts seek to record observable "traces" of unconscious mental processes, just as natural scientists seek to register the observable effects of natural events, using instruments designed for this purpose. James Strachey's 1934 paper on "mutative interpretation" classically described a psychoanalytic procedure for ascertaining and communicating unconscious mental phenomena. He described how the identification of small but cumulative discrepancies between a patient's attributions of certain qualities to his analyst's behaviour or demeanour, and the known actuality of it, can reveal to the analyst the influence of a patient's unconscious phantasies on his perceptions and beliefs. It may then be that through interpretation a patient will come to recognize a reality-obscuring propensity of his own mental life, and be able to change it in the light of this. Unconscious states of mind usually manifest themselves only in their effects on conscious states of mind or behaviours—they are "traces", in this sense. It is for this reason that it is mainly through their meticulous step-by-step investigation in the controlled conditions of the consulting room that phenomena shaped by unconscious mental life have been made visible (M. J. Rustin, 2001, p. 36).[4]

The purpose of maintaining the temporal and spatial boundaries of the analytic setting are, like the equivalent measures in the scientific laboratory, to enable differences and variances to be recognized. Weekend and holiday breaks serve as controlled disruptions to the mental state of patients, provoking and revealing unconscious anxieties—for example, about abandonment, perhaps experienced in phantasy as the repetition of a serious loss in early life. The space of the consulting room is maintained as far as possible as relatively "empty" and free of external disturbance, so that the phenomena manifested in it can be located and interpreted as the effects of the patient's state of mind. Where this space is invaded in unanticipated and uncontrolled ways and the phenomena "contaminated", such observations become difficult, if not impossible. Here, if patient and analyst and patient are to be able to attend to what is going on between them—or, it is hoped, will be going on between them—mobile phones really do need to be switched off.

The "techniques" through which psychoanalysis is conducted have become steadily more rigorous in regard to its boundary rules, at least in the "British School", since its beginnings. Modern conventions expect the relationships of psychoanalyst and analysand to be kept separate from those of close family or sexual links. This is different from the early days of the field, in which Freud and Klein both analysed their own children and Ferenczi his long-term lover and her daughter (Forrester, 1997, Ch. 2). One reason for this insistence on boundaries is the recognition of how difficult it is to discriminate the phenomena of the unconscious from foreground or background "noise", and how powerful the unconscious resistances are to the understanding of the unconscious. A psychoanalytic interpretation of someone's state of mind offered during a seminar, a committee meeting, or a dinner party is more likely to provoke embarrassment, outrage, or injury than enlightenment. The clinical consulting room has been designed as a setting in which both analysts and patients are as fully as possible prepared for what may be released into their world when the often dangerous materials of the unconscious and its resistances are exposed.

Intensive and extensive methods of investigation

Scientific laboratories have mostly been designed to investigate the fundamental structures and processes of the "objects" being studied, whether these are physical, chemical, or biological. The distinction between "intensive" and "extensive" designs for research is relevant to understanding the nature of laboratory investigations, including those of psychoanalysis in its "quasi-laboratory" (Smith, Harré, & Van Langenhove, 1995, pp. 64–67). "Intensive" studies investigate, through exploration (e.g., dissection) or experiment (e.g., inoculation to prevent infection of an organism) the complex properties of small numbers of an entity.[5] A first critical experiment may be only with a single case. Extensive studies investigate a small number of selected attributes of a large population of entities. For example, the investigation of the circulation of liquids in plants, or of blood in mammals, depended on the dissection and examination initially of small numbers of specimens, and of the relationship of the flows in question to the functioning of these organisms as complex entities. By contrast, the investigation of the effects of tobacco smoking on health focused on a small number of "variables" and their correlation with disease, as they occurred in large populations. The invention of statistical methods that enabled their attributes to be measured by probabilistic inferences from relatively small samples made extensive methods of investigation more feasible than they would otherwise have been.

However, even in the design and conduct of "intensive" studies, numbers and quantities are significant. An experimenter will need to know what degree of variation in an entity is a natural occurrence and what is the effect of a specific intervention, and this will be a matter for exact measurement. Outcomes found to occur in single instances of a phenomenon need to be repeated, to be sure that the single instance was not a mere anomaly. But experimental findings are very often tested through a procedure of "analytic induction" (Smith, Harré, & Van Langenhove, 1995, pp. 67–68) rather than by large-scale extensive investigation. Analytic induction consists of repeating an experiment on successive occasions, both to test whether its initial finding was valid and subsequently to understand the effects of specific modifications in the variables being experimented with. Once fundamental properties of an entity or causal relation have been established, there may be no need to revalidate them through additional experiments, although there may be value in investigating additional properties of the phenomenon in question.

These distinctions are relevant to psychoanalysis. Its clinical methods of study, based on the investigation of small numbers of cases, are "intensive" in their form, and proceed through "analytic induction" in their mode of "extension": that is to say, a specific discovery—for example, of the efficacy of Klein's technique of "play therapy" was validated by her making use of this method with successive cases. The total number of cases was limited by the number of child patients a single psychoanalyst can treat (especially if the treatment is "intensive" and prolonged in the psychoanalytic sense of several sessions per week over many months or years). Nevertheless, it became possible for many practitioners to establish that this method was efficacious in the treatment of children and to clarify in what setting and with what material resources—toys, drawing materials etc.—this was best conducted. There were advantages in "standardizing" this treatment setting and its techniques, since this established "parameters" (elements that remained constant) that then made it possible to observe and compare the different "variables", relating both to the patient's condition and the analyst's interventions, that comprise a psychoanalytic treatment.

The construction of artificial environments is of critical importance in establishing or validating experimental findings. To know what degree of difference in the growth of plants or their component cells is caused by alteration in elements of the environment—light, humidity, or nutrients, for example—requires the measurement of quantities. But there is also often a central qualitative dimension in laboratory investigations. Even single experimental cases may be informative. How many experimental mice needed to be killed through the withdrawal of oxygen from their atmosphere in order to establish that without oxygen to breathe, mice could not survive? And how many other mammals needed to be exposed to this intervention to establish that mammals were like mice in this respect. Of course many complementary investigations based on anatomical and physiological studies of the cardio-respiratory systems of animals were undertaken to elaborate and extend this fundamental theory.

What is to be noted, however, is that it was the close and detailed study of specific examples of an object of study (in this case an organism and its components), through various kinds of observation and experiment, that advanced this knowledge, not the statistical study of large populations and the correlations of variables pertaining to them. This distinction is important because of the ways in which valid research in psychoanalysis is often equated with the statistical investigation of the outcomes of treatments, while research into the structures and processes of the personality, which is fundamental to psychoanalysis, is disparaged as unscientific. There are serious issues in regard to the demonstration of the representative nature of phenomena discovered in consulting-room settings. In principle, quantitative measures are relevant to these. But in many situations, small numbers of instances are enough to establish the significance of a structure or a variation, in both the natural and the human sciences. These are reasons why the clinical consulting room has served well as the principal laboratory for psychoanalytic research.

"Actants" and "networks"

If one understands psychoanalysis by analogy with Latour's model of scientific discovery, the crucial "actant" that it has identified is the "unconscious". The question then arises of how its effects can be studied outside the clinical consulting room. Can they be traced through controlled observation, like the effects of gravitational attraction in the solar system, or have they been utilized (like electromagnetic forces) for purposeful modifications of the world? Have significant networks been discovered or activated to facilitate the transformative effects of the particular "actants" identified by psychoanalysis?

We can note both similarities with and differences from the transformative effects of the "actants" discovered in other kind of scientific discovery. The idea of the unconscious has certainly spread, like wildfire one might say, outside Freud's original consulting rooms. Its key elements—ideas of repression, oedipal desires, the transference, sublimation—have become part of the shared vocabulary of Western cultures. Freud's numerous writings have never been out of print and remain in wide circulation. Its central practices of psychoanalytic psychotherapy have become established in virtually every society whose political regime is liberal enough in its toleration of freedom of expression and association to allow them. However, these forms of transmission have been mainly "lateral" or, in Deleuze and Guattari's (1980) terms, rhizomatic. Psychoanalytic ideas and practices have become diffused largely in response to the choices of individual citizens, and in particular those located in particular social strata, especially the highly educated and those engaged in those forms of work that are focused on symbolic expression and human relationships.

Government health systems, and the professions involved with them, have incorporated psychoanalytic approaches, to a degree, within their mental health systems, with some concentrations in certain hospitals and outpatient clinics such as the Tavistock Clinic in Britain. However, in public systems of mental health in most nations, psychoanalytic ideas and practices occupy a minority position. At different times, the caring and educational professions such as social work and teaching have been influenced by psychoanalytic ideas and practices, though again usually only in specialized applications. Consultancy to organizations, in both public and private sectors, is another field where psychoanalytic approaches have developed.

But although the "actor-network" of psychoanalysis has achieved some extension to social institutions, it has encountered resistance in its attempts to extend its influence in society. There are many reasons for this resistance. The most important of these lies in the borderline situation of psychoanalysis. Its focus on the particularities of individuals, on the significance of emotions in human experience, and on the idea of unconscious states of mind make it seem closer to the forms of understanding more commonly located in literature and the arts than in the sciences. Divisions in some societies between the cultures of the arts and sciences have made this borderline position a precarious one.

Where approaches to mental life are mainly cognitivist and rationalist, and therefore uninterested in the emotional and "subjective" dimensions of mental life, psychoanalysis has struggled for recognition, even when wider publics have become interested in the domains of irrationality and emotional turbulence.[6] Yet psychoanalysis does claim to be intellectually rigorous and to base its theories on evidence. Its advocates believe that the effects of its treatments can be empirically measured. "Actor networks" in the humanities have been more significant in the diffusion of psychoanalytic ideas and practices than the medical and psychological sciences adjacent to it in its professional field. But nevertheless psychoanalysis has found some corroboration from its neighbouring sciences.[7]

The relative isolation of psychoanalysis from the human and social sciences has constrained its development and diffusion. The narrow understanding of the nature of science that dominated philosophical debate in the decades before the re-definitions of the field that emerged in the 1960s has contributed to this situation. The metaphor of the consulting room as laboratory, made possible by Latour's work, and his understanding of the role of ecological networks in the transmission of ideas and practices provide a new way of understanding of psychoanalysis as a field of science with its specific objects and methods of investigation.

What are the implications for research methodology of the metaphor of the consulting room as a laboratory? It enables us to understand psychoanalytic theories as the findings of a clinical research programme that began with Freud's case studies, including the self-analysis described in *The Interpretation of Dreams* (1900a). More scholarly attention should be given to the development of psychoanalytic knowledge as it has evolved in response to clinical phenomena. Psychoanalysis has always had its "research methods", even though these have often been disconnected from methodological discourses in other human sciences. It should be possible to bring about some greater retrospective understanding of these issues, through study of the historical development of psychoanalytic ideas in their clinical context of discovery.

It also becomes possible, in the light of these insights, to improve and refine methods of clinical discovery. In the terminology of research methodology, the clinical setting is a context of "data collection". The issue arises of what kinds of phenomena are best be captured by what forms of "data collection". For example, can audio transcripts or video-recordings of clinical sessions enhance the amount and quality of information that can be obtained, compared with the procedures of writing-up from memory that have traditionally been the principal source of clinical data?

Clinical data thus collected then become resources for data analysis. There has been a recent development of systematic methods of analysis, such as grounded theory and interpretative phenomenological analysis. Their purpose has been to increase the validity of inferences made from clinical material, both from specific moments within psychoanalytic encounters and over larger arcs of a treatment. These developments of method are further discussed in later chapters.

Notes

1. Another illuminating study of a key seventeenth-century debate about the significance of experimentation is Steven Shapin's and Simon Schaffer's *Leviathan and the Air Pump: Hobbes, Boyle and the Experimental Life*. This describes Hobbes' unavailing arguments against the validity of the experimental method, which, following Boyle's demonstrations, gained acceptance within the emerging scientific community. On the role of experimentation in the history of science, see also Ian Hacking's *Representing and Intervening* (1983).

2. In 1847 Ignaz Semmelweiss had discovered that puerperal fever in childbirth was greatly reduced by antiseptic handwashing by doctors, but the evidence he presented for this was rejected until Pasteur's research provided its theoretical justification, after Semmelweiss had died in an asylum in 1865.

3. A metaphor has the effect of transferring, in a single conceptual step, the attributes of one known field to one whose attributes are not understood. A great deal of understanding, both in the sciences and in everyday life, is achieved through the use of metaphors to make bridges or identify close similarities between one field and another (Black, 1962, Lakoff & Johnson, 1980). As we see in chapter 4, metaphors also have a large place in psychoanalytic understanding.

4. A similar view of clinical discovery has been developed by Judith Hughes (2004).

5. To understand the distinction between "exploration" and "experiment", compare Aristotle's study of the development of the embryo of a chicken's egg with Robert Boyle's investigation of the causal relations between the temperature and the volume of gases (Harré, 1981). Aristotle's only intervention was for the purpose of observation. He examined the growth of the embryo by breaking open and examining each of a cluster of chicken's eggs, at daily intervals between their being laid and their hatching. Boyle, however, modified each of his critical variables, to measure the causal effects of these variations on the others. In psychoanalysis, methods of

observation (e.g. infant observation, but also the observations that accompany and inform clinical practice) correspond to "exploration", while interpretations constitute a kind of experimental intervention. Interpretations may be characterized by "kinds" and their specific effects observed. For example "transference" interpretations—in particular those that take up a negative transference—may be observed to have specific effects on the state of mind of a patient.

6. Ernest Gellner argued, in *The Psychoanalytic Movement"* (1985), that psychoanalysis was correct in its recognition of the irrational elements in human experience, even though its means of understanding them were invalid, as Popper had suggested.

7. Note, for example, convergences between psychoanalysis and important strands in developmental psychology, attachment theory, and neuroscience.

CHAPTER FOUR

Philosophical realism and its relevance

The theoretical nature of psychoanalysis

In the public domain, whose province includes the authorities who make decisions about mental health and its treatments, psychoanalysis has long struggled for recognition as a valid form of knowledge. In part this is because of its assertion of the significance of the unconscious part of the mind, which has long been a matter of intense argument with its antagonists. It is understandable that the postulation of a sphere of mind that is not readily recognizable and puts up resistance to being known gives rise to scepticism. It seems to be only when experiences compel individuals to recognize that they have states of mind that are deeply troubling to themselves and others, and which cannot be readily understood, that the idea of an unconscious mind is likely to gain acceptance.

But the explanation of these difficulties of acceptance does not lie only with the idea of the unconscious. Psychoanalytic thinking is inherently theoretical in its nature, in so far as it refers to configurations of the mind that are not straightforwardly observable, as symptoms of mental disorder such as obsessions or phobias may be. Psychoanalytic trainees are taught psychoanalytic theory or theories and are expected to make use of these in their clinical work with patients. These theories identify and name entities such as the Oedipus complex, or the paranoid-schizoid and depressive positions. They also name "mechanisms" or interactive processes such as repression, splitting, and projective identification.

Ideas of this kind constitute the basic theoretical grammar of psycho-analysis. They are abstract "ideal typical" configurations, which have been found by psychoanalysts to give coherence and meaning to empirical phenomena encountered for the most part in consulting rooms. They have the property of generalizations or universals that have been found to be transferable from one "case" to another and thus constitute a field of theoretical and conceptual reference in clinical work. They amount to a "bank" of ideas on which clinicians can draw to identify those "kinds" of entity and experience that appear in their practice.

Psychoanalytic theories are deductive in their form—that is to say, they assert necessary relationships between their component elements. It is because of their deductive character that dependable inferences can be drawn from them, in their application in clinical situations. For example, oedipal desires are by logical implication accompanied by the desire to exclude "third parties", whether a rival parent or siblings. The paranoid-schizoid position definitionally entails the splitting of good and bad aspects of both objects and the self and the inhibition or distortion of rational thought.

Psychoanalytic theories have been in continuous evolution since the field's foundation, and there have been many divergences and disagreements about particular theories along the way. Much of this development has taken place in response to the specific phenomena that have manifested themselves in clinical situations. Many of the differences that have emerged in psychoanalytic theory reflect differences between the clinical phenomena that they have sought to explain and, indeed, from psychoanalysts' value-based interests in selected aspects of human nature.[1] But by no means all theoretical differences merely reflect actual differences in their objects. Some are disagreements about the nature of the same "facts". For example, whether or not infants are universally "object-related" from birth (as Klein believed), or develop this propensity only after an earlier phase of primary narcissism (Freud's original view) is one that requires a definite resolution, even though the broader theoretical implications of this question have made this resolution difficult. However, there have been long-standing theoretical disagreements and disputes in scientific fields other than psychoanalysis, although its critics often seem to suppose that in all other sciences perfect consensus reigns.

Psychoanalysis is a practical as well as a theoretical science—that is to say, its purpose is not only to generate a "universal" understanding of its field, as a corpus of connected theories validated by experimental or observational trials, such as one might believe characterizes the fields of the natural sciences, but also to make possible the understanding and treatment of the separate individuals who come to it as patients, and to take account in doing this of their uniqueness and specificity as individuals. This is, in part, a matter of the ethical and aesthetic dimensions of the psychoanalytic perspective. Psychoanalysis is interested not only in its objects of study as members of "kinds" (for example, those "kinds" named by psychiatric categorizations of mental disorder), but it is also interested in them as persons with their own potential for growth and development as individuals. Of course, psychoanalytic therapists will wish for their patients to cease to be depressed, or pathologically anxious, or disabled from living satisfying lives, for whatever reasons. In this respect their therapeutic goal is no different from those of other mental health practitioners. But their interest in and commitment to their patients goes beyond this. Their therapeutic purpose is to support in their patients the growth of their particular capacities for thought and feeling, such that they can fulfil their own purposes and potentialities. The aim of psychoanalytic treatment is as much to enable development in patients as to "cure" them.

This goal, together with the naturally occurring diversity of human character and experience, is why there is never a perfect "fit" between the "ideal typical" formulations of psychoanalytic concepts and theories, and the phenomena that analysts encounter in their consulting rooms. The correspondences between clinical facts and the theories that can give explanatory meaning to these are always approximate. The "normal science" of clinical psychoanalysis thus often consists of extending the explanatory reach of a theoretical schema in its application to a specific patient. Therapists will often find that this is far from an intellectually tidy process and may well find themselves drawing on more than one theoretical subparadigm to bring understanding to the immediate clinical situation. It is a matter for judgement and empirical assessment whether the best clinical outcomes are achieved by psychoanalytic psychotherapists who choose to work within the framework of a single theoretical paradigm, or whether eclecticism and theoretical bricolage can work as effectively.

The fact that psychoanalysis is committed both to the generation of new knowledge and to clinical practice with individual patients gives rise to misunderstandings about its nature as a science. Psychoanalysts are called upon to make fresh discoveries in almost every moment of their clinical practice. But for the most part these are discoveries of a very particularistic and "low-level" kind—such as, "what is the meaning of what is happening between my patient and me here and now?" . . . "What does this tell me about the state of mind, or even the developmental history, of my patient?" Such "local" discoveries may well draw on and instantiate broader psychoanalytic ideas. But they will mostly have neither the purpose nor the outcome of developing these ideas in ways intended to have a more universal relevance or application. It is enough, for most clinicians, most of the time, to hold to their task of understanding their particular patients and, as its essential purpose, to enable their patients better to understand themselves. The revision and advance of psychoanalytic theories is not the day-to-day activity of the majority of psychoanalysts.

However, sometimes psychoanalysts and psychoanalytic psycho-therapists do engage in the additional kind of investigation involved in theory generation. When this happens, it goes beyond the understanding of an individual patient or patients, although it is often arises from it. This is where psychoanalytic concepts and theories themselves become the critical object of the analyst's attention and study. The question then becomes, is a new concept or theory needed to take account of this clinical phenomenon, or of this patient? Or, to put it another way, do the conceptualizations and theories that are available and seemingly applicable to this situation actually fail to explain or predict what is happening? And if they do fail, can a new concept or theory be discovered or invented that better explains the phenomenon in question? My contention is that it is through such questioning of existing theories and their consequent revision that psychoanalytic understanding has advanced and its theories have evolved (M. J. Rustin, 2001). This process is surprisingly close to the idea of progress through theoretical conjecture and empirical falsification prescribed for science by Karl Popper.

Now, this apparently abstract and "theoretical" nature of psycho-analytic thinking goes against the grain of common-sense thinking, and especially the "common-sense psychology" that dominates public discourse. What is found contentious and sometimes obnoxious is the reference within psychoanalysis to entities and configurations of the mind that are not simply observable, as, for example, a particular phobia or obsession may be. Recognizing that a person may be made anxious by a particular object or experience (e.g., the presence of dirt, or the idea of eating or sex) seems to be straightforward. Behavioural symptoms may be easy to see—sometimes even hard not to see. The explanatory difficulty comes when a psychoanalyst insists on looking beyond what she sees as a symptom, to the underlying structures of the mind where she believes its underlying cause may lie. While it is true that the structures of mind with which psychoanalysts are concerned are deemed by them to be "unconscious" in their specific, dynamic sense of the term, it is not only this unconscious aspect that is an object of suspicion in psychoana-lytic thinking. The broader idea that causal powers may be located in theoretically defined structures that are not immediately observable in themselves is itself a matter of contention in the philosophy of the sciences. It is here that philosophical realism, in its relation to the sciences, is relevant to understanding the nature of psychoanalysis.

The realist conception of scientific knowledge

The modern realist philosophy of science emerged in the 1970s as a movement of dissent from the prevailing orthodoxies of empiricism, the effect of whose domination, the "new realists" contended, was to misunderstand science, nature (including human nature), and society.

Two of its founders, Rom Harré and Roy Bhaskar, first sought to define their positions through revising the understanding of the natural, not the human, sciences, even though the human sciences were their principal focus of interest. According to them, it was through misrepresentations and misunderstandings of the methodologies of the natural sciences that the human sciences had been led in false directions. They sought to show that if the procedures of the natural sciences were correctly understood and appropriate conclusions drawn from them, then the human sciences (psychology in Harré's case, political economy and sociology in the view of Bhaskar and his realist associates) could be properly reconstituted.[2] The realist philosophy of science adds a further dimension to the critique of the empiricist ways of thinking that dominated the human sciences until the 1960s and 1970s and was explored in chapters 2 and 3.

Realist philosophy defined its antagonist as the empiricist and, in its strongest terms, "positivist" view of science,[3] which claims that no phenomenon that is not directly observable can be recognized as an object for science, nor can scientific theories or explanations have any basis other than that of the constant conjunction of observed entities. The most influential figure in philosophy to set out this view was David Hume (1739, 1777). He was laying down a basis for the investigation of the natural world by methods of empirical observation and logical reasoning, rejecting what he saw as the "metaphysical" (i.e. beyond sensory observation) of the pre-scientific philosophers and theologians. His aim was to clarify and provide philosophical legitimacy for scientific modes of inquiry, to superseding the religious frame of reference that had dominated Western society until the seventeenth century. Hume was himself a sceptic in matters of religion. He wrote:

> All reasonings concerning matters of fact seem to be founded on the relation of Cause and Effect. By means of that relation alone we can go beyond the evidence of our memory and our senses.

> I shall venture to affirm, as a general proposition which admits of no
> exception, that the knowledge of this relation is not, in any instance,
> attained by reasonings a priori, but arises entirely from experience when
> we find that any particular objects are constantly conjoined with each
> other. [Hume, 1777, Section 4, Part 1, ¶ 22 and 23]

The realists rejected these Humean assumptions. They argued against
the view that nature is understood merely as an infinity of discrete
empirical objects that we connect in causal laws inferred from our
observation of their constant conjunction. An example of such a conjunction is that of the phases of the moon and the ebb and flow of the
tides. This correlation was observed centuries before there could be
an adequate scientific explanation of their causal connection, which
depended on the theory of gravitational attraction. Gravitational
attraction is an example of a theory that asserts the existence of a deep
structure in nature that is known through its many observable effects
but is not identical with any of them. Harré proposed that we come to
understand nature as composed not of infinities of particular objects
or phenomena, linked in contingent ways as mere "constant conjunctions", but as composed of "kinds", embodying complex attributes and
possessing specific causal powers. Scientists have developed theories
of great explanatory power that explain causal powers of these kinds
and the relation of these to one another.

One example given by Harré and Madden (1975, chapter 1) is that
of the chemical elements and their properties, for example, copper.
Copper is an entity that possesses certain observable attributes—colour,
brittleness, conductivity etc.—but also less directly visible underlying
properties (e.g., those of atomic weight and valency), which explain its
observable qualities. Copper comes to be understood as a distinct, "real"
entity that possesses these attributes, which become part of its definition
as a "kind". The periodic table is a miracle of such scientific explanation, since it enables the many observable properties of the discrete
chemical elements to be correlated as effects of their fundamental atomic
structure, even to the degree that the properties of elements that were
empirically unknown were able to be theoretically predicted before they
could be observed in nature. Harré holds that much scientific knowledge is of theoretically constituted kinds of entity.

Harré argued that analogues and metaphors had an important function in the development of scientific knowledge—that is to say, science
did not merely advance through inferences from observed facts, but also
through the transfer of structured kinds of understanding from one field
to another. Harré's idea of "source analogues" asserted the significance
of metaphors. A metaphor transfers what is known in one field to another

and functions as a hypothesis about the properties of the unknown field (Black, 1962). Such metaphors or analogies can vastly extend the scope and power of explanation, sometimes in a specific moment of illumination. We become able to understand one "domain" of knowledge by transposing our existing knowledge of another, such new knowledge then requiring its empirical verification.

Harré gives many examples of this pattern of theoretical discovery. He cites Darwin's theory of natural selection. As well as reflecting on what he observed on his expeditions, Darwin made use of a "source analogue"—the selective breeding of stock-breeders or gardeners—to understand the process of natural selection. By taking away the idea of purposeful intervention, made by a breeder or designer to enhance or diminish specific attributes in a species, Darwin realized that naturally occurring variations, in an environment of reproductive competition, could explain the selection and survival of the fittest in their particular ecological niche. Another source analogue for Darwin was Malthus's population theory. Malthus had argued that populations would expand until they reached the limit of resources to support them. Darwin extended this idea to apply to natural species and their relation to their environment.

Harré gives other examples from the history of science of metaphoric transfers of understanding from one sphere to another. With Robert Boyle's theory of gases, the source analogue was the idea of a coiled spring whose volume expands as pressure upon it is reduced. In Newtonian physics, solid objects are imagined as having the properties of billiard balls, which are motionless except when force is imparted to them. Gravitational forces, operating in three dimensions, can, by this analogue explain many forms of motion. Later on, atoms become modelled as miniature solar systems, with particles revolving round a nucleus. The idea of a computer virus transfers the attributes of the viruses known to biology to the sphere of computers, usefully because both have the properties of "infecting", by reproducing themselves rapidly and parasitizing their hosts. Preventive ("hygienic") measures in the biological sphere are shown to be relevant by analogy to the cybernetic. The explanatory power of this metaphor arises from the fact that biological and computer viruses are both carriers of information, through genetic and software "codes", respectively.[4] The theory of "Artificial Intelligence" has modelled the brain according to the properties of the computer. In the reverse direction of transfer, computer scientists seek to design computers with more of the capabilities of human brains.

An example of theoretical understanding through metaphor (Harré, 1979, 1986) from the field of social science is Goffman's concept of the performative "team", acting in order to make a positive impression on an audience. Instances he gives of this are the "front-stage" and "back-stage" locations of a restaurant, or a family preparing its home to receive visitors. Goffman described a criminal form of team performance in an essay that described the technique used by confidence tricksters of duping their victims and then "cooling them out" into the false belief that nothing untoward has happened. The film *The Sting* dramatized this kind of performance. Harré's "theory families" evolving from "source analogues" resemble Kuhn's paradigms (Harré, 1986, Ch. 11).

Roy Bhaskar (1975), like Harré, proposed that the sciences postulate theories to explain nature at a level more abstract than that of empirical observation. Bhaskar also asserted that theoretical entities exist, and have causal properties that give rise to the observable phenomena that we perceive through our senses. In the non-organic, physical sphere, examples of such theoretical entities are gravity, electromagnetic energy, and subatomic structures and particles. They are theoretical constructions whose existence is inferred from their observed effects. He proposed that reality is known to science in three stratified levels, which consist of the real (causal mechanisms that generate actual events); the actual (events that occur); and the empirical (that part of the actual that we actually perceive). This view is consistent with Harré's example of the chemical elements and the invariant relation between their fundamental atomic structure and their various physical and chemical properties. The sciences were able to evolve through theoretical deduction as well as through cumulative observation because of the invariant relations embodied in their theories.

Harré's substantive adversary was the doctrines and methods of empiricist psychology, which sought experimentally to demonstrate correlations between certain observable attributes of human behaviour without giving attention to its underlying intentional and rule-governed structures and processes. Bhaskar believed that recognition of the causal powers of deep structures, including those of the rational human mind, could lead to an understanding of science as a means of emancipation through enhancing human agency and freedom. The obscuring of the real powers underlying capitalism by attending only to the apparent freedoms of participants in markets—not least labour markets—was one of the instances most important to Bhaskar.[5]

Realist theories of science re-focused attention on the objects of scientific investigation, in contrast to the means of perception and observational evidence by which these entities became known to science. Crucial to philosophical realism was a distinction between the philosophical concept of *ontology* (the study of what is, or "being"), and that of *epistemology* (the study of the means by which knowledge is gained). Both Harré and Bhaskar, in their different ways, re-affirmed the significance of ontology to science in a twentieth-century philosophical climate in which it had been dismissed as virtual nonsense. Ontology, or the study of "being", was dismissed as referring to a merely "metaphysical" sphere, with no tangible meaning or empirical referents "Metaphysics", which encompassed the idea of ontology or "being", had been forcefully rejected during the philosophical defeat of idealist philosophy in the early twentieth century by logical positivism and its more nuanced empiricist successors, who included the Wittgensteinian philosophers of "ordinary language". The dismissal in British philosophy, over several decades, of the entire field of "continental philosophy" was a related aspect of this empiricist and positivist hegemony.

Realism and psychoanalysis

What, one may well ask, has all this to do with psychoanalysis? Why is "realism" in the philosophy of science, in the terms set out by advocates such as Harré and Bhaskar, relevant to psychoanalytic inquiry? The principal reason is that psychoanalysis is distinctive for its postulation of theoretical structures of the mind, which are known largely primarily through their observable effects, including those states of consciousness and "meaningful" forms that psychoanalysts seek to understand and change through interpretation. Bhaskar's view of reality as inherently "stratified" into "levels" that include surfaces known through observations and "depths" that are known through theoretical inference has a specific application to the central theoretical postulates of psychoanalysis. This affinity arises from the fact that the psychoanalytic unconscious, in Freud's dynamic sense of that term, is specifically blocked off from consciousness through the mechanisms of repression and of projection, splitting, and projective identification in later theoretical formulations. Psychoanalysts believe that these levels of these mind exist, and their separation is the outcome of quasi-intentional processes—for example, repression—that are located in the unconscious mind itself. Thus "the unconscious" in its psychoanalytic sense is a theoretical entity, with definite attributes and powers conceptually attached to it, just as we have seen that attributes and powers were assigned by Harré to chemical elements in his arguments for scientific realism.

What forms do psychoanalytic explanations take in practice? This question invites us to examine the differences that separate psychoanalytic understanding from other approaches to the mind, including those which dominate contemporary mental health services. Contemporary clinical psychological and psychiatric practices are for the most part "positivist" in their methodological assumptions. The *Diagnostic and Statistical Manual of Mental Disorders*, now in its fifth version as *DSM–5*, is essentially a classification of symptoms, set out without theoretical explanation or justification. (In fact, in the original identification and definition of these symptoms, psychoanalytic ideas were influential, though the *DSM* does not incorporate their theoretical underpinning and explanation.) In this health environment, the theoretical rationale for the definition of a disorder, or for the development of a treatment that may offer a remedy for it, is of much less account than the "constant conjunction", if one can be established, between the disorder that has been defined by its symptoms, and the standardized treatments that are offered as potential cures.

In physical medicine, immense scientific attention is given both to questions of the immediate effectiveness of treatments and to establishing empirical evidence for them, and to the investigation of the underlying structures and processes that are causally responsible for illness and health. Although the evidence base for treatment effectiveness is assigned great importance, "fundamental" medical science and the many subdisciplines on which it draws (e.g., immunology, embryology, virology, anatomy, biochemistry, etc.) also occupy a large place in this field.

In the field of mental health, it appears that the dominant focus of attention is different. Psychoanalysis is unusual in its practitioners having always been most interested in the fundamental structures and processes of the mind and in the differences as well as the similarities and uniformities to be found in its objects of study. The central theoretical findings of attachment theory, regarding the four distinctive patterns of mother–infant attachment, have been validated in several thousand empirical studies. Psychoanalysts might ask, why undertake so many studies to verify the existence and causes of only four or five distinct patterns of behaviour, when one could be investigating the immense variety of configurations of mind and emotion that need to be understood if there are to be effective psychotherapeutic treatments? Developments in neuroscience, in laboratory studies of developmental pathways, in evolutionary psychology, and in the study of affective systems, are, however, examples of "fundamental" kind of research that are taking place in the field of mental health, from which one might hope to see some convergence with psychoanalytic theories concerning the mind.

However, the predominant demand in current mental health services is for "evidence-based" therapies, and this pressure has crystallized the methodological issues in dispute. "Evidence" is taken to refer to what can be empirically demonstrated, through the factual correlation of one observable fact with another—for example, the correlation of a symptom (or symptoms) with an intervention (like the administration of a drug) that will cause, or seem to cause, its disappearance. Neither the condition being treated, nor the remedy provided for it, have to be understood in theoretical terms for such trials to be instigated, and for their findings to become the grounds for prescribed treatments.

Here is an illustrative instance. Suppose we have a child patient—it is more likely to be a boy than a girl—with symptoms that lead him to be defined as suffering from attention deficit hyperactivity disorder (ADHD).[6] (This diagnostic term refers to two associated symptoms, designated as a disorder.) Suppose that a drug, or a drug family such as Ritalin, is administered to this patient in an appropriate, experimentally trialled dose and is shown to reduce his symptoms. We then have the kind of proven cause-and-effect relationship that meets the specifications of "evidence-based medicine". All that one needs to know for an explanation to suffice in this framework is that two observable entities— the cluster of distressing behaviours and the drug that can alter it—can be found to exist in a constant conjunction.

A psychoanalytically minded clinician is unlikely to be satisfied with this kind of understanding. Furthermore, this form of explanation departs so far from psychoanalytic beliefs about the human mind that she is not likely to have confidence in the lasting effectiveness of its remedy, even though in some trials it has been shown to have improved the behaviour and state of mind of patients. Even if the psychotherapist has been convinced that admission of this drug can help a particular patient, she is still likely to want to explore further, to find "deeper" reasons for the patient's difficulties and a means of addressing these in psychotherapy. What reasons or causes might these be, and where might the psychoanalyst look for them?

One question to be asked in such a case might be about the nature of the patient's "attention deficit", and his "hyperactivity". Attention or inattention to what, the therapist might ask, and hyperactive in what ways and to what purpose? Here is a patient who is unable to attend to his lessons at school (this is one common reason for referral) or to what is said to him at home, to the point that he is persistently disruptive even in doing the ordinary things of life—for example, at meal-times or with his mother in the supermarket. A psychoanalyst might surmise that the behaviour is not the outcome of a mere deficit of attention (e.g., to mother's words) but may, rather, be the effect of a serious disturbance of his attention, perhaps unconscious in its origin and cause. A hypothesis might be that the child is so upset by his "internal" state of mind, his "phantasies" about himself, and his relationship to those around him (his "internal objects") that there is no mental space left within him for listening to his teacher or responding sensibly to what she says. Similarly, being endlessly restless and active in all sorts of ways that other people find disturbing may serve as a distraction, a way of creating a mental space separate from that in which disturbing and distressing thoughts and feelings might otherwise emerge.

In other words, the psychotherapist may imagine such symptoms to be the effects of some deeper structural causes, located, perhaps as unconscious phantasies, within the mind of the patient. The problem, from a psychoanalytic perspective, is to find out what this "something" is, and perhaps, then, by enabling the child himself to understand its meanings, to lessen their unconscious influence on his mind. One says "unconscious" in part because it is almost certain that a child with these symptoms has no conscious understanding of what their cause might be. The various terms that I have introduced in this sketch—an inner world, mental space, unconscious phantasy, internal objects—are "theoretical" terms, that is to say, they have virtually no meaning outside a model of the mind that one cannot directly capture through observation, but which psychoanalysts have rather built up conceptually and inferentially, as a hypothetical "structure" with its own "mechanisms" and processes.

Additionally challenging for those who take the view that knowledge is essentially the representation in concepts of phenomena perceived through the senses is the fact that psychoanalytic explanation is highly metaphorical, both in its theoretical structure and in its interpretative practice. The "internal world" of the mind is not like the inside of a box, or even the inside of a human head, even though something is certainly going on neurologically to bring about mental phenomena. The concept of an "internal" world makes use of the "source analogue" of the inside and outside of physical objects. Bion's model of the maternal mind as a container, and of the container–contained relation that follows from this, is a metaphor that posits two imagined "boxes" in which certain mental processes occur, with various kinds of communication between them. The ideas of projection, evacuation, and toxicity are drawn from source analogues of a physical and biochemical kind, which are deployed to describe mental processes. "Mental space" is also a metaphor. It is an imagined location in which thoughts, feelings, and mental images occur, not a space in which physical objects exist.

Psychoanalytic theory and practice is saturated with metaphorical equivalences of these kinds. It is this quality, as well as its elaborated and complex theoretical vocabulary, that differentiates it from the theoretically and conceptually minimalist languages of empirical psychology, whose prescriptions have widely debarred psychoanalysis from scientific acceptance. The recognition that the sciences have to take account of forms of "being" as well as forms of "seeing", of ontological structures as well as epistemological practices, is thus indispensable to psychoanalytic understanding.

Notes

1. It seems in part a matter of national culture and temperament that lead some analytic schools to have focused more on destructive aspects of the personality and others on its more positive dispositions. Both clearly identify attributes that exist.

2. "Critical realism" has had its advocates in several social science disciplines. There has been, however, surprisingly sparse consideration of its great relevance to psychoanalysis (but see M. J. Rustin, 1991a; Will, 1980, 1986).

3. The distinction between the two is that, for an empiricist, theories do have an independent existence and heuristic function, though they depend on empirical validation. Karl Popper thus valued the role of imaginative conjecture in the invention or discovery of theories; for "positivists", theories are no more than explanatory laws inferred from empirical observations by inductive procedures.

4. The sociologist of education, Basil Bernstein (1975) referred several times in his writings to the promising explanatory conjunctions of biological (genetic) and cultural codes.

5. I believe that Bhaskar was trying to rescue at this metatheoretical level the relevance of a Marxist theory of emancipation that was becoming difficult to defend in substantive terms because of the complex configuration of class structures and relations at the time he was writing, which was far from the polarization that Marx had predicted.

6. There is a large literature on ADHD and its treatments (see, for example, Fonagy & Target, 1994; Gilmore, 2000; Lange, Reichl, Lange, Tucha, & Tucha, 2010).

CHAPTER FIVE

Meanings and causes in psychoanalytic explanation

What is an explanation in psychoanalysis? Is it the same as, or different from, an explanation in physics, chemistry, or biology? Or is it like an explanation in a social science, like economics, sociology or anthropology? Or is quite different from all of these kinds of "scientific" explanation, and more like the explanations we might try to give of the meanings of a novel or a poem? These are fundamental questions: we can hardly hope to understand the nature and methods of research in psychoanalysis if we don't have a clear idea of what kinds of understanding or explanation psychoanalysts are looking for.

Each of these kinds of explanation is relevant and important to the study of human lives. The laws of physics, chemistry, and biology all have relevance to this understanding: their application in many domains, not least medicine, has transformed lives for the better. Although the social sciences generally achieve less certainty and finality than the natural sciences, nevertheless most people would accept that economics has thrown some light on the functioning of markets; sociological research on the social divisions of class, gender, and race and their effects; and investigations in anthropology on the social functions of rituals. But we can hardly claim not to have learned as much about human nature from writers such as Euripides or Shakespeare and the imaginary characters they have created as we have learned from social scientists and psychologists, even though in quite a different way. The difficulty is to clarify the similarities and differences between these forms of understanding and, having done so, to locate the theory and practice of psychoanalysis among them.

These issues have been problematic for the psychoanalytic field from its inception. Freud wished psychoanalysis to be recognized as a science like any other, and in his early work developed models of explanation, based on somewhat mechanical source-analogues, that were consistent with this ambition. Thus in his initial topographical model, desires were repressed almost as if they were physical forces, which sometimes broke through these barriers. Freud's early metaphorical model of desires and repression has been described as hydraulic, an analogy of liquids moving under pressure. But in *The Interpretation of Dreams* (1900a), his method of explanation was interpretative, as well as causal. A dream was a representation of repressed desires. It could thus be seen as an effect of a certain kind of causal mechanism. But its more important and special significance lay in its meaning, what it expressed in a symbolic form. The terms "condensation" and "displacement", referring to the transformations of objects of desire or fear under the influence of repression, are metaphors that evoke physical events. But the particular meaning that Freud assigned to them referred to the semantic attributes of language. The meanings that Freud attributed to dreams and symptoms were both in the domain of effects of certain causes and were also transformations of a symbolic kind, which he understood through their interpretation—that is, by a kind of "translation" of meanings that have been allowed to come to the surface, from their consciously intended meaning to their deeper symbolic significance as representations of the unconscious mind. Freud's *The Interpretation of Dreams* (1900a), *The Psychopathology of Everyday Life* (1901b), and *Jokes and Their Relation to the Unconscious* (1905c) are full of such "translations" from overt to covert kinds of significance, each revealing an underlying reality of unconscious desires and conflicts.

Both during and after Freud's lifetime, it became difficult for psychoanalysts to defend his original claim that psychoanalysis should be recognized as a new science. There were various reasons for this. One of these was the deep split that developed, especially in the English, but less in the German-speaking world, between the sciences and the humanities.[1] Since psychoanalysis retained a deep affinity with the interpretative modes of thought of literature and the humanities, to which Freud remained strongly attached, this made some analysts feel uncomfortable with the idea of their field as required to follow the rules and assume the characteristics of a science. A further reason for this difficulty was the restrictive idea of the scientific method, which adopted theoretical and experimental physics as its normative model, which became dominant in the early and middle years of the last century. As we have seen, psychoanalysts found it difficult to defend themselves against the attacks that were launched on it from that philosophical position. The field suffered, in effect, an intellectual defeat, and this induced its leading figures mostly to withdraw into a professional psychoanalytic and/or psychiatric enclave, mostly outside the universities. When its place in public mental health services came under serious challenge from the 1990s onwards from governments' demands for "evidence-based medicine", psychoanalysis found itself ill-prepared to undertake the kinds of research or provide the empirical findings that would meet these requirements. Indeed, it found that "scientific research" was being defined in such a narrow way as to doubt whether there had been much previous research in psychoanalysis at all.[2] The traditions and methods of knowledge-generation through which the entire corpus of psychoanalytic theories and techniques has developed over more than a century and the method of discovery on which they have been based were dismissed as scientifically inferior and irrelevant. But, paradoxically, the treatments that the current vogue for outcome studies seeks desperately to measure could only have been developed through these denigrated methods of investigation. The purpose of clinical methods of discovery in psychoanalysis has been to investigate the fundamental structures and processes of the mind, not merely the effects of psychoanalytic treatments. Without such knowledge, there would be nothing for "outcome studies" to investigate and measure.

I have argued in previous chapters that crucial developments in the philosophy and sociology of science have transformed the understanding of science and its methods in ways that have large implications for psychoanalysis. These developments have now made it possible for psychoanalysis—the investigation of the unconscious—to take up its proper place in the field of the human sciences. An equally important development concerns the dimensions of meaning and cause introduced at the beginning of this chapter as giving rise to contrasting kinds of explanation.

Meaning and cause in the social sciences

The difference between meanings and causes became important in the social sciences in the nineteenth century well before they arose as an issue for psychoanalysis. A distinctive attribute of the social sciences is that their objects of study are human beings who give their own definition to and interpretations of their world, and that these "subjective meanings" are constitutive elements of their worlds. The fields of study of material objects and processes that constitute the natural sciences are different from the self-reflective and self-interpretative nature of the objects of the human sciences, of which psychoanalysis is one.

Human actions are determined by motivations of which people ("social actors") can give their own account and upon which they can reflect (Davidson, 1963). Animals, even plants, can be said in a sense to have "motivations" too, to seek food, reproductive partners, or light. But what they cannot do to is to give an account of these in a symbolic form and to modify their behaviour through changes that are effected in the sphere of symbolism. It might be argued that some animal behaviours, and some animals' relationships with human beings, are mediated by symbolic exchanges of limited kinds, but these are much less complex than the symbolic life of human beings.

The social sciences, as they developed in the eighteenth and nineteenth centuries and as they sought to define their identities separate from those of the natural sciences, were obliged to take account of this symbolic, cultural, and subjective dimension of their object of study. They did this in different ways, according to their "disciplines" and specific objects of attention. The economists adopted the assumption that human beings were motivated by rational interests in optimizing their satisfactions, construing market exchange as one of the principal spheres in which optimization is pursued. Quite a lot of market behaviour can indeed be explained through this model, although there is also a significant field of economics that is devoted to exploring the limits of these rational-interest assumptions.

The sociologists developed more descriptive and open-minded models of motivation, noting that values and motivations were variables, not constants, and seeking to explain how and why they did vary. A formative work in this respect, in regard both to substance and method, was Max Weber's *The Protestant Ethic and the Spirit of Capitalism* (1930), and the methodological essays that accompanied it (Weber, 1949). Weber proposed that satisfactory explanations in the social sciences had to take account of explanations of a kind that *both* established the relations of cause and effect (the normal goal of the sciences) *and* explained in an interpretative way the meanings of social actions to those who performed them. Weber's argument, a partial rebuttal of Karl Marx' "materialist" explanation of the origins of capitalism and preceding social systems in terms of their modes and relations of production, was that the emergence of Protestantism, a variety of religious belief, had a major causal role in capitalism's rise.[3] He demonstrated the causal dimension of this relation by showing that capitalism had developed far more fully and quickly in

Protestant societies (e.g., the Netherlands and Britain) than in Catholic ones (e.g., Spain and Italy). He demonstrated the connection at the level of meaning and interpretation by describing those rational or logical implications in Protestant systems of religious belief and practice that would encourage or enforce "capitalist" behaviours among Protestants. Such beliefs, the argument was, would give rise to a compulsive desire to "prove" individual worth and a person's divine election and entitlement to salvation through the evidence of their worldly success, their abstention from sensual pleasures, etc. Weber argued that explanations both at the levels of cause and of meaning were necessary for the full understanding of the origins of capitalism to be complete. By implication, both these levels were essential for all social scientific explanation.

Unsurprisingly, the arguments of Weber's *Protestant Ethic and the Spirit of Capitalism* were disputed. For example, it was argued by some Marxist historians, such as Christopher Hill (1961, 1991), that Protestantism, though associated with capitalism, was more its effect than its cause. It was argued that there had been proto-forms of capitalism in Catholic societies, such as the city states of Italy, and that the Calvinist theory of predestination, which Weber associated with capitalist motivations, might as well have led to fatalism as to compulsive striving among its believers. But none of these substantive issues called into question the idea that the structures of religious meanings and values that prevailed in precapitalist and capitalist societies were relevant to understanding them, and that these needed to be understood interpretatively as symbolic systems that had ruleful and logical implications for their believers, in order for their causal effectiveness to be understood.

This idea that the interpretation of "subjective" or cultural meanings is an essential element of a sufficient explanation has remained central to sociology ever since it was first enunciated, and it has been defined and elaborated within many subsequent schools of sociological thought (e.g., symbolic interactionism, phenomenology, and ethnomethodology), as well as in the cultural or interpretative anthropology of influential writers such as Clifford Geertz (1973, 1983) and Victor Turner (1974). Differences of focus and emphasis remain important in this field. On the whole, those committed to quantitative research methods adopt "causal" rather than "interpretative" methods of explanation. However, correlations of causal variables established through objective and statistically valid methods (for example, between social class and ill health or educational achievement) invariably invite, and require if they are to be sufficient, a further level of explanation at the level of motivations, meanings, and beliefs. A correlation of variables that seems to make no interpretative sense or contradicts conventional understanding of motives and purposes merely demands further investigations to resolve the apparent anomaly or deficiency of explanation. Qualitative researchers are mostly more committed to an "interpretative" approach, sometimes even believing that if a convincing and detailed explanation can be provided of behaviours in terms of intentions and motives, additional empirical verification to prove causal connections is redundant. After all, in everyday life many assumptions have to be made about what is causally connected to what. These assumptions are based on observations of the causal consequences of actions, but also on interpretative understanding of people's motivations and beliefs and how these shape their behaviours. There is not time and resources to subject every such assumption to empirical test. It is usually only when we find that our taken-for-granted picture of reality is false that investigation of the real facts is called for. No one needed empirical research to prove that smoking cigarettes was relaxing and pleasurable—research only became necessary once it was realized that it might also be leading to illness and death.

A compromise that is often struck between causal and interpretative perspectives (often corresponding to quantitative and qualitative methods) is to propose that interpretative, descriptive methods may be productive and informative in the generation of theories but are inadequate at the level of proof. It is often held that hypotheses that have been inferred using qualitative methods of study need subsequently to be tested by methods that can empirically test correlations of variables to establish relations of cause and effect. This is sometimes referred to as the distinction between the "context of discovery" and the "context of justification" (Popper, 1934).

It is important to note that psychoanalysts have mostly believed that their clinical practice provides them with sufficient evidence of the effectiveness (and sometimes ineffectiveness) of what they do, despite the common absence of quantitative measures of this. They believe that their capabilities in their practice with patients attunes them to evidence of development and change in them, or its absence. (Analyses are sometimes reported in professional presentations to have got stuck, or go nowhere.) They hold that theories and techniques have advanced in their field because of clinical evidence of "what works", or at least works better, and that the literature in their field evidences this. Their professional view is that there is more than one method of assessing effectiveness and value, of which the empirical[4] or, at its most rigorous, the randomized controlled double-blind trial is but one of several. An analogy can be drawn with the works of creative artists and writers whose effects and influence are sometimes very substantial, but are scientifically unmeasured.

Interpretation and causality in psychoanalysis

These issues in sociological explanation have their close equivalent in psychoanalysis, although, as always, with the additional dimension of the unconscious to be taken into account. Psychoanalysis mainly locates itself at the interpretative end of this methodological spectrum. What psychoanalysts mostly do is, after all, to try to understand the meanings of their patients' communications, whether these are made in words, play, gesture, behaviour, or as they are understood through the "countertransference"—that is to say, when an analyst infers that her own state of mind may be reflecting unconscious communications from the patient.

Interpretation of this kind calls for the development of a particular sensitivity to subtleties and nuances of meaning, especially when in a psychoanalytic context it may be expected that patients may not say what they mean, or mean what they say. Psychotherapists have to become "specialists" in this kind of sensitivity, a capability different from that required from most social scientists or even psychologists. This is because psychotherapists' practice is focused on individual patients, their particular states of mind and feeling, and their development within the context of a therapeutic relationship. And also because a psychoanalytic interest in unconscious dimensions of the mind, and the ways in which these make their presence felt in the transference relationship, calls for a distinctive kind of attention and discrimination. Only with the utmost delicacy can unconscious meanings be identified and brought convincingly to the attention of a patient. There is need for a psychoanalytic therapist to be able to stay with the experience of an individual patient, and to resist premature impulses to theorize and generalize, for fear that the particular moment or quality of an experience will be missed. There are kinds of interpretative social science, such as in socio-biographical and narrative studies, that also seek this kind of closeness to experience—some of them influenced by psychoanalysis (Hollway & Jefferson, 2012). But this is not the case for most social science research, where there is a greater pressure to move from an initial attention to phenomenological experience and qualitative description, in doing fieldwork and acquiring data, towards more abstract and theoretical ways of thinking, during the operations of data analysis and writing-up. One reason for this difference of approach is that psychoanalytic clinical research is indissolubly linked to the responsibilities of clinical practice, whereas most social scientific research has a more detached relation to its subjects. The methods of "action research", where researchers may have participant as well as researcher roles in a setting, is one exception to this researcher's rule of detachment.

The sensitivity to symbolic and expressive meaning and their inter-pretation that is so valued in psychoanalytic work finds its nearest equivalent not in the social sciences, but in the humanities. The subtleties of tone, contextual implication, and evoked feelings that are called for in the reading of a work of literature, or in response to the performance of a play, are closer to psychoanalytic practice than they are to most research in the social sciences. When the field of Cultural Studies was founded in the 1960s, seeking to bring different forms of popular culture within the sphere of academic study, its starting point was the application of the methods of literary criticism, hitherto developed in the context of classi-cal literature, to more popular forms, such films or popular music. The exceptional quality that one of its founding figures, Richard Hoggart, brought to this kind of research before its later more theoretical develop-ment was said to be his exceptional sensitivity to "tone". Hoggart wrote, in *The Uses of Literacy* (1967) from his own autobiographical experience, as well as about "texts" drawn from both classical literature and the popular arts. Such a capacity to write from experience, and in response to varied kinds of "texts", also characterizes psychoanalytic work at its best, where the symbolic materials are those that emerge in the interac-tions of the consulting room.

Nevertheless, although there are similarities between the humani-ties, such as literature, and psychoanalytic practice, there are significant differences between them in the sensitivities to meaning and feeling that they both require. The knowledge that has been accumulated and ordered in the scientific literature of psychoanalysis is not merely an accumulation of particular clinical experiences and case studies, even though these have a central place in psychoanalytic writing. From its beginning, psychoanalysis sought to conceptualize and generalize its findings, and to formulate them as descriptions of *kinds* of phenomena and their relation to each other. Psychoanalysis has evolved a rich con-ceptual and theoretical lexicon, in relation to which its "cases" serve as instances or exemplifications and as records of their clinical validation. Its concepts and theories, within their different schools of thought, have evolved in a (relatively) systematic way, in response to their own logi-cal implications, to the pressure of clinical evidence, and to the ways in which changes in culture and society (for example, attitudes to sexual-ity) have brought new issues and concerns into the consulting room.

Generative concepts in psychoanalysis: the transference

Consider, for example, the development in the Kleinian tradition of the understanding of the transference. Initially, Freud's concept referred to the relationship in what we would now call unconscious phantasy that patients developed with their analysts. In his seminal paper "The Nature of the Therapeutic Action of Psycho-Analysis", James Strachey (1934) described how understanding and change could be brought about in an analysis through the recognition of discrepancies between a patient's unconscious beliefs about his analyst and what the patient could come to recognize as an analyst's actual qualities. In this way— usually only in very small steps because of the power of unconscious resistance to self-understanding—a patient could be brought to an awareness of the misperceptions brought about by the influence of unconscious phantasy. In this paper Strachey elaborated in detail, by reference to his own clinical experience, a crucial implication of Freud's original theory of the transference.

How the transference related to the process of interpretation was one "puzzle" (to use Kuhn's term) raised for psychoanalysis by its transference theory. Another was the question of what happened on the other side of this relationship to the analyst. The initial idea was the analyst would simply do her best to understand and interpret what was happening in the session and in the mind of the patient. Since the transference was a projection of feeling between one person and another, it must be expected to have some effects on its recipient. The original idea was that such emotional effects on analysts should be dealt with in such a way as to minimize any disturbance in their capacity to attend to and think about their patients. If analysts found themselves being unduly upset or disturbed, this was an indication that their own analysis had not equipped them with sufficient self-insight for all of their work. Perhaps such experiences of disturbances were a sign that more personal analysis, or at least clinical supervision, was necessary.

Then, in 1950, Paula Heimann reflected on her clinical experience in a different way. Melanie Klein had been recently writing about the idea of projective identification, which added a further dimension to the unconscious processes that a transference relationship was likely to involve. Heimann had been struggling with the emotional disturbance she had been experiencing with a particular patient, and she had the idea that this might not merely be an indication of her own vulnerability or clinical inadequacy with this patient but might, rather, be the effect of an unconscious projection into her by her patient. Not only might its content consist in what it conveyed to her about her own state of mind, but it might also be understood as an unconscious communication to her by her patient, conveying information to her about his troubled state of mind as well as hers. This idea even has a precedent in the eighteenth-century philosophers' theory of moral sentiments (Smith, 1759) that were evoked by our "sympathetic" responses to the emotions of others. Thus the expression of pain in others can arouse pain in ourselves.

Thus the seminal idea of the countertransference as a central resource of clinical understanding found its first expression in the psychoanalytic literature. It became substantially extended in subsequent years. Bion's clinical and theoretical writing and Esther Bick's development of the method of psychoanalytic infant observation led to an integration between the theory of infant development and that of psychotic states of mind. It was proposed that in the first months of life the mother–infant relationship depended on the mother's capacity to receive the intense projections of her infant and to process and thus "contain" these. Evidence of the nature of this interaction was also to be found in the consulting room, notably in Bion's understanding of the nature and meaning of his psychotic patients' projections while they were in a state of mind or mindlessness that resembled—indeed, in his view recapitulated—the disorganized mental states of early infancy. In this way another implication of the original theory of transference was identified. The scientific "puzzles" to be to be solved here were as follows: What kind of communications took place in a transference–countertransference relationship? What was the relation between the emotional interactions of infants (the distinction between conscious and unconscious levels of experience can hardly yet have emerged in the minds of small babies) and their mothers, and those that take place in the clinical consulting room?

Many further elaborations of theory of the transference and countertransference relationship followed these early investigations and discoveries. The scope of the "transference" became extended, in the writing of Betty Joseph (1985), to encompass all that happened within an analytic relationship. It became recognized that countertransference experiences were a potential resource for understanding many kinds of patient in analysis, not merely those suffering the most psychotic kinds of disturbance, whom Bion had described. And what about transference and countertransference phenomena in non-clinical settings: for example, in relationships between teachers and pupils in a school—might these be relevant to understanding their interactions also?

Many of the central concepts of psychoanalysis, such as oedipal relationships, the transference and countertransference, the container–contained relation, and the states of mind denoted by the concepts of the paranoid-schizoid and depressive positions (a "position" in this model is a potentially recurrent configuration of mind, not merely a phase in an infant's development) have been found during the evolution of psychoanalysis to be immensely generative—that is to say, their power to identify phenomena and to understand their relation to each other has been found to be far greater than was evident when the phenomena to which they referred were first identified and named. One could say, in the light of a "realist" view of scientific knowledge, that these concepts each identified a distinct field of psychological reality, whose structure and content it became the work of at least a generation of psychoanalytic researchers to investigate and clarify. The development of such theoretical structures takes place both at the level of meaning, as the logical implications of concepts are clarified, and of empirical investigation (usually in the context of the consulting room) of relations of cause and effect. The relevance of the countertransference of the analyst in understanding a patient was a logical implication of the idea of projective identification. (Heimann tells us that it was this conceptual connection that led to her discovery.) Similarly, the distinction Rosenfeld came to see between libidinal and destructive narcissism can be understood as the discovery of a further implication of Freud's distinction between the life and death instincts, in a new context of application. Both of these important new ideas, once discovered, were then tested out by their originators in work that they then reported as evidence of their validity. It is mainly through clinical investigation that the hypotheses that emerge as possibilities within a theoretical structure are put to evidential test, to discover whether or not they can explain additional phenomena.

The core theories and concepts of psychoanalysis are similar in respect of their generative potential to the ideas that lie at the centre of other great scientific paradigms. The theories of gravitation, or of natural selection, or of the atomic composition of the elements have each led to immense programmes of both theoretical and empirical elaboration. In sociology, the forms of social solidarity identified by Emil Durkheim had a comparable potential for theoretical elaboration and empirical extension. A realist would say that these ideas lead us to an understanding of the deep structures in nature, including human nature. Actor-network theory might lead us to believe both that nature, although existing as a reality, can be understood in more than one way, and that our understanding of it can be transformative in its effects.

Knowledge in psychoanalysis and in the humanities

As we have said, in the apprehension of its central phenomena, the transference relationships of the clinical consulting room, psychoanalysts call on sensibilities and skills very close to those that are involved in the understanding of imaginative literature and art. Yet the concepts and theories that psychoanalysis has evolved have no equivalent in the domain of the humanities. In a sequence of poems, novels, or plays, even when they are written by the same author, every work has its own particularity and creates its own imagined world, although there are often elements of repetition and overlap in a writer's work. Indeed, such partial repetitions may be an essential element in its evolution.

The fields of literary criticism and literary theory somewhat blur this boundary between the general and the particular, since such critical theories generalize and order literary artefacts in terms of their kinds and properties. The distinctions made in such work are often informative. For example, understanding the generic attributes of the dramatic forms of comedies and tragedies may enhance understanding of what a dramatist has achieved and the conventions he has followed in writing a particular play. (*Hamlet* can, for example, be understood as a revenge tragedy in which the act of revenge is endlessly deferred because of the troubled state of mind its central character.) Such understandings may even inform the creative work of dramatists in their own reflections on the genres of work or convention they are working with. But for the audience or the reader, response to the exemplary realization of a genre such as tragedy in imagined characters such as Macbeth and Lady Macbeth, Othello or King Lear is more important than the abstract understanding of a genre. It is the particular "instances" created and realized by artists and the "family resemblances" (Wittgenstein, 1953; *Stanford Encyclopedia of Philosophy*, 2002) between them from which we learn most, not from the generalizations or theories that we may infer from them.

Psychoanalysis is different from literature in this respect, since although its ideas are grounded in particular kinds of experience, it is a theoretically systematic and cumulative enterprise, even though it is dependent on sensibilities and habits of mind that are commonly learned through the humanities.[5]

Meanings as causes

One can consider meanings and causes as two complementary modes of explanation in the human sciences, both "levels" being deemed necessary, as Weber proposed, for a complete understanding. An alternative approach argues for their integration, understanding "meanings" and intentions as a particular kind of cause that is essential to the explanation of human action.

This idea corresponds to evident facts. Suppose that one understands a human action to consist of the bringing together of a desire with a belief in a state of affairs within which that desire might be realized (Davidson, 1963; *Stanford Encyclopedia of Philosophy, 2014*). If the desire gives rise to a decision and action then follows to fulfil the desire, then

the desire can be understood, in conjunction with the subject's definition of the situation, as the cause of the subsequent action. For example,
I have a desire for an ice cream. My belief is that the shop on the corner
sells ice cream. If I make a decision to go and buy one and do so, it seems
clear that in this case the desire and the decision were the causes of my
purchasing the ice cream.

The role of unconscious states of mind as the causes of behaviour can
certainly be framed in these terms (Wollheim, 1993a). One can include
the idea of desires and beliefs that are unconscious to the subject but
nevertheless influence his conscious thoughts and actions, to give this
psychoanalytic model explanatory force. To give an example, let us
say that unconsciously I am deeply envious of someone's success. This
makes me hate them and wish them harm, although I disavow this and
am not aware that this is what I feel. In a context in which I believe that
this person will be sensitive to what is said about them I nevertheless
find myself saying quite spiteful things, without my recognizing that
this is what I am doing.

What informs this model of explanation is the idea of a parallel
unconscious script running in the mind (McDougall, 1986), in which
unconscious motives, intentions, decisions, and beliefs play the same
part as causes of behaviours as conscious decisions and beliefs normally
do. In this instance, we should be attentive to mental as well as behavioural effects, since the first line of influence of unconscious desires and
beliefs is likely to be on conscious thoughts and wishes, through which
behaviours are normally mediated. (Dreams can be unmediated expressions of unconscious desires and terrors, as with Bottom's dream in *A
Midsummer Night's Dream* and Lady Macbeth's nightmares in her sleep-
walking scene.)

It seems that in everyday life we think of beliefs, intentions, and
decisions as "causes" of actions, even though the causal relation may
also be one of logical implication as well as of an empirical "constant
conjunction". Drinking is a meaningful as well as an empirical concomitant of thirst. From a psychoanalytic perspective, what is relevant is that
unconscious beliefs and desires may also be related, both logically and
causally, to behaviour. One can act on unconscious and unrecognized
feelings and beliefs—for example, about particular persons—as well as
upon conscious and recognized ones. One of the primary aims of psychoanalysis is to bring such unconscious beliefs and desires within the
sphere of conscious understanding.

Psychoanalysts ask themselves, if I make this interpretation, or
decide not to do so, what will its effect be on the patient? A decision
whether or not to cancel a patient's session will routinely involve

consideration of such a decision as the potential cause of certain effects in the patient, including some that may be experienced unconsciously. The patient may tell us about the "conscious" aspect of his response: "That is not a problem—as you are not going to be available, I can leave earlier for my weekend away." But the patient may not recognize or be prepared for his unconscious response, which may be to feel cast out and abandoned.

It is a property of "meanings", understood both as causes and effects, that they are often extremely complicated. The particular capability of psychoanalysts, and of creative writers, is to be able to recognize their multidimensional and interconnected nature. It is the particular virtuosity of some novelists, like Jane Austen or Henry James, to be able explore such complexities of motive and response, showing their readers how beautifully subtle such interactions of meanings in the mind—and between minds—can be. "Poetry", as Terry Eagleton has put it,

> has a minimum of "redundancy"—of those signs which are present in a discourse to facilitate communication rather than to convey information—but still manages to produce a richer set of messages than any other form of language. . . . Every literary text is made up of a number of "systems" (lexical graphic, metrical, phonological and so on) and gains its effects through constant clashes and tensions between these systems" [Eagleton, 2008, pp. 103–105]

The teasing out of complexities of meaning, in their patients' and their own minds, is indeed one of the special things psychoanalysts also do and describe in writing about their cases. If this were all they did, this would be similar to what novelists or dramatists do, except that rather than working out how imaginary characters might think, feel, and behave, they are trying to understand how actual people, including they themselves, are thinking and behaving within and outside their clinical setting.

It is because of these similarities that psychoanalysts can believe that what they are doing belongs exclusively in the sphere of meaning and interpretation (both conscious and unconscious) and can disregard the significance to their work of causes and effects. They may disregard the role of "causality" and feel closer to creative writers than to scientists in their work, because they may not fully recognize that states of mind, both conscious and unconscious, have causal properties and powers. Relations of cause and effect may seem to belong to an "external" or scientific context of understanding, which has nothing to do with human subjectivity. From an interpretative perspective, acting to alter states of mind with drugs or through narrowly cognitive programmes of behaviour modification may seem to ignore or violate essential capabilities of human beings.

Does this conception of "meanings as causes" resolve the problem of reconciling the causal and meaningful dimensions of explanation in psychoanalysis? For some practical purposes, it does. An "interpretative" model of their work leaves analysts and therapists free to attend to the complexity of what their patients say, and to rely on everyday under- standings—"ordinary language", in Wittgenstein's term—of the ways in which thoughts, feelings, and decisions shape actions. Other "external" conceptions of causal relations may then seem unnecessary, or to get in the way of the true psychotherapeutic task of searching for meaning.

Suppose, for example, than an analyst has the idea that "abuse in childhood" is a cause that often has terrible effects on subsequent per- sonality development and believes that her patient had been abused when young. There is a risk that this "general idea" of a cause and effect relation will have too much influence on the analyst and will lead her to disregard the complexity of the patient's actual state of mind. There is no invariant relation between early abuse and character development. Does this mean that analysts should disregard all gen- eralized theories of a causal kind in their work and just stay with the particular complexities of each of their cases? Matters of explanation and research in psychoanalysis would be simpler if this were so. An apprenticeship in the deep reading of great novels, plays, and poems could then be all that analysts would need by way of training, perhaps with the addition of learning the therapeutic techniques of how to be with and give interpretations to a patient.[6]

But psychoanalysis, and especially the generation of knowledge in psychoanalysis, isn't just an activity of interpretation of particular "lived" phenomena. Psychoanalysis also has concepts and theories that denote kinds and types of phenomena. In their training, analysts learn about these as a body of knowledge. If they eventually write papers, they may even seek to revise or add to these ideas, providing clinical and other empirical evidence for doing so. The question is, how do the issues of meaning and cause bear on this "generalizing" lexicon of ideas? If one explains a state of mind or behaviour as oedipal, or paranoid-schizoid, or "borderline", is this attributing meaning to the state of mind, or refer- ring to its causal properties, or both?

The answer to this is that psychoanalytic, like sociological, expla- nations require both of these dimensions. The central concepts and theories of psychoanalysis summarize and condense the accumulated knowledge of the field. Just as capital, in Marxist economic theory, is the accumulated product of labour, or "dead labour", so one may say that the theories of psychoanalysis—its "cultural capital" in Bourdieu's (1984) term—are the accumulated product of its clinical and theoretical labour, selected through processes of reflection and competition and surviving as those that have been found to have most explanatory power.

What do such concepts and theories condense and summarize? On the one hand, they refer to sets of complex causal relationships. The Oedipus complex denotes, in general terms, the forms of desire, repression, splitting, and internal conflict that are liable to arise from the emotional experiences of infants in relation to their family constellation. Once a situation is identified as belonging within this theoretical constellation, we can predict certain of its properties: who will have what kinds of unconscious feelings for and beliefs about whom, and what their effects are likely to be. The theory becomes usable as a summary description of a complex, causally interconnected totality. The same can be said for the other central theories of the field. Thus, in the paranoid-schizoid position, there is a certain combination of attributes; in the depressive position, there is a different one.

The idea that unconscious feelings and beliefs are concomitants of these configurations of mind and personalities reminds us that they denote subjective states of mind, as well as entities with causal powers. The paranoid-schizoid position is constituted by a particular pattern of thought and feeling—namely, one in which the good and the bad are deeply split off from one another. It has further probable concomitants of thought and behaviour, which are effects of this configuration of mind. But a pattern of thought and feeling has a "subjective" meaning that is accessible, in principle, to interpretation. Indeed, one of the principal kinds of causal relation in which psychoanalysis is interested are the effects of interpretations on patients. Each of the central concepts of psychoanalysis "predicts" both causally interconnected patterns of thought and action and "structures of feeling", to adopt Raymond Williams's (1977) term, whose meanings are susceptible to understanding.

The central concepts of psychoanalysis are, in other respects, similar to those of the natural sciences. Just as the elements classified in the periodic table definitionally possess certain definite properties, known from the development of empirical knowledge about them and from knowledge of their atomic structures, so key psychoanalytic concepts have come to acquire the properties of structures found in (human) nature. What is distinctive about the concepts and theories of psychoanalysis is that they are only of much explanatory value where they are instanced or realized in individual cases. Certainly this is the case for their use within psycho-analytic therapy. One gets nowhere clinically with concepts like oedipal or paranoid-schizoid states, except where these can be found to give meaning and coherence to the states of mind of individual patients. This is why it is seldom helpful to psychoanalytic treatment when patients refer to themselves, in generalizing theoretical terms, as a case of some named psychopathology, summarized in a diagnostic label. A dialectical relationship between general concepts and their particular realizations is what distinctively characterizes psychoanalysis.

In subsequent chapters I examine the kinds of causal and meaningful explanation that psychoanalysis develops through its methods of clinical research.

Notes

1. Criticism of the English translation of the *Standard Edition* of Freud's works arises from this difference between Anglophone and German-speaking cultures. It is argued that the choice of "technical" scientific terms over everyday language ("ego" for "I", for example) is a consequence of this more rigid separation between different kinds of knowledge in Anglo-Saxon culture. A series of new English translations was initiated in 2007 with this in mind (Phillips, 2007).

2. Urgent demands from within psychoanalysis for a new research agenda have thus emerged (Fonagy, 1993, 2003; Wallerstein & Fonagy, 1999).

3. Tawney's *Religion and the Rise of Capitalism* (1926) developed a related view.

4. "Empirical" is a contestable term, often mistakenly appropriated to refer only to quantitative methods of investigation.

5. The distinction, made in Aristotle's *Poetics*, between knowledge derived from particulars (Greek tragedy was his exemplar of this) and from "universals" (generalizing ideas) lies at the origin of these differences.

6. It is sometimes held, with good reason, that an education in literature equips analysts to work with patients better than does one in scientific psychology.

CHAPTER SIX

On classification

There may be a widespread assumption that the classification of mental conditions and their treatments, and the typologies and procedures that follow from them, have little to do with psychoanalysis and psychoanalytic psychotherapy. It certainly is the case that the term and topic rarely appear in the psychoanalytic literature—there are few papers, symposia or books that take classification as their explicit theme, whereas in the other mental health professions and in medicine classification, both of disorders and their remedies, seems to be absolutely fundamental, the basis of knowledge and sound practice. One of the reasons for this difference in approach is that in the self-described "scientific" fields of mental health, the necessary first step is always to identify the type and kind of disorder that is confronting the practitioner, it only then being possible to choose what treatment to offer. The purpose of initial assessments is precisely to make a "diagnosis" of what the condition in question might be and to locate it within one of many possible classifications to which it might correspond. The classifications themselves are the outcomes of ongoing scientific research. It is because such systems of classification are deemed to be so well founded and reliable that it becomes possible to believe that computer-based methods of diagnosis might be more reliable than those of human practitioners. The role of some practitioners may have become that of mediators between the patient and the information that can be gathered about him, and the banks of ordered knowledge held in electronic databases in which his "kind" of disorder and its known causes can be located. Doctors routinely now access computers to assist their own diagnostic practice, even in the presence of their patients. Those who perform initial diagnoses in response to inquiries made over the phone, to service users who are scarcely yet anyone's individual patient, surely largely depend on classificatory algorithms that they access by computer, which hopefully enable them at least to discriminate minor from serious symptoms reported to them.

Psychoanalytic practice is somewhat different from this. There is a prevailing belief in this field that real understanding of a patient is only achieved in the course of the therapeutic process and cannot, for the most part, precede it. Even psychoanalytic assessments may have as their primary purpose not to locate and define the patient's precise problems or disorders, although as much of this kind as possible is attempted, but as much to investigate whether a prospective patient seems likely to respond to a psychoanalytic "talking" therapy. Assessments are often something like an initial trial stage of treatment (M. E. Rustin & Quagliata, 2004)—this can give rise to the problem that a patient becomes attached to the therapist who has performed the assessment and would prefer to be treated by them, not passed on to someone else.

Of course, the boundaries between treatment and assessment are rarely absolute. Medical as well as psychological treatments are always liable to reveal, as they proceed, new dimensions of an illness. Nevertheless, the distinction being made here, between assessments in fields that are largely reliant on pre-existing classifying systems and those in psychoanalysis in which they have a lesser role, is valid. The difference between these approaches is, to an extent, explained by the fact that the object of investigation and treatment in psychoanalytic practice lies in the unconscious or inner world of the patient and therefore by definition can only become fully known in the context of a therapeutic relationship, often based on the transference.

It would, however, be false to conclude from this difference in approaches to mental illness that "classifications" have no significant presence in psychoanalytic theory and practice. The reality is, on the contrary, that psychoanalysis has evolved immensely complex and informative "classifications" of its own—of configurations of mind, patterns and pathways of development, "mechanisms of defence", and therapeutic techniques, among others. In fact, because of its distinctive commitment to the understanding of human individuals and their personal uniqueness, the systems of classification of psychoanalysis are more intricate and differentiated than those of its neighbouring psychologies. For example, the central diagnostic or classificatory product of "attachment theory" is a small number of kinds of attachment—in children these are four—secure, avoidant, ambivalent, and disorganized. Psychoanalytic descriptions of the kinds of mental structure and process relevant to a patient are markedly more differentiated than this.

There can be no theory without concepts, and a concept is, in essence, a classification, the designation of a "kind". The task of this chapter is to show how important classification is to psychoanalysis, but also to show that its method, form, and use is substantially different from the classificatory practices of other mental health disciplines.

The most widely used system of classification found in the field of mental health, the *DSM–5* (APA, 2013), is a typology of the many forms of mental illness, primarily organized by reference to their symptoms. The World Health Organization's *ICD–10* (WHO, 2016) has a chapter on mental health. These systems, devised and maintained by the professional institutions of psychiatry, have followed, or attempted to follow, a medical model in which symptoms are identified, classified, and discriminated from one another, in order that specific treatments that can address them can be devised and applied. Diagnostic Manuals of this kind also have a large place in the practice of physical medicine, although in that field diagnostic categories are supported by a much more substantial base of research and explanation than is the case for psychiatric medicine. Many of the diagnostic categories of the *DSM* seem to be coterminous with, or to overlap, the theoretical concepts of psychoanalysis and have partly been informed by psychoanalytic ideas. Nevertheless, classification in psychiatry has a different function from its use in psychoanalytic practice, and to understand psychoanalysis, these differences need to be recognized.

One major difference arises from the applicability, or otherwise, of a "medical model" to understand and treat mental illnesses. The issue is: how is mental illness best understood, and is an approach largely based on typologies of symptoms sufficient?

Even in regard to physical medicine, there is some space for disagreement regarding the definition and measurement of health and illness. For example, the rise of obesity to the status of a serious medical problem is recent. It reflects both changing patterns of life regarding food intake and exercise, and the epidemiological evidence of their consequences for long-term health. There is also, in these assessments, an element of aesthetic or cultural evaluation of physical characteristics and appearances. In societies where material scarcity predominates, the signs of being well-fed can signify high social status. In societies where malnutrition ceases to be an issue for most of the population, a higher value may be placed on a disposition to defer immediate satisfactions, and "slimness" may become the preferred bodily ideal. The exceptional thinness that seems to be mandatory for fashion models and that influences ideals of appearance may have yet have yet other explanations. Some have suggested that it expressed an unconscious hatred of femininity, while pretending to be its opposite. Other medical definitions of good and bad health may also be influenced by broader cultural norms—for example, the idea of physical "fitness" as a desirable quality may not have a mainly medical explanation. But despite this wider sources of variation, there is a high degree of consensus regarding definitions of physical health and illness. The substantial advances of physical medicine in the prevention and cure of illness—measured, for example, by longer average life-spans although the causes of these are by no means only medical—have given authority to doctors in maintaining these definitions.

However, so far as social consensus and professional authority is concerned, the fields of mental and physical illness are distinct. Mental illness is, as sociologists have demonstrated, in part defined as a deviation from prevailing social norms. Mental illness is attributed to persons on grounds of their irrational, inexplicable, strange behaviours and because these can give rise to disturbance and intolerant reactions among those who are in contact with them (Goffman, 1969; Spillius, 1976, 1994; Szasz, 1961). Often, sufferers from mental illness become acutely aware of the troubling aspects of their states of mind, to themselves and others, and seek treatment. But sometimes they are not, and sequestration and/or treatment is administered to them against their will. Sufferers from physical illness are rarely subjected to sanction and compulsory treatment in this way, although this can occur when illnesses threaten to infect others.

Psychiatry and the other mental health professions have not achieved the demonstrable successes of physical medicine in their "technologies" of diagnosis and treatment. Nor have they been as successful as the practitioners of physical medicine in achieving professional consensus—or a hegemony of their explanatory schemas—regarding the ruling paradigms and practices of their field. Differences concerning the understanding of mental health and illness even reflect differences of beliefs and values in a society, relating to conceptions of what are to count as good and fulfilled lives. What is deemed to be a normal and satisfactory condition of life from some points of view may be regarded as shallow and alienated from others. For example, the phenomenon of the widespread dependence on the consumption of prescribed drugs as a condition of normal social functioning is taken by some to be evidence of a serious deficit in the mental health of a significant part of the population. But others may see this apparent dependence is no more problematic than the taking of aspirin or Panadol to deal with headaches or the symptoms of colds.

"Classifications" can themselves be powerful instruments of social control. Foucault's critique of the repressive role of the social sciences in the modern West is organized around his central idea that forms of knowledge become forms of power, articulated and institutionalized in the fields of medicine, criminology, psychiatry, and in the social constructions of sexuality (Foucault & Rabinow, 1991). Ian Hacking's *The Social Construction of What?* (1999) describes the "active" role certain classifications can have in the social construction of a phenomenon (e.g., "madness" or "child abuse"), which then come to have important practical consequences to those whom these categories are ascribed. Psychoanalysts have believed that they have their own specific "classifications"—ones that enable individuals and groups to achieve greater self-knowledge and thus freedom. Critics of psychoanalysis such as Foucault (1997) and Nikolas Rose (1999) have viewed psychoanalytic forms of knowledge as more psychologically invasive than others, and therefore no less controlling. In its early days, when in 1948 the Tavistock Clinic joined the National Health Service, its Chairman, Hugh Crichton-Miller, envisaged the development of a model of psychodynamic community mental health provision that would be engaged with the mental suffering from illness of both children and adults. He hoped that this might be the template for a nation-wide community mental health service and was related to a larger post-war project of social reconstruction and repair, in which the idea of universal education through improved and expanded schooling was another element. This conception evolved as the Tavistock's multidisciplinary approach to mental health, with many kinds of therapeutic intervention, most of them informed by psychoanalytic ideas. The idea of community mental health was linked by the early Tavistock Clinic and Tavistock Institute of Human Relations (in effect, its research division) to an idea of enhanced societal as well as individual well-being. Its researchers, such as Wilfred Bion, Eric Trist, and Fred Emery, embodied this in a conception of democracy that would go "all the way down", from formal political institutions into the daily life of the workplace.[1] But while the Tavistock institutions attempted with some success to implement their democratic conception, it was not, for the most part, taken up more widely as a model of mental health provision. In recent years, different models of mental health and ill health have become adopted and, indeed, imposed by governments. Their principal aim is to find cost-effective treatments that can reduce disabling symptoms and support the operations of a functioning economy through the supply and psychological maintenance of its workforce. From this perspective, even the existence of unconscious mental life is often disputed. This is a contemporary example of the differences of theory and practice that are found in the field of mental health and its treatment. The origin of these lies in divergent conceptions of individual and social well-being.

The most important difference between the *DSM* diagnostic model and the perspective of psychoanalysis concerns their respective understanding of symptoms. The psychiatric perspective is essentially descriptive and pragmatic. Its classifications differentiate between observable patterns of disturbed or dysfunctional behaviour and mental condition, and they seek to correlate these with remedies that are effective in curing or alleviating them. It is not primarily concerned, as psychoanalysis is, with whatever "underlying" mental processes may be the causes of symptomatic or behavioural states, although the development of neuroscience has produced a new interest in such explanations within psychiatry. Conjectures about the relation between brain function and consciousness and behaviour are deemed to be more susceptible to empirical test than those that posit unconscious mental states as causes, although it is a matter of opinion whether this is really the case. What matters, within the dominant psychiatric and psychological perspective,[2] is what "works" and can be shown to work through "hard" evidence of clinical outcomes.

The psychoanalytic perspective by contrast regards symptoms, whether of behaviours or states of mind, as the effects of structures of the mind that are, in part, unconscious and therefore accessible only with difficulty. The basis of mental illness and health, within this perspective, lies in the configuration and usually the early origins, of these "internal" structures. The purpose of psychoanalytic treatment is to gain understanding of them, by analyst and patient, in the belief that only this, where there is deep and persistent psychological disturbance, can give rise to deep-seated and lasting change. The fundamental belief of psychoanalysis is that access to unconscious structures of mind is best obtained through the experience and observation of the transference–countertransference relationship. The unconscious, according to this view, gives up its secrets only gradually and reluctantly: this is the cause of patients' "resistance" to interpretation and understanding.

It follows that the concepts and classifications that are of most relevance in psychoanalysis are those that map the internal, unconscious structures of the mind, not only the symptoms of mental illness. Psychoanalytic theories set out a large and complex system of concepts, which exist as frames and points of reference for analysts as they seek to find meaning in their observations and exchanges with their patients.

Psychoanalysts conduct analysis in the belief that it is mainly through the development of the transference relationship—"the gathering of the transference", in Meltzer's (1967) terms—that the "material" will emerge that reveals the configuration of the "internal world" of the patient, that is, his or her unconscious states of mind. This "material" includes the analyst's observations of a patient, the patient's reported dreams and associations, and the analyst's countertransference experiences, which may convey understanding of a patient's projected states of mind. It follows from this view of psychoanalytic treatment that to adopt classifications or "diagnostic labels" to describe patients preceding some experience of them in analysis is to start the process of understanding in the wrong place. This will be the case whether the classifications in question are taken from the lexicon of psychoanalytic concepts and theories or from the more symptom-based classificatory systems of medical psychiatry. It was the view that psychoanalysts came to their understanding through "learning from experience"—which essentially means from the transference relationship in the consulting room—that led Bion to propose that analysts "eschew memory and desire" and prior theoretical preconceptions in their clinical practice (Bion, 1967a, 1970, 1980).

Nevertheless, classification is a fundamental to psychoanalytic practice, and it is through classifications that the psychoanalytic paradigm and its component (and indeed partially divergent and conflicting) theories are constructed. Major texts in the field, such as Laplanche and Pontalis's *The Language of Psychoanalysis* (1967), Hinshelwood's *A Dictionary of Kleinian Thought* (1989), and the *New Dictionary of Kleinian Thought* by Spillius, Milton, Garvey, Couve and Steiner (2011) provide systemic codifications of the classificatory systems of psychoanalysis, structured by concepts and theories and, additionally, by the contributions of major psychoanalytic authorities. These invaluable books provide an explanation of each of the concepts they select, locate them within an evolving body of psychoanalytic theories, and identify the primary textual sources in which the origin and meaning of these ideas was first explained. One can see these works as a distillation of the core concepts and theories of the psychoanalytic traditions on which they have focused. Collections of papers that reprint key articles and review theoretical developments in particular subfields provide parallel guides to the source literature and provide other means by which practitioners can access generative and framing ideas in their fields.

I have argued in earlier chapters that psychoanalysis is a scientific paradigm similar in many of its attributes to other paradigms, even though, like others, it has its specific object of knowledge, its own theories, methods of observation, and means of representing its discoveries—its "inscription devices", in Latour and Woolgar's (1979) term. All sciences develop systems of classification—ordered concepts that define their field. Their theories are constituted through the empirical and logical relations of their classifications.

Classification in different fields of science

Despite the similarities to one another of all forms of scientific investigation (it is these that give them their identity as scientific forms of inquiry), there are differences between them. One of importance lies in the domain of classification. Some sciences have mainly sought explanations at the level of universal laws that capture elements of nature at the highest level of generality. Physics is the prime example, with its immensely powerful laws—for example, Newton's laws of motion, which explain gravitational attraction; the "gas laws" explaining the behaviour of gases in relation to their pressure, volume, and temperature; the laws of thermodynamics; and Einstein's special theory of relativity, summarized in formula, $E = mc^2$. The core concepts of each of these theories are classifications, defining the phenomena that have been discovered to be in a definite causal relation to each other.

A greater attention to a multitude of differences and particulars characterizes the field of chemistry, one of whose purposes was to explain the different properties of the many elements found in nature. The first step in this process of discovery was the development of atomic theory in the nineteenth century, by John Dalton. He discovered a remarkable uniformity in nature. Elements, he found, are made of extremely small particles, which he called, following the ancient philosopher Democritus, atoms. Atoms of a given element are identical in their size, mass, and indeed all their properties. Atoms of different elements differ in these attributes.

Atoms, it was once believed, cannot be subdivided, created, or destroyed. Atoms of different elements combine in simple whole-number ratios to form chemical compounds. In chemical reactions, atoms are combined, separated, or rearranged.

A further major development was to classify elements by reference to their major properties, and to explain these "kinds" by reference to their elementary atomic structures. In 1869, on the basis of an extensive correlation of the properties and the atomic weights of the elements, Mendeleyev proposed the periodic law and devised a tabular arrangement of the elements to show the observed relationships. The periodic table made it possible to observe many types of chemical relations hitherto studied only in isolation.

Periodic Table

Key:
- Relative atomic mass
- Symbol
- Atomic number

Those numbers appearing within brackets are the mass of common isotopes
Those elements underlined are radioactive

N element is a gas
Hg element is a liquid
Li element is a solid

at room temperature and pressure

1	2											13	14	15	16	17	18
1.0 **H** Hydrogen 1																	4.0 **He** Helium 2
6.9 **Li** Lithium 3	9.0 **Be** Beryllium 4											10.8 **B** Boron 5	12.0 **C** Carbon 6	14.0 **N** Nitrogen 7	16.0 **O** Oxygen 8	19.0 **F** Fluorine 9	20.2 **Ne** Neon 10
23.0 **Na** Sodium 11	24.3 **Mg** Magnesium 12	3	4	5	6	7	8	9	10	11	12	27.0 **Al** Aluminium 13	28.1 **Si** Silicon 14	31.0 **P** Phosphorus 15	32.1 **S** Sulphur 16	35.5 **Cl** Chlorine 17	39.9 **Ar** Argon 18
39.1 **K** Potassium 19	40.1 **Ca** Calcium 20	45.0 **Sc** Scandium 21	47.9 **Ti** Titanium 22	50.9 **V** Vanadium 23	52.0 **Cr** Chromium 24	54.9 **Mn** Manganese 25	55.8 **Fe** Iron 26	58.9 **Co** Cobalt 27	58.7 **Ni** Nickel 28	63.5 **Cu** Copper 29	65.4 **Zn** Zinc 30	69.7 **Ga** Gallium 31	72.6 **Ge** Germanium 32	74.9 **As** Arsenic 33	79.0 **Se** Selenium 34	79.9 **Br** Bromine 35	83.8 **Kr** Krypton 36
85.5 **Rb** Rubidium 37	87.6 **Sr** Strontium 38	88.9 **Y** Yttrium 39	91.2 **Zr** Zirconium 40	92.9 **Nb** Niobium 41	95.9 **Mo** Molybdenum 42	(99) **Tc** Technetium 43	101.1 **Ru** Ruthenium 44	102.9 **Rh** Rhodium 45	106.4 **Pd** Palladium 46	107.9 **Ag** Silver 47	112.4 **Cd** Cadmium 48	114.8 **In** Indium 49	118.7 **Sn** Tin 50	121.8 **Sb** Antimony 51	127.6 **Te** Tellurium 52	126.9 **I** Iodine 53	131.3 **Xe** Xenon 54
132.9 **Cs** Caesium 55	137.3 **Ba** Barium 56	138.9 **La** Lanthanum 57	178.5 **Hf** Hafnium 72	181.0 **Ta** Tantalum 73	183.9 **W** Tungsten 74	186.2 **Re** Rhenium 75	190.2 **Os** Osmium 76	192.2 **Ir** Iridium 77	195.1 **Pt** Platinum 78	197.0 **Au** Gold 79	200.6 **Hg** Mercury 80	204.4 **Tl** Thallium 81	207.2 **Pb** Lead 82	209.0 **Bi** Bismuth 83	(210) **Po** Polonium 84	(210) **At** Astatine 85	(222) **Rn** Radon 86
(223) **Fr** Francium 87	(226) **Ra** Radium 88	(227) **Ac** Actinium 89	(261) **Rf** Rutherfordium 104	(262) **Db** Dubnium 105	(263) **Sg** Seaborgium 106	(262) **Bh** Bohrium 107	(265) **Hs** Hassium 108	(266) **Mt** Meitnerium 109									

* 58-71 Lanthanide series

140.1 **Ce** Cerium 58	140.9 **Pr** Praseodymium 59	144.2 **Nd** Neodymium 60	(147) **Pm** Promethium 61	150.4 **Sm** Samarium 62	152.0 **Eu** Europium 63	157.3 **Gd** Gadolinium 64	158.9 **Tb** Terbium 65	162.5 **Dy** Dysprosium 66	164.9 **Ho** Holmium 67	167.3 **Er** Erbium 68	168.9 **Tm** Thulium 69	173.0 **Yb** Ytterbium 70	175.0 **Lu** Lutetium 71

† 90-103 Actinide series

232.0 **Th** Thorium 90	(231) **Pa** Protactinium 91	238.1 **U** Uranium 92	(237) **Np** Neptunium 93	(244) **Pu** Plutonium 94	(243) **Am** Americium 95	(247) **Cm** Curium 96	(247) **Bk** Berkelium 97	(251) **Cf** Californium 98	(252) **Es** Einsteinium 99	(257) **Fm** Fermium 100	(258) **Md** Mendelevium 101	(259) **No** Nobelium 102	(260) **Lr** Lawrencium 103

FIGURE 6.1

Published by
ICIEducational Liaison

This classification system had gaps in the elements that could not be filled by observation or experiment. Mendeleyev successfully predicted that these gaps would be filled through the empirical discovery of the "missing" elements. Higher atomic numbers originally denoted increasing atomic weights, but from the early twentieth century it came to be recognized that the periodic law was better explained by reference to the electronic structure of atoms. The atomic number (also known as the proton number) is the number of protons found in the nucleus of an atom. We can see that in this theory, a model based on the causal powers of a small number of variables, belonging to the domain of physics, is able to predict and explain the properties of the large number of different chemical elements.

Whereas physics had as its early aim to discover the fundamental laws that would explain the universal properties of nature, biology was always as occupied with the task of describing and classifying the immense variety of life as with discovering laws that would explain its common properties. The creation story in the *Book of Genesis* was one source of this tradition, first describing the making of the different forms of life by God, then narrating how they were saved from the Flood. The Biblical creation story retained a lasting influence on biological studies. Not only did it inhibit and delay Darwin's publication of *The Origin of Species* through his fear of being attacked and ostracized by Christians, but it continues today through Creationist beliefs among fundamentalist Christians, notably in the United States. Aristotle's theory of nature as composed of kinds with distinct powers and potentialities was another significant representation of the idea of a fundamental diversity.

The great achievement of early modern biological classification was that of the Swedish botanist, Carl Linnaeus [1707–1778]. His major work, *Systemi Naturae* (1735), ordered the forms of living nature into a hierarchical structure of three kingdoms, subdivided into classes, and these, in turn, into orders, families, genera, and species, with an additional rank lower than this. Linnaeus's taxonomy is based on the structural properties of animals and plants and does not propose theoretical or causal explanations of their differences.

Charles Darwin [1809–1882] gave an explanatory dimension to the descriptive and classificatory schema of the Linnaean approach to nature. Following his grandfather, the geologist Erasmus Darwin, he came to believe that the diversity of nature was the outcome of evolution over long periods of time. He proposed (at the same time as William Wallace) that the different attributes of living species could be explained as the outcome of "natural selection". This was the process in which selection took place of the variations of attributes that occurred in the biological process of reproduction, according to their contribution to a species' success in competition for reproductive survival within its environment—the "survival of the fittest". Darwin's famous tree diagram is a simple representation of the evolution of species, which results from this process. Darwin's theory of natural selection is a general law. It states that random variation (what we now understand as genetic variation) leads in minute stages to species variation, and that the comparative reproductive success of the variants determines the evolutionary pathways of species. It is a universal law that finds its empirical validation in myriads of particular cases, each different from the other.

This diagram illustrates how evolutionary branches terminate at a point of maximum adaptation to their "fitness landscape"—for example, at the point when the length of a giraffe's neck, or the ornateness of a peacock's tail, achieves its maximum advantage for the species of giraffe or peacock. Any further development of this characteristic would have had costs in regard to competitive fitness and survival, which would have outweighed its benefits. Darwin's theory of natural selection made possible a multitude of specific descriptions, classification, and explanations—for example, how a particular species evolved, how it was fitted to its particular environmental niche, how it lived in symbiosis (predator–prey, parasite–host) or in competition with

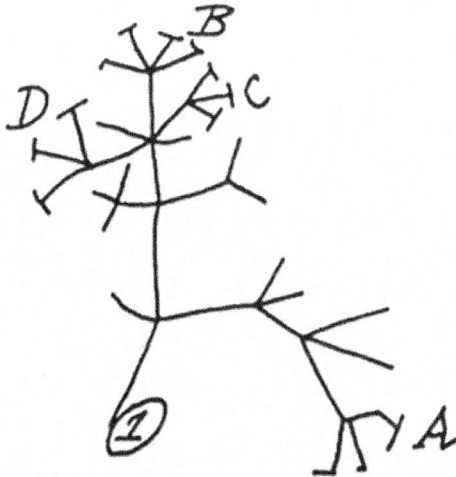

FIGURE 6.2 *Darwin's original tree diagram* (from Darwin's First Notebook on "Transmutation of Species", 1837)

other species. The relation of species to their environment came to be known as ecology. Darwin's theory became filled out with explanations of processes and mechanisms that were unknown to him. First was the genetics of Mendel [1822–1884]—the idea that distinct units of reproductive material (genes and chromosomes) were the transmitter of inherited characteristics. Then came the opening up of these "black boxes" when molecular biology (and its new research instrument, X-ray crystallography) revealed the physical structure (the "double helix") and the biochemistry of DNA and RNA, the protein molecules central to the reproduction (and mutation) of inherited characteristics. "Genes" now became theorized as information carriers. (A virus is a parasitic carrier of instructions to host cells.) These developments in biochemistry bring evolutionary biology closer to the more generalizing forms of explanation of physics and chemistry, specific organic attributes being causally correlated with the combinations and structures of protein molecules, which give rise to their transmission. But even so, this does not displace scientific interest in the characteristics and behaviours of the species themselves, whatever we may learn about the biochemistry of their reproduction. Their differences and specificities remain important objects of study in the biological sciences. In her studies of modern scientific laboratories, Knorr-Cetina (1999) has found that divergent focuses on diversity and uniformities continue to differentiate the biological from the physical sciences.[3]

Classification and explanation in psychoanalysis

A comparison may be made between the law of natural selection discovered by Darwin and the theory of the unconscious mind discovered by Freud. Each asserts laws of universal application, but in each the manifestations of the laws are particular and are adapted to the differences in the objects to which they apply. The "general law" of natural selection explains almost infinite numbers of attributes and their origins and functions, but it is of little explanatory value merely as a generalization. Whereas the relevance of objects to Newton's laws of motion depend only on their attributes of mass, velocity, and distance from one another, the entities whose behaviour is explained by Darwin's law of natural selection have many particular attributes that are necessary to demonstrate the law's explanatory power. Evolutionary theory needs its system of classification, with its many hierarchical subdivisions, to explain its differential applications. Scientific natural history, such as in its many television presentations like the *Planet Earth* series, amounts to a continuing demonstration of how these principles function in relation to particular environments. A recent example from *Planet Earth 2* showed how it is the distinctive adaptability of the leopard as a species (compared with the other big cats) that has enabled it to colonize urban environments in India, which other "big cats", its metaphorical cousins, have not (so far) been able to do, although it seems that mountain lions do now roam the suburbs of Los Angeles.

Psychoanalysis is similar to evolutionary biology in its attention to particularities and differences. The "universal law" that the oedipal situation will be, in one way or another, encountered and will have psychological consequences in every human life gains its meaning and power from the fact it is instanced in particular ways in individuals—in every life and in every society, according to the theory, although this has famously been disputed (Malinowski, 1927; Mead, 1928). Roger Money-Kyrle's (1968, 1971) formulation of the "facts of life"—of differences of generation and gender that have to be faced in some way by every human being—is an articulation of this idea. But in psychoanalytic theory, these instances are an infinity of individual particulars, accumulated case by case but giving rise to the recognition of distinct "types" or "kinds". There are, for example, several different forms of psychopathology that have been the outcome of unsuccessful negotiations of the oedipal situation. Freud's great case studies are of lasting significance in psychoanalytic theory because they each identify and explain a major "variety" of psychopathology understood as an outcome of this fundamental developmental challenge. These were the hysteria categories in the Dora case (Freud, 1905c), and the obsessional anxieties and phobias of Little Hans (1909a) and the Rat Man (1909b). Each of these contributed a major element to the early classificatory scheme of psychoanalysis. Any theory that explains the relation between one entity and another requires that they be identifiable through their attributes. For each area of psychoanalytic theory, whether concerned with stages of development, psychopathology, or therapeutic technique, classifications are required.

In the development of psychoanalytic theory the elaboration of such classifications has been central. Each "concept" is an element in a system of classification; each "theory" asserts a relation between them. Most often new concepts, thus new elements in a classificatory scheme, emerge when a phenomenon that cannot be captured within the boundaries of meaning of existing concepts manifests itself. Usually this recognition of a hitherto unknown phenomenon occurs within a clinical setting. When Herbert Rosenfeld (1971, 1987) identified the phenomenon of "destructive narcissism" and began to explore the meaning of the state of mind it identified, he stated that in order to arrive this idea, he had first struggled with the inadequacy of the accepted definition of "narcissism" to describe the actual mental state he was encountering in his patient. Often in the development of psychoanalytic theory new concepts are forged through bringing into juxtaposition more than one classificatory frame, in relation to the clinical problems posed in the treatment of patients. For example, the pre-existing dichotomy set out in Freud's and Klein's writings between the life and death instincts was found relevant by Rosenfeld in his differentiation between libidinal and destructive narcissism, the idea of narcissism having its origin in another region of Freud's theory. Britton's (1989, 1998b) idea of a "third position", as related to the individuation and autonomy of the personality, brought together the theory of the Oedipus complex with Bion's theory of the development of the "mental apparatus" (O'Shaughnessy, 1981). Britton's discovery was that the recognition of this "position" depended not only on the containing functions of maternal care, but also on the ways in which the mental pain that unavoidably occurs in the oedipal situation is negotiated during development.

One therefore understands the development of psychoanalysis not only as a research programme giving rise to a body of systematic theory, but also as the evolution of a complex system of classifications. One may see this as parallel to the structure and development of Darwinian evolutionary theory. Some might hope that the discoveries that brought an understanding of the biochemical processes involved in genetics as an integration between the biology and chemistry involved in species variation will eventually have their equivalent in psychoanalysis, through the discoveries of neuroscience concerning the brain. It may become possible to explain differences in human character and behaviour by reference to brain functions, as it is possible to correlate the attributes of biological organisms with the segments of the relevant species genome. However, one may wonder whether the phenomenological qualities of conscious and unconscious states of mind will ever be accessible by those means.

There is an important difference between the function of classifications and theories in psychoanalysis and their functions in evolutionary biology. The central object of interest and explanation in evolutionary biology is the species, or "type". It is a variety of fungus, or tiger, or plantain, for whose attributes, behaviours, and relations to its environment explanations are sought. Usually the particular fungus, tiger, or plantain—that single organism—is of scientific interest only as an example or specimen of its kind. If it turns out to be significantly different from others in the species category to which it was believed to belong, the outcome may be the discovery of a new species or subspecies. In a sense, in evolutionary biology there is no such thing, from a scientific point of view, as an individual. Descriptive classification and theoretical (causal) explanations of the kinds of entity denoted by such classifications are the goal of this and other natural sciences.

Psychoanalysis has a goal that is different from this. Its clinical object of concern is the individual, not types of individuals. Psychoanalysis is essentially rooted in and governed by its therapeutic purposes and practices. Its primary aim is to make use of the classificatory and explanatory resources of its field in order to understand and support the psychological and emotional development of a particular patient. It is not to make use of the particular patient (like a laboratory fruit-fly or rat) for the purpose of developing its scientific theories and classifications. The study of particular patients does sometimes give rise to the discovery of new "types" of phenomena and thus to additions to or revisions of classificatory schemes and theories. We have referred to notable instances of such discoveries. Freud's Dora, Schreber (1911c), and Little Hans were real individuals who became famous because they were the locus of an important discovery. In the same, way the observation of a single instance of a biological species can amount to the discovery of a new "kind", as we see sometimes when a hitherto unknown organism or fossil is discovered. But the balance of purposes in these two forms of science is different—it is almost reversed.

It is also the case that the primary value of new discoveries in psychoanalysis does not lie only in their extension of a theory or classificatory scheme, as an addition to knowledge. Their relevance is also that they may be relevant for the better understanding of patients in future therapeutic work. Patients cannot be regarded, in psychoanalysis, as expendable objects of scientific investigation. "Never mind what happened to the patient, think what I contributed to psychoanalytic theory", is not a defensible position for a psychoanalyst to adopt.

This ethically driven patient-centred approach creates significant difficulties for the development of psychoanalysis as a science. For example, the fact that the subjects of psychoanalysis recruit themselves to the patient population has the effect that the psychoanalytic patient population, unlike most other subjects of scientific investigation, comes to the scientific field unsorted and uncategorized. We have already suggested that the theoretical foundations of psychoanalysis make for considerable problems in patient pre-selection and sampling. It is mostly only through experience of therapy that the psychoanalytically most significant attributes of a patient are revealed. It is hard to systematically develop a theory referring to "types" of pathology if the patients most relevant to the investigation of such a "type" occur only infrequently among a psychoanalyst's clinical cases and are therefore difficult to compare with each other.

One such solution has been found in the "clinical workshop" model of study long practiced at the Tavistock Clinic (M. E. Rustin, 1991). These are set up to examine a specific clinical problem or manifestation—for example, patients suffering from autism, anorexia, or borderline person-alities, or psychotherapy with severely deprived children. Therapists bring reports to such workshops on ongoing clinical work with patients of these kinds, enabling the longer-term effects of therapies to be observed. This comparative study has led to significant developments in theories and classificatory concepts in various subfields of psychoanaly-sis and child psychotherapy. An advantage of this approach has been that the selection of patients as relevant to a chosen field of study can be made by therapists themselves from a psychoanalytic understanding of patients gained through the treatment process, rather than by assess-ment procedures prior to treatment that may be poor at capturing the most psychoanalytically relevant differences.

The development of larger-scale studies of the outcomes of psycho-analytic treatment, for specified categories of patient, has offered other opportunities for clinical research. Such researches have been motivated mainly by the need to demonstrate in aggregated terms the compara-tive effectiveness of treatments—that is to say, they have been directed more towards the justification of psychoanalytic treatment within an "evidence-'based'" environment than towards the goals of fundamen-tal research. Nevertheless, there has been sufficient correspondence between the psychiatric diagnostic categories employed for the selec-tion of treatment samples and those of psychoanalytic relevance (severe depression in adolescents, for example) to have to make the sample population wholly appropriate for psychoanalytic study. The standardi-zation of diagnostic and treatment conditions required in such studies, the role of clinical supervision, and the accurate session reports made possible by audio-recording and by meticulous write-ups by clinicians have led to the production of high-quality data for subsequent analy-sis, with large samples of comparable cases. It is to be hoped that this resource will be used not only to measure treatment effects, but also enhance understanding of the particular clinical conditions and the treatments that have been selected as the objects of these studies. These possibilities are further discussed in a later chapter.

The classificatory schemes and theoretical understandings of psy-choanalysis will continue to be used as explanatory resources for therapists, available to be drawn upon as they are found to be relevant in their work with individual cases. Many "kinds" of unconscious structure, psychopathology, and issues of clinical technique will be described and classified in this literature. Nevertheless individual patients may not correspond in any straightforward ways to such "kinds", as these are set out in "pure" or ideal-typical forms. Analogy with a similar clinical instance may often be a better source of insight than a procedure of "deduction" from an established theory. The therapeutic aim of psychoanalysis is to treat patients in their individuality and particularity, not to investigate them merely as specimens of a kind. Psychoanalytic theory and classification is an indispensable resource for therapeutic practice, but because human beings do not present themselves as pure instances of psychoanalytic types, there will always be a substantial element of "bricolage", of imaginative synthesis and combination, in the uses of psychoanalytic knowledge in treating them.

Learning takes place in this practice as much through the recognition of similarities and "family resemblances" between cases as through the perception of the conformity of a case to the "ideal type" of its category. The ways in which psychoanalytic knowledge is primarily used in sequences of particular applications also explains why the skills of the clinical practitioner are so important, since it is through descriptions of clinical practice that practitioners learn the use of psychoanalytic ideas, not mainly by deduction from theoretical texts.

In music, there is a role or function for composers who invent and write new music, and for performers who enable it to be listened to on specific occasions. In psychoanalysis too, there may be roles for "composers"—the inventors or discoverers of theories—and "performers"—who demonstrate their usefulness in their understanding and work with patients. Music is written in order to be performed, not merely read and studied in the mind, and many of meanings and effects are discovered only in performance. By analogy, written musical scores are mainly of value when they are played, and psychoanalytic concepts and theories are mainly of value in clinical practice. Psychoanalysis is, in Toulmin's (2001) terms, a field oriented towards practice, not a "pure" science. Most original theorists in psychoanalysis have been clinical practitioners, although most clinicians are not original theorists. In a tradition like the British School, which gives such emphasis to clinical practice, it is to be expected that these roles will be combined in the same persons, since without good clinical capability it is unlikely that therapeutically useful discoveries will be made.

It is because of the central importance of the particular instance—the individual within his or her context of relationships—that psychoanalysis has as much affinity with the sensibility of writers of fiction, who seek to understand the individuality of an imagined person in his or her milieu, as with the generalizing and typifying perspectives of the natural sciences.

Notes

1. On this history, see Dicks (1970), and for a summary visit https://tavistockand portman.nhs.uk/about-us/who-we-are/history

2. With the influence of mental health programmes such as Improved Access to Psychological Therapies (IAPT), the balance of influence between clinical psychology, the advocates of cognitive behaviour therapy, and psychiatry has shifted in favour of the former. The generic orientation to "cases" of psychiatrists and the role as the managers of interdisciplinary teams has sometimes led to open-mindedness regarding different therapeutic approaches, often lacking in the protagonists of specific clinical approaches. Curiously, the leading figure in the IAPT movement, Richard Layard, is a labour economist, not a psychologist.

3. Scott Atran (1990) provides an extensive account of the development of biological systems of classification, from Aristotle to Darwin. Anna Pavord's (2005) *The Naming of Names* is a beautiful illustrated history of botanical classification.

CHAPTER SEVEN

Case-study methods in psychoanalysis

T he psychoanalytic field is often criticized for its reliance on clinical case studies as its primary research method. If psychoanalysis is to establish its place among the mainstream psychological sciences, it has been argued, it needs to abandon its reliance on its traditional approach to knowledge generation and adopt methods, such as the randomized double-blind controlled trial, that are more likely to achieve scientific respectability.

But why, if case studies are of such limited value in providing statistical evidence of the effects of psychoanalytic treatments, have they nevertheless proved so productive in generating new knowledge and understanding over the entire history of psychoanalysis? To understand this, it is useful to understand the larger place of case-study methods in scientific research.

Contexts of case study research

The fields in which these methods have proved most fertile in the generation of knowledge share certain characteristics, as a substantial literature explains (Byrne & Ragin, 2012; Ragin & Becker, 2010; Smith, Harré, & Van Langenhove, 1995; Stake, 1994). These are fields in which the objects of study are complex in the interrelationships between their component elements. They have a high degree of specificity and therefore difference from other apparently similar objects of study. They are often subject to substantial change and variation over time.

Mostly it is in the biological and especially the human sciences where such complex and singular entities are objects of investigation, because it is in these fields that interest in differences between objects of study is paramount. The unending process of "speciation" that Darwin noted to be the outcome of natural selection has given rise to innumerable different species, each living in its particular ecological niche. Although there are many attributes common to different species, in their genetic structure, anatomy, behaviour patterns, and so on, species are, by definition, distinct from one another (they are defined by their capacity to reproduce only within their own kind), and they evolve different modes of adaptation and survival. For this reason, the study of particular instances of a species in its environment has remained an illuminating kind of scientific inquiry.

The observation and filming of giant Wels Catfish feeding on pigeons at the waterside, shown in the last episode of *Planet Earth 2*, or of leopards making themselves at home in the city of Mumbai, are accessible examples of cases of new kinds of ecology, with their own effects on their environments. The Mumbai catfish have learned to prey on birds on the riverside instead of, as would be normal for their species, on fish in the river. No doubt in the struggle for survival, their prey will learn to avoid these predators and may further evolve so that this capacity is genetically given to them. Or perhaps the catfish will significantly reduce the size of the pigeon population in cities whose waters they have colonized, as they have already destroyed most of its fish-stock.

Even highly empiricist and quantitative studies of species behaviours may have case studies as their initial starting point. The observation of even a single species anomaly may give rise to larger-scale investigations of its frequency, causes, and effects. A principal reason for the persisting relevance of the case study to research is that until a phenomenon or a characteristic has been identified and specified, it is inaccessible to investigations of more generalizing kinds. Quality necessarily precedes quantity, since until the attributes of an object of study are specified, instances of it can neither be identified nor enumerated. Such initial identification and specification is often best done through the "close-up" approach of a case study.

In the human sciences case-study methods have tended to be adopted where particular entities or kinds are the object of research. Singularity or difference, when it is found, is often the outcome of a specific location in space and time. Geographical isolation of human communities has led to a kind of social speciation, parallel to the biological speciation of plants and animals. Some writers (Dawkins, 1976; Runciman, 2009) have proposed that "memes" are the carriers of cultural variations as genes are of biological ones. Human societies change their form over time, over generations, and now faster than this. It follows that generalizations about social phenomena are likely to be restricted in their scope of application. It may be reasonable to regard an entire phase of development of a social system as a "case", because of its complex, distinctive, and interrelated features. Some social scientists contrast an early phase of capital accumulation of capitalist societies with a later phase of mass consumption, as "types" of social formation to which particular societies to a degree conform. It has been argued that Freud contributed to the emergence of the mass consumption phase of capitalism through his identification of the consequences of sexual repression (Gellner, 1995; Marcuse, 1958).

Case-study methods have been significant in the social sciences. Ethnographers in anthropology and sociology, life-history researchers, organizational researchers, management scientists, and consultants all use case-study methods, even though their "cases" may be communities and institutions rather than individual subjects. There is a medical tradition of the clinical case study, seen, for example, in the work of psychiatrists and neuroscientists such A. R. Luria (1972), Oliver Sacks (1985), and Antonio Damasio (2000). Jurisprudence concerns itself centrally with "cases". In the field of law, the application of general principles has always to be applied to particular instances—"cases"—where the relevance to them of this or that law has always to be determined by investigation and argument. An influential practice of legal education is based on the study of cases (Harvard Law School, 2018). The practical and ethical reason why attention should be given to "cases" in medicine and law is that individuals, and therefore "cases", matter in their own right. Individuals receiving medical care, or being tried by the courts, are recognized as of value in themselves, and not only as instances of some larger category.

Historical research implicitly uses case-study methods, even though its "cases" may be sequences of events that have occurred in specific places and times. Historical subjects can be described as "cases" since they are significantly different from one another and embody complex causal relations. They rarely conform exactly to theoretical types or general laws. While sociologists and economists seek to identify the theoretical "kinds" to which phenomena correspond, historians more often aim to produce exact descriptions of their objects of study, sometimes taking account of historical actors' subjective experience of their place in their world.[1] Although in such work concepts and abstractions are unavoidable and quantitative measurement has a place, these may be secondary to narrative and holistic descriptions, connecting the different elements of a situation in their unique configurations in time and space.

The fields of business and organizational studies and the practice of organizational consultancy also make substantial use of case-study methods.[2] This is because their objects of study are both complex and significantly different from one another. The study of organizations requires that attention be given both to widely shared attributes and practices (such as types of leadership, the functions and dysfunctions of bureaucracy, formal and informal organization, the characteristics of socio-technical systems) and to particulars, when the problem is, for example, to understand the conditions in which certain organizations succeed and others fail. A knowledge of "types" and exemplary instances may as valuable to an organizational researcher as to a clinician in the medical or mental health field.

A kind of case-study method was the staple investigative form of anthropology during the period when its main object of study was remote communities or "tribes". Such studies usually began with observations and descriptions by anthropologists who spent time "in the field", which they then developed as classifications of kinds of social phenomena (such as kinship systems and religious rituals) and their inter-relationship within specific kinds of society. Out of such studies generalizable classifications and models emerged—for example, the ideas of social structure and of culture—which then served to guide further investigations. But anthropologists are nearly always concerned with specificities—and thus "cases"—since the societies they study are constantly subject to processes of differentiation and "speciation", just as biological species are.

The essence of the matter is that these methods are well adapted to investigating complex interconnections and interdependencies within bounded objects of study that are, in certain respects, particular and unique.

Research designs: experiments, surveys, and case studies

Case-study methods should therefore be understood to be not as an inferior and outdated kind of investigation, but as one in a large array of research methods, each appropriate to its object of study. The following schema, adapted from Gomm, Hammersley, and Foster (2000, p. 4) and extended is instructive:

Experiments

» A relatively small number of cases.
» Information gathered about small number of features of each case.
» Cases structured to allow important variables to be controlled.
» The quantification of data a priority. However, not all experiments require quantification for their outcomes to be evaluated.
» An aim of either theoretical inference—the development and testing of a theory—or of the evaluation of the effects of an intervention.

Clinical trials and outcome studies in psychotherapy aim to meet the specifications of this model.

Surveys

» A relatively large number of cases.
» Information gathered and analysed about a small number of features of each case (e.g., frequencies of variables that correlate drinking and road accidents).
» Study of a sample of naturally occurring cases; selected in such a way as to maximize a sample's representativeness in relation to a larger population.
» Quantification of data is a priority.
» The aim is empirical generalization from a sample to a finite population, although such a finding may be a platform for a theoretical inference, or be a basis for further investigation of a more theoretical kind.
» Statistical methods, enabling valid inferences about finite populations to be drawn from findings from selected samples, are an essential basis of survey methods.
» Epidemiological studies that seek to discover the factors related to the incidence of diseases make use of such methods.

Case studies

» A small number of cases (even a single case).
» Information gathered about large number of aspects (or "variables") of each case.
» Case studies may give attention to naturally occurring phenomena, in their relative "impurity"—"impure", that is to say, in contrast to laboratory conditions, within which experiments are undertaken with "pure" examples of the objects of study, in closed systems from which extraneous variables are excluded, as far as possible.

» "Action research" and "participant observation" may be forms of case-based research in which the effects of a researcher's presence or activity may be an aspect of the object of study.
» Quantitative data are not a priority in case study research, in which qualitative data may be considered superior, since its purpose is to capture and describe the specific attributes of objects.
» A main concern may be to understand a case itself (e.g., a patient), with no interest in theoretical inference or empirical generalization. But there may be an aim of generalization too. Inferences regarding "kinds" of phenomena may be drawn from specific cases, which may then be tested through wider observation. This process has been termed "naturalistic generalisation". It is related to what in psychoanalysis is called "learning from experience" (Bion, 1962).

Clinical case studies in psychoanalysis frequently have these attributes.

Psychotherapy patients are "naturally occurring phenomena", and rarely constitute instances of "pure" kinds. Even though either diagnostic (ADHD, PTSD) or more theoretical (e.g., "destructive narcissist" or "paranoid-schizoid") categories may be applicable to them, such categorizations need to take account of the particularities of individual patients in clinical practice. Furthermore, "co-morbidity" (the presence of more than one pathological condition) is common in this field, and such co-morbid conditions may well interact with one another.

Case-study methods in psychoanalysis and their limitations

Since Freud's first invention of psychoanalysis, the clinical case study— and sometimes initially a single-case–study—has been its primary location of discovery. *The Interpretation of Dreams* (1900a) is, in effect, such a study, whose subject is Freud himself. His six most famous case studies—Anna O (1895d) Dora (1905e), Little Hans (1909b), the Rat Man (1909d), the Schreber case (1911c) and the Wolf Man (1918b)—are where some of his most important theoretical discoveries were reported and where the clinical method of psychoanalysis was first displayed at length. Klein's theoretical discoveries were largely made through her clinical cases, and her *Narrative of a Child Analysis* (1961) was where she set out in detail her analysis of a particular child. There are rather few examples in the literature of full accounts of psychoanalytic cases,[3] though doctoral research theses are now adding to their number.[4] In psychoanalysis in Britain clinical cases are strongly relied upon as providing the evidential grounds for innovations in theory and technique. This is so for each of the three principal schools of psychoanalysis in

Britain—the Freudian, the Kleinian, and the Independent—and also to a degree in psychoanalysis in the United States in its Freudian and Relational traditions.

Yet for all their centrality to psychoanalysis, case-study methods have been under attack for many years, both from within and from outside the field. One line of criticism has arisen from a change of focus in the never-ending critical debate about the scientific value of psychoanalysis. In an earlier phase, the main controversy concerned the validity and truth of its principal ideas. More recently, the question has become its effectiveness as a mental health practice. The former line of critique came primarily from philosophers of science, such Karl Popper (1963) and Adolf Grünbaum (1974, 1993), the latter now comes as much from competing mental health professionals, such as the advocates of cognitive behavioural therapy. But also influential in these debates have been psychoanalysts whose aim has been to bring psychoanalysis closer to what they see as the scientific mainstream, with the stated purpose of defending it against external attack—even, in some formulations, to save it from virtual extinction. For example, Peter Fonagy:

> Psychoanalytic practice has profound limitations as a form of research. Psychoanalytic theory precludes the possibility that psychoanalysts can be adequate observers of their clinical work. The discovery of the pervasiveness of countertransference has totally discredited Freud's clinician–researcher model. In the absence of a genuine research tradition, academic disciplines will appropriately distance themselves from psychoanalytic study, in much the same way that they hold journalism at arm's length. [Fonagy, 2003, p. 74]

Case studies are often said to have a low degree of scientific credibility. In the "hierarchy of evidence" (Akobeng, 2005), the randomized placebo-controlled trial comes top as the "gold standard" (Wesseley, 2001) and the single-case study rather low down. Where the aim is to establish the outcomes of a specified kind of intervention, the randomized trial is no doubt the optimal research method. It consists of a set of linked procedures, which include accurate sampling, the standardization of interventions, a non-treated control group, defined base-lines to identify pre-treatment conditions, and end-of-treatment and follow-up measures, with statistical techniques that can track significant variations in sampled populations. Most medical trials of drugs are undertaken according to these protocols, and the licensing for use of a specified drug depends on their evidence.

It is possible to organize comparable trials of psychological treatments, including those that are psychoanalytic, for specified kinds of mental illness, although to achieve uniformity at each stage of this process—the definition of the illness and the collection of the sample, the standardization (e.g., through "manualization") of a treatment intervention, and the measurement of its outcomes—is more difficult than for many conditions in physical medicine. Significant randomized controlled trials of psychoanalytic therapies have recently been undertaken in England, with outcomes that have been to varying degrees positive. (Three of these are discussed in chapter 13.) The evidence from these is now enabling psychoanalytic therapies to be included in NICE recommended treatment paths, more than was the case in their absence. These trials have become essential if psychoanalytic treatments are to be remain licensed and funded within the public health system.

It must be acknowledged that normal psychoanalytic clinical practice is ill suited to provide valid and reliable measures of treatment outcome. Its cases arrive at the request of prospective clients, rather than through scientific selection by analysts. Whereas with medical conditions, diagnoses and the classification of patients by category of illness are made before treatment is decided, in psychoanalytic work a full assessment of the condition of a patient may only emerge during a therapy itself. In most clinical settings, standardized records of initial condition, the specific nature of a therapy, and its clinical outcomes are rarely maintained in a form that meets the purposes of research, although requirements upon state-funded services to follow audit procedures to monitor their work may be changing this situation to some degree. But while audit is a useful practice, there are considerable difficulties in standardizing the essential variables—initial diagnosis of patient, treatment mode, measured outcome—to achieve standards comparable to those of a clinical trial. And even if adequate measures of outcome can be achieved for small, selected patient groups, there are great difficulties in drawing larger inferences from them. If one cannot reasonably assume that the larger population possesses the same attributes as a treatment sample, one cannot validly predict the outcome of a treatment if it were "scaled up".

There are similar issues with "treatment equivalence". A well-conducted psychotherapeutic programme may achieve good outcomes in one setting but may be difficult to reproduce with exactness in others. Standardized and manualized treatment "packages" are widely advocated as a solution to this problem, especially where authorities are concerned about the cost-effectiveness of therapies. The difficulty is to incorporate within standardized models of treatment the complexity and open-ended responsiveness that characterizes the psychoanalytic method. It easier to measure some types of therapy than others, and measurability does not coincide with therapeutic value.

Some of the current demands for evaluation and measurement in mental health clinics may, in fact, be contributing to a worsening rather than an improvement in mental health care, since the time required to be devoted to record-keeping (as in other professions too) may drain resources from treatment itself.

Psychoanalytic case-study methods and the generation of knowledge

Case-study methods in psychoanalysis have been of limited value in providing verifiable evidence of clinical effectiveness. From this perspective, the field's historical reliance on these has been held to be a grave problem. Yet, on the other hand, these methods have been central to psychoanalytic discovery and to the generation of new knowledge over the entire history of psychoanalysis.

In psychoanalysis, "cases" are studied for different purposes, only some of which are concerned with the development of theoretical knowledge. The purpose of most clinical practice with cases is to do no more than understand the particular individuals who are in analysis or therapy. Psychoanalytic concepts, theories, and techniques are likely to be drawn upon by clinicians as resources for this work, but may neither intend nor effect any revision or development of the ideas they find clinically useful.

However, clinicians may find themselves asking questions that are of wider significance than the qualities of their particular patient. They may find that their case is an instance of a type of character, or a psychological difficulty, or a transference phenomenon notable for demonstration of a significant psychoanalytic idea. A specific contribution to knowledge by an analyst may be the recognition that her particular case provides evidence that instances an idea that is not yet routinely accepted in its field. When discoveries are announced by an analyst for the first time—for example, in a paper that may refer to a single case—practitioners' recognition that cases that they know are similar to it, and that a new idea has explanatory power, can be significant. A principal means by which psychoanalytic ideas are tested and validated in their fields is through such a process of clinical confirmation or "disconfirmation". Single clinical instances, whatever their apparent significance, are unlikely to lead to a development of theory if others that corroborate this are not found. Such a process of testing by example, and of finding points of similarity and difference between cases, is the most normal kind of "normal science" in this field.

There is the further question of how significant new ideas are discovered in the first place: such discoveries are infrequent but important. It seems that such innovations require clinicians to be able to think not only about their patients, but also about theories and concepts. Sometimes this involves a procedure of deduction, of working out hitherto unrecognized implications or extensions of a theory. (Much of Freud's work proceeded through such theoretical deduction, often based on the evidence of very few cases.[5]) It may also involve the recognition of significant discrepancies between what a theory says should be the case, or of what "ought" to have been captured by a concept, and the discrepant phenomena of an actual case.

When she was trying to find meaning in the states of mind that led to her discovery of the countertransference, Paula Heimann (1950) recognized a crucial causal and explanatory link to the idea of projective identification, which Klein had recently formulated. But she also found that the idea that countertransference might mainly reflect insufficient self-understanding in an analyst might not explain the emotional disturbance she was experiencing—she came to see that this might be an effect of her patient's unconscious projections into her. Similarly, when Herbert Rosenfeld struggled to understand one narcissistic patient and his non-responsiveness to interpretations that focused on his self-love, the idea came to him that narcissism might take both a libidinal and a destructive form. He was here recognizing that an established concept did not sufficiently fit clinical facts, and that an additional idea would be needed to give meaning to them. But he seems also, consciously or not, to have drawn upon Freud's fundamental distinction between the life and death instincts to create a more adequate concept of narcissism, which he now saw to be of two distinct kinds. The fact that the patient responded in an active way to interpretations of his hatred and envy of his objects was evidence for Rosenfeld that he had made a genuine discovery, one that became influential in post-Kleinian psychoanalytic theory.

One might expect a method of research that compares several cases to be superior to the intensive study of single cases. As we see in a later chapter, the "constant comparative method of analysis" (Glaser & Strauss, 1967, pp. 101–115) enables variances to be investigated in many instances and to gain in validity and reliability through this procedure. The "method of agreement" and "method of difference" that originate in the work of Francis Bacon (1620) and John Stuart Mill (1843) enable conjunctions of variables and their relations of cause and effect to be traced (Gomm et al., pp. 239–252). However, it is likely that with comparative case studies in psychoanalysis, many attributes will need to be specified if a case is to be assigned accurately to a theoretical category. The move from "ideal typical" or conceptually pure models to the phenomena of actual cases is always practically difficult when dealing with human and social subjects. It is the particularity of cases that makes clinical judgement so important in psychoanalysis.

It is feasible even for single-case studies to be analysed in a methodologically rigorous way. One can do this because it is possible to treat different elements or segments of a case as separate instances, whose differences and variations over time can be identified and compared. A single-case study of psychoanalytic psychotherapeutic work, conducted even on a once-weekly basis over two years, may generate as many as 80 separate clinical records, each providing a detailed description of a clinical session. Events such as a transference interpretation, or one that refers to a patient's negative feelings, may be investigated in multiple occurrences even within in a single case.

Fonagy and Moran described this kind of procedure in their papers "Psychoanalysis and Diabetic Control: A Single Case Study" (Moran & Fonagy, 1987), and "Selecting Single Case Research Designs for Clinicians" (Fonagy & Moran, 1993). "What is needed", Fonagy and Moran (1993) wrote, "is a means to enhance the internal validity of the data gathered in the clinical setting, so that the canons of scientific objectivity can be met, while at the same time preserving the subtlety and complexity of clinical phenomena" (p. 63). To achieve this end, they operationalized and independently rated analytic themes in each week of the five-times-weekly psychotherapy. They related this to the weekly index of the diabetic balance of their patient. "Two themes of psychic conflict were held to predict short-term changes in diabetic control. In the long term the verbalization of conflict was strongly associated with improved diabetic control" (Moran & Fonagy, 1987). The study was both quantitative and qualitative. It was valuable that there was an objective medical index of improvement against which to measure the progress of the therapy. This was feasible because monitoring intakes of medication was a routine practice for a patient with this condition and did not interfere with the analytic therapy in the way that conducting independent psychological assessments at similar intervals might have done. The study is exemplary in showing the rigour with which single cases can be analysed. Its concept of "verbalization" may have contributed to Fonagy and his colleagues' later focus on the idea of "mentalization" as a psychological function, and on its enhancement as a principal aim of treatment.

The clinical case study as an inscription device

A valuable concept in Bruno Latour's studies of science is that of the "inscription device" (Latour & Woolgar, 1979). This refers to the notations or symbolic forms in which scientists' experimental and other interactions with nature are formulated as descriptions, and from which theories are built. Latour's argument is that the different "objects" of science will each give rise to their own methods of investigation, their own conceptualizations, and their own forms of representation of findings. Thus, astronomers have depended on visual observations and their enhancement though telescopes and on their records of the appearance and movement of heavenly bodies. Inferences were made from these concerning the causes of these patterns of movement, such as those formulated in Newton's laws of motion or in Einstein's theory of special relativity. Geographers, when attempting to understand land forms, found graphical representation in maps to be indispensable. Epidemiologists, seeking to find correlations between different variables as causal conditions of human health and disease, depend overwhelmingly on the representation of quantities whose causal significance depends on correlations through statistical procedures based on theories of probability. For a long period, the primary inscription device through which zoologists and botanists registered their findings were descriptions drawn from observation, often also rendered as drawings, and later as photographs.

This relation between forms of inscription and the specific objects of science being investigated explains why the descriptive clinical case study has been so important in psychoanalysis. The analyst's observations and record of her transactions with patients in clinical sessions provide the crucial data for psychoanalytic reflection. There is a particular aspect of psychoanalytic investigation that makes these records of such importance. Its most significant phenomena are those that reveal the unconscious desires, phantasies, and interactions of patients and their analysts. Written records of communications are crucial to other forms of case investigation too—for example, in the field of law—but from a different perspective.

One might infer that a fully accurate record of such verbal exchanges, such as might be obtained from audio-recording, is all that is needed to provide adequate clinical data. However, what can be captured in such a verbal record is not all that may be psychoanalytically relevant. Some of what is learned about patients may emerge from what is not said by them, in surprising periods of silence, or from their bodily movements, appearance, and mood. In the psychoanalysis of children, where the observation and interpretation of play is so central, the dimension of the "non-verbal" in the clinical context is especially important. It seems that video-recordings could improve on audio-recordings from this point of view, although these would not be without practical difficulty.[6] But the limitations of literal records of exchanges between patients and therapists, whether aural or visual, as sources of data have a deeper cause.

A particular methodological difficulty derives from the phenomena of the transference and countertransference. These constitute dimensions of the analytic relationship that are unlikely to be fully captured in the textual record of what is said in clinical sessions. Analysts make verbal interpretations, describing a feeling or a situation in words, and these will be part of a verbal transcript. But sometimes they will refrain from speech, in the belief that at that moment an interpretation would be unhelpful. Furthermore, what is going on in an analyst's mind can be as relevant to understanding what is going on in a session as what the analyst puts into words. Given the phenomena of the countertransference, the analyst's state of mind may be a container of important information about the patient. Influential developments of psychoanalytic theory, for example, Bion's understanding of psychotic states of mind (Bion, 1967b), have emerged from his self-reflections in therapeutic situations where few words seem to have been spoken.

Thus, when analysts or clinical researchers reflect on the meaning of an analytic session, their own feelings and associations of ideas may be as relevant to their understanding as a written session transcript. Some analysts have described unconscious aspects of the communications with patients, comparing them to a dream-like experience (Bollas, 1995; Meltzer, 1984). A full understanding of what happens may require taking account of these elusive dimensions.[7]

The fact that psychoanalysts seek to understand unconscious meanings creates problems in making its interpretative procedures transparent and accountable. The "subjectivity" of the analyst is a necessary resource in their observation and understanding of patients. But how can this subjective and introspective aspect of perception be reconciled with the standard requirement that scientific observation be objective and impersonal in its approach? It is necessary that such a reconciliation between the subjective and the objective be achieved for psychoanalysis, given that its primary field of study is unconscious mental life. We have earlier argued that sciences adopt methods of observation and report that are appropriate to their specific objects of study. The methods of data analysis appropriate to register and report the distinctive unconscious phenomena of psychoanalytic "cases" is discussed in a later chapter.

The understandings that can be achieved from case study research can sometimes be convincing in their its own right, without larger-scale trials. Case study evidence is likely to be more conclusive where the relations of cause and effect that are in question are unmistakably large. One hardly needs to detonate an atomic weapon on a city to know what damage it would cause. Examples of the knowledge that can be gained from singular case studies are to be found in the neuroscientific research of Antonio Damasio (2000). His research examined the functions of different physical areas of the brain and their effects on subjects' consciousness. In his clinic, he was able to take advantage as a researcher (he was also a clinician) of incidences of severe brain damage in patients where these had been the result of traumatic accidents. He was able to investigate what mental capabilities were left to patients who had suffered damage to specific areas of their brain. This research work was based both on clinical interactions with patients, designed to investigate, with their active help, the capabilities remaining to them following brain injuries, and also on knowledge of the brain and its functions obtained from neurological research.

Another example of such an influential case study was the discovery by John Bowlby and his colleagues, James and Joyce Robertson, of the effects on the emotional state of young children in hospital when they were separated from their parents (Bowlby, 1952; Bowlby, Robertson, & Rosenbluth, 1952; Robertson, 1952, 1958). The powerful "inscription device" of film was used by the Robertsons to record and represent this situation and its effects. The distress of these children was so obvious and harrowing to viewers that it did, in effect, tell its own story. This study was supported by others which confirmed that the absence of parents could cause severe distress to young children and which were able to track the typical "stages" of children's response to this situation of their perceived abandonment. It scarcely required a large sample survey of children's treatment in hospitals to validate the initial finding. The chosen mode of representation, a documentary film, itself had an impact on policy and public understanding. It is now routine and mandatory in British hospitals to allow and, indeed, encourage parental access to children's inpatient care in hospitals. Bowlby's "attachment theory"—his research into the dynamics of attachment, separation, and loss—was the main theoretical foundation for these findings and has been supported and developed in many empirical studies.

A further question of psychoanalytic interest raised by the children-in-hospital research concerns the processes of "not-seeing" and denial that contributed to the apparent non-recognition by hospital staff of states of distress that became so obvious once they were reported and persuasively represented on film. We can understand this state of "not-knowing" by noting that the camera observed a child throughout his experience of separation, and that its film record could be studied in its totality, and in slow-motion detail, by the researchers. However, it seems likely that the hospital staff had learned to keep themselves at some distance from child patients who were suffering in this way. This distance was, no doubt, sometimes physical (through rotation of nurses around the wards) but must also have been psychological, affecting what staff were able to notice or bring to others' attention. A psychoanalytic literature on denial and not-seeing or "turning a blind eye" related to the idea of a narcissistic personality organization (Britton, 1998b; Steiner, 1993b) has developed since that study was undertaken, bringing understanding to many other kinds of disavowal (Cooper & Lousada, 2005).

The tendency to disparage the value of "case studies" and the more informal knowledge gained from clinical and other practical experience is strong in the current climate of "evidence-based practice". The belief among authorities is that if a practice or procedure has not been validated by a randomized controlled trial, it has no validity. The effect of this belief system is to discount practice-based forms of knowledge, skill, and understanding.

In the mechanical servicing of motor cars or aircraft, which have been manufactured to a high uniform specification, it is no doubt feasible that every maintenance procedure should follow a prescribed pattern and be set out in a manual. We should all be grateful that modern automobiles and aircraft work with such wonderful reliability. But in the lives of human beings, such uniformities do not obtain and are, in any case, undesirable. It is important that teachers should have a defined and proven method of teaching literacy, but also that they should be capable of understanding and interacting with particular child who does not learn, in situations when teaching performed by the teachers according to a teaching manual has little meaning for a child. Such a child may be a "case" not in a clinical sense, but because he needs to be understood in his own particularity and complexity.

Psychoanalysis is a practice-driven field of knowledge. Most of its understandings have emerged from therapeutic work with individual patients. Analysts' clinical work is with "cases" located within a field of internal and external relationships with others. It is because of this practice-based focus that case-study methods of research have always been and are likely to remain the primary source of psychoanalytic knowledge. The research need is not to do without them, but to do them better. How this may be accomplished is discussed in later chapters.

Notes

1. The idea of "History from Below", a narrative of the lives of ordinary people rather than their rulers, has been a democratic version of this approach.

2. Case studies are central means of instruction in business schools, such as those of Stanford (Stanford Graduate School of Business, 2018) or Harvard (Harvard Law School, 2018).

3. Others are Winnicott (1980) and McDougall (1969).

4. *New Discoveries in Child Psychotherapy: Findings from Qualitative Research,* edited by M. E and M. J. Rustin (forthcoming) will report eleven such cases.

5. Anna Bentinck van Schoonheten (2016), in her biography of Karl Abraham, contrasts Freud's practice of developing theories from single cases with Abraham's reliance on a broader clinical experience.

6. When one recalls the skills needed by film directors and cinematographers, including the makers of documentary films, to represent the emotional meanings of a scene, one can see how difficult it might be to make use of video recordings to capture the reality of clinical sessions.

7. In the recent IMPACT study of adolescent depression, two forms of record of clinical sessions were maintained. One of these was an electronic recording, the other the conventional post-session process notes of the therapists, maintained in part for purposes of clinical supervision. A valuable doctoral research project by Miriam Creaser (2015), a child psychotherapist, has compared these two forms of record and their differences, with valuable findings (discussed in chapter 10).

CHAPTER EIGHT

Parts and wholes: different kinds of explanation

T his chapter is about the differences between "causal" explanations, which describe the relations between discrete causes and effects, and "part–whole" or holistic explanations, which describe how one understands a specific phenomenon in relation to a larger totality or system of which it is a part. The former kind of explanation belongs within an "atomistic" or "mechanistic" frame of thinking, the latter within a "holistic" or organic perspective. Explanations in the physical sciences commonly aim to set out causal relations between discrete entities in law-like terms. Explanations in the biological and, sometimes, the human sciences often make use of holistic models, such as those of "systems" of interrelated and interdependent parts. Where explanation requires understanding the meaning of symbolic communications, complex relations involving a holistic perspective almost invariably arise, as should have been clear from the earlier discussion of meanings and causes.

What is it to find an explanation in psychoanalysis? What is a psychoanalyst or psychoanalytic psychotherapist looking for when they try to understand a patient, or a moment or episode in the treatment of a patient? This seems to be a simple question, but it is not simple at all. My contention in this chapter is that, whether or not its practitioners have regarded it as a science, psychoanalysis has, for most part, adopted a holistic conception of its object of study. It is necessary for this aspect of it to be recognized.

Atomistic forms of explanation

In everyday life what we often mean when we say we have explained something is that we have identified its cause. "Why has someone in our family caught this virus?" one may ask, on a winter's day. "They caught it from the baby? Where did the baby catch it? It came from the day nursery, viruses are always going around there, everyone catches them." This is surely a familiar and persuasive line of reasoning. Its purpose is to discover the relationship between a specific cause and a specific effect. In this case, we focus on the ideas of infection and proximity of physical contacts as the source of an illness. We are trying to locate a chain of causes and effects, for the reason that if we can locate this chain, we may be able to break it by keeping ourselves away from those infected with the virus and keep those infected with the virus out of contact with as many other people as possible. We try, in many circumstances, to identify the "efficient cause" of something, which can enable us to prevent what would otherwise be its effect.

Of course there is an enormous amount that can also be said about infections in which viruses are involved—for example, about immunity and general health, as factors that might explain why infections don't happen, even if there is contact between an infected person and others, and for this reason exposure to a virus. And further about the way that viruses operate in the body, about the effects they can have on an entire organism, about the illnesses they give rise to and the further consequences that these can have. The field of viruses and their behaviours and effects is a very complicated one. But when we are thinking in everyday life about the "efficient cause" referred to above, we put all that aside as irrelevant. All we are practically interested is the link between cause and effect that we may be able to break.

The idea that explanation is primarily concerned with establishing causal connections between variable x and variable y is an extremely influential one in our culture. It represents the common-sense version of a dominant view of science and scientific methods, one of whose influential proponents was the philosopher David Hume (1777), already referred to in chapter 4.

> I shall venture to affirm, as a general proposition, which admits of no exception, that the knowledge of this relation is not, in any instance, attained by reasonings a priori but arises entirely from experience, when we find that any particular objects are constantly conjoined with one another. [*Enquiry Concerning Human Understanding*, Section 4, Section 4, Part 1, ¶ 23]

To attribute causal agency is to do no more than to refer to such observed conjunctions, and assertions of such causal relations need always be open to correction if observation (what Hume refers to as "experience") requires this. This model of science was atomistic in its presuppositions. Since its purpose was to establish constant conjunctions and the causal relations that could be (provisionally) inferred from these, it became essential to specify the entities between which conjunctions could be observed. An atomistic view that perceived nature according to its elementary components or entities facilitated the scientific procedures through which a new understanding of nature could be built.

Following this procedure, many apparently indivisible entities that were essential to life—for example, air and water—later became intelligible as combinations of simpler elements: nitrogen, oxygen, and carbon dioxide in a physical relation in the former case, hydrogen and oxygen in a chemical relation in the latter. It could be shown that these simple elements could be combined with one another in different ways—water is not the only molecule that can be built from atoms of hydrogen and oxygen, just as carbon dioxide is not the only molecule that can be built from atoms of carbon and oxygen. Both an atomistic ontology and an analytic epistemology were central to the development of this new scientific world view. The "realist" perspective I outlined in chapter 4 argues, however, that what may initially have been recognized as "constant conjunctions" of empirical attributes may later be understood as the theoretical terms of "natural necessity"—that is as the invariant properties of distinct substances. These may become elements in a more comprehensive theoretical structure, such as that represented in the Periodic Table of chemical elements (Harré & Madden, 1975).

In setting out his philosophical understanding of causality, with his characteristic and engaging scepticism, Hume was providing the rationale for a scientific revolution. He sought to overthrow a prevailing metaphysical perspective on the world, whose theories depended on received knowledge and abstract theories, not on empirical observation. He also wished to displace teleological conceptions about the innate powers and dispositions of objects and entities, which were incompatible with this new view of science as concerned only to establish correlations capable of being tested by observation. Hegel's theory of historical development as driven by the working out of the logical implications of emergent ideas—particularistic claims to rights becoming universalized to all of humanity, for example—is a late version of an earlier purpose-driven (teleological) view of the world whose original philosophical advocate was Aristotle.

Ernest Gellner (1975, 1994) a philosopher and sociologist, described the momentous impact of this "modern" world view as enabling the human environment to be remade, both conceptually and in practice, through the demand that all explanations be validated by criteria of fact and logical consistency, and not by reference to received beliefs or traditions. Gellner described this as a revolution in thought, the development of a "modular" perspective in which the elements of nature and society could be broken down analytically into their separate elements and then re-assembled in those patterns and relations that could best serve the purposes of scientific and technological understanding, and of social betterment. Gellner saw this development as a source of liberation, which both allowed and required human beings to take responsibility for their understandings of the world and, through science and technology, conferred on them enormous powers to intervene in nature for their benefit.

The conception of science that has come to dominate modern societies has been deeply influenced by the idea that the discovery of causal connections makes possible the application of science to serve human purposes. The discovery and utilization of "efficient causes" is central to this vision. An "efficient cause" becomes the agent by which a desired effect can be achieved. Most of the major fields of discovery of "pure science" have turned out to be capable of exploitation for human ends. Thus the theory of gravitational attraction became deployed for many mechanical purposes, including engineering and military ballistics; the theory of electromagnetism became the basis for machines based on electrical power; atomic physics made possible nuclear bombs and reactors.

Karl Popper's (1934, 1963) "falsificationist" model of science, according to which science proceeds by formulating universal laws that assert the causal relations between entities, was a development of Humean principles in some—but not all—respects. He held that scientific laws were validated not by their positive correspondence with observed facts, but by a test of their negation—that is to say, whether they could survive empirical (experimental or observational) tests capable of falsifying them. This was a development of Humean principles, since the idea of constant conjunction remained at its core. However, it added to this falsificationist principle the idea that the laws of causality, once validated, could become the building blocks in ordered bodies of theory, which thus acquire more complex and substantial attributes than singular conjunctions. He also believed that major scientific discoveries could as well have their origin in imaginative speculation as in inductive inferences from experience. "Conjectures", through which hypotheses were formed, were distinct in his view from their empirical testing, through his procedure of falsification. This insight reflected a scientific environment around the turn of the century in which established "Newtonian" and "Galilean" cosmologies had been revolutionized by the discoveries of quantum theory and relativity— neither the outcome of direct observation. Popper, however, held on to Hume's insistence that correspondence with observed facts was the decisive criterion of their validity. Scientific laws were, of their essence, universal in their logical implication and entailed predictive relations where specified conditions of application were present.

The questions that Popper asked of psychoanalysis were: what are its universal laws, within what specifiable conditions do these apply, and what falsifiable predictions can be made according to these principles? Popper held that psychoanalytic theories could not meet these criteria in the way that the natural sciences, and, even with a limited scope of application, the social sciences, could do. Psychoanalysis was therefore in his judgement false in its claim to be a science. Popper dismissed it as a "pseudo-science."

In the evidence-based culture that dominates modern health services, the explanations that are believed to matter are those that specify the "efficient causes" characterized above. There is the question of what causes explain this or that psychological disorder, but there is also the question—to which greater practical importance is attached—of what specific treatments or interventions might bring about their alleviation or cure. In the field of mental health, it is believed to be more feasible to locate "efficient causes" that might achieve, if not a cure, than at least an alleviation of the severity of mental illnesses, than it is to identify the causes that are responsible for bringing them about. Even in some fields of physical medicine, if an "efficient cause" can be found that has positive therapeutic effects, it may not even matter much, for the time being, what theoretical connection this may have to the understanding of the original illness. Thus a drug used for one medical purpose (e.g., aspirin, for reducing superficial symptoms) may be discovered to have benign effects of a different kind (in lessening the incidence of heart disease). If this effect is shown to be robust, then the drug can be prescribed for this new purpose, even if no one can explain—i.e. identify the specific causes of—this effect.

The common contemporary definition of scientific research in psychoanalysis as the investigation of the outcomes of psychoanalytic treatments is implicitly framed within a conception of science whose aim is to establish laws that connect causes and effects. The evidence that matters concerns "efficient causes" (e.g., therapies or drugs) that can bring about desired effect; how it does this, if it does, is of little concern. Since psychoanalysis has always been primarily concerned to understand the deep structures and processes of the mind, this perspective disregards much of what it is about. This shift towards a highly instrumental conception of knowledge has contributed to the precarious standing of psychoanalysis.

Holistic and organic perspectives

There is, however, a conception of science that is different from that outlined above. Its sources lie in the biological rather than the physical sciences—that is, in the study of living forms. In this view, biological organisms are conceived as holistic entities, whose components are causally interdependent with one another and whose natural state is a homeostatic (self-maintaining) equilibrium. It is this self-maintaining capability that ensures their persisting existence as bounded totalities over periods of time and over generations, since one attribute that living species possess is that of self-reproduction—for example, through a specialized subsystem of the body. The chemical elements and molecules that constitute the body of an organism have different properties and causal relations with each other when an organism is alive than when it has died. Explanations in terms of homeostatic or self-regulating systems are relevant not only to the functioning of individual organisms, but also to larger "ecological" environments. An ecological system of interdependencies between species and the materials on which they depend for life may also be self-equilibrating. This has become a matter of intense interest as human actions are disturbing equilibria that have persisted for long periods. The largest entity now being understood in these terms is the planetary environment itself, in the discovery that the stable life-supporting properties of the atmosphere depends on organic processes—such as the production of oxygen by plant-life. The "Gaia Hypothesis" is one version of this idea.

The use of biological analogies to explain the functioning of social systems has been criticized, on grounds that they neglect the significant differences that exist between the "natural" (genetically given) equilibrium states of organisms and the purposeful, value-driven, conflict-rich potential of social systems. However, while this critique points to significant differences between biological and social systems, the similarity remains that both can display self-maintaining and self-equilibrating properties. They may share these homeostatic properties, have boundaries across which exchanges take place with an "external" environment, and have "functional" interdependences between their parts. The analysis of socio-technical systems by researchers at the Tavistock Institute of Human Relations has enabled institutions to be modelled in ways that identify their specific tasks, the boundaries between them and their environment, and the inputs and outputs that are required to take place across them, if they are to survive or flourish (Miller & Rice, 1967).[1] The understanding of both organic and social systems is insufficient if these attributes are not recognized.

Thomas Scheff's model of part–whole analysis

Thomas Scheff's (1997) model of part–whole analysis or "part–whole morphology" (morphology is the science of structures) is a valuable point of entry into these methodological issues. Scheff suggested that botanical morphology employs the method of part–whole analysis, since it relates the "least parts" (the tiniest details of the individual plant) to the "greatest wholes": the structures and processes of plant communities and their relationship to their environment. He drew here on the philosophy of Spinoza (1677), which proposed that human understanding requires "relating the least parts to the greatest wholes". Spinoza's idea was that the analysis of causal connections will reveal an underlying meaningfulness and connectedness in Nature, which he understood as the expression of the will of God. (Pantheism is the name given to this belief.) Spinoza's view was opposed to the mechanistic atomism of Hobbes and the English empiricists, in which values came to be understood not to be innate in Nature but, rather, subjective attributions to Nature made by human beings.[2]

Scheff proposed the method of part–whole analysis as a resource for the human sciences, in various domains, which include family systems, international relations (including the diplomatic exchanges that culminated in the outbreak of the Great War, and psychotherapy.) He traced the practice of part–whole analysis back to the German writer and scientist, Goethe. Goethe was, among his other interests and talents, a collector of plants and an investigator of their form and function, and Scheff held him to have anticipated some features of Darwin's theory of evolution. Goethe wrote this about organisms:

> In every living thing what we call the parts is so inseparable from the whole that the parts can only be understood in the whole, and we can neither make the parts the measure of the whole nor the whole the measure of the parts; and this is why living creatures, even the most restricted, have something about them we cannot quite grasp and have to describe as infinite or partaking of infinity. [Goethe, 1790, quoted in Scheff, 1997, p. 43]

Goethe's view was part of a larger reaction in his time against atomistic and mechanistic theories of nature, and to the idea that only observed "constant conjunctions" could establish a relation between the discrete objects of perception and experience.[3] His reference to the "infinite" points to the spiritual and religious dimension of experience which Romantics like Goethe, Blake and Wordsworth believed were ignored by scientism. Blake denounced the great empirical scientists, Bacon, Newton and Locke, for example, and wrote

> "Art is the tree of life
> Science is the tree of death."

Coleridge's view of science was more nuanced than Blake's but nevertheless upheld the value of a holistic in contrast to an atomistic perspective:

> A poem is that species of composition which is opposed to works of science, by proposing for its immediate object pleasure, not truth; and from all other species (having this object in common with it) it is discriminated by proposing to itself such delight from the whole as is compatible with a distinct gratification from each component part.
>
> For, if the definition sought for be that of a legitimate poem, the parts must mutually support and explain each other; all in their proportion harmonizing with, and supporting the purpose and known influences of, metrical arrangement. [Coleridge, 1817, p. 172]

A holistic (part–whole) perspective was introduced into the study of the mind by the Gestalt psychologists, whose ideas were elaborated philosophically, especially in regard to symbolic expression, in the work of Suzanne Langer (1942, 1953). Scheff argued that a contrast between atomistic and holistic models of thought is significant in the field of sociology. He cited C. Wright Mills as an advocate of a human science that sought to integrate "least parts and greatest wholes", in opposition to monodisciplinary perspectives that tended analytically to separate them. Mills advocated a sociology that moved from representative individual experiences, to social character, to institutional processes, to wider societal forces.

The sociological imagination, Mills wrote, is

> The capacity to shift from one perspective to another—from the political to the psychological; from the examination of a single family to comparative assessment of the national budgets of the world; from the theological school to the military establishment; from considerations of an oil industry to studies of contemporary poetry. It is the capacity to range from the most widespread and impersonal transformations to the most intimate features of the human self, and to see the relations between the two. [Mills, 1959, pp. 13–14]

Especially hostile to the separation of the psychological—the sphere of the mind—from the sociological—the sphere of social relations and society—in social science was Norbert Elias (1991), whose "configurational sociology" sought to maintain their connection. Elias was unusual in having trained not only as a sociologist and a historian, but also a group analyst.[4] Elias achieved one of the deepest integrations between psychoanalytic and sociological perspectives to be found in the field of sociology.

In recent decades a significant re-orientation of the human sciences in a holistic direction has taken place, represented, for example, in the work of Gregory Bateson (1972) and of Fritof Capra (1997). Many developments have accompanied this movement of ideas: for example, the ecological perspective on the natural and social environment referred to above and the emergence of "complexity theory", which is discussed in chapter 9.

Part–whole relations in psychoanalysis

These two contrasting models of explanation—what one might describe as the atomistic and the holistic, or the mechanistic and the organic—both have relevance to psychoanalytic understanding. When a psychoanalyst asks herself about a phenomenon encountered in her clinical practice, she may bring to mind two different kinds of question. On the one hand, she may ask herself, what was the cause of a specific effect, observable in the thoughts, feelings, or behaviour of a patient? Such questions may be asked about phenomena at different levels of scale and significance. On the smallest scale, might a patient's extremely angry state of mind have been the effect of the analyst's ill-judged interpretation? Or, is a child patient's apparent withdrawal from contact with his analyst today, or this week, the effect of the long summer break in the analysis, which has just ended? Or, on a still larger scale, can we best explain a particular child patient's extreme distrust of his analyst and, indeed, of most of the adults in his life as an effect of early years in which he was abandoned by his parents and had no adults in his life who appeared to care for him?

But there is also another kind of question that an analyst is likely to ask—namely, what relation does this specific entity or experience have to a larger structure of personality and a recurring way of relating to others to which it may be connected? And if so, how may such a structure and pattern of relationships explain its meaning now? These kinds of larger (holistic) connections can be made at different levels of detail and scale. They may be asked of a moment of a session, of an uttered phrase, a clinical symptom, a type of personality, or a pattern of development.

For example, why did a patient fall silent at that moment? The explanation of this might be found to lie in a particular memory having been evoked in a patient, whose significance for him only becomes fully apparent over time. Why does a patient persistently come late to her sessions and, furthermore, appear to be unwilling to think about why she does this? Or, why does this child patient find it difficult to make friends at school, or to play with the materials provided for her in the therapy room? It is surely clear that, in order to answer these questions, it will not suffice to look for the conjunction between a single cause and a single effect. The memory that disturbs, a habit of persistent lateness and a reluctance to think about it, an inability to make friends, an unwillingness to play are all complex states, each requiring a "holistic" explanation. Each of these specific phenomena has its explanatory location in some kind of persisting pattern or "system". This particular disturbing memory, this difficulty with session times or with relationships or with play, may be persistent as actions or dispositions and may well be found to be resistant to change. There may well be no simple "button"—for example, a suggestion, an instruction, or even an interpretation, which, if pressed, will have the desired effect, in the way that an antibiotic kills (or used to kill) the bacterium, or awarding the young pupil a gold star for his achievement may make him feel for a time encouraged and good about himself. One reason why psychoanalysts might hope that an interpretation or a trustworthy relationship with a therapist might have more lasting and profound effects than mere advice is because they may have a deeper influence on the way in which patient sees and experiences the world.[5]

Within a broad understanding of causes and effects, one may believe or hope that psychoanalytic treatment is itself a "cause" that can have the "effect" of enabling the patient to change for the better. "Outcome studies" of psychoanalysis look for evidence of such demonstrable causal connections. But measured correlations or constant conjunctions of this kind between a therapeutic input and a curative output may tell us next to nothing about how such an effect, where there is one, has come about.

For example, as we see in chapter 13, IMPACT was a large randomized control of three different treatment modalities—short-term psychoanalytic psychotherapy, cognitive behaviour therapy, and specialist clinical care—used to treat severely depressed adolescents within a system of delivery that was designed ensure their comparable use of therapeutic resources and thus facilitate measurement of their relative costs and benefits. Its outcome was that all three treatment modes achieved comparable levels of benefit, although the procedure of the randomization of cases—so that patients were unable to choose, or be selected for, the treatment that they or professionals believed was best suited for them—probably diminished the average gain from all three treatment methods. But what this expensive investigation neither revealed nor was designed to reveal was in what ways these different forms of treatment modalities affected their patients. Yet for each treatment, and in every single case, many continuing interactions between clinicians and patients, between support workers and patients' families, and with the researchers, took place. The principal design even of an ambitious "outcome study" like this one leaves the processes by which any "outcome" is or is not achieved largely uninvestigated.

Psychoanalytic models of the mind

A notable feature of psychoanalytic models of the mind is how exceptionally inclusive they are of its different dimensions and of the relations between their different elements. Psychoanalysis lies largely outside the disciplinary boundaries maintained by the academy, belonging securely within neither the psychological nor the social sciences and often disregarded by both of their mainstreams. For example, psychoanalysts do not regard "cognition" and "emotion" as separate fields for investigation or therapeutic intervention. Within a psychoanalytic perspective, cognitive functions and emotional states are closely connected from their infantile origins onwards, and for this reason therapies focused on either of these, separate from one another, are believed likely to be superficial in their effects. Injunctions to "think positive thoughts", to refer to a fashionable therapeutic idea, seems to psychoanalysts to be an unlikely solution to serious difficulties in living. From their point of view, the need is to understand what it is that inhibits ways of thinking and feeling of a sufficiently positive kind.

The inclusiveness and multidimensionality of the psychoanalytic model of the mind is in considerable part due to its theory of the shaping effects of unconscious phantasy and the inner world on patterns of thought, feeling, and behaviour. Plainly, outside the field of psychoanalysis, scepticism about the existence of the unconscious or its relevance to human science, has had a large role in the rejection of the psychoanalytic model. From the psychoanalytic perspective, understanding of human lives requires the integration of the domains of mind and body, of thought and feeling, of conscious and unconscious, and of self and society. These totalities or wholes are relevant to the explanation of the particular phenomena of experience. In fact, this idea of totality is more commonly found and exemplified as a form of understanding in works of the imagination than in the human sciences.

It should be acknowledged that psychoanalysis has proved to be capable of its own kinds of reductionism—for example, where its proponents have denied the relevance to mental disorder of causes which seem to lie outside its own theoretical frame. The damaging division in the 1970s and 1980s between "attachment" and "psychoanalytic" perspectives arose in part from a seeming psychoanalytic insistence on the priority of the phenomena of the internal world, to the exclusion of the "external" relational environment, in the approach to mental illness. Yet the "internal working models" of attachment theory are close to the idea of unconscious mental processes, and most psychoanalysts recognize that "internal" mental states exist in a context of relationships with the mental states of others, both at intimate and larger levels.[6] It is possible for psychoanalysts to focus on the investigation of unconscious mental states as the object of their specific form of understanding without disregarding other influences—biological, social, and cultural—on well-being and illness. The problem is to avoid a situation in which appropriately selective and specialized points of view become mistaken for the entire reality—a part being mis-read as the whole.

Psychoanalysis needs not to choose between "causal" and "part–whole" models of explanation. It needs, instead, to hold both of these and their relation to one another in mind. Psychoanalysts in their practice reflect both on specific causes and effects as they arise in the therapeutic process and on the relation of these specificities to the larger patterns of behaviour and personality, which they aim, with their patients, to understand. Without a concept of a totality, or system, there can be no understanding. But a system cannot be understood except through grasping the relations of causal interdependence that sustain it, and which can lead to a personality's change and development as these relations are understood.

Notes

1. A review of this literature is in three large collections of key Tavistock papers (Trist & Murray, 1993a, 1993b, 1993c).

2. A link can be made between Spinoza's philosophy and a psychoanalytic world-view. In his *Ethics* (1677), Spinoza proposed that human beings could experience peace of mind or serenity if they were able to comprehend the meaning of phenomena, including their own emotions, in their widest causal relations. Bion's idea of the containing functions of the mind seems thus to have an affinity with Spinoza's view. Some would say that as an idea of "spirituality" is common to both.

3. An overview of the romanticism and its commitment to organic ways of thinking is given in M. H. Abram's classic study *The Mirror and the Lamp* (1953).

4. Elias worked with his fellow exile from Frankfurt, S. H. Foulkes, who was one of the founders of group analysis.

5. Holistic issues of context, pattern, and meaning are usually central to a psychoanalytic approach to a clinical phenomenon. When writing about "selected facts", Britton and Steiner (1994) were surely referring to the holistic pattern within which such a "fact" had its meaning.

6. In M. E. Rustin and Rustin (2017, pp. 121, 170) it is shown that Melanie Klein, criticized in the past for her alleged disavowal of the "environmental" dimension of young children's development, did not in fact disavow this.

CHAPTER NINE

Complexity theory and psychoanalysis

In chapters 7 and 8, on case studies and on part–whole relations, respectively, I have argued that biological and "organicist" forms of explanation are more applicable and relevant to psychoanalysis than physical and mechanistic models of explanation. This is not primarily because of the transferable content of these explanatory systems—for example, in regard to the psychosomatic basis of psychological experience, real as this is—but, rather, because of their contrasting explanatory form. It is the holistic, relational, time-dependent, process-oriented aspects of biological explanations and their respect for particularities and differences that correspond to the ways in which in which psychoanalysts think. This affinity is reflected in many of the spheres of psychoanalytic explanation. These include personality development, the study of individual patients and their pathologies, and the dynamics and evolution of clinical sessions and analytic treatments. The extraordinary elegance and universality of the principal laws of physics do not, by contrast, seem to have much in common with the explanatory achievements of psychoanalysis. It has always been found extremely difficult to justify psychoanalytic methods of explanation by reference to criteria that take the physical sciences and their search for deterministic laws of ever-increasing scope as their model.

Chapters 7 and 8, on case-study methods and on part–whole relations, and in a different way the chapter on meaning and interpretation, have sought to explain some of the specificities of psychoanalytic explanation. They have shown that its frame of reference is more particularistic, relational, and process-oriented than that of the atomistic and variable-focused sciences, even though the constant conjunctions and cause-and-effect modelling of the natural scientific and medical models also have a place in psychoanalysis. A theory and practice one of whose purposes has always been to treat mental illness can no more afford to be indifferent to its effectiveness than the medical sciences which treat physical illness. Nevertheless, psychoanalysis as a field seems to have been surprisingly slow to understand the relevance of relational and organicist scientific perspectives to its own theory and practice, possibly because of the hegemony which physical and mechanistic models of science have exercised over the human sciences.

The emergence of the perspectives of chaos theory and complexity theory[1] in the last 30 years or so has added a new dimension to this debate. Its essential challenge has been to the mechanistic, atomistic view of nature that has dominated the sciences throughout the "modern" era. There have been two elements in this challenge. One is the discovery that relational and systemic models of explanation (in contrast to atomistic and variable-focused models) have application to important elements of "physical" nature, beyond the biological and social spheres to which they have been more often recognized to apply. The second is methodological and arises from advances in the capacity of mathematicians and computer scientists to quantify and explain complex systems. We have learned that there were kinds of regularity in the behaviour of "natural" systems that had been unobservable and unmeasurable with the mathematical techniques that had been available to the scientists of the mechanical and atomistic universe of Galileo, Newton, and Descartes, but which can now be recognized and understood.

There are connections between the world views espoused by the sciences at given historical periods and the mathematical techniques that have been available to investigate nature. The scientific model that for long hypothesized an inert, mechanical universe, in relation to which human beings were mainly powerless observers, was both the product and the producer of a particular "technology" of calculation and measurement through which its properties were defined and measured. In recent decades, new technologies of calculation have become available, which have enabled hitherto unrecognized properties of nature—in particular the propensity for the self-organization of physical as well as biological phenomena—to be understood and measured. In this phase of science, just as in the past, the relation between the means of conceptualizing and measuring and the defined nature of the "objects" being studied is one of reciprocal influence. There seems little doubt both that a new "cosmology" is emerging, with an ethical and aesthetic perspective different from that of early modern mechanistic science, and that this "cosmos" is being made intelligible through the development of new methods of investigation and measurement. Not for the first time, epistemology and ontology are being transformed through a process of interaction with one another.

The central idea of complexity theory is that of the ubiquity and significance of complex self-organizing systems, in the physical as well as biological worlds. These systems have the property of being time-irreversible, in contrast to the fundamental property of Newtonian scientific models according to which causal relations between entities are, in principle, if not always in practice, reversible. Biological evolution is a prime example of such a time-irreversible process. The 99% of species that once lived on earth and have become extinct are never going to return in their original form (although it is imaginable that "empty" ecological niches could be filled by evolutionary developments similar to those of the past). Second, self-organizing systems need to be understood as mobile processes rather than as structures. Structures are the determining material entities located in space and time within which processes take place, but they are not identical with them. (We might think of brains and minds as structures and processes in these terms. They are neither identical nor reducible to one another.) Processes are relationships between the elements of a system and between a bounded system and what lies outside it. Third, they exhibit different kinds of pattern and regularity, modelled on the idea of "attractors" of different kinds. In the lexicon of concepts of complexity theory there are, for example, periodic attractors, oscillatory attractors, and "strange attractors", each of which has the effect of pulling a specified system towards its own characteristic kind of equilibrium. A fourth attribute is that of self-similarities within a system, such that its distinctive form replicates itself at its different levels of scale and magnitude. For example, the patterning of root systems in trees, or tributary systems in river basins, or capillary systems in the circulation of the blood, each displays replications of form. There may be similarities of form and pattern between entities of different substantive kinds (for example in the branching patterns of trees and river systems) and patterns may replicate at different magnitudes within the same system—for example, the marine erosion of coasts giving rise to recurring, self-similar patterns of land-form (Mandelbrot, 1983).

Such recurring patterns depend on innumerable iterations of similar but slightly changing relations of variables. The effect of their causal action is to reproduce constancies of pattern within systems that nevertheless evolve in response to changes in their component variables or attractors. It was the development of computers capable of modelling immense numbers of possible interactions between related variables, and of recognizing patterns resulting from these variations, that made these discoveries possible. The modelling of Newtonian physics was, in essence, deductive—from certain fixed laws (e.g., the laws of motion or thermodynamics) deterministic consequences were inferred, where the relevant conditions of application (e.g., of mass, distance, and velocity) could be specified. Newton's invented mathematical resource for understanding the outcome of gravitational forces was the calculus. By contrast, the modelling undertaken within the framework of complexity theory is inductive. Its method has been to calculate the effects of ongoing variations in certain elements of an otherwise constant system and observe the self-similar but evolving patterns that emerge. Such patterns can be calculated abstractly in mathematical form, but they may also describe certain regularities occurring in nature. Without modern computers, such numbers of iterations and possibilities could not be calculated or graphically represented. There are now familiar kinds of computer-derived images and models that depict examples of such swirling, evolving relationships changing over time and displayed as recurring complex shapes and forms (Mandelbrot, 1983).

Naturally occurring instances of such self-organization are the patterns observed in the "murmurations" of immense flocks of starlings, and their mathematical representation, and the similar patterned movements of shoals of fish. The "organizing principle" (perhaps the "strange attractor") of these formations lies in the genetically programmed responsiveness of each member of the flock or shoal to the movements of those individuals in close proximity to it.

A fifth attribute of self-organizing complex systems lies in their propensity to undergo processes of "phase change", and for the bifurcation of systems that can occur when they arrive at a point of disequilibrium. "Phase" is a mathematical concept that denotes a state of relative constancy in the relationship of the elements of a system—this can be described as an equilibrium state. "Phase change" is what happens when a system moves or "leaps" from one stable or recurrent state to another. These are complex multivariate, interactive processes, like meteorological cyclones or climatic seasons, not mechanistically organized structures. A sixth attribute of such systems, within this theoretical frame, is the idea of the "disproportionate" or unexpected effect of a specific event or change of variable on the dynamics of an entire system, if it arrives at a state of disequilibrium or chaos. This is the famous idea of a "tipping point"—when, for example, just a single extra grain of sand causes a hitherto stable sand-pile to slide, or a single off-piste skier causes an avalanche. Each of these "catastrophic changes" is likely to have as its outcome the establishment of a new stable state. Prior to this "turning point", the effect of the movement of what became the critical sand particle or skier would have been imperceptible. The "butterfly effect", according to which the flapping of a wing of a butterfly in the Amazonian rain forest could (in theory) set off a tropical storm, is the most famous metaphorical representation of this idea.

These ideas have been stimulating ones for social scientists, since they have thrown light on phenomena in their fields that had hitherto seemed to defy explanation within the frameworks of causal determinism. An example of this application can be found within the theoretical perspective of Marxism. Here the "complexity theory" idea of "phase changes", and of the contingent effects of a single small event in bringing about large changes in a system is analogous to the concept of "conjunctures" in the twentieth-century Marxist theories of Gramsci and Althusser, which they used to understand potential transformations in social systems (Henriques & Morley, 2017, Part II). The "standard theory" of orthodox Marxism to which these ideas were a revisionist challenge was somewhat mechanistic and deterministic. It had been believed that the working class would grow in its numbers and power, through its indispensable role within the capitalist economy, until it arrived, through its own aggregation and through increasing conflict with the forces of capital, at a moment, revolutionary or otherwise, when it would seize power from its bourgeois oppressor.

However, these deterministic "laws of motion" did not explain how and why the first major revolutionary transformation that modelled itself on Marxist principles, the Bolshevik Revolution of 1917, actually occurred. The industrial working class had by 1917 by no means arrived at demographic or economic dominance in Russian society—it comprised only a small fraction of the population. According to the formulations of Marx's theory, this revolution was therefore extremely premature, as Lenin himself recognized. A specific conjunction of historical particulars had been necessary to bring about these dramatic events. Its most contingent feature was the decision, in April 1917, of the German High Command to send Lenin back to Russia in his "sealed train". The High Command's purpose was that Lenin would, on his arrival in Moscow, instigate a revolution, which would cause Russia to withdraw its armies from the Great War and ensure the victory of Germany. This is essentially what happened. It has been convincingly argued that without Lenin's capability as a leader, the Bolshevik Revolution would not have been taken place. However, although the German leaders correctly estimated how Lenin's insertion into Russian politics would influence the war to their advantage, they failed to foresee the larger transformations that the October Revolution would bring about and its consequences for the world (Merridale, 2016).[2] The theory of "conjunctures", arising from the writings of Gramsci and Althusser (and of "combined and uneven development" in those of Trotsky, 1932) was developed in recognition of the actual complexity and multidimensionality of class struggles and with the aim of identifying the specific conditions in which political action by Communists (especially those in the West) could be effective. This was a variety of complexity theory before its time.

Sociologists such as David Byrne (1998), John Urry (2003), and Sylvia Walby (2009) have sought to make use of the idea of complexity to understand the dynamics of contemporary social systems. One motivation for this lies in concerns about the instability of present-day social arrangements, in the face of the potentially catastrophic changes arising from phenomena such as climate change, the exhaustion of natural resources (e.g., "peak oil"), and the disorganization of economies through financialization and uncontrolled flows of capital. Climate change has brought the agendas of the natural and social sciences into close connection with one another, as changes to the natural world brought about by human action become impossible to ignore.

The models of complexity theory have application to self-organizing systems in the domains of biology and ecology to certain non-organic, physical phenomena and to human societies. As we shall see, one of these spheres of application, now explored in a considerable literature, is psychoanalysis.[3] What has become recognized is the causal connectedness between these different spheres, so far as the earth is concerned. As a consequence, a shift in cosmology is taking place. Newton's laws of physics described phenomena of nature essentially unaffected by the laws of biology or human science. But we can now see that the self-organizing systems of climates, erosion cycles, and plant, animal, and human ecology are causally connected. The biosphere of the earth itself now has to be understood as a dynamic self-organizing system. The "equilibria" that can be observed in many natural systems on earth—the proportion of gases in the atmosphere (oxygen, nitrogen, and carbon dioxide); the relative stability of its temperatures; the cycles of growth decay and recycling of organic matter—are products of complex processes operating at a planetary scale. This is, in essence, James Lovelock's "Gaia hypothesis", although one may not wish to attribute agency to "Gaia" as a transcendental entity. However, the earth is without doubt a self-organizing system. The central fact is that the systems that maintain the atmosphere, the oceans, and the surface of the earth in their relatively constant state depend on biological life-forms.

Thus it is not just that complexity theorists have established that the idea of self-organizing systems extends beyond the biological to the non-organic domain, they have also shown that what we once saw as the "physical" or material sphere is, as far as the earth is concerned, essentially bio-physical in its nature.

Psychoanalytic complexity

One of the early explicit connections between complexity and psychoanalysis appears in Bion's writing. In his work with patients whose minds were in extremely disorganized states, Bion found himself searching for coherence and pattern in what seemed to be almost meaningless fragments of material. He adopted an idea he found in the writings of a mathematician, Henri Poincaré [1854–1912], that of the "selected fact", as a way of identifying the order in what could seem to be a state of chaos. Poincaré's work later became influential in the mathematics of chaos and complexity theory. Bion quoted Poincaré (1908, p. 375) thus:

> If a new result is to have any value, it must unite elements long since known, but till then scattered and seemingly foreign to each other, and suddenly introduce order where the appearance of disorder reigned. Then it enables us to see at a glance each of these elements in the place it occupies in the whole. Not only is the new fact valuable on its own account, but it alone gives value to the old facts it unites. Our mind is as frail as the senses are: it would lose itself in the complexity of the world if that complexity were not harmonious; like the short-sighted, it would only see the details, and would be obliged to forget each of these details before examining the next, because it would be incapable of taking in the whole. The only facts which are worthy of our attention are those which introduce order into this complexity and so make it accessible to us. [quoted in Bion, 1962, p. 72]

Bion found Poincaré's account of how a mathematician can recognize a new kind of meaningful order in an apparent chaos of facts a suggestive one. It represented for him not only his own experience as a psychoanalyst, seeking meaning in his patients' obscure communications, but also the processes of mental life and meaning-making more generally. The experience of not-knowing, and thus of potential chaos, was, in Bion's view, an essential aspect of the mind's development. The container–contained relationship between mothers and infants was a context in which meaning was created out of chaotic emotional experience.[4] Oscillation throughout life between paranoid-schizoid and depressive states of mind was another instance of experiences of disorganization—"catastrophic change"—which had to be survived if mental development was to take place. Poincaré was at pains to insist that a great deal of mathematical learning took place unconsciously, "subliminally" as he put it, and this was a further point of affinity for Bion, writing many decades after him.

Poincaré anticipated the perspectives of complexity theory through his interest in "complex causes", understood as probabilities and as the outcome of many interacting variables but nevertheless possessing a latent order capable of being recognized. He developed mathematical approaches that sought to account for these relations. Bion believed that laws of cause and effect, as these are conventionally framed, had little relevance to psychoanalysis—indeed, for him they were looking for meaning in the wrong place. Although he did not formulate a theory of complex causation himself, this is implicit in the structures and processes of mind (the container–contained relation, for example) that he came to define and describe.

In fact, psychoanalytic theory, from its beginnings with Freud, has developed models of mental life and of unconscious mental process that are based on ideas of the self-organization and internal coherence of the mind. The idea of "pathological organizations" developed by Rey (1994), Rosenfeld (1971), and Steiner (1993b) to understand borderline and narcissistic states of mind denotes the functioning of self-organizing systems. Bion's experience of coherent patterns of mind being discerned amidst apparent disorder and chaos may have influenced that idea of a persisting mental organization. But the psychopathologies that Freud described—for example, hysteria, obsessional neuroses, phobia, and mania—are no less pathological organizations—defences against mental pain and a fear of disintegration—than those identified by the post-Kleinian theorists. Klein's paranoid-schizoid and depressive positions are similarly self-organizing and self-reproducing structures of mind. They refer to real phenomena, not merely to theoretical mapping tools. These "organizations" are "intentional" in so far as these mental states have definite "objects", whether these are feared and hated, loved and cared for. It is because of this assumption of a self-organizing complexity of the personality, shaped by the unconscious desires, anxieties, and defences of subjects, that many of the concepts developed in the broader literature of complexity have relevance to the psychoanalytic field.

One such concept is that of self-similarity in the manifestations of pattern and form in personalities. Such recurring patterns of constancy and change in nature are formulated mathematically as repeated iterations of a form in which only certain variables are subject to change. It is these iterative variations that give rise to the fractal or self-similar structures described in the complexity literature. In psychoanalysis, we can think of the manifestations of symptomatic behaviours or of unconsciously determined patterns of personality, in these terms, as the successive enactments of internal compulsions. These are the identities and similarities that analysts learn to recognize in their patients' presentations to them. They enable them to understand the constant features within evolving (perhaps unstable) personalities and the unconscious forces or structures that persistently shape these. In the qualitative analysis of session material in clinical research, such similarities, and the desires, defences and ideations that give rise to them, are revealed through coding procedures that identify recurrent themes[5] and through the "constant comparative analysis" that this makes possible.

What we do not have in psychoanalytic research are meaningful ways of quantifying the elements that constitute such mental structures, and of representing in a mathematical form the "parameters" (constant elements) and "variables" of which a personality might be said to consist. It seems that the degree of "sameness" on which quantification of variables and constants depends (which is found, for example, in the medical measurement of changes in organs or their component cells) cannot be established for useful purposes from a psychoanalytic perspective— except, that is, in the more limited kinds of measurement represented by the recognition of presence or absence (1/0) of greater and lesser frequencies or magnitudes, or of increases or decreases over time. All clinicians intuitively make use of such basic measures of quantity as an extension of the reasonings found in everyday life. It may, indeed, be important to note, for example, that the frequency, duration, or intensity of phobic anxiety in a patient has increased or decreased, and to establish the correlates and causes of this, even if it is not feasible attach numbers to these changes. It is possible that at some point the quantitative measurement of such variables could come to be of value in the analysis of clinical data, or indeed in clinical work with patients.

In the study of the measurable effects of treatments, quantification of mental states, through the application of varieties of indicators and scales, has become important and widely practiced. In outcome trials, the task of such measurement is often assigned to researchers, and its outcomes are withheld from clinicians in order to avoid influencing the treatments whose outcomes are being investigated. It is, however, possible to envisage a greater integration of quantitative measurements of personality changes with ongoing clinical practice. The purpose of such integration s would be initially to see if such measurement could be a resource for psychotherapists. How far can psychoanalytic models of personality and personality change be usefully formulated in quantified terms?[6]

A problem in testing and measuring patients' states of mind during the course of a therapy is the disturbance this may cause to a therapeutic process. However, it has been found in one recent study—the Tavistock Adult Depression Study (TADS)—that regular contact between researchers who periodically administered psychological tests to patients to monitor the effects of therapy and the patients was often positively valued by the patients. This seems to have been experienced as an additional expression of concern for and commitment to them and was in this way implicitly therapeutic. There are specific aspects of such concurrent involvement by researchers in clinical practice that merit study—questions, for example, such as the frequency of such interventions and the consequences for good or ill of feeding back to clinicians such independently gathered information about their patients. Psychoanalysts are often initially suspicious of interference with the seclusion of their clinical settings. But whatever preconceptions about this there may be, it seems that knowledge of these questions can only be advanced through investigation and experiment.

A second "complexity" concept of relevance to psychoanalysis is that of psychic equilibrium and its possible disruptions. The concept of "phase change" can be deployed to model the oscillations that occur between conflicted states of mind, such as movements between paranoid-schizoid and depressive states. These can be observed at high tempo, within specific clinical sessions, or can be plotted as the more gradual outcomes of a prolonged therapeutic process, even though such developments are never continuous or uninterrupted. The equivalent of the "butterfly effect"—small perturbations/events producing very large effects—can be found in the triggering of disturbed or anxious states of mind by what might seem in themselves to be only mild provocations. Such "routine" disturbances might be an unexpected interruption of a clinical session and its timing or physical setting, or it might be caused by an interpretation that is exceptionally disturbing to a patient. Such unexpected effects may reveal that an earlier apparent equilibrium was unstable and may enable attention to be focused on why this was so. In selecting samples of clinical session records for detailed study, reports of instances of "extreme" states of mind may generate more information than those that describe sessions that are closer to the norm for a patient.

A third idea of particular relevance to psychoanalysis is that of the "attractor", which refers to that apparent "force" which brings and maintains order to an otherwise apparently disorganized or chaotic field. The complexity literature describes different kinds of "attractors" whose effects explain regularities in systemic organization. Of special interest for psychoanalysis is the idea of the "strange attractor".

This has a specific resonance for psychoanalysts (Quinodoz, 1997) because the idea of "strangeness" evokes the unconscious internally generated forces in the personality. These are seen to exert pressure on personalities to maintain persisting patterns of mind and behaviour, without the conscious recognition or decision of subjects. One can, indeed, think of the investigation of unconscious or inner worldly states of mind as the search for the "strange attractors", which organize both the personality of a patient and the transference–countertransference relationship of patient and analyst.

A fourth valuable idea put forward by Quinodoz (1997) in his reflections on the relevance of complexity theory for psychanalysis is that of the "tuning variable". He has in mind the role of the analyst, and, indeed, the mother's containment of the infant, in maintaining a state of relative equilibrium, or emotional calm, which is a precondition for the psychological and emotional development of infants and in the clinical setting of patients. This metaphor of modulation is a suggestive one and offers a way of reflecting on the meaning and effects of specific therapeutic interventions in a therapeutic process. In an analysis undertaken or retrospectively studied as research, these can be identified and mapped through coding procedures, such as those of grounded theory. One can similarly reflect on the significance of mother–baby interactions in the infant observation context by reference to this metaphor of "tuning", which has an affinity with the idea of "attunement", which has been developed to describe mother–infant relations in an adjacent field of research (Stern, 1985).

A theoretical issue to which this "tuning variable" metaphor draws attention is the necessary place of a containing as well as an interpretative function in the psychoanalytic process, and the choices that have invariably to be made, consciously or otherwise, regarding the balance to be struck between them. The experience of dependability and attentiveness on the part of a therapist is therapeutic in itself and may help to explain how therapists can be successful with patients even when they work within quite different theoretical paradigms. But the psychoanalytic tradition of active interpretation is usually an essential dimension of the therapeutic process. The question is, then, what place within the "containing" or "holding" function of a therapeutic relationship, should interpretation have.

This distinction between interpretation and containment is not, however, entirely clear-cut. In Bion's view, a containing function, performed by mothers to their infants or analysts to their patients, depends on emotional understanding, whether or not this understanding is conveyed through words. An analyst may not need to make an explicit interpretation to convey to a patient that a communication of information or feeling from them has been understood. But containment usually depends on more than merely being there.

The idea of "turning points" in psychoanalytic treatments, formulated by Gunnar Carlberg (2007) and described in different terms by Quinodoz (1997), should also be included in the lexicon of concepts useful for understanding the complex patterns of self-organization that psychoanalysts can identify in patients' personalities and in therapeutic processes. Margaret Lush (2011) made this connection in her doctoral research, which was a single-case study. She identified in her patient's material—most vividly in his drawings—a significant "turning point" in his therapy. This was where her patient, who suffered from autism, began to acquire a more multidimensional sense of himself. One of the indicators of this was the appearance in his drawings of both colours and identifiable human forms, where previously his pictures had been monochrome and robotic. The therapist understood these pictures as representations of her patient's inner world.

Case-study methods, part–whole relations, and complexity theory and the idea of self-organizing systems are closely connected in this book's conception of psychoanalytic research. What is being proposed here is not a new set of rules that would prescribe how psychoanalytic research should be done. I am setting set out a description of the approaches that clinical researchers in psychoanalysis have in great part actually followed in their practice, even if often without a clear articulation of their research method.

Of course, psychoanalysts have always described "cases" and produced written "case studies". Their preferred mode of explanation has not been to identify discrete connections of the "linear causal" kind that specify that variable x is associated with variable y in certain conditions, according to an explanatory law. Actual persons and therapies are too complex to be adequately described in such simplified terms. Psychoanalytic explanation usually takes the form of describing configurations of personality in which the relations of its inner world elements to one another best explain the states of mind and behaviour of whole persons.

Finally, one can surely see that many of the ideas that have been described above, drawn from the vocabulary of complexity theory, correspond to the ways in which psychoanalysts already understand their fields of study, even though they do not usually make use of these explanatory terms. Ideas of self-organization, self-similarity, "catastrophic change", and the unconscious "attractors" that shape a personality are very close to those that are already implicit in psychoanalytic theory and practice.

What remains to be discovered is how far advances in research might become possible if these parallels were better understood. Although there is now a significant research literature that links psychoanalysis and complexity theory,[7] there has not yet been a concerted exploration of how its concepts might illuminate psychoanalytic clinical research, if they were thought about in a more systematic way.

Notes

1. These theoretical frameworks are closely related. Chaos theory arose from the mathematical work of Henri Poincaré, whose work influenced Bion. Its principal discoveries concerned the properties of complex self-organizing systems, and the idea of chaos is a limit position "the edge of chaos"—not the central object of attention. There is a large literature, both technical and in the genre of "popular" science (see, for example, Mandelbrot, 1983; Mitchell, 2009; Prigogine, 1996; Prigogine & Stengers, 1984; Ruelle, 1991; Waldrop, 1992).

2. Catherine Merridale's *Lenin on the Train* (2016) describes these events in a compelling narrative.

3. See, for example, Carlberg, 2007; Galatzer-Levy, 1995, 2005, 2009; Lush, 2011; Mahoney & Moes, 1997; Miller, 1999; Moran, 1991; Perna, 1997; Perna & Masterpasqua, 1997; Quinodoz, 1997; M. J. Rustin, 2002; Seligman, 2005; Shigeru, 1999; Shulman, 2010; Spruiell, 1993; Verhulst, 1999.

4. Here is John Milton's idea of primordial chaos:

> Before their eyes in sudden view appear
> The secrets of the hoarie deep, a dark
> Illimitable Ocean without bound,
> Without dimension, where length, breadth, and heighth,
> And time and place are lost; where eldest Night
> And Chaos, Ancestors of Nature, hold
> Eternal Anarchie, amidst the noise
> Of endless warrs and by confusion stand.
>
> [Milton, *Paradise Lost*, Book II]

5. These might be termed "variables" of measures of frequency of intensity where appropriate; but psychoanalytic analysis of clinical records is more often qualitative than quantitative in its approach.

6. The work of researchers in the Tavistock Adult Depression Study, who measured at specified intervals the mental state of patients in treatment, has produced quantified data, from which kinds of depression have been modelled (Rost, Luyten, & Fonagy, 2018). The theoretical frame in which this modelling has taken place is psychoanalytic in its origins, but it is different from that which has for the most part informed the specific clinical practice whose outcomes were being studied. It would be valuable to bring the theoretical perspectives of the researchers and the psychoanalytic clinicians into a closer conjunction with one another.

7. See, for example, sources listed in Note 3.

CHAPTER TEN

Clinical facts

One of the most significant methodological debates to have taken place in the psychoanalytic field in recent years concerns the nature of "clinical facts", which was the subject, in 1994, of a special seventy-fifth-anniversary double issue of the *International Journal of Psychoanalysis,* edited by David Tuckett. This debate was a response to a number of overlapping anxieties about the scientific status of psychoanalysis. One concern was why there were such apparently irresolvable differences between schools and perspectives in the psychoanalytic movement.[1] There were issues of translation to consider too—how had the sense and meanings of Freud's writings in their original German been seriously modified through, for example, their translation into the English *Standard Edition* (Steiner, 1994)? There were the problems of evidence, and issues of validation of hypotheses and theories. Critics within psychoanalysis, such as Robert Wallerstein (Wallerstein & Sampson, 1971), Donald Spence (1982, 1993, 1994, 1998), and David Tuckett (1993), have pointed out the problems of reliance on analysts' reports of clinical sessions. It was pointed out that it was often virtually impossible to differentiate between theoretical formulations and the imputed evidence for them. The clinical vignette, standard in psychoanalytic writing, was deployed more often as an illustrative or persuasive device than as systemic evidence, which could validate or invalidate a theory, according to a scientific procedure. Spence put it thus:

> Whereas we would not take seriously any paper on art history that did
> not present reproductions of the painting or art object in question, we deal
> constantly in hearsay reports of clinical happenings that are undoubt-
> edly influenced by the author's need to sharpen his point, or improve the
> fit between evidence and theory. Our clinical literature can be described,
> from one point of view, as doing art history without present the slides,
> and what is remarkable is that, to date, no one has pointed to the prob-
> lem of presenting the missing data. [Spence, 1994, p. 918]

The belief underlying the IJPA Symposium was that if an understanding could be achieved of what observable facts were in psychoanalysis,
it might become more feasible to establish the parity of psychoanalysis
with other forms of science. The idea of a distinctive kind of "clinical
fact" was put at the centre of the discussion, because psychoanalytic
theories have mostly originated in the clinical consulting room, and
because case material has been commonly cited, from Freud's work
onwards, as providing the central evidence on which psychoanalytic
theories are based. The question for the symposium contributors was:
what is a clinical fact?

Considerable progress was made in answering this question.
Most significant—for example, in the papers by J.-M. Quinodoz
(1994) and Edna O'Shaughnessy (1994)—was the idea that a clinical fact was essentially one that emerged from the phenomena of
the transference–countertransference relationship between patient
and analyst. Since psychoanalysis is essentially the investigation
of unconscious mental processes, and since the transference and
countertransference were found to provide the best access to states
of unconscious phantasy, "clinical facts"—those most crucial for
psychoanalysis—were those that could be observed within that
relationship between analyst and patient.

O'Shaughnessy's paper put forward this view in a discussion of
three substantial vignettes of clinical material from three sessions
taken from the last days of her analysis of a 10-year-old boy, in which
she showed how "clinical facts" of this kind could be recognized and,
indeed, made the object of interpretations to the patient.[2] Few papers in
the symposium provided the clinical detail of O'Shaughnessy's paper,
which, even in this instance, was set out in only a few paragraphs. The
symposium was stronger in its arguments about the significance of
clinical facts than in its demonstration of how they can be recognized,
or in clarifying the functions they may have in the discovery and validation of psychoanalytic theories.

The nature of clinical facts

The methodological arguments of earlier chapters in this book are relevant to further clarifying the idea of clinical facts. In the first place, the idea of the "facts" as the starting-point for a methodological debate in psychoanalysis is more problematic than it seems. The idea that "facts" are the decisive arbiter of scientific truth carries an implicit echo of the philosophical tradition of "English empiricism". David Hume canonically proposed that empirical understanding must have, as its point of departure, facts and their "constant conjunction" where these can be observed. In conjoining such observed entities, the laws of logic must be respected (for example, by definition, entities cannot both be and not be, and they must occupy distinct locations in space and time). Hume argued that if observations are accurately recorded and logical procedures followed, all that can be known will be known. Valid knowledge (what we now think of as scientific knowledge) can thus be built up afresh from the foundations of perception itself. Those illusory forms of knowledge founded on conjecture and abstract reasoning alone, which Hume deemed to be "metaphysical", could thus be swept away, and, indeed, in the English empirical philosophical tradition this is what largely happened.[3]

David Tuckett followed this essentially Humean programme in his European Psychoanalytical Association research project, which followed his initiation of the debate about clinical facts. His idea was to begin psychoanalytic inquiry with the analysis of clinical material (i.e. arrays of "clinical facts"), avoiding their usual pre-coding in conceptual and theoretical terms. The aim was then to see whether, from the "constant conjunctions" that could then be observed, a minimal sufficient apparatus of theoretical ideas could be built up. The aim was to proceed by inference from "observations" alone, stripped of unnecessary—he might say dogmatic or "metaphysical"—legacies from the different psychoanalytic schools.[4] In this proposed psychoanalytic "reformation" the Tower of Babel of overlapping, confused, and conflicting theoretical discourses of the international psychoanalytic movement (not to mention the disputatious British tendencies) might be bypassed, and a fresh start be made. It was hoped that this might set the psychoanalytic movement onto foundations more consistent with those of mainstream science, as had been advocated by "internal" critics of psychoanalysis such as Fonagy and Wallerstein.

Tuckett and his European Psychoanalytic Federation colleagues recognized that the specifically unconscious attributes of "facts" of a psychoanalytic kind needed to be identifiable through their investigative methods.

However, there are serious problems in apprehending unconscious phenomena without recourse to prior psychoanalytic conceptualization. Take, for example, the clinical facts of the countertransference—those states of mind of analysts that are understood to be the effects of unconscious communications taking place within an analysis. Do analysts recognize such phenomena merely by observing "constant conjunctions" between their states of mind and those of their patients? Such constant conjunctions are necessary but not sufficient conditions for the recognition of countertransference events. The idea of countertransference is a theoretically complex one, linked to the idea of projective identification and the understanding of that "mechanism" as a defence against anxiety. When analysts seek to understand their response to a patient, they must reflect both on their own state of mind and the patient's, to establish which concepts best enable them to understand what is taking place between them. As Paula Heimann (1950) discovered, a state of disturbance in an analyst can be an effect of a communicated disturbance in a patient and can be informative for this reason. But it may also be the effect of unrecognized disturbance in an analyst's mind that may be confusing their understanding of their patient. To make therapeutic use of this theory requires close attention to transference and countertransference phenomena, to "clinical facts". Testing the validity of the theory itself is an even more demanding task, since it requires unpicking and then examining each separate link in this chain of unconscious phenomena and testing the evidence for their causal connection.

How far is it feasible to reconstruct or reassemble psychoanalytic theories from a "ground zero" of theory-free observations, as the EPF project has been attempting to do, in part as a remedy for what some see as the excess of overlapping and unproved theories in psychoanalysis? Is it possible to rebuild from a small base of core concepts—for example, the unconscious and the transference—and from the evidence of "clinical facts" a conceptual system to which virtually all psychoanalysts could subscribe? Is this the way that a new "scientific revolution" or "paradigm shift" in psychoanalysis could come about, by means of suspending existing theoretical beliefs in order that more solidly based theories could be inferred from "clinical facts" alone?

The idea of rebuilding psychoanalytic theories from a state of "ground zero" is challenging. However, it may be misconceived. Established paradigms in science consist of complex assemblages of connected hypotheses, linked together conceptually and resting on the base of multiple sources of evidence. Theories within a paradigm are often related to one another as a core of central propositions and a periphery of specific implications or hypotheses. Revisions can be made at the periphery of a paradigm which need not bring into question its core theoretical assumptions. For example, the interruptions in the evolutionary path that were found to have been caused by various mass extinctions gave rise to the theory of "punctuated evolution" and modified previously held gradualist assumptions (Gould, 2007). But these events and the changed understanding of the evolution of species that followed did not call into question the laws of natural selection, the core of the Darwinian paradigm.

Development in theories can take place through extensions of both scope and depth. In Darwinian evolutionary theory, developments in "scope" include the discovery of new species and ecological systems, and a development in "depth" is exemplified by the discovery of DNA and genetic codes. Paradigms incorporate and depend on auxiliary theories concerning, for example, the validity of the findings of their observational instruments.

The complexity of psychoanalytic theories, and the interlocking assumptions of which they consist (e.g., concerning infant development, transference relations, and the causes and meanings of psychopathologies), are not different in character from those of other scientific fields. Even though there have been significant weaknesses in the transparency of the procedures by which psychoanalytic theories have been grounded in evidence, it is unlikely that the entire reconstruction of psychoanalytic theories from the foundations of clinical observations alone will resolve these methodological problems.

Robert Hinshelwood's (2013) project to subject psychoanalytic theories to neo-Popperian tests of falsification has attempted in a different way to meet the challenges to psychoanalysis that have been made by empiricists. Hinshelwood's point of departure was the Popperian theory of falsifiability, rather than a Humean model of inductive inference from the observation of conjoined facts. (Popper once contemptuously rejected this model of inference as a "bucket theory" of knowledge.) Popper believed that the function of empirical observation was to test the correspondence between hypotheses and reality, rather than to be the prime source of theoretical conjectures. He recognized the importance of theoretical and mathematical reasoning in physics, noting that new conjectures could emerge in the first instance from moments of intuition and imagination. He held that the scientific theories set out law-like relations between entities that were universal in their claims (within the specification of their scope of application). Their validity was established not by their corroboration through positive instances of their occurrence (by a method of inference) but, rather, by submitting them to empirical tests deduced as hypothetical implications of a theory. If such tests failed, a theory would be falsified (hence Popper's "hypothetico-deductive method").

This was a somewhat heroic conception of scientific investigation, on both sides of the theoretical/experimental divide, in that it recognized both the importance of imagination and even genius among theoreticians and the role of the decisive observation or experiment in assessing the truth or falsity of a theory. Since the Popperian critique of psychoanalysis and its adaptation and development by Adolf Grünbaum has been so destructive to its scientific credibility over decades, it is admirable that Hinshelwood should have sought to demonstrate the defensibility of psychoanalytic theories by reference to these widely accepted criteria of validity.[5] Hinshelwood's programme prescribes that psychoanalysts should set out clear theoretical hypotheses, identify the conditions that specify their scope of application, and then subject clinical material (from analytic cases) to rigorous examination to enable the validity of such hypotheses to be tested. Hinshelwood asserts that if a clearly formulated hypothesis failed to explain (retrospectively) or to predict (prospectively) its specified outcome, then the hypothesis in question would be *ipso facto* falsified. Hinshelwood sought to demonstrate, through some detailed examples based on records of clinical exchanges, that well-designed experiments (whose data was the phenomena recorded in textual descriptions of clinical sessions) could validate or invalidate specified psychoanalytic hypotheses. In particular, he sought through this procedure to demonstrate the validity of certain of Klein's theories (of which Hinshelwood is a leading scholarly exponent).

The problem, however, is that the grounds for having confidence in Klein's explanatory schema (or, indeed, of any other well-established subparadigm in psychoanalysis) does not rest on its validation in the context of a singular empirical instance, however finely this is specified. An empirical test of this kind might fail not because of the falsity of the theory being tested, but because conditions of application specified within the theory were not met, or because of some other operative causal force. Single instances of falsification are rarely decisive in determining the validity of a theory, although there are experiments and observations that are famous in science for having had this significance. The proven usefulness of the psychoanalytic theories of Klein—and of other psychoanalysts whose contribution has been equally influential—derives from the multiplicity of clinical instances in which key ideas have been found to give meaning to clinical phenomena, not from singular decisive empirical tests. The validity of such understandings is characteristically established when they are put to clinical use—for example, in the formulation of interpretations that are found to be generative for the mental life of patients, as they recognize their truth and relevance to themselves. It is important, however, to note that it is not analysand's agreement with an interpretation that demonstrates that it has captured a truth but, rather, its effects in enhancing an analysand's capacity to think and feel. Such realizations most often happen in the context of a transference relationship, in which the existence and effects of a particular mental state become most evident.

Furthermore, within the process of a particular psychoanalytic case, it is unlikely that single demonstrations of the existence and functions of an unconscious mental state will of themselves carry full conviction, either to analyst or to patient. However, the many sessions in an analytic treatment provide many opportunities to study clinical phenomena and to determine what theoretical conjectures or models of the mind are most relevant to understanding them. These phenomena include states of mind evoked by memories or current experiences in life and interactions in the transference situation. Analysts there have opportunities to deepen their observations of a patient and to test their conjectures about his or her state of mind on many occasions.

Subtle discriminations are involved in such clarifications of meanings in the events of mental life. To give an example, consider the distinction an analyst may believe to be relevant between the state of mind known as jealousy, in which hostility to imagined rivals may be in question, and envy, which consists of hatred of "objects" to which value is ascribed.

The distinction between the ideas of jealousy and envy may, in any case, be theoretically contentious. It is within Klein's theoretical perspective in which there is belief in innate dispositions to destructiveness and hatred that the idea of envy first gained its psychoanalytic currency.[6] The idea of jealousy presupposes that there is a loved object that is at risk of being lost or stolen to a rival of some kind—the oedipal situation is deemed to be the original source of this anxiety. But while the presence of jealousy does not in itself call in question the existence or worth of objects of love or desire, envy is constituted by hatred of objects, however seemingly desirable or virtuous they may be. Whereas in the state of jealousy, antagonism is directed in the first instance towards rivals for a loved object, in the state of envy it becomes focused on the object itself.

Discrimination, in a psychoanalytic situation, between these two states of mind may be far from straightforward. A perceived absence of love, by or for a person, can be a most painful and desolate state of mind. Without it there can be no hope. The idea that other people are in possession of the good implies the possibility that some form of it exists somewhere. But where the very existence of the good is denied,[7] there is a more catastrophic situation. In a psychoanalytic treatment, one of the objects whose goodness is liable to be envied and attacked is the integrity and capability of the analyst, and analysis itself.[8] Demonstrating to a patient the presence of such envy is liable to be exceptionally difficult. Who will believe a message from a messenger who is deemed be without credibility? Envious states of mind, in other words, bring with them their own powerful defences against their own recognition.

I have set out this example in order to show how the recognition of a distinct state of mind in the psychoanalytic process, and its discrimination from one closely linked to it, usually requires the investigation of many clinical instances. These may be within specific analytic treatments, which are made up of many sessions, or may involve comparison between many treatments. It should also be noted that a key concept like this is necessarily located within a complex network of ideas. The onset of envy, for example, may be understood through its genesis in a developmental pathway, and/or through its observable effects on a person's mental life and relationships, and/or in its manifestations in a transference relationship. While each element in such a chain of causes and meanings is in principle subject to separate investigation by reference to "clinical facts" of the kind just illustrated, they do not exist in isolation from one another but are linked in terms of both cause and meaning.

In setting out to assess the validity and usefulness of an entire sub-paradigm in psychoanalysis, it is not always easy to determine which concepts and theories are core and which are secondary or auxiliary in their function. One can observe in the broader British psychoanalytic tradition a process of convergence, through which some initially contentious ideas of Klein became widely accepted while others remained in dispute. The ideas of projective identification and the analytic relevance of the countertransference, for example, gained wide acceptance (Sandler, 1988). It is also now recognized that the psychoanalytic treatment of children even as young as 2 years old can be undertaken successfully, through the invention by Klein of the technique of "play therapy", even though this idea was originally received with scepticism. However, other of Klein's ideas—for example, that of the death instinct, which she adopted from Freud, and the significance of innate dispositions to hatred and envy—remain contentious.

It seems probable that the most relevant question to ask about psychoanalytic theories concerns less their validity than their scope of application. The repeated testing in clinical practice of hypotheses that have characterized psychoanalytic practice throughout its history make it likely that most of its ideas that have achieved currency have been able to demonstrate their validity and usefulness in *some* specific conditions of application. Descriptions and conceptualizations that may accurately fit some clinical and developmental phenomena are unlikely to be true of *all*. One reason for the plurality of and apparent incommensurability between psychoanalytic theories may lie in the inclination of each psychoanalytic school to overgeneralize its findings and models, beyond the contexts in which their relevance has been clinically demonstrated.

At one time, Freudians tended to insist that the key to all clinical understanding was oedipal phenomena, in their various manifestations. A Kleinian revision to this perspective focused more intensely on the earliest relations between mothers and their infants, in which the oedipal "third" was initially a shadowy presence. A third revision of this perspective came with a "rediscovery of Oedipus" in the work of post-Kleinian analysts such as Bion, Britton, and Steiner, who argued that the toleration and actualization of "triangular" relationships during early development and afterwards is a precondition of psychological integration. (This development represented a "return of the father" to the psychoanalytic theory of development, after a phase in which Klein and her mainly female psychoanalytic colleagues had held the initiative.) What has taken place here is an evolutionary "speciation" of knowledge often driven by clinical encounters and discoveries, in which different phenomena have been successively brought within the scope of understanding.

In the discipline of sociology, a valuable distinction was made by Robert Merton (1968) between "general theories" (these were at the time mainly those of "structural functionalism) and "theories of the middle range", which were those that offered explanations of domains of social life at a level of generality mid-way between the nature of society as such and more local understandings. The theory of deviance and its relation to the larger social system was one such "middle-range" theory. It may be useful to think of psychoanalytic theories in this way, differentiating between their common and universal presuppositions (for example, concerning the existence of repression, the unconscious, and the transference) and their more circumscribed spheres of application (the understanding of different life stages, such as infancy or adolescence, psychopathologies such as psychosis or anorexia, or group phenomena such as those characterized by Bion's "basic assumptions"). Within each of these "middle-range" fields, different concepts and theories provide explanations of phenomena. There can be substantive overlaps and interconnections between them (for example, in a developmental understanding of the origins of eating disorders) but without these amounting to a unified theory of the human mind.

Such a combination of universal explanatory concepts and principles, with specific, differentiated, and indeed changing contexts of application, characterizes all those social sciences (for example, sociology, anthropology, historiography) that are attentive to differences among human beings and societies and embody different value-orientations towards them.

The theoretical framing of clinical facts

For various reasons, it has become widely understood that "facts" in science do not exist independently of the conceptual frames through which they are discriminated. Different theoretical insights have contributed to this understanding. One of these is the central idea of Ferdinand de Saussure's "structural linguistics" (1916), that meaning arises from identifying differences within a conceptual field and that words do not represent the unproblematic essences of what they name. A second insight most relevant for psychoanalysis is Kuhn's historicization of scientific knowledge, as evolving fields of concepts and categories that were selective in the attributes of nature they sought to name and understand and, to a degree, "constructed" them in relation to human and scientific interests. Even the primordial facts on which the English empiricist philosophers sought to base their new understanding of nature can be shown to have been selective in certain terms—for example, in discriminating the supposedly "objective" primary qualities of mass, volume, and location in time and space from the "secondary qualities" of colour, texture, and the like, which rested on more subjective perceptions. "Gestalt" theories of perception, such as that set out by Suzanne Langer, argued that the world of experience is constructed and integrated by reference to the choices and interests of human subjects. Understandings are thus constituted through human relationships to nature and other entities and are not merely their passive reflection or the imprint of its attributes on our minds. Hume's theory of understanding as a progression from impressions, to ideas, to recognition of their causal conjunction is thus insufficient.

Thus one may observe or study an area of vegetation—for example, a field—from different points of view or perspectives, whose criteria of relevance will determine what will count for us as its significant "facts". A botanist, a geologist, an entomologist, a farmer, an ecologist, a landscape painter, an archaeologist, and a property developer are all likely to "see" a field in different ways, and to mobilize different concepts and theories to make sense of what they see. Many of these domains of knowledge may, in principle at least, be related to and relevant to one another. For example, it may be of interest to a property developer to know that a field (or the zone within which it lies) is infested with biting midges. Or one may see the yellow-flowered plant called ragwort either as a colourful addition to the landscape, or as poisonous to horses, or as the food plant of the burnet moth. But despite such interconnections of understandings, it is surely clear that there are many theoretically informed perspectives through which a single field of vegetation can be observed. ("There were lots of birds on the lake", I said appreciatively to the young woman who worked at the boat-hire in Regents Park, London, when our short excursion was finished. "Do you know the different species?" she asked me, sadly regretting that she did not.)

O'Shaughnessy's "clinical facts"

It is instructive to examine Edna O'Shaughnessy's (1994) paper in the IJPA "Clinical Facts" symposium to see how embedded her own clinical observations are in a psychoanalytic frame. Here are her summary accounts of three clinical sessions.

> My patient, whom I call Leon, will soon be 14 years old. At his request, his analysis is ending. Only fifteen sessions remain.
>
> Session 1
> Leon puts the large box containing his drawings, paper, pens, etc. up on the table so that it forms a barrier between him and me when he sits down. He looks tense and fearful. He has brought with him a carton of Ribena, a children's drink, on which, in big print, is written "FIFTEEN FREE EXTRA". Through a straw he starts sucking the drink. He looks no more a schoolboy, but every bit a baby as he empties the carton, which is collapsing in a grotesque shape. Desperately, he sucks for the last drops. Then he hurls the carton violently away into the rubbish bin. I speak to Leon about being near the end of his analysis, of how he feels like a baby whose drinking causes such collapse and ugliness that he must get free—and free of me he will be in fifteen days. I also speak about how he is not satisfied, and desperately still needs and hopes for something more, "extra". There is a long silence. Then, very anxiously, he peers round the box to look at me, retreating instantly. I speak of his terror that I am like the collapsed Ribena carton, and of his being so afraid that he cannot see how I really am. His breathing becomes distressed and he starts to wheeze. It is most distressing to hear. He transmits to me absolutely rending pain and anxiety. And suddenly he falls asleep—it is so unendurable.

Session 2

The next day Leon was different—every inch a schoolboy, a highly defended one. He again made a barrier with his box, and then pulled out a pile of books from his schoolbag and spread them out ostentatiously. He read out his homework assignments loudly. For a brief moment he began to wheeze as if his lungs were again collapsing in agony, but he threw it off, and went on reading continuously in a loud voice bits from various schoolbooks. There seemed no way to make contact with him. I found myself feeling hopeless; I could do nothing but endure his loud blocking reading. I spoke of his need to free himself of a helpless baby who has to endure fear and pain by getting rid of it into me. Leon's response was to print his name on a sheet of paper in big letters and tear it in half, and continue even more loudly with his blocking talk. However, when I later interpreted his terror that I would make his schoolboy self disappear and be lost to him, a striking change came about. Leon was quiet and he put away his schoolbooks.

Hidden by his box, he stayed silent for a long time. I asked him what was happening. He was about to answer, then did not. I spoke of his fear that I would use what he might tell me to say something that would disturb him too much. He then started pushing his chair into view so he and I could see each other and then moving it away so he was again hidden by the box, doing so several times. I was reminded of something he had told me two years before—how he felt half-human and half-bird, that is, half like a human who stays in touch with humans and half like a bird who flies away. When I spoke to him in these terms he was visibly moved. He agreed it was so and then took down the box barrier.

Session 3

He made no box barrier this time. He sat down, openly hard and nasty. He took off his watch and started to draw it. In an exaggerated, mocking way he measured everything with a ruler. I first spoke about the watch being time of which he was so aware in these last days. His nasty performance continued and I then spoke about how he was giving a caricature of me as a cruelly measuring watcher. I went on to say that I thought he knew it was a false picture. Leon continued in the same spoiling way. Suddenly he announced with sarcastic emphasis "I was going to draw it exactly, but I have decided not to", and he stopped. He drew the watch now in a straightforward way, and he started to bring his lips gently near to his hand several times as if to touch it with a kiss. I understood him to be showing the affection he feels when he thinks I know he needs me both to be gentle and not force him and also not to be weak and let him take bad advantage and make a mockery of me. He said "Yip". Then, with an effort, he said a clear "Yes", going very pink.

This is my record of the clinical facts as I saw them. [O'Shaughnessy, 1994, pp. 939–940]

O'Shaughnessy's description of these three sessions is deeply theoretical, even though she makes no explicit of psychoanalytic concepts in these vignettes. [This theoretical abstinence may be related to the fact that she reports the analysis of a child. In such work there is an especial necessity to use "experience-near" (Geertz, 1983, pp. 57–58) language in communicating with patients.]

However, this clinical description is nevertheless deeply informed by theoretical ideas. These include:

» the transference and belief in its influence on the state of mind of and enactments of the patient
» the countertransference—the analyst's understanding that her state of mind reflects unconscious projections into her by the patient—she describes Leon as transmitting to her "absolutely rending pain and anxiety"
» ideas of "splitting" (Kleinian in their origin) and of the "parts of the self" that are brought into being by this mental process
» the idea of unconscious defences against mental pain and anxiety
» the belief that interpretation and understanding, over a long period, can relieve pain and bring about self-understanding and greater integration of the self
» the belief that virtually all of what was observed of the patient communicated meaning to the analyst about his unconscious states of mind (in the context of the transference relationship that had been established within this long analysis, it is assumed that such communication to his analyst was consciously or unconsciously intended by the patient)

One of the boldest elements of this presentation lies in the significance that the patient's analyst attaches to his bringing into the consulting room a Ribena carton. Its written notice "Fifteen Free Extra" corresponded in its number to his fifteen remaining sessions, and Ribena is a drink mostly consumed by young children. O'Shaughnessy suggests that it is for this reason the carton becomes the object of her patient's agonized enactment of infantile pain. A psychoanalytic sceptic might suspect that this was a mere coincidence, being exploited by the analyst to make a theoretical point. O'Shaughnessy's description of these three last sessions with her patient is clear and moving, with its revelation of the different aspects of the patient's personality, and in her sensitive understanding of him, However, one might still ask, how substantial is the evidence provided by this material of the theoretical ideas that the writer has chosen not to set out discursively, even though they are plainly the theoretical subscript to the description of the paper?

O'Shaughnessy is at pains to make limited but nevertheless precise claims for her paper. She holds that its understandings and interpretations of her patient are for the most part true and valid, with one specific exception.[9] She states that there might be different theoretical understandings of this material that could also be true—the implication is that other aspects of a patient or treatment might be also validly grasped—however, in ways which need not dispute the truth of her account.

It can be noted that O'Shaughnessy's clinical descriptions, and her inferences from these, are extremely succinct and compressed. A question that can be asked of this paper, and *ipso facto* of others, is: how might the grounds for drawing theoretical inferences from clinical evidence be made more substantial? How might one be given more reasons for confidence in the understandings of a patient than O'Shaughnessy offers in this paper? What is at issue here is the larger one of how far the development of psychoanalytic theories from the evidence of the clinical consulting room—the entire practice of clinical psychological research—can be defended as a valid scientific practice.

There are two responses to this question. The first of these lies in the domain of the collection and presentation of clinical data. The second is in the analytic methods we employ. The procedure of theoretical inference that O'Shaughnessy follows in her paper could, in principle, be strengthened and augmented by making more data available for investigation: for example, more clinical sessions could be presented and these in fuller detail. In addition, more explicit methods of making and justifying theoretical inferences from clinical particulars than those demonstrated here by O'Shaughnessy could be developed.

Considerable progress has made been made since the "Clinical Facts" symposium was published in addressing these issues. In particular, this has been by child psychotherapists. A practice has been adopted, in part to meet the methodological demands of the funders of large-scale research, of audio-recording and subsequently transcribing entire sequences of clinical sessions. Psychoanalysts have always placed substantial reliance on the adequacy of post-sessional write-ups from memory of clinical sessions, and such "process records" have been one of the major resources for the clinical grounding of psychoanalytic discoveries. But there has also been a question latent in this procedure—namely, how accurate is the record-from-memory of an analyst, and how liable to omission or distortion may it be? The practice of audio-recording of sessions (sometimes feared and resisted because of its potential interference with the therapeutic relationship) makes it possible systematically to compare the literal "mechanical" record of a therapeutic exchange with the therapist's own recalled and written-up memory of it.

It is surely certain that a transcribed mechanical record will provide a more complete and accurate report of the words spoken in a clinical session than a therapist's own retrospectively written-up account of it. Even though analysts in the British psychoanalytic and child psychotherapy traditions are trained to be meticulous recorders of what they observe and experience,[10] the write-up from memory of what may often be a complicated dialogue is bound to be both incomplete, in terms of the detail of what is remembered, and selective. Published psychoanalytic papers in this his tradition frequently contain reports of sequences of clinical exchanges, and, despite the unavoidable limitations of clinical recall, the analytic community has long relied on the "good-enough" fidelity of such reports, as well as on the trained sensitivity of experienced analytic readers to their relative accuracy. This analytic sensitivity to the truthfulness or otherwise of what is written has similarities with the sensibilities of capable readers of poetry and other imaginative literature.

Psychoanalysts have good reason to believe that there are dimensions of the psychoanalytic process that cannot, in any case, be completely captured by even the most literal electronic record of what has been said in a clinical session. Non-verbal communications take place within analytic—and, indeed, most—relationships. An analyst's own counter-transferential feelings and insights are likely to constitute active elements of the clinical relationship. A further source of relevant information may be an analyst's own associations and interpretations of clinical material which she has chosen not to share with a patient, at a given moment, but which may still be a potential source of understanding. There has been concern that while the audio or audio-visual recording of clinical sessions would add to the literal accuracy of any description of it, such recording may intrude too much on the clinical setting and its context of confidentiality and trust to be clinically justifiable.

Nevertheless, for all these understandable qualifications, it is remarkable that there has been so little investigation hitherto of the similarities and differences between remembered and electronically recorded descriptions of sessions. A recent study by Miriam Creaser (2015), for her child psychotherapy doctoral thesis at the Tavistock Clinic, in which she compared clinical write-ups with audio transcripts of sessions, has proved revealing and interesting. She notes in the first instance the obvious but little regarded fact of the inevitable compression of the reported material provided in a therapist's write-up from memory of a session, compared with the volume of what is usually actually said. The word-length of a written-up record may amount, in its quantity of words, to only a quarter the number of those actually spoken and recorded. Creaser asked, what actually happens when such a "reduction" of quantity, or process of "reduction" or "abstraction" from a total volume of clinical material, is made?

She found inaccuracies of sequencing and significant omissions even of issues that seemed to have involved intense feelings during sessions in their written-up record, when this is compared with their transcription. Especially interesting has been her discovery that in the cases she studied, clinical write-ups were shaped by a distinctive "narrative logic", distinct from the mere compression of a total record. She found that the child psychotherapists had in their clinical notes focused selectively on what they perceived to be aspects central to the transference relationship between their patients and themselves. Thus the therapists' accounts were found to have their own narrative structure, influenced by their implicit conception of what was most psychoanalytically relevant. Creaser found that this selection for significance by therapists had been made as they described what had taken place in a session, usually very soon after its completion when it was fresh in their minds. (These therapists often had fortnightly clinical supervision, which gave them particular reason to provide as detailed as possible write-ups of sessions.) The element of "selectiveness" that Creaser found in these reports (comparing them retrospectively with session transcripts) was likely to have been largely implicit and even unconscious—the therapists had no independent record with which their own account could be compared or by which it could be checked for accuracy. However, memories do become filled out in the act of writing and in supervisory discussion of clinical material. Creaser showed that therapists' memories of earlier sessions, and their evolving sense of narrative "arcs", which gave sessions a developmental meaning, could also influence the process of writing up. We have seen such a theorized narrative "shaping" of session reports in the material presented by O'Shaughnessy, although there we have no literal transcript of the sessions with which to compare her account.

Some might see the discovery of significant discrepancies between the literal and the therapist's record as almost scandalous in its implications for the accuracy and veracity of most psychoanalytic clinical writing. But it is clear that these issues now need further attention. To understand the content and meaning of a psychoanalytic treatment necessarily requires substantial selection and abstraction from a large volume of clinical material. Even a once-weekly analytic treatment of 28 weeks, of the kind trialled and "manualized" in the short-term psychoanalytic psychotherapy intervention, might generate as many as 96,000 words of clinical transcript (8 sessions × 12,000 words).

A five-times-per-week psychoanalysis conducted over five years (which is by no means exceptional among in the British Psychoanalytical Society analysts), if it were electronically recorded and transcribed, might generate as many as 12 million words of transcript![11] Even the analyst's post-sessional write up of such sessions could amount to a quarter of this (i.e. 600,000 words.)

It is obvious that analysis of such material cannot be accomplished without a procedure involving selection and abstraction, and without preparedness to sample from the totality of the clinical material that may, in principle be accessible.[12] The question is not *whether* a selective approach to such material should be taken but *what kind* of selection this will be. By what criteria can selections from clinical material be made that enable a truth-bearing account of a patient and his analysis to be conceived and justified by reference to facts? It seems inevitable that such selections will always be made by reference to criteria of theoretical relevance, as they have been throughout the history of psychoanalytic case studies.

The question is how to make such selective procedures more transparent and accountable than they have hitherto been for the most part. The pioneering value of Creaser's (so far) limited study of only three STPP cases is to have shown how illuminating it is to have the two separate data sets of the electronic record and the therapist's notes from memory available for comparative study. This investigative approach provides a means by which clinical researchers can reflect on the explicit and implicit beliefs that shape their understanding of their clinical data and, indeed, their practice. Its development should enable psychoanalytic theories and techniques to be set on to a firmer empirical ground. It is clear that the stated belief of some psychoanalysts that an electronic record of clinical sessions could add nothing to their trained recollection needs to be put to further test.

The approach described above to enhancing the validity of the analysis of clinical material belongs primarily in the domain of data *collection*. But it has now also been amply demonstrated that systematic procedures for the *analysis* of clinical records can enhance their transparency and accountability. "Line-by-line" and "sequence-by-sequence" analysis of clinical material enables it to be subjected to close scrutiny. Systematic sampling and comparison of segments of clinical material can enable changes and turning points to be identified, and uncertainties regarding the meaning of what has taken place in a clinical process to be resolved.

Two methods, in particular, have come to be widely employed for this purpose, following their development in other domains of "qualitative" social science. These are the methods of grounded theory and of interpretative phenomenological analysis. The origin of the former lies in the discipline of sociology, a field that has usually been receptive to holistic theoretical ideas. The origin of the latter lies in psychology— its principal focus has been more on the explication of the meaning of experiences to their individual subjects, and less on the generation of holistic theories. However, these perspectives can be complementary. Their value is that through their focus on specified, contextually situated details of a clinical process, they make it possible to identify unconscious dimensions of meanings in the communications between patients and analysts.

The adaptation of these systematic methods of qualitative research to the study of the clinical facts of psychoanalysis and their necessarily unconscious dimensions are further explored in chapter 12.

Notes

1. Those senior analysts who had been most involved in the international activities of the psychoanalytic field, such as Robert Wallerstein and David Tuckett, seemed the most inclined to be disquieted by this apparent "Tower of Babel" (Steiner, 1994; Wallerstein, 1988, 2005): the coexistence of many mutually uncomprehending tongues. By contrast, analysts who remained within the confines of their national schools seemed to be less concerned about these differences of tradition.

2. O'Shaughnessy defines as a clinical fact one that is both perceived and understood by an analyst in the transference and is then successfully interpreted to a patient. However, it seems to me that the accurate understanding of a patient's state of mind is distinct from finding the most effective way of conveying this to a patient at a given moment. It seems an unduly restrictive definition of a clinical fact that it must fulfil both of these criteria—one of understanding and the other of clinical technique.

3. Hume intended and largely achieved a philosophical reformation of the foundations of knowledge following the controversies and wars of the religious Reformation and Counter-Reformation of the previous centuries. Ernest Gellner (1975) argued that Hume's separation of arguments from factual correlation from those depending on metaphysical presuppositions laid the basis for the "modular" ways of thinking on which modern understandings of the properties of nature and society are based. Thus, in Gellner's view, the facts and the moral choices human beings can make in the light of the facts, can now rule unimpeded by dogma.

4. Note that the "schoolmen" were also Hume's negative point of reference: "If we take in our hand any volume: of divinity or school metaphysics for instance: let us ask, Does it contain any abstract reasoning concerning quantity or number? No. Does it contain any experimental reasoning concerning matter of fact and existence? No. Commit it then to the flames, for it can contain nothing but sophistry and illusion" (Hume, 1777, Section Xii, Part III, 132).

5. Popper's falsificationist theory has, however, become more subject to dispute than Hinshelwood seems to have recognized. Lakatos has been a major revisionist from within a Popperian perspective. Stove's (1982) objections are more fundamental.

As we have shown in early chapters, the Kuhnian development called into question Popper's model of the linear advance of science towards an ever-growing understanding of nature. Following Kuhn, sociologists of science drew attention to the greater diversity of the sciences and their methodologies.

6. Elizabeth Spillius (2007) notes parallels between Kleinian understandings of envy and Catholic theological doctrines.

7. Or even turned into its opposite: "Of us out-cast, exil'd, his new delight, Mankind created, and for him this World. So farewell Hope, and with Hope farewell Fear, Farewell Remorse: all Good to me is lost; Evil be thou my Good" (words spoken by Satan in Milton's *Paradise Lost*, lines 108–110).

8. It seems likely that some of the hostility and rancour associated with attacks on the credibility of psychoanalysis is an outcome of particular psychoanalytic treatments that have disastrously failed.

9. The exception, in her view, is the interpretation she offered of her patient's infantile anxiety, which, she believes, had the effect of both overwhelming him in the first session and provoking the defended and cruel state of mind that we see in the second and third sessions. This relates to the distinction made above between the recognition of a clinical fact and the true understanding of a patient's state of mind that may be learned from it, and how this may be communicated to a patient. I've suggested that these are distinct functions, which it requires training and experience to bring together.

10. Developing capabilities for observation, recall, and accurate writing up of what has been observe and experienced is one of the main purposes of the practice of infant observation in pre-clinical analytic trainings.

11. The calculation is: 5 sessions × 40 weeks × 5 years × 12,000 spoken words in each session.

12. Such procedures of abstraction, compression and selection from large volumes of data are by no means specific to psychoanalytic case records. Consider, by way of comparison, the records of anthropological or ethnographic field-studies. In those fields, too, large volumes of data may be collected by researchers, for example in the form of descriptive reports. Where such investigations have been open-ended and have not been structured by pre-defined protocols, meaning has to be assigned to data after its collection.

CHAPTER ELEVEN

Grounded theory in psychoanalysis and child psychotherapy

Problems of evidence in psychoanalytic research

T he main purpose of debate about clinical facts in the psychoanalytic literature has been to establish the kinds of evidence by which claims to psychoanalytic knowledge can be validated. Its argument was that since psychoanalysis is a distinct sphere of scientific inquiry, there must surely be distinct kinds of "fact", or empirical evidence, by which its theoretical claims can be justified. Clinical facts—namely, those located in the phenomena of the transference–countertransference relationship—have been proposed to constitute this relevant kind.

What was expected to follow from this clarification, in so far as it had been achieved? Many of the limitations in the presentation of evidence to test or support psychoanalytic theories had always been practical ones, arising from the circumstances of clinical work and its description. These limitations have included:

» The dependence of most session reports on clinicians' memory of what has taken place
» the small amount of clinical material that it is usually feasible to present in journal articles of the usual length
» the elision in many written clinical reports between factual descriptions of what had taken place, and their conceptualization in theoretical terms

» the absence of any explicit selection criteria in the sampling of clinical material from a case or cases
» even assuming that the findings of case-study methods were valid for those cases, the problems of making valid inferences from single cases or small numbers of cases to larger populations

Merely to identify these as methodological issues is by no means to resolve them. The question is, is there a way in which the psychoanalytic field can continue to make use of clinical, case-based approaches as its major source of new knowledge while at the same time responding to criticisms of their methodological inadequacy? How can the justifiable demands for more transparent and accountable evidence to support theories be met?

Psychoanalysis had to a considerable degree been protected from questions of this kind by its isolation from the academy and from other fields of science. While its writings had been undertaken mainly for the psychoanalytic community, it achieved considerable advances within its own field of knowledge according to its own criteria of validity. Challenges to its intellectual legitimacy from outside were difficult to respond to but did not greatly affect creative work within the field itself. But in recent years this situation has changed. The demands for "evidence-based medicine" have required psychoanalysts to demonstrate empirically the efficacy of their treatments, or else find themselves excluded from public health services. Additionally, the need for psychoanalytic psychotherapists to achieve parity of qualification with other mental health professionals has driven psychoanalytic training institutions to seek academic accreditation for their programmes. At doctoral level, academic regulations require students to undertake original research and to adopt methods of research comparable to those of other disciplines. For these purposes the traditional forms of clinical writing, which have served psychoanalysis so well throughout its history, are insufficient.

One response to this problem has been to introduce into psychoanalytic training research methods that bring psychoanalysis closer to "mainstream science". In practice, it is usually psychology that is taken as the norm—a restricted choice from the wide spectrum of the sciences. The "evidence-based" climate of contemporary health policy-making has been a strong driver in this respect. The standardization of patient assessments, treatments, and measures of benefit are elements of this evidence-based approach. The risk in these measures is that in trying to measure the psychoanalytic process, they may change its character for the worse. The aims of treatment may shift from the psychoanalytic goal of modifying structures of character to merely alleviating symptoms. Demands for "cost-effective" treatments may require that only short-term and non-intensive kinds of therapy are undertaken, even though psychoanalysts believe that for some patients intensive and long-term work is necessary. The measurement of outcomes may include demands for assessments of progress session by session—an expectation that negates the entire psychoanalytic model of treatment. From that perspective, patients may need to experience greater conscious mental pain if their problems are to be understood and recovery made possible. For good therapeutic work, the transference relationship with the therapist must have space to develop which is not unduly intruded on. It is often now proposed, for reasons for cost, that manualized treatments conducted by inexperienced practitioners are preferable to therapies provided by fully qualified therapists. Although greater transparency in treatment provision has its benefits, the insistent demand for measurement can impact destructively on service quality. Psychoanalytic therapies are liable to become merely a provision of last resort, offered to patients who are so ill as to have already failed to benefit from other treatments, or who have been found to be untreatable. (Psychoanalytic therapists have developed particular capabilities in working with severely disturbed patients, arising from their understanding of the unconscious meanings of extreme behaviours.) But although psychoanalytic therapies can be of benefit to the most seriously ill, they are also often beneficial for those with less acute or chronic difficulties—in fact, they may be preferred by such patients.

An alternative response to the scientifically demanding culture of the present day has been to seek to preserve the essence of psychoanalytic practice, while making their procedures more systematic and accountable. The crucial development has been of qualitative research methods. It has been possible to adapt approaches first developed in the social sciences for psychoanalytic purposes.

Both in sociology and psychology, fierce battles were fought from the 1960s onwards against the domination of "positivistic" and largely quantitative research methodologies (Keat & Urry, 1975). The debates, discussed in earlier chapters, on methods based on interpretation and meaning, case studies, part–whole analysis, and complexity theory all came about in part as a critical reaction to earlier positivist orthodoxies. Two specific approaches to qualitative empirical research have emerged from these debates which are of particular relevance to psychoanalysis. One of these, whose origin lies in sociology, is the method of grounded theory. The other, whose origin lies in psychology, is interpretative phenomenological analysis (IPA).

Grounded theory

The Discovery of Grounded Theory was published in the United States in 1967 by two sociologists, Barney Glaser and Anselm Strauss. It was a challenge to an orthodoxy that defined research as a procedure for the empirical testing of hypotheses formulated as deductions from prior theoretical models. One of those dominant models of the time was the theory of structural functionalism, which set out a theory of the entire social system and the contributions of its different components, positive or negative, to its supposed equilibrium state.[1] But other "general theories" from which hypotheses could be deduced and empirically tested were also called into question, by implication at least.

In opposition to this sociological orthodoxy, the grounded theorists recommended that research be undertaken not from the perspective of preconceived theories but, rather, by drawing inferences from empirical experience—that is, from data gathered in a field setting. There was a latently ethical or political dimension to this perspective, in so far as deductive theory-derived research methods were seen to reflect the "top-down" perspectives of those in authority, whose view of the world tended to be encoded, for reasons of funding and political power, in the dominant theoretical models. Thus a functionalist conception of "normal" and "pathological" aspects of society could readily frame policies designed to manage and control varieties of criminality and deviance. By contrast, researches based on observations or dialogues with ordinary human actors could be understood as representing *their* perspective on the world, a view "from below". This perspective resonated with other countercultural challenges of the time—for example, in the fields of criminology and the sociology of education, where to describe and sympathetically report the experience of offenders or under-achievers challenged the "official" sociologies that saw offending and under-achieving mainly as social problems requiring solutions.[2]

There had been an earlier tradition of ethnographic research, notably in the Chicago School of Sociology in the United States, in which field observation and individual case studies had been among the principal methods of research. However, the main influence of this work came from the descriptive vividness of its studies and its illumination of hitherto unknown social worlds, rather than from codified methods of research. Indeed, it was common in these studies for little attention to be given to research methods as such, or to the validation of findings, or to the problems of generalizing from particular observed cases or contexts to larger populations. The persuasive powers of these texts depended mainly on their descriptive capture of roles, milieus, or patterns of interaction more than on methodological justifications of how such discoveries could be reproduced. These ethnographic studies had something in common with brilliant journalistic reportage, even when they were the outcome of researchers' immersion in a social world.

The emphasis of Glaser and Strauss and their successors was a different one. There were essentially concerned with methodological procedures, not with the particular findings or insights to which these led. Although Glaser and Strauss did significant field research while developing and using their own methods (e.g., on what they observed as the social construction of the experiences of patients dying in hospital), it is the method of grounded theory and not their substantive findings that was their main invention and achievement.

The grounded theorists' idea was that it was possible to develop theories from the interrogation of data that had not been pre-selected or organized according to existing theoretical principles. Researchers should begin, they recommended, with a broad question in their mind, in relation to their field of study. But they should only seek to formulate explanatory theories once they exposed themselves to a situation and its phenomena—for example, as passive or participant observers—and had allowed their data to acquire meaning in their minds.

Glaser and Strauss saw this initially as an inductive method, in contrast to a hypothetico-deductive approach. The idea was that from the observation of instances, laws, or generalizations that connected them in patterns of cause and effect could be inferred. But it has emerged that C. S. Peirce's concept of *abduction* better describes the procedure that Glaser and Strauss recommended than their initial use of the idea of *induction* (Gallie, 1952; Locke, 2007; Reicherz, 2007; Strübing, 2007). The latter refers, in Hume's terms, to the "constant conjunction" of observed phenomena; because it leaves the observed and conjoined phenomena unmodified except in their correlation, it is theoretically minimalist in its approach. What Peirce meant by "abduction" was the location of an observed fact in an illuminating field of meaning, whatever that context might turn out to be. This is a theoretically more generative process than Glaser and Strauss's inductive model, since it recognizes that pre-existing ideas can help in finding meaning in what is being learned about from observation. Abduction is neither a formally deductive procedure, nor is it purely inductive. It does not begin with an *a priori* established theoretical model and then seek to deduce empirical implications from it. Nor does it merely gather up data and infer generalizations from repeated instances and from the observation of correlations between them. Instead, its purpose is to relate observations to whatever concepts, theories, and empirical analogues are found useful for understanding them, thus making possible the development of existing fields of knowledge.[3]

Somewhat contrary to their own formulations of their method as inductive, Glaser and Strauss can themselves be shown to have followed an "abductive" procedure in their own substantive grounded-theory research. For example, in trying to understand the meaning of the situation of the dying patients, families, and nurses whom they studied in hospital, they drew on concepts such as role and status, which were part of the basic grammar of their field of sociology. Glaser and Strauss thus found the best "fit" between the phenomena they observed and theoretical concepts that were already available to them. But new discoveries emerged from their substantive research too, in so far as they were able to identify connections and correlations that they had not anticipated. The idea of an "abductive" method of analysis allows for the discovery of both correspondences between observed data and existing conceptual schemes as well as for the development of new concepts and theories.

It was of particular importance to the grounded theorists to devise procedures through which researchers could proceed from descriptions of observational particulars to the development of themes and categories and, ultimately, to the generation of theories that relate concepts to one another in explanatory ways. They set out this procedure as a sequence of stages.

The first is data collection. Standard positivist models that required hypotheses to be formulated, tested, and then generalized from samples to larger populations required each stage of a study to be designed *ab initio*, according to protocols that are then followed. Within this conception of research, the collection of data is largely separate from its subsequent analysis, in order to ensure that its selection is not biased by preconceptions. It may be that those doing that data collection—for example, as interviewers—will have no part in its subsequent analysis. Sampling methods are designed to ensure that valid inferences can be made from a sample to the larger population of which it is statistically representative. Psychoanalytic outcome studies, as we see later, also adopt these procedures.

Grounded theory proposed, by contrast, an exploratory open-ended approach. Its aim was not to test hypotheses that had been previously formulated according to theoretical principles, but to discover from investigation what new hypotheses might throw most light on a problem or situation. They recommended, both for the collection and the analysis of data, a method of "theoretical sampling", which meant not the selection of a sample to represent the presumed average kind of behaviour being investigated but, rather, one that might reveal its

162 RESEARCHING THE UNCONSCIOUS

most unexpected aspects, and thus those that would be most likely to challenge existing ideas and generate new ones. Although in many investigations the collection and analysis of data may be undertaken as separate stages, there are contexts in which these phases of research intermingled. For example, in a prolonged field study, the selection of issues to be studied may arise from what is encountered during an investigation. (This might be a kind of theoretical sampling undertaken during the process of data collection.)

In both their collection and their analysis of data, grounded-theory researchers were recommended to proceed with sampling only to the point of "theoretical "saturation". In the context of data collection, this might involve deciding how many subjects of a given kind to interview. Rather than persisting with further instances of what has already become familiar, it may become preferable to seek out instances of a contrasting kind. In analysing interview data, the question might be to decide how many transcripts of a given kind need to be analysed in depth. At the point when a sample is yielding no new information, it may be desirable to move on to a different sample.

The primary focus of grounded theory was on the collection and analysis of qualitative material, although Glaser and Strauss did not exclude quantitative data. Thus field observation, semi- or unstructured interviews, the analysis of documentary records of various kinds (e.g., court reports), media materials, life-history narratives, even photographic records were the kinds of data the grounded theorists had in mind. They recommended that it was often useful to bring different sources of data together, in order to produce what they referred to as "triangulated" view of the field.[4]

The crucial methodological step, once an archive of data had been assembled, was its line-by-line or segment-by-segment analysis, or "coding". The task was always to move from particulars—an observation, a reported statement or remark, a response in an interview—to a "kind", at a higher level of abstraction and generality. The grounded theorists saw this as a sequential, one-step-at-a-time procedure, to ensure that concepts which emerged from analysis, as the building blocks of a "grounded theory" remained firmly grounded in the data itself.

One serviceable way of conducting this procedure is through setting out data in a tabular form, in rows and columns. In the first column, the samples of raw material to be analysed may be displayed. In the second and subsequent columns, alongside the segments of material to which they relate, themes, concepts, and categories are identified, at increasing levels of abstraction, until in the final column concepts are joined up to constitute the "grounded-theory" product of an investigation. It can be illuminating to undertake such a sequence of steps. Its effect is to focus attention on each single item of an array of data, enabling the significance of particulars and their relation to each other to be examined.

Glaser and Strauss recommended the use of the "constant comparative method" (derived from John Stuart Mill's model of analysis of causal relations) to identify patterns of recurrence and correlation of items in a data set. In this way valid "conjunctions (or causal relations) could be identified. Recurrences of correlations between phenomena could indicate causal connections; unexpected correlations could reveal unseen causes, or hidden variables. Charmaz (2006), a leading second-generation exponent of grounded theory, recommended a procedure of "axial coding", by which particular categories are identified as the "axis" around which connections and relationships can be identified. She sees the analytic process as requiring both the initial "fracturing" of data, through line-by-line coding, and its re-assembling to enable theory-building to take place.

Glaser and Strauss further suggested that as the gathering and analysis of their data proceeded, researchers engage in "memo-writing"—a way of making connections between their data and what is already known in their field of study. Such "memo-writing" can also be valuable in developing concepts. This procedure is consistent with the method of "abduction", later imported into grounded-theory methodology (Charmaz, 2006; Reicherz, 2007), since it enables researchers to enlarge the frames of reference that give their data meaning.[5] Glaser and Strauss's model set out to address the central problem of nearly all qualitative research, which is how to convert what is often an immense mass of descriptive, particularistic data into a manageable summary or model of some kind, by a method that is not arbitrary in its procedures.

Before proceeding to discuss the relevance of these ideas to psychoanalytic research, I provide a brief illustration, drawn from a socio-biographical study, of how grounded theory methods can throw light on an unstructured kind of qualitative research data.

A grounded-theory analysis of an extract from a biographical narrative interview[6]

This is an extract from the audio-transcript of the beginning of an interview undertaken as part of a research project—Social Strategies in Risk Societies (SOSTRIS)—in seven European countries, between 1997 and 1999. The data were gathered through use of the Biographical Narrative Interview Method (BNIM). With this method, the interviewee is asked only a single "prompt" question, and from this starting-point is encouraged to

tell their own life-history in their own words. The interviewer is expected
to provide the response of a sympathetic listener, but to ask no further
questions until a second-stage interview, at which specific questions can
be asked, but only to take up omissions and ambiguities arising from
the earlier interview. The material that results from the audio-taped and
transcribed interview is thus shaped as far as possible by the interviewee
alone. In this respect it has some similarities with the material provided
by patients in clinical psychoanalytic sessions, although psychotherapists,
unlike BNIM interviewers, respond actively, for example, with interpretations, to what patients communicate to them. Within the BNIM method,
there is a complex multi-stage procedure for analysing biographical interview data, but for the purpose of this chapter a simpler grounded-theory
approach has been chosen.

The interviewee is a British Caribbean subject, a woman who was in
her thirties at the time of the interview. The research project had selected
its interview subjects by reference to six categories of "social exclusion",
one of these being a single parent. This is indicated in the opening
prompt question. It may previously have been mentioned to the subject when she was asked whether she was willing to be interviewed as
part of the study. Retrospectively, the researchers wondered whether
Janette might have told her life-story in a different way if she had not
been made aware of our interest in the experiences of single parenthood.
For example, had we chosen her as a member of our "ethnic minority"
category, and told her this, would her narrative have taken a different
course? (See "Opening section of narrative by Janette.")

Opening section of narrative by "Janette"

The researchers in their analysis of this interview material, of which
this is the opening passage, found many aspects of interest. The subject presented an articulate and forceful account of her experience of
herself as a "single parent". She sets this in the context of a family
history, which the researchers are able to relate "abductively" to the
frequent occurrence of female-headed black families in the Caribbean.
They noted also the anger the subject expresses towards her father,
who she describes as having been absent from her life from when she
was 18 months old to her adulthood. She later on describes his unexpected visit to her family, when she rejected him, saying she owed
him nothing. She describes her dismay at the chaos of her family,
through which she feared that sexual relationships between cousins
whose family connections were unknown to them might have unwit-
tingly arisen. She refers to her mother's remarriage to her stepfather,

Interview transcript

Interviewer's initial statement	Initial comments	Theoretical inferences
We are interested in the biographies of people living in different European countries, of different ages, and of different life situations. In this context we are interested in people who became single parents. And so I'd like you to tell me your life story, and you may begin wherever you want. **Janette:** (giggles) My life story? **Interviewer:** And I'm interested in everything that has been important to you. **Janette:** mhm **Interviewer:** and, erm, take the time you need and I'll not interrupt you, I'll take some notes and I'll ask you later. . . . **Janette:** *Line 7* I think I'll start off by saying that I am, probably, third generation single parent.	"I'll start off by" implies that the subject already has an idea of how her interview is to unfold. The research team were amazed to find that their own category of "single parenthood" was immediately being responded to reflectively by the subject. What does "probably" refer to—the subject's uncertainty about whether she is using these concepts correctly?	It seems that the initial question prompted an already "theorized" life story from the subject—the idea that single parenthood is a recognizable "way of life".

Interview Transcript (continued)

Interviewer's initial statement	Initial comments	Theoretical inferences
Line 18 My grandmother was a single parent, and she was a nurse, she came to England in the early fifties, with my mum, my, my grandfather didn't eh come with her, he chose to stay back, so she was actually a single parent while she was here, and . . .	Grandmother defined as "single parent". Her working status established. The history of her and her mother's migration to England given at the start. Her grandfather chose not to come to England. Thus grandmother's single parent status established in this initial account.	The history of mother-centred black families in the Caribbean (and the United States) came "abductively" to the researchers' minds.
My mum was raised here, with my grandmother, and subsequently as she grew up she got— well she didn't get married.	So mother raised in single-parent household with her mother. "She got—well she didn't get married" this hesitation suggests some tension here.	Later Janette refers to her mother "remarrying". It seems that she earlier believed that she had been married to her father.
She had four children, and, I think the last time I saw my dad (before I had been an adult) was when I was eighteen months and	These four children are probably those by Janette's father. Mother had two more with her subsequent husband. This complicated family story is not altogether clear in the narrative. Janette says her father absent from when she was 18 months to when she was adult. Suggestions of reproach/ anger towards him.	The reproach towards her father later becomes vivid in the interview, when he visits her and is rejected because he has abandoned them.
my mum managed with all four of us, right, that is going back to college, she then became an accountant and she's now reached –	Description of strong and capable mother "managed with all four of us, right". ! Then back to college, became an accountant, she's now reached (incomplete passage, perhaps a higher position).	Admiration for her capable mother.
she's now married—but it's to somebody else and erm I think I've always felt –	Married "but to somebody else"—that is, not her father.	
I'd, I've never ever felt the need for like the norm of a family situation because all the women in our family were quite strong women,	Here is Janette's story of herself as part of a line of strong women—grandmother, mother. . . herself.	

and what my mum has always said to me was that there's not a woman in our family that wouldn't have been the shrew in *The Taming of the Shrew*. Women in our family we're always tend to rise, we don't like su- . . . suppression, and I found that,

especially when she remarried, my stepfather, I was eleven at the time, when she remarried, and instantly I had conflict with him, I couldn't take orders from him,

and it wasn't just because erm some people said it was because of he was not taking my mum's attention.

I didn't have that attention from my mum, because there was four children, and erm in terms of when my mum had my two younger brothers erm myself and my two sisters, erm we were like, we were the parents of my two brothers

Line 59 . . . and my older brother who is now in the States

we were the parents of my younger brothers.

Regardless of whether my stepdad was there or not we took over the parenting roles, and that's when the conflict came, was when my mum left to go to work of a day. I was in charge, if I was the only person in the house other than their dad, I felt that I was in charge, and I would tell them to do whatever needed to be done, and their dad didn't like it. And there'd be arguments.

Heroic narrative of women in her family, with literary reference from mother. In Shakespeare's play, "the shrew" (Kate) is eventually "tamed" —do Janette and her mother know this?

She twice says "remarried". But later there is a question of whether she was ever married to Janette's father.

She shows she is aware of interpretations of her jealousy of her stepfather, but rejects them.

This lack of attention isn't presented as a problem for her, just the way things were.

But she tells us later that she did undertake a conventional marriage, which later broke down.

So an implicit reference to psychoanalytic discourse is part of the narrative.

One can see Janette and her sister's adopting a "parentified" response to the lack of attention from her mum, and the absence of her father. Mobile family from Caribbean—grandmother and eldest brother in United States.

(continued)

Interview Transcript (*continued*)

Interviewer's initial statement	Initial comments	Theoretical inferences
Line 72 I've never felt that erm (right) I've never ever felt that I have met a person that is my equal partner, even my children's dad, erm, I suppose yeah there was love and there was all of that but I never felt that he was my equal, oh yeah, yeah, as in my partner, I never felt that he could ah. . . . I gave power to him, he didn't actually have power over me, I felt that I gave power to him, erm I don't know what it was I uh (exhales) I've discussed it with so many people because I felt that I was so strong.	Now goes on to describe arguments over power between herself and her husband.	Where does this narrative of relationships defined by power come from? Power issues between women and men discussed with "so many people". This a reference to feminist conversations?
Line 83 I actually became the housewife in the house, making a conscious effort to iron clothes, making a conscious effort to make proper dinners, to cook proper meals, and he actually put on a heck of a lot of weight because of it, in fact we all did, but erm, but I knew, I mean I knew that that wasn't me, I knew that that was what, I felt was supposed to have been the norm, I wanted to fit into that little, that's how it's supposed to be, you know what society wants it to be a kind of nuclear family, you know, and it was only when I realized that I couldn't live that life any more, erm, and I knew that I was dead as a person it wasn't the real me, it was like a forced erm forced environment, really erm I mean I gave up my identity in that relationship, erm	Describes her "housewife" self". Contrasts conventional social expectations—"nuclear family" with "real self".	Narrative becomes torrential, as if recalling period full of turbulence for her. Echo of psychological discourses of real and false selves, as well as repudiation of conventional norms.
I wasn't able to do the things that I did before—I was very creative before, I used to do amateur dramatics. . . .	This begins the description of the way she changes her life.	

but that she had learned, to her dismay, that her mother had not been married to her father.

The researchers became interested in the experiences which had led the subject to describe her life-story as she did. Later in her interview she referred to a local government strike in which she was a shop-steward, and her decision to change career from work in a housing department, to undertaking a social work training, on the advice of friends who had taken up careers in education.

She refers to reading books, in contrast to tabloid newspapers, to her political disagreements with her conservative policeman husband, and her rejection of his conventional approach to their marriage. She mentions meeting Maya Angelou (a famous American black feminist writer) as a highly memorable moment in her life. The researchers inferred that she had formed her new ways of thinking in a milieu influenced by feminism, probably black feminism, though she refers little in this interview to ethnicity and race as such.

Although the subject insists on the virtues of female strength and independence, admiring her mother and grandmother, her life-journey has been in some ways a difficult one. She has fought with her stepfather, rejected her father, and separated from her husband, after having tried to make a conventional marriage. She talked of wanting to find an "equal partner", where issues of power would not dominate. Although she is at times highly critical of her husband and his conservative outlook, we learn that he has continued to be an active father for their daughter, even though they are now divorced and he has a new family. The researchers admired the courage and determination with which this subject sought to understand and describe some of the central experiences of her life and its ongoing struggles.

From a psychoanalytic perspective, it seems that the experience of the interview may have provided "Janette" with a space to work through some of her experiences and feelings. She seems to have an implicit—perhaps unconscious—ideal of a kind of family system that would be more harmonious and less disrupted than hers had so far been. The line-by-line analysis of the transcript gave rise to an understanding of this subject which was initially sociological and cultural in its framing, but which subsequently acquired a psychoanalytic dimension.

Interpretative phenomenological analysis (IPA)

I will not say a great deal in this chapter about the method of interpretative phenomenological analysis (Smith, Flowers, & Larkin, 2009), which has been the most-often used alternative to grounded theory in clinical psychoanalytic and especially in systemic family therapy research. Its origin lies in academic psychology. It made the same kind of challenge to positivist orthodoxy in that discipline as grounded theory had to its equivalent in sociology. Its point of departure was to insist on the central importance of the subjective meaning of human actions, as essential to psychological understanding, in opposition to models of mind and behaviour which sought to study these in objectified, "thing-like" terms, according to models drawn from the natural sciences.

As its name implies, the purpose of interpretative phenomenological analysis is to capture the ways in which human subjects construct their own worlds through language and in other forms of symbolism, and to make sense of social interactions in these terms. Analysis with IPA methods is above all an investigation of patterns of motive and intention. The data which it gathers and analyses is largely qualitative. Like grounded theory, it proposes a method of systematic "coding", designed to abstract generalized "kinds" of phenomena from often unstructured masses of data, drawn from open-ended interviews or observations. This method is able to capture significant patterns of structured intention and interaction, from the interpretations which subjects themselves give to their experience.

It can be argued that IPA is largely interchangeable, as a method of data analysis, with grounded theory. This is because the analysis of clinical data with each of these methods involves the elucidation of conscious and unconscious meanings and intentions, within transference–countertransference relationship. Each infers "categories" or "themes" which represent a level of abstraction or typification, from sequences of particulars having the form of descriptions or narratives. There is no insuperable difficulty in extending the IPA notion of interpretation from the sphere of conscious to that of unconscious meaning. (This is what the term interpretation mainly refers to in psychoanalysis.) Neither the IPA nor the grounded theory founding figures seem to have considered psychoanalytic applications of their method, and there are similar problems for both approaches in taking that step.[7]

There is, however, a difference between these methodological frameworks which may confer a comparative advantage on grounded theory in psychoanalytic research. This is because psychoanalytic theories are not concerned exclusively with the elucidation of meanings, with subjects' conscious or unconscious definitions and interpretations of their situation. They are also concerned to understand mental structures (e.g., the Oedipus complex or the paranoid-schizoid position) and entities (e.g., "the total transference situation") which are understood to have causal powers distinct from the conscious or unconscious intentions of individuals. It may be that a fairly complete translation can be made between these two lexicons of explanation. After all, psychoanalytic explanation, even where it postulates mental structures, also has to account for subjective states of mind. Even so, the attention given to structures and causes, as well as to the phenomenological experience may give it a larger scope of application to psychoanalytic data than is readily accessible within the IPA protocols.

Grounded theory and psychoanalysis

There is a striking similarity between the analytic methods of grounded theory, and the procedures by which knowledge has been acquired through clinical practice in psychoanalysis. Janet Anderson (2006) has well described these research- and clinically oriented methods as "well-suited partners". Among the essential procedures of grounded theory are the following:

»   The gathering of open-ended and unstructured qualitative data
»   its "fracturing" through line-by-line analysis and its subsequent re-assembly in the form of conceptual "kinds" and theoretical models
»   its use of "abductive" procedures to locate the meaning of particular observed entities in a larger conceptual field
»   the almost invariable "grounding" of its theoretical discoveries in observed (clinical) data

Each of these phases corresponds to the methods which psychoanalysts have used to develop psychoanalytic knowledge from their experiences in the consulting room. These equivalences become particularly visible in the context of psychoanalytic training. Clinical supervision can be described as the routine practice of an implicit grounded theory method. Material is presented for supervision in its "raw" form of written-up clinical sessions. Supervisors go through material with their supervisees, often line-by-line. The questions being addressed are: what is going on here? What "kind" of phenomenon, or process, or interaction, exactly is this? How does this relate to what happened previously? (Which might be just now, or last week or a year ago.) Here an implicit constant comparative method of analysis is employed to identify similarities and differences, connections and correlations between relevant facts, perhaps specifically "clinical facts". A supervisor might recommend a supervisee to read items of literature, in order to facilitate the discovery of meanings through "abduction". Such observations and the discussion which may follow them may have the function of "memo-writing", accompanying the detailed analysis of the clinical narrative. Of course there are clinical as well as investigative issues at stake when such analysis has a supervisory function. A supervisor may observe that it might have been better if the supervised therapist had said more, or something different, at a certain moment. She might offer a prediction from clinical material of what she sees as a possible future enactment, and might advise a supervisee to take account of this prospect. Where supervision is taking place in a seminar group, other seminar members may well add their own questions and comments. The material may provoke unconscious dynamics in the relationship between supervision group members, which may become a further topic for reflection and interpretation.

Psychoanalysts in their personal reflections on their own work may well engage in a reflective, analytic process similar to this, when they come to write up a case for a presentation or publication. Their clinical notes are usually their essential resource in such writing. Their clinical records are likely to be (implicitly) "theoretically sampled", with selections made of those episodes which are most illuminating in respect to the argument they are making. In most published clinical writing, no formal or systematic method for generating theoretical inferences from the session material is usually described. It is left to be inferred that meticulous reflection on the material has taken place, with the quality of "fit" between exemplary clinical particulars and conceptual "kinds" offering grounds for confidence in the validity of an argument. However, what is usually explicitly set out in clinical writing are the relations between concepts and clinical instances and some existing literature relevant to the topic. In effect, psychoanalytic writers rely on the experienced judgement of their peer-readers to find meaning and relevance in what they write. In his seminal book *Second Thoughts* (1967b) Bion states that he expects only psychoanalysts to fully understand what he has written.

It is important, however, to insist that this unsystematized method of knowledge generation in psychoanalysis has been productive in the generation of new knowledge, and in the extension or "speciation" of the psychoanalytic paradigm. Many analysts believe that since these practices have served their field well, there is little reason for changing them. Some hold that attempts to formalize such methods and to demonstrate their similarities and comparabilities with the research methods of adjacent fields of study, is at best pointless, and at worst threatens to compromise the primary work of psychoanalysis itself.

However, once it was decided that psychoanalytic psychotherapists needed to seek forms of academic accreditation comparable to those of other professions, attention to questions of methodology became unavoidable. Various options were available in response to this challenge. One choice was to undertake studies whose methods were close to those of conventional psychological or social science, while their subject matter was nevertheless relevant to psychoanalysis. Examples of such scientific mainstreaming are investigations which measure treatment outcomes, or investigations of patient satisfaction which employ structured forms of interview. Some universities which have accredited clinical trainings have insisted that only such established research methods be used in psychoanalytic doctoral research.

A more specifically psychoanalytic option was base research on data which was gathered through normal psychoanalytic clinical practice, but then to develop methods of sampling, recording, and analysis which would meet a more formal research purpose. It is through work of this kind that the good fit between grounded theory methods, and the clinical practice of psychoanalysis was recognized. It has proved possible to adapt the qualitative methods both of grounded theory and interpretative phenomenological analysis for research purposes. Many doctoral studies have been successfully completed which have made use of these methods, which have themselves become a field of debate (Anderson, 2006; Midgley, 2004, 2006; Midgley, Anderson, Grainger, Nesic-Vukovic, & Urwin, 2009). One advantage of these studies is that they have allowed, indeed required, the presentation of clinical and other case material in much greater length and detail than is customary in published clinical writing. Full case studies (like those by Klein, 1961; McDougall, 1989; Winnicott, 1978) of the psychoanalysis of children have been relatively infrequent, but correspondingly highly valued. Clinically based research theses have provided opportunity to add to this kind of detailed case-description.

Questions arose in the adaptation of grounded theory methods for these purposes. The original grounded-theory model proposed that investigators should engage with their research questions and their data without theoretical preconceptions. Research in the field was supposed to commence from a theoretical blank slate. The IPA methodology was similar in its eschewing of a priori theories, its preferred approach being that the research subjects' definition of their situation would become the main source of understanding. However, it was obvious from the start that a psychoanalytic approach to clinical work was necessarily shaped by the ideas of psychoanalysis, if it were to capture phenomena relevant to the psychoanalytic field. How could these seemingly opposed approaches be reconciled?

Significant developments both in grounded-theory methodology and psychoanalytic thinking, contributed to the resolution of this contradiction. As grounded theory evolved, and was taken up by researchers from different disciplinary perspectives, it became clear that investigations of virtually any phenomena depended on prior presuppositions about what was of research interest, and what was not. A psychoanalyst studying the first two years of life of a baby in a family would come to her subject with a certain frame of reference, while an economist researcher visiting a family to study its changing patterns of economic behaviour with another. A specialist in forestry would be likely to frame his understanding of a pinewood in a way different from that of an ornithologist or an entomologist. It was clear reading the pioneering empirical studies of Glaser and Strauss that their focus on patterns of interaction with terminally ill patients in hospital were framed by their sociological sensitivity. Kathy Charmaz in fact acknowledged that researchers were always likely to bring a theoretical orientation to their field, and noted that Glaser and Strauss had themselves acknowledged this. David Tuckett (1994b) made a comparable assertion in regard to "clinical facts" in psychoanalysis.[8]

From the psychoanalytic point of view, convergence with grounded theory perspectives arose from the early commitment of psychoanalysts to the need for an open-ended responsiveness to clinical experience. This was Freud's idea of "evenly hovering attention" in the consulting room, and the belief that it was the flow of "material" (dreams, free associations, later unconscious projections and states of projective identification) which needed to guide the process of learning and understanding. Later insistence by Bion and other analysts that essential for understanding disturbed states of mind in patients was the analyst's receptivity to their unconscious communications gave additional force to this idea. Bion's idea of "learning from experience", his famous aphoristic instruction to analysts to "eschew memory and desire" (Bion, 1980), and the emphasis on the "here and now" of the psychoanalytic situation (Joseph, 1985) were formulations which emphasized the need for the avoidance of theoretical preconceptions in undertaking clinical work.

However, these prescriptions did not mean that analysts were supposed literally to forget everything they had ever learned, in working with patients. It was rather that their knowledge of theories and of other cases, and of earlier moments in work with a current patient, needed to be kept in the background, while the immediate experience of a session was absorbed and attended to. The function of the psychoanalytic tradition and its literature then becomes that of a memory-bank or archive, available to be called on by analysts when it is needed, but which is invoked only when its relevance is made evident by actual clinical experience.

The idea of "abduction" seems to correspond both to the grounded theorists' and to the psychoanalytic approach to understanding the theoretical significance of phenomena. For example, what gives this clinical "particular" a meaning? To what conceptual field does it belong? What similarities and differences does it bring to mind? To what "whole" does it relate as a "part"? Does the idea of metaphorical equivalence help us to understand what is going on? To take the phenomenon of anorexia, for example, can we best understand the literal refusal of food as a refusal of "mental nourishment too, in a refusal to accept any form of offered understanding?

Because the procedures of grounded theory, and those of clinical research in psychoanalysis are already so close to one another, questions can be asked about how much grounded-theory methods can add to the generation of knowledge in psychoanalysis. In many influential papers in the psychoanalytic literature, there are close correspondences between clinical descriptions and the new theoretical concepts and "kinds" which they are held to exemplify. How far can such processes of inference from particulars to "kinds" be facilitated by the meticulous procedures of grounded theory? Doctoral theses which have been completed in the Tavistock's child psychotherapy programme suggest that it can be.[9]

The next chapter presents an example of the use of grounded-theory methods in analysing material from the case of two siblings who were seen for a four-session psychoanalytic assessment.

Notes

1. Its leading figure was Talcott Parsons, *The Social System* (1951), its comprehensive formulation.

2. In the period of the 1960s and 1970s when a democratic spirit was abroad, many redefinitions of academic subjects took place—for example, assertions of the value of popular culture, in the work of the Centre for Contemporary Cultural Studies; the idea of "history from below" in the *History Workshop Journal*; even the writing of military history from the point of view not of generals and strategists, but of ordinary soldiers (see John Keegan's *The Face of Battle* (1976)).

3. Further clarification of the concept of abduction can be obtained from the *Stanford Encyclopedia of Philosophy: Abduction* (2017). In *The Sign of Three: Dupin, Holmes, Peirce*, Eco and Sebeok (1988) enjoyably link Peirce's procedure to that followed by great fictional detectives such as Sherlock Holmes.

4. This concept (Denzin, 1970) derives by metaphorical transfer from the field of surveying. One can also compare the resonance of "triangulation" as a source of understanding with the psychoanalytic ideas of a "third position" (Britton, 1989).

5. A procedure of ongoing file-making, analogous to memo-writing, was recommended in an Appendix "On Intellectual Craftsmanship" by Mills (1959). One can see some affinity also with the psychoanalytic idea of "free association", as leading to greater understanding.

6. Later analysis of this material revealed issues of psychoanalytic interest, as "Janette" was understood to be experiencing and enacting internal conflicts rising from what she had experienced as her father's betrayal of her as a child, and her family. While working on this project, the research team had decided not to pursue psychoanalytic approaches to their topic, feeling themselves to be poorly qualified to do this.

7. There is no reference to psychoanalysis, in the 623-page *Sage Handbook of Grounded Theory* (Bryant & Charmaz, 2007).

8. "In the fifteen years I spent doing research work in social science and psychiatric epidemiology, I was repeatedly made aware that there is no observation, and therefore no fact, that in any absolute sense stands outside the theoretical framework within which it is perceived" (Tuckett, 1994b, p. 866).

9. *Discoveries in Child Psychotherapy: Findings from Qualitative Research*, edited by M. E. and M. J. Rustin (forthcoming, 2019) consists of papers drawn from such doctoral research.

CHAPTER TWELVE

Grounded theory in child psychotherapy: an example

This chapter presents an example of a grounded-theory analysis of three sessions of a child psychotherapy assessment of two children, which were conducted and reported by an experienced child psychotherapist, Margaret Rustin (M. E. Rustin, 2004). The previous chapter has described the use of grounded-theory methods, adapted for psychoanalytic purposes, and their value in drawing out and making accountable inferences from the kinds of relatively unstructured material which provide the principal data for clinical research. Such "material" derives from the experience of a therapist with a patient. It will usually consist of a written-up record of the proceedings of clinical sessions, which will include observations of the patient, and reports of what the patient and therapist said, did, and, in so far as can be ascertained, felt during the sessions. It is also likely to include an amount of background information concerning the patient, and about the context of the work in question.

The advantages of presenting and analysing three sessions of a child psychotherapy assessment for this purpose are several. One is that an assessment is a self-contained piece of clinical practice. Its purpose in investigating, learning and coming to a conclusion has to be fulfilled within this limit of a few sessions. The disadvantage of the possible alternative of selecting a similar number of clinical sessions, with or without reference to the longer treatment of which they may have been a part, is that it would be more difficult in such a case to establish the context of such material, and the significance of what can be learned from it, than in a specifically focused piece of work such as this.

A second advantage is that the method of child psychotherapy assessment demonstrated in this chapter is in fact quite close to the approach a child psychotherapist uses in clinical work with child patients. The setting of the work is similar, and the technique followed (with limited play and drawing materials provided for the children) is close to that originally developed by Melanie Klein, and widely followed by child psychotherapists since then in their clinical work with children. One reason for this similarity is that this model of assessment is intended to explore how a child responds to a therapeutic setting, like that which a child would then encounter if therapy were recommended. In a sense, an assessment like this is designed in part to function as a kind of "trial" of a child's likely response to therapy, which is best done by providing an initial experience of it. Although reference in this material to the children's relationship to the assessing therapist is restrained and cautious, some reference to transference and countertransference phenomena is nevertheless present in the material, as it needed to be if the "testing out" purpose of the assessment was to be fulfilled.

The research questions that are likely to arise in clinical cases emerge from the experience of the work itself, and do not ordinarily precede it. With assessment work like this, the "questions" are rather more clearly defined at the outset, since an assessment will usually have been set up for a definite purpose: to answer certain questions. With the cases reported here, where there was a context of a considerable involvement with an adoption process, there was some knowledge of the past and present circumstances of the two siblings being assessed before the assessment took place. The assessment was therefore undertaken with some specific initial questions in mind.

There was an assumption, based on prior clinical experiences of children who had been in the care-system after their difficult beginnings and who were now being adopted, that the children might well have some emotional difficulties liable to give rise to problems, both for the adoptive parents and the children themselves. One question being explored here was whether psychotherapy might help with these difficulties, which had already begun to appear. A second question arose from what was known from the referral about the relationship between the two siblings. As this relationship had so disturbed the preceding foster parents that the foster placement had been discontinued, a second focus was on this sibling relationship. The assessing psychotherapist designed an approach that involved first seeing the two siblings together, then each of them separately, in order to explore both the children's individual states of mind and their relationship with each other.

This assessment was undertaken in normal clinical circumstances, not as a designated research project. Nevertheless, it was written up as a chapter of a book on child psychotherapy assessment and therefore received an amount of attention after the assessment similar to that which might have been given in a more formal research study.

The material presented in the initial column of the tabulated analysis is taken from the session material, which was reported in the published paper. The previous chapter has described the close affinity between the line-by-line approach to understanding followed by psychoanalysts and the grounded-theory method of research. Although the child psychotherapist in this case had not presented her analysis of the case in a tabular form, her reflections on the material, both in the real time of the session and in the later writing-up, involved close scrutiny of the text. It might be mentioned also that assessments like this, in which a great deal has to be learned from a very brief quasi-therapeutic interaction with a child or children, call on a high degree of skill from therapist/assessors, as there is little time with this kind of work, as there might be in more extended treatments, to learn gradually from experience.

The tabulated analysis that follows seeks to discover, and demonstrate, as grounded-theory methodologists recommend, how conceptual and theoretical inferences can emerge and be inferred (by "induction" and "abduction") from line-by-line study of sequences of material. These tables are organized in five columns: (1) the original session material as reported by the therapist; (2) issues arising from the therapist's interventions; (3) issues arising from the children's words and actions; (4) reflections arising from these (corresponding to the grounded theorists' advocacy of "memo writing", a researchers' kind of "free association"; and (5) a setting-out of the concepts and theoretical issues that arise from the material, which become visible as recurrent elements in the assessment process. The final column is presented, for purposes of this chapter, as a summary of the more abstract categories that emerge from the material, among which are these.

1. Classification of different kind of intervention or commentary by the therapist assessor. These include interpretations of the unconscious meanings of the children's play—sometimes spoken and sometimes retained in her own mind; questions to elucidate further thoughts from the children; explanations of the setting, etc.
2. Identification of the states of mind of the children—for example, their anxieties and defences and their uncertain and sometimes

bewildered transference response to the therapist. Sometimes we see that her closeness to them makes them anxious, at other times that her attention and understanding calms them. This is accomplished through observation of their way of being with the therapist and in the room, and by interpretation of their play and drawings, in the "classic" child psychotherapy approach. Although explicit distinctions are not made here between conscious and unconscious mental processes, the method of proceeding from description of what the children say and do in the therapy room to inferences concerning its meaning enables attributions of unconscious states of mind to be grounded in detailed evidence.

3. Observations of the children, visually and aurally, and the therapist's emotional and countertransference response to them are important in the process of understanding them. The report does not try to identify the evidence drawn from a self-aware emotional response to the children as against the unconscious communications of the countertransference, but in some places in the narrative the countertransference dimension of what is happening is clear.

4. Towards the end of the report, the therapist's own reflections on what she has learned are given in the initial transcript column. I have drawn attention only to a few additional theoretical concepts that emerged in this summary, since the therapists' summary of her work is self-explanatory.

I hope it will be seen that even a rather brief sample of clinical work conducted and reported by a child psychotherapist reveals, when examined in detail, a considerable complexity of meaning of a theoretically informed kind and enables a clear understanding of the children being assessed to be formed, with valuable implications for subsequent clinical decisions concerning them. When accounts of much longer therapeutic treatments are reported and analysed in this way, a much greater volume of material is available for analysis, providing fuller grounds for inferring theoretical conclusions from clinical evidence. But a condensed therapeutic assessment like this shows how instructive a grounded-theory analytic procedure can be.

While material presented in this tabular form may appear forbidding, I have found on many occasions that it is the explanation of a detailed example that brings the method of grounded theory alive for clinicians.

Tabulated report and analysis of three child psychotherapy assessment sessions, of two siblings

1. The setting for the assessment

Transcript of sessional material	Summary of issues from point of view of therapist undertaking the assessment	Aspects of reports concerning the two children being assessed	Notes and "memos" (a grounded-theory procedure)	Concepts and categories emerging from grounded-theory analysis
Lorraine and David, aged 14 and 10, were referred by their social worker and prospective adoptive parents, with whom they were already living. There was a fairly detailed history available: the children had been removed from their unsupported mother's care aged 5 and 1, together with another sister aged 3, who had been badly hurt in an accident in the home when the children were left alone. This episode followed many previous occasions of neglect and abuse. The injured child was placed for adoption, following hospital treatment. The other two remained together, and had been in children's homes and in a long foster-placement which ended in their being very hurtfully rejected. A psychiatrist	Background of two children being assessed. Removal from unsupported mother's care, injury to third child following previous incidents of neglect, children's homes and hurtful breakdown of long foster placement of long foster placement are salient elements in background. They are living with prospective foster parents, who are committed to therapy for children.	As in previous column.	Context of assessment one reason why considerable background information available. Traumatic history of neglect and Vulnerability. Idea of psychotherapy has come from both social workers and parents. Issue is to assess suitability for this.	Starting point is children from overwhelmed single parent, and difficult experience of care and foster placement. Question of what assessment will discover.

(continued)

1. The setting for the assessment (*continued*)

Transcript of sessional material	Summary of issues from point of view of therapist undertaking the assessment	Aspects of reports concerning the two children being assessed	Notes and "memos" (a grounded-theory procedure)	Concepts and categories emerging from grounded-theory analysis
colleague had already met with both social worker andadoptive parents to discuss the children's earlier lives, their current difficulties, and the long-term care plans, which were for adoption to go ahead. Both children were in some difficulties at school and were not easy to live with, and the parents hoped that therapy might help them to make better use of the family life they were committed to offering.				
I decided to begin by seeing both children together, since the one constant factor in their turbulent lives had been their living together. I wanted to observe the nature of their involvement with each other, and then planned to see them individually on a later occasion, I had not by any means anticipated the tumultuous session that took place.	Plan for sessions described. Decision to see them together since this the most constant feature of their lives.	Not in published report, but learned that foster parents had previously tried to keep Lorraine and reject David— placement had been ended by social workers who did not agree with separating them.	Evidence of strong professional involvement, in this case in reference to how placement was ended, psychiatrist's involvement, social workers involved in referral to Clinic	Therapist has given priority to nature of the sibling relationship, given the history with the foster family.

2. The assessment session with both siblings together

Transcript of sessional material	Summary of issues from point of view of therapist undertaking the assessment	Aspects of reports concerning the two children being assessed	Notes and "Memos" (a grounded-theory procedure)	Concepts and categories emerging from grounded-theory analysis
David was small for his age, fair-haired, neat, a live-wire child.	Therapist provides description of two children and how they present to her	Information from therapist's observation		Role of *observation* in assessment process
Lorraine, by contrast, big, gawky, dark, and looking younger than her years.	Contrast between siblings	Information from therapist's observation	How significant is the difference between them going to be?	
They had been looking at a "baby" book in the waiting room, with Lorraine sitting in a baby chair, and were joking about who was the baby.		Baby book, baby chair, "who is the baby?"	Children bring baby aspects of themselves into the Clinic, even in the waiting room.	Psychoanalytic idea of infantile *parts* of self seems on the agenda from the start.
David made an immediate impact, anxious about what to do with the drink he had been given from the vending machine and passionately demanding to go down to my room in the lift.	Therapist reports her strong response to David.	David anxious about drink he has been given, and wants to use lift to go to therapist's room.	Why is the lift important to David?	*Anxiety* already present, in both one of the children and the therapist in response to this in them.

(continued)

2. The assessment session with both siblings together (continued)

Transcript of sessional material	Summary of issues from point of view of therapist undertaking the assessment	Aspects of reports concerning the two children being assessed	Notes and "Memos" (a grounded-theory procedure)	Concepts and categories emerging from grounded-theory analysis
I felt it was urgently necessary to get a firm grip and said that we would walk down but could come up by lift at the end.	Therapist feels it is important to maintain control of situation, and tells David what they will do.	David has aroused therapist's anxiety about losing control		Boundary setting in response to anxiety and potential loss of control.
I had put out a selection of small toys on a low table in the middle of my room, and drawing materials on the desk by the window.	Therapist describes usual setting for child psychotherapy. Small toys and drawing materials are standard Kleinian play-therapy materials.	Child-friendly setting prepared		Child psychotherapy play therapy setting is set up in room.
David headed for the toys but then saw that Lorraine had sat down, so did likewise.	Therapist's attention at this point is on David—she sees Lorraine through his eyes.	David responds to play-setting, but then follows sister's example in sitting down. David's attachment to sister already clear. He follows her lead.	Link between siblings already evident. We recall that social workers had insisted on keeping sibs together, against wishes of foster-parents.	Sibling relationship theme begins already
I spoke briefly about this being an opportunity for me to get to know them, and indicated that the toys and drawing things were for them to use.	Therapist now tells them why they are there and invites them to use the play materials.			Brief explanation by therapist.

Their eyes met and a prolonged giggle broke out. David's giggle was violent and loud, and gave the impression of his progressively working himself up to a high. There were noisy mutual accusations: "You're making me laugh."	Therapist's observations important. Although describing how they are, also picks up emotional tone (violent, loud, "a high", "noisy accusations").	Children are showing anxiety, through giggling, and are anxious that they are doing something wrong, out of control perhaps.	*Close observation as resource for therapist/ assessor. Children's anxiety pushed from one to another in mutual projections (through eyes meeting and giggles).*
As the giggling persisted, I spoke about the pleasure of having a good giggle together, probably much nicer than wondering about me whom they did not know or wondering what they should do here.	Therapist sympathetically interprets their enjoyment but also notes that they are a little worried about her and what they are supposed to do in her room.	Children's giggling continues.	*Therapist's reference to herself and the children's feelings about her. An early interpretation and transference reference to herself.*
Infectious outbursts continued apace so I talked about their embarrassment, and after a while on the theme of their noisy laughter filling up the room and leaving no empty space.	Therapist now refers to the children's embarrassment and to the idea that they are filling up the space with their giggling.	Children's giggling still more or less out of control (infectious outbursts).	*Interpretation is the key activity here.*
		Therapist's method is interpretation of their feelings, and of the effect/purpose of what they are doing.	

(continued)

2. The assessment session with both siblings together (*continued*)

Transcript of sessional material	Summary of issues from point of view of therapist undertaking the assessment	Aspects of reports concerning the two children being assessed	Notes and "Memos" (a grounded-theory procedure)	Concepts and categories emerging from grounded-theory analysis
This remark made contact, and they began to investigate the toys.	Therapist observes and records.	Children respond to this interpretation, and feeling less anxious, turn to toys in the room.		The effect of an interpretation.
The chaos and noise was tremendous, however, and rivalry dominated everything. They squabbled, snatched and chattered abusively. David was full of dirty talk and kept up a torrent of verbal abuse of Lorraine and she retaliated by hitting his head.	Therapist observes chaotic and quite aggressive behaviour of children.	Report of chaos, noise, squabbling, snatching, abusive chatter, dirty talk, torrent of abuse by David of Lorraine, and her physical retaliation. The children do take possession of the space offered to them, but enact their quarrelsome relationship.	We are reminded that the foster-parents found the siblings too much and wanted to separate them and keep only one. What is the significance of David being so verbal, and Lorraine, the bigger one, resorting to retaliation by hitting. Dirty talk by David may indicate one of problems for foster family.	What is to be understood of the sibling relationship is the issue here.

Surveying the scene, I felt I had two very wild toddlers in the room, in overgrown bodies.	Therapist's response in psychoanalytic terms—observation and countertransference response to children as "wild toddlers" but in "overgrown"—i.e. children's—bodies.	"Wild toddlers" suggests Klein's concept of infantile parts of the self.	*Infantile parts of the self—* how is therapist going to respond to this?
And David then launched into the story of the injury sustained by the third sibling. Mother was silly, he said, she had gone out and left them alone.	David now tells therapist about something troubling, the injury and his mother's failure to look after her children.	David is able to use the assessment setting to tell the therapist something which is important to him.	The sibling's injury is now evidently in David's mind. Lorraine is no doubt hearing this too.
I managed to get reasonably clear their picture of what had happened despite many interruptions and to find out about current contact with this sister.	Therapist indicates they she has asked about this and eventually got some information. Also about current contact with the sister—third younger sibling whose separation from them is now part of the situation.	Therapist wanting information—needed in an assessment.	Therapist asks for *information from the children*—from questions it seems, to fill out for her the situation the children are in, and what is in their minds. *Finding relevant facts is an aspect of the assessment process.*
I said something about how horrible and frightening this must have been.	Therapist names their feelings about the sister being hurt.		Back to *interpretation* of the children's feelings.

(continued)

2. The assessment session with both siblings together *(continued)*

Transcript of sessional material	Summary of issues from point of view of therapist undertaking the assessment	Aspects of reports concerning the two children being assessed	Notes and "Memos" (a grounded-theory procedure)	Concepts and categories emerging from grounded-theory analysis
to which they agreed, but any attempt to get them to go on with the story of what happened next met with a blank wall and further waves of excitement and noise.	Therapist tries and fails to get them to go on with their story.	Children seem to agree with interpretation, but then block out further exploration by therapist.		*What the children cannot bear to think about.*
The children decided to draw. This also became an argument, each wanting the other's pencil which seemed sharper than their own, and this despite the presence of a sharpener.	Therapist observes how the children cannot really draw/play, because of their rivalry.	Children do turn to the drawing materials, but cannot sustain this. Rivalry over pencils takes over. They are unable to use the realistic solution of the sharpener. Thus rivalry is the main issue, not the sharpness of the pencil.	Every detail (e.g., the non-use of the sharpener) carries meaning if one observes closely.	Interpretation has only had a momentary impact. *More observation as resource.*
David was very restless, and interfered with Lorraine who drew slowly and carefully, and with enjoyment.	Therapist reporting her observation of the children together.	David restless and anxious, Lorraine has settled to draw carefully		*More material showing differences between the siblings. Therapist's observations a crucial resource for her.*

David drew a witch with a spider coming out of her nose saying "kill me". I asked to whom was she saying it.	Therapist asks who the witch is asking to kill her.	Drawing is a turn to symbolic expression by David.		Therapist encourages David to say what is happening in his drawing.
And he said "to Lorraine", pushing the picture at her.	Therapist reports his answer, notes that the picture is pushed towards Lorraine.	David oriented towards sister.		
. "What would happen?" I asked.	A follow-up question by therapist.			More gentle questioning by therapist, encouraging him to say more to clarify for therapist what he is thinking.
"She'd be frightened", he replied.		Lorraine is to be frightened. But by the spider coming out of the witch's nose, or the witch saying "kill me"?	Someone has to be frightened. Is the witch the therapist? Who is to be killed and why?	David saying that his sister to be frightened.
He then drew a giraffe with measles, "a special disease that only farts get", he announced.	More observation by therapist.	More symbolic representation by David.	Does the giraffe (tall, long neck) stand for the therapist, who is then insulted?	Covert insult to therapist?

(continued)

2. The assessment session with both siblings together (continued)

Transcript of sessional material	Summary of issues from point of view of therapist undertaking the assessment	Aspects of reports concerning the two children being assessed	Notes and "Memos" (a grounded-theory procedure)	Concepts and categories emerging from grounded-theory analysis
Then he scribbled a horse, in imitation of Lorraine's carefully drawn horse.	More observation by therapist.	David moving from one image to another. He is now imitating his sister's careful drawing. But what does the description of "scribbled" indicate?	David's rapid succession of different drawings, perhaps all with some nastiness in them. He seems to want to communicate through drawings, but moves quickly from one to another.	*Drawing materials used as one might hope in a child psychotherapy assessment.*
Lorraine had drawn two horses, the first a show-jumper "whose head was too big", she said, the second a patchwork horse "tired after a long ride". She did not know whether its head was down because it was tired or because it was eating, but then added grass and said the horse was like a lawn-mower.	Therapist now gives her attention to Lorraine.	Lorraine now producing symbolic material. Both horses are imperfect. One is tired and very hungry. What do they stand for? Herself? A show-jumper horse (what she would like to be) but with too big a head. Or a tired patchwork horse?		Now Lorraine draws, and gets some attention from the therapist. In the assessment, essential to observe and interact with *both of the siblings.*

She talked about going horse-riding herself. Her arm was recently broken as the result of a fall, and she showed me her distorted arm.	Lorraine now describes her injury. How serious is the "distorted" arm in terms of her bodily identity? She shows her injury to the therapist.	Horse riding is something her new adoptive parents have no doubt given her.
She handed both pictures to me and said, "They're for you". She was quiet now, and basking in my attention. This hopeful turning towards me had a most touching quality.	Lorraine now turns to therapist and enjoys her attention. Therapist notes the quality of her turning towards her.	
Meanwhile David went to play with the bricks. I sat between the children trying to watch and listen in both directions.	Therapist between the children observing them.	Problem the new parents must be having to keep both of them in mind?
David's play had two phases. First, there was a lengthy game of building shaky towers, bulldozing them down with cars or simply using his hands to sweep them to pieces. The pleasure seemed to be in this moment of smashing it all up.	Therapist observing what David is doing, and its emotional quality.	

(continued)

2. The assessment session with both siblings together (*continued*)

Transcript of sessional material	Summary of issues from point of view of therapist undertaking the assessment	Aspects of reports concerning the two children being assessed	Notes and "Memos" (a grounded-theory procedure)	Concepts and categories emerging from grounded-theory analysis
He began to talk about the leaning tower of Pisa and why it leaned, and both children got involved in speculations about this—what would happen if it fell?		Leaning Tower of Pisa brought up by David, Lorraine joins in. What would happen if it fell? An actual horse has hurt Lorraine—perhaps by being too much for her.	Something perhaps unsafe towers over them. Does this refer to Lorraine being overwhelmed by what is happening to her?	
Gradually, David's manic delight in the crashes faded and he began to get frustrated and a bit miserable that he could not build higher.	Therapist observes that David's manic state is fading and he becomes miserable.			*Failure of manic defence by David.*
I now felt I could formulate an anxiety they both shared and had expressed in their own ways.	Therapist sees opportunity to interpret both children's state of mind.			
And I spoke about their both feeling there was a problem about things not balancing well—Lorraine's horse's head was too big, David's towers got too top-heavy. Was something a bit too much to manage?	Therapist interprets in terms of things not balancing well.			*Interpretation by therapist. She thinks they have conveyed to her something important about how they feel.*

I was thinking of an image of a head/mind that could not contain something so burdensome.	In the report, therapist explains what she means about the children's minds being overloaded.	*A countertransference dimension in the therapist's understanding.*
Of course they had shown me this problem in a direct way, in that the question I myself had been faced with was whether I could manage them! I had certainly been oppressed by thoughts of how much the racket they were making would be disturbing nearby colleagues and other patients.	Therapist describes her own feelings of being overwhelmed, worried that the children—in her session—would be disturbing colleagues and patients. This makes her anxious.	
After this intervention, David's building techniques improved, and he enjoyed his success hugely.	David responds to interpretation—he finds he can build better.	Anxiety has been contained by the therapist. Impressive that David now feels better about his building. *Interpretation by therapist has an effect.*

(continued)

2. The assessment session with both siblings together (*continued*)

Transcript of sessional material	Summary of issues from point of view of therapist undertaking the assessment	Aspects of reports concerning the two children being assessed	Notes and "Memos" (a grounded-theory procedure)	Concepts and categories emerging from grounded-theory analysis
I thought that I had perhaps contained his anxiety adequately through this interpretation.	Therapist in her own report explains what she thinks had happened.		Containment through interpretation— containment does not always require interpretation to take place.	
Lorraine meanwhile was talking about her trouble with thick catarrh and the doctor's plan to deal with it.		Lorraine's reference to a doctor's plans for her suggests that she is hopeful of being helped. She has responded to the interpretation too.	A helping doctor.	
I wondered in my own mind about thoughts she might have about the Clinic— might there be something done for her here too, which would make her feel better?	Therapist thinks that maybe doctor = the Clinic where the assessment is taking place, but does not say so. Does not want to encourage transference to the Clinic at this early stage in the assessment before it has been decided whether she will be offered therapy there.			An unspoken interpretation.

She moved over to the table where David was working and played briefly with the little dolls and animals. There was another episode of snatching each other's things, but then David concentrated on a particularly elaborate building and both children became involved in this.	Therapist still observing closely.	Lorraine goes to table where David is, and starts snatching again, David is concentrating on his building and Lorraine is able to join in.	Mood has changed— children are in a calmer state.	*Children are responding to this taste of this therapeutic setting and the interpretations of the therapist.*
A much quieter tension now held the air as I wondered whether this building too would be demolished.	Therapist notes changes of mood, but from "quieter tension" (i.e. there is still tension) she wonders if this building would also be knocked down.		Buildings seem be representations of their fragile containment.	
In fact the vehicles were driven round at a dangerous pace with accompanying screeches of brakes etc., but with dramatic swerves, like cars on a race track avoiding skids, and they would be brought to a halt inches from catastrophe. While this was proceeding both children were at the small table engaged in the same game.	Therapist reports more observations.	Narrow escapes from catastrophe in this car game. But the two children are playing together.	There are still risks being created and demonstrated, but the crashes are avoided, unlike the buildings which earlier were knocked down.	

(continued)

2. The assessment session with both siblings together (continued)

Transcript of sessional material	Summary of issues from point of view of therapist undertaking the assessment	Aspects of reports concerning the two children being assessed	Notes and "Memos" (a grounded-theory procedure)	Concepts and categories emerging from grounded-theory analysis
I had noticed the shape of the building and when they asked me what I thought it was called I replied straight-forwardly that it had made me think of Buckingham Palace. David confirmed with delight that I had guessed correctly.	How did therapist guess rightly that the building was Buckingham Palace?	Children ask her what their building is called. David delighted that she is right—that therapist is in touch with them.	Remarkable that building was identifiable to therapist—to do with its unconscious meaning perhaps?	
I was sure that this game held a shared meaning for them and I surmised that this concerned the depth of their preoccupation with the issue of whether this "palace", which I felt represented the admired and overwhelming material and emotional riches of their new home, was strongly enough built to survive the impact of their destructiveness.	In another unspoken interpretation, to herself and the reader, therapist connects the Palace with their new home, in both its material (middle-class, she knew) and emotional aspects. She thinks the children are worried that their destructiveness will destroy it.		This is an assessment, not treatment, so many actual interpretations are not appropriate. Purpose is not to begin a treatment with them, or "gather a transference" with them.	Another unspoken interpretation, valuable for the therapist/ assessor's think even if not tested out in words with the children.

Also in question was whether their feelings of wonder and gratitude at what they were being offered would be able to contain their powerful impulses to attack and spoil, to test to destruction.	Therapist wonders about the potential conflict between their wonder and gratitude and their impulse to attack and spoil.	
I was much impressed in this session by the joint defences these two had constructed—excitement powered by hilarity and obscenity held anxiety at bay quite effectively, and their mutual clinging relieved potential loneliness and the terror of facing so many worries about themselves and their future.	Therapist's conclusions from the joint session with the children.	Note that therapist able to think about meaning and function of obscenity and manic excitement, and not be unduly disturbed or prevented from thinking by it.	*The children's main defences noted—manic excitement and clinging to each other. Also pushing feelings back and forth. There is also a significant response to the therapeutic setting and to the limited interpretations offered.*

3. The therapist/assessor had decided to have one session with the children jointly, and two further sessions, separately with each of the children. Here is Lorraine's individual assessment session

Transcript of session material	Summary of issues from point of view of therapist undertaking the assessment	Aspects of reports concerning the two children being assessed	Notes and "Memos" (a grounded-theory procedure)	Concepts and categories emerging from grounded-theory Analysis
Lorraine began uncertainly. And I spoke about the discomfort of David's not being there.	Therapist responds to Lorraine's uncertainty with an interpretation about her brother's not being there.			Therapist's interpretation, but recalling the children's previous joint session.
After a brief conversation recalling the joint session—"those bricks!" she giggled—she began to draw.		Lorraine remembers earlier session with David with some warmth and begins to draw.	Therapist's remembering of earlier session is containing for Lorraine.	Therapist's holding in mind of past sessions reassuring and containing for the child.
She sketched a complicated chart of the universe, earth, sky and the planets and got lost in trying to remember the names of the planets.		Lorraine draws complicated chart of universe and gets lost.	She can't locate herself. A metaphor for her state of mind.	

Setting this aside, she drew an Easter picture which she said came out the wrong way round: "I always do that", she added. Next she made an Easter card.

I talked to her about the chart being an attempt to show me a picture of the world she felt of the world she lived in, both the outside world and the world inside her, her memories, the past and the present, her first family and now her new family. She was showing me how many gaps there are—it doesn't quite make sense to her. I reminded her of the long gap of years in the story of their lives as they had told it to me.

Then draws Easter picture, and this is wrong way round. (Horse in earlier picture was wrong too—head was too big).

Quite a long interpretation by the therapist connecting the chart of the universe with her confusions—internal and external, about what has happened when, her two families, etc.

Therapist goes to the point with her *full interpretation* of Lorraine's state of confusion, which she feels has been indicated to her in her chart and Easter picture and card material.

(continued)

3. Lorraine's individual assessment session (*continued*)

Transcript of session material	Summary of issues from point of view of therapist undertaking the assessment	Aspects of reports concerning the two children being assessed	Notes and "Memos" (a grounded-theory procedure)	Concepts and categories emerging from grounded theory Analysis
She then drew my attention to a mistake she made, writing "4" instead of "E".		Lorraine responds by pointing out mistake—writing "4" instead of "E".		
Which I took as a possible entree to more talk about the new family of four.	Therapist understands this as allowing her to talk about her new family of 4.			
However, Lorraine did not really listen to me.		Lorraine does not really listen.		
And the amazing thing was that despite the peace and calm of the session, in contrast to the tumult of the earlier one, I was now feeling concerned at the degree of her deafness—she had been able to "hear" far more in all that noise than she could now!	Therapist says that she is surprised to feel that Lorraine is deaf—that she could hear more when it was noisy with her brother. Does she mean physically deaf, or more that she is hard to get through to?			
She involved me in a companionable game with the animals in which I was to make a zoo for the wild ones while she made a farm for the domestic animals.		Domestic farm animals for Lorraine, wild animals for therapist.	Why the allocation of wild and tame to therapist and Lorraine? Therapist has to look after the wild parts.	Therapist's understanding (not spelt out) of inner world meaning of children's play—splitting function here.

We could be quite cosy together on the basis of ignoring any difficulties and any painful feelings and playing a little girl game together.	Therapist notes that while they are quite cosy together, this is on the basis of difficulties being kept out—this is a little girl game.	Little girl game is therapist's description of it.	Blocking out of deeper contact with therapist by child—a kind of *regressive defence*.
This was evident as she packed up when she said "till next time".	Therapist thinks her out-of-touchness is conveyed by her saying "till next time", which she has said is not to be the arrangement.	Lorraine's "till next time". Confusion or hope?	
This seemed to negate all the work I had put into explaining that I would be seeing her just this once to help me think with her parents about whether coming to the Clinic regularly to see someone else might help her.	Therapist disconcerted that Lorraine ("negating all her work") has not remembered or understood what she had set out as their arrangement for the assessment.		Therapist seems rather disappointed with the difficulty of making contact with this child. Rather less detail given in the report, compared with the other child. Issue of how the therapist responds to the different children and how interested she feels in each of them.

(continued)

3. Lorraine's individual assessment session *(continued)*

Transcript of session material	*Summary of issues from point of view of therapist undertaking the assessment*	*Aspects of reports concerning the two children being assessed*	*Notes and "Memos" (a grounded-theory procedure)*	*Concepts and categories emerging from grounded theory Analysis*
I was left with considerable anxiety: her limited intelligence and somewhat shallow capacity for attachment seemed manifest, but I also had evidence that a great deal of blocking-out was going on which would make it difficult to make contact with the troubled child within. She did not feel anxious and she certainly did not want to have to, at this point.	Therapist summarizes her feelings of anxiety about Lorraine. Refers to her blocking our and her absence of suppression of anxiety. However, the material given is very brief, compared with the joint session. There is little material given to show this conclusion was arrived at.		*Is there evidence for* all these limitations in the material presented? An alternative explanation is that the therapist has produced too indigestible an interpretation in commenting on the meaning of the charts, which Lorraine found too much to take in. The qualifiers "somewhat" and "rather" in therapist's comments suggest that she has doubts about what she is saying, which seems rather dismissive of Lorraine's capacities.	

4. Here is David's individual session

Transcript of session material	Summary of issues from point of view of therapist undertaking the assessment	Aspects of reports concerning the two children being assessed	Notes and "Memos" (a grounded-theory procedure)	Concepts and categories emerging from grounded theory Analysis
David on his own, by contrast, was openly worried and talked about how nervous he was without Lorraine. "It was better when she was here", he said.	Therapist very focused on the child's state of mind.	Contrast with Lorraine. David is openly worried in contrast to Lorraine avoiding worry. David is open about wanting Lorraine to be with him.		*Lorraine, the elder sister, has been holding anxiety for David as well as herself, perhaps. He seems to depend on her more than she on him. This may explain why she is less responsive to interpretations of anxieties. A specific focus on the differences between the children. Their relationship was a key question for the assessment, as it had been said to be a source of concern earlier.*
	Therapist notes that he is quiet and confiding, but also afraid of his own anxiety.			
He spoke in a quiet confiding voice, and I felt he was afraid to hear and feel his own anxiety so clearly.				
His voice had become absolutely tiny.	Therapist notes that his voice is very tiny.	Child's tone of voice very expressive.		

(continued)

4. David's individual session (continued)

Transcript of session material	Summary of issues from point of view of therapist undertaking the assessment	Aspects of reports concerning the two children being assessed	Notes and "Memos" (a grounded-theory procedure)	Concepts and categories emerging from grounded theory Analysis
He went back to the bricks, and tower-building, and more crashes caused by the cars. The destructive car was driven by Lorraine, he announced, and he, David, was driving the dump-truck. It was quite clear that he was the good one and she the bad one.		Return to more violent play of the two together. But now David assigns good role to himself and bad one to Lorraine.		Splitting between the two children, with David saying how it is he that is the good one, and she the bad. *Is there evidence of splitting by David?* No reason to think that Lorraine is more destructive in fact, is there? *Children's play* important here and earlier as evidence of unconscious states of mind of child.
I wondered about some feelings of his own about smashing things up which he had showed me last time.	Therapist thinking to herself about previous session, and connection between them.			
He then constructed an elaborate building. Again Lorraine's vehicles approached dangerously, and David with his ally Superman worked at protecting it.		He makes an elaborate building; this time Lorraine is the threat to it and David and Superman protect it.		Building as metaphor again. Now Lorraine as destructive vehicle. David has Superman as ally.

I tried to link this with his worries about things falling to pieces in his life more than once—and referred to the missing years of their narrative.	Therapist interprets his worries in terms of his life having fallen to pieces.		*Interpretation of play scenario created by David,, as an unconscious representation of his experience.*	*Further splitting. Function of superman in dealing with anxiety shown here.*
"It's too private", he said. "I can't talk about it."		David says he can't talk about it, but is acknowledging that therapist is talking about something real to him.		*Interpretation can have meaning for patient even if patient says it is too much to talk about.*
His voice had become absolutely tiny and I was thus made aware of how small and frail he felt in relation to really overwhelming worries about the destructive potential within himself and Lorraine.	Therapist notes how tiny David's voice had become. Interprets thus (to herself) in relation to his and Lorraine's destructive potential.	David's tiny voice.	Idea of destructive potential relates back to Buckingham Palace/new house, and idea that adopted children can be very destructive in their new families because of their internal objects (Henry, 1974, was the beginning of this understanding, much amplified in subsequent child psychotherapy writing).	Therapist believes main anxiety is about child or children's fear of their own destructiveness in their new family situation. *Observation of child and therapist's countertransference as resources for understanding his deep fears.* Therapist refers to destructive potential of himself and Lorraine. David has given Lorraine destructive role in the game—but is *she* really destructive?

(continued)

4. David's individual session (continued)

Transcript of session material	Summary of issues from point of view of therapist undertaking the assessment	Aspects of reports concerning the two children being assessed	Notes and "Memos" (a grounded-theory procedure)	Concepts and categories emerging from grounded theory Analysis
The game changed to going into space, to search for a lost star. He spoke of a mystery. "When it comes to earth, something will come to life again."		David interested in the universe too. The lost star and the idea that something will come to life when it comes to earth. Is David the lost star?		More interpretation of meaning of David's play.
When I picked up his questions about himself, his own story, what had got lost.	Therapist asks him about what he has in mind.			Therapist asks questions, in hope that child will elaborate his phantasy.
He became quite anxious—when will he come here again? How long is he going to stay?		David becomes anxious—will he come again, how long will he stay? Is this adventure in the mysteries of the Clinic and this assessment part of being lost?	But David has also had the single appointment explained to him too. Therapist noted that Lorraine had forgotten this, but does not take it up that David has too.	David is a little overwhelmed with anxiety when asked to think about what has happened to him.
I talked about the possibility of ongoing work at the Clinic.	Therapist now brings up the idea of ongoing work at the Clinic. It seems it was too early to put this to Lorraine in her assessment session.		Only David has this possibility put to him. As the session is written up, there seems to be greater interest in and sympathy for David than for Lorraine, including in the amount of detail which is given of their two sessions.	

And he said "With Lorraine would be better" and then wanted to leave early to get home in time for Tarzan on TV.	David again clear that he would prefer to be with Lorraine if he comes again. He wants to leave for his Tarzan programme. Made anxious by uncertainty about what happens next.	*Sibling tie important to David. Dependence on his elder sister.*
I tried to encourage him to stay.	Therapist tries to encourage him to stay.	*Therapist tries to persuade David to stay—she is quite pro-active here.*
And he produced a stream of drawings of TV heroes. "They help people", he said, as he hummed the theme tunes.	David describes importance of TV heroes to him, giving help to people, with the music emotionally reinforcing the heroic /helping message he likes. He seems to be explaining why Tarzan on TV might feel like a help to him.	*More vivid play and talk material—TV heroes—from David.*

(continued)

4. David's individual session (*continued*)

Transcript of session material	Summary of issues from point of view of therapist undertaking the assessment	Aspects of reports concerning the two children being assessed	Notes and "Memos" (a grounded-theory procedure)	Concepts and categories emerging from grounded theory Analysis
Feeling safe again with his omnipotent protectors close at hand.				*Omnipotent protectors' idea of therapist—relevant to understanding heroes for children and their function in phantasy, in relation to anxiety. In this case a boy's and girl's might be different.*
On the back he drew a steam train with lots of coal and smoke, and at this unconscious allusion to the anal preoccupations more evident in the earlier session he became really anxious to leave.	Therapist interprets to herself the anal/destructive preoccupations and why they make him anxious. Perhaps he is worried about the damage he might do here too.			*Another theoretical idea by therapist—unspoken—anal-destructive preoccupations expressed in drawing.*
These sessions provide abundant material relevant to the questions raised in my model of assessment. Both children had affected me powerfully with a wish to help them, though I knew that I	Therapist refers her to the purpose of the work, and also to its relevance to her "model of assessment", in connection with which this report was first published.		Therapist could remember the sessions very fully, consequence in part of their emotional impact, also of her close observation and attention during the sessions.	Therapist is reflecting on and describing her own method of assessment in these segments of the report.

could not undertake the ongoing therapy personally. The evocative, even haunting quality of their play and verbal communications lodged in my mind.

I would understand this as a communication received by me in the countertransference of their wish to be helped, as well as of their anxieties about themselves.

In the sessions, much of the impact on me was registered fleetingly, and it was in the subsequent reflection on the interaction that some of the unconscious aspects of the countertransference

Therapist refers to her countertransference and the information about their wish to be helped and their anxiety about themselves that she believed it communicated to her.

She refers to the fleeting impressions at the time of the sessions, and the value of being able to reflect on the sessions later, including their countertransference

(continued)

4. David's individual session (*continued*)

Transcript of session material	Summary of issues from point of view of therapist undertaking the assessment	Aspects of reports concerning the two children being assessed	Notes and "Memos" (a grounded-theory procedure)	Concepts and categories emerging from grounded theory Analysis
could be brought to mind and made use of in my understanding. This mulling over of the experience of the session is a fundamental part of the assessment process. Allowing time to think over what has happened, to let it gather meaning gradually, is necessary for the conscious and unconscious material to be integrated in the mind. Premature formulations need to be avoided, and the structure of the assessment appointments offered can facilitate access to the process of reverie (Bion, 1962).	aspects. She warns against premature formulation (in the assessment process, not just with the children.) Refers to Bion and reverie.			

I had evidence of the extent to which the children's actual capacities were being crippled by maladaptive defences, predominantly manic hyperactivity, with unmodified splitting and projection. I had also learnt something of the pressure of anxiety about strength and survival in the face of impulsive destructiveness with which the children and their adoptive parents were likely to be faced.	Summary of the main issues concerning the two children.	*Manic hyperactivity, unmodified splitting and projection. And anxiety about strength and survival in the face of impulsive destructiveness which children and adoptive parents would be likely to face. This both draws on and contributes to this therapist's wider experience of and writing about adoption and its problems (M. E. Rustin, 1999, 2006).*
My experience of being together with the two children in a room for one hour gave me a vivid glimpse of a clash of cultures: the two formed a sort of little	Gang and Group. Gang is an important psychoanalytic idea, from Herbert Rosenfeld and Donald Meltzer.	*Gang and group mindedness, important concepts.*

(continued)

4. David's individual session *(continued)*

Transcript of session material	Summary of issues from point of view of therapist undertaking the assessment	Aspects of reports concerning the two children being assessed	Notes and "Memos" (a grounded-theory procedure)	Concepts and categories emerging from grounded theory Analysis
gang (Waddell, 1999) which parental figures might find it very difficult to penetrate. The level of anxiety and frustration this might engender in adults trying to find their feet as parents of their children was not hard to imagine.				
Becoming a family, in the sense of the children being able to trust the parents to respond to their more infantile dependent needs, and help them to separate their own individual personalities gradually from the enmeshment I could observe, was going to be a tough challenge.	Therapist/assessor anticipates future difficulties in settling in new family.			
What therapeutic approach was indicated?	Therapist raises crucial question arising from assessment sessions.			

Despite the difficulty of fighting through the confusion and speed of events in the joint session, I thought I had in fact made more contact with the children's anxieties when I saw them together. They seemed to feel safe enough, when protected by their well-rehearsed repertoire of joint defensive manoeuvres, to listen to me from time to time.	Believes that made more contact with children when they were together—because they could protect each other they could also listen to therapist sometimes.	Crucial psychoanalytic idea of unconscious defences.	*Unconscious defences expressed in the children's holding on to each other.*
In the individual sessions, despite excellent evidence for interpretive linking, I had encountered Lorraine's tendency to block, a sort of deafness, and defensive quasi-stupidity, and David's very easily unbearable degree of anxiety.	Notes Lorraine's "sort of deafness" and defensive quasi-stupidity, and David's easily unbearable anxiety.	Is there enough evidence to support this view of Lorraine? But even if not in the written transcript, therapist will have had an emotional impression, perhaps beyond what is recorded here.	Idea of *"parentification"* of elder sister.

(continued)

4. David's individual session (continued)

Transcript of session material	Summary of issues from point of view of therapist undertaking the assessment	Aspects of reports concerning the two children being assessed	Notes and "Memos" (a grounded-theory procedure)	Concepts and categories emerging from grounded theory Analysis
Some disentangling of their mutual defensive system seemed a pre-requisite for useful individual psychotherapy to be possible.			Idea of possible "parentification" of Lorraine, as taking the role of big sister to her anxious but livelier younger brother, is not raised in this account, though therapist has elsewhere said that this was the case.	
The idea that a therapist could paradoxically have more space to engage the children in thinking in joint sessions matched an important external factor. Over the next year, the children's placement would be facing the strain of being tested for durability, and the legal processes of adoption would add to this stress. I thought it could be very helpful for the children to have a place	Therapist notes potential stress of early days of adoption, with legal processes a possible source of anxiety. Thought it might help the children to be able to be together while this "life crisis" was worked together, with space to think about it. Suggests that individual therapy work might follow.		They have already suffered the breakdown of one long-term placement. Likely to be anxiety about a repetition.	

to express their feelings about this shared life-crisis, and that this would be protective of the placement. Individual work could well follow at a later date.

In conclusion I will make a few brief points. Most important is that assessment of any child is only well based if the past and current context of their life is held in mind. This means that we have to explore both the family structure and functioning as it now is, and create a dialogue with parents about their concerns, as well as use the individual sessions with the child to get a picture of the child's internal world.

Therapist describes what assessments like this need. Past and present context, dialogue with parents, and sessions with child (or in this case children) need to go together.

(continued)

4. David's individual session (*continued*)

Transcript of session material	Summary of issues from point of view of therapist undertaking the assessment	Aspects of reports concerning the two children being assessed	Notes and "Memos" (a grounded-theory procedure)	Concepts and categories emerging from grounded theory Analysis
For children with disrupted experiences of care the inner world will be peopled by figures and stories which can show us what the child has made of his life, how the events in his history have been understood by him.	Inner worlds of children significant—therapy can access these.			
This is a unique individual matter, as the very different personalities of Lorraine and David exemplify.	Different children experience traumatic histories like this differently.		What explains differences between David and Lorraine? Perhaps birth order is most important factor. Lorraine as the older child had to face these anxieties before her brother. He may have been supported by her, has thus remained more expressive and able to feel his anxieties openly. Gender difference important.	*Birth order* as explanatory factor in explaining differences in children's responses to their traumatic history. Also *gender differences.*

Paying attention to what a child can tell us through play, drawings and their overall response to our close attention is the essence of what a child psychotherapist's assessment offers.	What children communicate through play, drawing and their response to therapist's close attention is what child psychotherapist's assessment offers. Note that no protocols or schedules of questions or indicators for this.	Core ideas for psychoanalytic child psychotherapy.	*No protocols* for this kind of assessment, either in its practice or its record. Descriptions, with theoretical and practical inferences drawn from them.
Integrating the perspectives of the inside and the outside, the individual and the family, is what we aim to do and what can lay the basis for appropriate treatment.		Integration of internal and external important, in Margaret Rustin's thinking.	*Internal and external aspects both important* in this conception of child psychotherapy and its form of assessment. Not the excessive preoccupation with the internal world sometimes ascribed to Klein-influenced psychoanalysts.

I would like to thank Sharon Novara for her help in setting out the table.

CHAPTER THIRTEEN

Outcome studies

Much of the demand for research in psychoanalysis in recent years has arisen from the wider insistence on the need for a scientific evidence base for medicine, and for other public services, such as education. Even the culture of evidence-based medicine is relatively recent in its dominance. Earlier, professional consensus among doctors was more likely than scientific trials to determine what treatments were offered for many illnesses. One of the leading forces in this later development has been the pharmaceutical industry. Procedures of research to find new drugs involving clinical trials, followed by licensing by the state and funded forms of treatment that create markets for patent-protected drugs, have become standard in physical and psychological medicine. In physical medicine it has been possible to demonstrate the effectiveness of this model of medical provision. "Survival rates" for many diseases have improved in response to trialled medical remedies, and overall increases in life-expectancies contribute to public confidence in this system.

But even so, scientifically calibrated medical interventions are only one determinant of health and illness. Epidemiological data show large discrepancies in susceptibility to disease and life expectancies, related to variables of income and region (Marmot, 2016; Shaw & Smith, 2008). While there have been some successes in public health measures (such as the diminution of tobacco consumption, despite the obdurate resistance of the tobacco industry) there are new epidemics the causes of which lie in the cultures of consumption. Obesity, with its attendant consequences for health, and atmospheric pollution from automobile exhausts are two of the most significant of these. Inequalities of wealth and income are closely correlated with differential susceptibility to illness: life expectancy varies between English boroughs of different average income levels by margins of several years. Important epidemiological studies have shown not only that economic disadvantage is a cause of ill health, but that in more equal societies health and well-being (e.g., the incidence of crime) is improved for nearly everyone (Wilkinson & Pickett, 2009). Measures to effect improvements in health often face resistance from, for example, those with economic interests in products harmful to health. Many of those who enjoy relative advantages in society have no objection to inequality and will defend the systems that maintain it.

The evidence-based medical model of treatment that can claim a high degree of success in the sphere of physical medicine is assumed by some to be equally applicable to the field of mental health. But physical and mental health and illness are different. Although drug therapies for various conditions of mental illness can produce significant alleviation of symptoms, they may require prolonged use and rarely give rise to a return to a sustainable state of full mental health. They can be addictive and may fail to achieve improvements for many for whom they are prescribed. A recent major review of the research literature demonstrated that anti-depressant drugs were more effective than placebos, contrary to earlier findings, but even so the claim—to be better than nothing—was a modest one (Cipriani et al., 2016). The movement to develop psychological therapies ("Improved Access to Psychological Therapies" or IAPT), which in practice has mostly meant cognitive behavioural therapy on grounds of its allegedly superior evidence base, to replace excessive reliance on drugs was a response to the failure of pharmacological treatment in relation to many forms of mental illness (Layard & Clarke, 2015). An earlier chapter referred to the sudden rise of diagnosis of attention deficit hyperactivity disorder (ADHD) and its pharmacological treatments as an instance of the irrationalities and distortions that can follow from the failure to understand the complexities of mental states and their definition as illnesses.

The evidence-based system has set up a field of competition between different means of defining and treating diseases by reference to apparently objective criteria of success and failure. The application of "evidence-based" criteria to the field of mental health has created a situation in which proponents of different models are required to justify their treatments through scientific trials of their effectiveness. This situation has created competitive relationships between practitioners of different forms of treatment, which involve issues of ideology and professional competition (for funding, clinical contracts, licenses to practice, etc.) as well as scientific measures. Indeed, scientific methods become matters of contention in this situation.

In this context, long-standing arguments about the validity of psychoanalytic, biochemical (pharmacological) and cognitive behavioural therapy (to name only three) have been renewed and vigorously pursued. The underlying grounds of the argument between these diagnostic viewpoints are in part "cultural", based on different views of human beings and what constitutes well-being. Psychoanalysis embodies a view of human nature that emphases its complexity and vulnerability to conflict and disturbance. Its therapies are strategies to enhance self-understanding as a resource in managing vulnerability, of which mental ill health is an extreme expression. This perspective has always been part of the life-world of a cultural minority, mostly located among those with higher levels of formal education and disproportionately engaged in symbolic and expressive kinds of work. The post-war welfare state saw the extension—its advocates saw this as a democratization—of this vision of human need and purpose, through the activities of its sympathizers in the fields of education and other fields of work most concerned with human relationships as well as in health. But "the psychoanalytic movement", as Ernest Gellner (1985) has characterized it, has always had its determined opponents, as well as being somewhat distant from the experience of most people.

The development of the culture of evidence-based treatment has somewhat altered the terms of the long-standing debate about the relevance of psychoanalysis. What in an earlier generation was principally a debate about the validity—the "truth claims"—of psychoanalysis as a form of knowledge has recently become more of an argument about its "effectiveness" as a form of treatment. This research climate has been greatly influenced by policymakers. However, the necessity to engage in outcome research has become widely recognized, especially by practitioners working in publicly funded clinics. It is seen as an essential resource in defending psychoanalytic psychotherapy against attack, perhaps even for avoiding its extinction. Three examples of outcome research involving substantial numbers of randomly assigned patients, in which the clinical work was undertaken by well-qualified and supervised practitioners, are described below.

Necessary as this work has been, one must take note of the kinds of research in psychoanalysis that it leaves out. The investigations through which the fundamental concepts, theories, and techniques of psychoanalysis have been developed since its beginnings have not been those of systematic outcome studies. One can see this in relation to the most significant psychoanalytic discoveries that followed Freud's own invention of the field. As examples of these we can identify these additions to the core psychoanalytic lexicon of concepts, theories, and techniques:

»   the idea of identification with the aggressor (Anna Freud)
»   the understanding of the punitive superego (Klein)
»   the nature and meaning of projective identification (Klein, Bion, Sandler)
»   the container–contained relationship in infancy, in psychoanalysis, and in other settings (Bion), and the idea of the "holding environment" (Winnicott)
»   the discovery and therapeutic use of the countertransference (Heimann, Brenman Pick)
»   the idea of transitional phenomena and transitional space (Winnicott)
»   the distinction between libidinal and destructive narcissism (Rosenfeld)
»   the origin and functions of "borderline" states of mind (Britton, Steiner)
»   the nature of autistic phenomena and levels of experience (Tustin)

These have all been major additions to psychoanalytic knowledge. They are cited because of their omnipresence in contemporary psychoanalysis and psychotherapy. They are additions to earlier formative ideas, which included the Oedipus complex, the transference, the unconscious meanings of dreams and children's play, the pathologies of hysteria, obsessional neurosis, and psychosis, and the paranoid-schizoid and depressive positions. It is difficult to imagine contemporary psychoanalytic therapies taking place that do not make use of these classifications and explanatory theories (among others) to give meaning to the phenomena of the consulting room.

But by what methods of investigation were these fundamental discoveries made? It is a paradox that the outcome studies on which the future of psychoanalysis is said to depend measure the effectiveness of therapies that were discovered within the disparaged research tradition of the clinical case study. Without such discoveries, over a long period of time, there would be no outcomes of psychoanalytic therapies to measure. We have argued in earlier chapters that investigations of unconscious structures and processes through clinical methods can be made more rigorous and accountable and have described qualitative methods of research for doing this. However, trials following the medical model do measure the effectiveness of psychological treatments for specific disorders, and are of value for this and other reasons.

Large-scale outcome studies also provide opportunities for clinical psychoanalytic research. They make clinical records available for large numbers of cases that are similar in their initial diagnosis. This contrasts with standard clinical situations where it is more usual to undertake studies of single cases whose similarities and differences can only be established retrospectively. Systematic outcome studies demand, through their design and clinical supervision, a greater consistency of technique than can commonly be assumed among clinicians. For the IMPACT study of Depression in Adolescents, which included short term psychoanalytic psychotherapy among its three treatment modalities, an *STPP Manual* was prepared to ensure that clinicians followed similar prescribed methods in their treatment of their patients. This has subsequently been published for the guidance of the larger child psychotherapy profession (Cregeen, Hughes, Midgley, Rhode, & Rustin, 2017).

A requirement of the outcome research projects described below was that clinical sessions be audio-recorded and transcribed, in part to enable compliance with treatment protocols to be assessed, and in part to facilitate later research on the case records. Session records were also written up in detail by clinicians, according to the usual psychoanalytic approach.

The existence of both audio-transcribed and clinicians' written records of sessions makes it possible to address one aspect of case study research that has long been deemed problematic by its critics (Spence, 1993): namely, the accuracy of recalled clinical notes. Since psychoanalytic theories have always been substantially based on the evidence provided by such clinical material, it is valuable that its qualities can be investigated. It was always likely that literal audio-transcription and clinical process notes would each have strengths and limitations as evidence. While verbal accuracy is the clear advantage of the audio-recording, other dimensions of the psychoanalytic process—states of feeling, non-verbal behaviour, and the play and other activity of children, and the unspoken reflections of the analyst—may be better captured by the clinician's session report. At all events, the co-existence of these two kinds of record, for considerable numbers of similar cases, provides a resource for investigating these issues.

These outcome studies thus create opportunities to generate and test hypotheses concerning both treatment effectiveness and clinical processes themselves. Innovations in treatment patterns required for purposes of an outcome study have been found to be of intrinsic clinical interest. IMPACT required that psychotherapy be offered to patients on a once-weekly basis, and for a limited period of time (28 weekly sessions for the child psychotherapy arm of the study). Although once-weekly sessions are commonly offered in public mental health services, in part because of resource constraints, and although most offers of treatment of adolescent patients are in fact taken up for less than 28 weeks, these limits of frequency and duration were initially seen as being restrictive by many child psychotherapists.

But interesting questions were raised by this framing of the project. For example, what difference does it make to the practice and experience of psychoanalytic treatment when it is offered on a once-weekly basis, and for a pre-determined number of weeks? In response to this question, it was recognized on the basis of clinical experience in this project, even before its quantitative outcomes were known, that fixed-term once-weekly psychoanalytic psychotherapy for adolescents was an intrinsically valuable form of treatment. It has indeed now been adopted as an integral element of the training of child psychotherapists, with the *STPP Treatment Manual* providing its guidelines.

Other issues were raised by this investigation. How significant is therapeutic or supportive work with the parents of child or adolescent patients, accompanying the treatment of their children, within an outcome trial? How important is it to insist on reflecting with patients on the pre-determined termination of treatment during the course of a therapy? Does the predominance of transference-based interpretation, or reliance on the countertransference, or the interpretation of negative feelings in the transference, make a difference to the development of the patient? Can one identify those attributes of patients (for example, educational attainment, relationships within a family) that are conducive to psychoanalytic treatment, and those that work against it? Can one identify distinctive and hitherto unrecognized personality structures in patients which relate to different therapeutic outcomes?

Questions of these kinds have often been asked of individual cases, and explorations through group supervision have provided scope for comparison between them. But the greater measure of standardization and the increase in scale made possible by outcome studies goes further than this, in making possible systematic study. Until now, most of the financial resources available for psychoanalytic research have been directed towards the measurement of effectiveness, not the study of clinical processes. More "fundamental" kinds of research in psychoanalysis have usually depended on the unpaid commitment of the therapists to be undertaken at all. But there is now a large archive of recorded clinical data potentially available for such research.

Outcome studies and randomized controlled trials

It is often held that the "gold standard" for the scientific validation of medical—and indeed other—interventions is the "randomized controlled trial". The prerequisites of a valid study are held to include:

» the standardization and representative nature of samples
» the randomized allocation of subjects to the procedures being trialled
» the existence of non-treated or placebo-treated "control groups"
» standardized measures to assess condition at outset, during and after treatment
» the full separation of researchers from clinicians in the conduct of a study
» follow-up measures after an adequate period post-treatment to assess long-term effects ("sleeper effects")
» adequate statistical procedures to measure the factors affecting outcomes

There are significant problems in devising trials for mental health treatments that meet all these criteria. These include difficulties at the level of diagnosis: "co-morbidity"—the conjunction of more than one pathology in individual patients—is one. Ethical constraints around offering "no treatment" to a control group is another. The problem of "random assignment" to treatment modes is a third, since the denial of choice of therapies to patients may depress their average outcomes. Furthermore, there may in the context of mental health be a lack of consensus about how well-being and recovery are defined.

Nevertheless, in recent years there have some significant outcome studies, conducted according to the principles of the randomized controlled trial, to measure the effectiveness of psychoanalytic psychotherapy. Three of these, in which the Tavistock and Portman NHS Foundation Trust has been involved with other partners, are briefly described. Each was designed to measure the comparative effectiveness of different treatments in comparison with one another, thus addressing the question of which of the competing treatments should be licensed and funded.

The Childhood Depression Project

The Biomed/ERC Outcome Study on Childhood Depression was a European Union-funded study, directed in London by Judith Trowell, David Campbell, and Maria Rhode. Its purpose was to compare individual psychoanalytic psychotherapy (IPP) with systemic family therapy (SFP). This was its design:

» Patients aged 10–14 were selected for treatment following their assessment as severely depressed, using standard psychological measures.
» A sample of 72 patients was chosen, 24 in each of three centres (in London, Athens, and Helsinki).
» Half of each centre's sample of 24 were randomly assigned to the family therapy, and half to the individual psychoanalytic psycho-therapy groups. In the individual psychoanalytic psychotherapy cases, parents were seen every two weeks by social workers for sup-portive work.
» A fixed period of once-weekly treatment (30 sessions) was offered to each patient having IPP, with 15 sessions of supportive parent work; 14 fortnightly sessions were offered for those assigned to SFP.
» Qualified psychotherapists were employed in the study, and they received high-quality supervision.
» Sessions were audio recorded in the IPP cases, video-recorded in the SFP cases.
» Assessments were made of changes in patients at the end of therapy, and at a six-month follow-up.

Findings of the study

Patients in both the IPP and SFP samples achieved significant average improvements in their mental health and social functioning, far greater than would have been predicted without treatment, given the severity of the original condition. Improvement in SFP cases was more rapid, but improvement in the IPP cases was shown by follow-up measures to have been sustained over a longer period after the conclusion of the therapy. In other words, the improvement curve measuring symptoms in the family therapy cases fell more steeply but then levelled off; in the individual psychotherapy case it fell more gradually but continued to fall for longer. Similar patterns were seen in all three European centres where the study was conducted.

Many of the child psychotherapists conducting the treatment ini-tially believed the time-limited, once-weekly pattern of treatment to be unduly limited, given the severity of the condition being treated, and also expectations within the professional field that treatment for such patients might need to be both of longer duration and of greater frequency. From this perspective, the outcomes of the study were all the more impressive. They provided sufficient evidence of the effectiveness of time-limited psychoanalytic child psychotherapy to justify the commissioning of the larger "Improving Mood with Psychoanalytic and Cognitive Therapies" (IMPACT) study into severe adolescent depression, which followed it between 2011 and 2015. The findings of these studies have led to the recognition in the National Institute of Clinical Excellence (NICE) guidelines of psychoanalytic child psychotherapy as an admissible treatment for severe childhood and adolescent depression.

Limitations of the research design

There were significant limitations in the design of this study:

» The total sample size of 72 is smaller than the minimum size of 100 conventionally required to achieve statistical significance. This disqualified reports of the study from being published in some high-ranking journals.
» The study compared one mode of psychotherapy with another by random selection of patients, but lacked a control sample that would have compared these treatments with "no treatment" (deemed ethically unacceptable) or a standardized "treatment as usual" model (which could have been included). The consequence of this choice was that the research could not compare the improvement achieved against that which might have taken place in the absence of the specialized interventions being trialled.
» The shortfall below the required statistical threshold of 100 cases had a circumstantial cause in problems with patient recruitment to the study. However, because the degree of improvement obtained was so far from marginal, it seems unlikely that much difference would have resulted from an increase of 30 in the sample size needed to reach the standard statistical threshold.

One impressive feature of this research was its demonstration that a study deploying quantitative methods to measure outcomes could provide not only gross measures of treatment effectiveness, but also new understandings of the treatment process. The method of fixed-term once-weekly psychoanalytic psychotherapy, which had been adopted as a necessity for the outcome study, was initially a challenge to many psychotherapists' beliefs about what was appropriate treatment for seriously depressed patients. The discovery from the research, and from clinical experience within it, that this pattern of treatment could be especially suited to adolescent patients in their transitional life-stage has been significant.

It is clear that detailed analysis of the clinical records of the treated cases could provide further insights into the treatment process, relevant to the crucial question of "what works for whom". The book (Trowell, 2011) that reports this research includes several chapters in which child and family psychotherapists and their supervisors review clinical cases. These are perceptive discussions of the clinical process and contain many suggestive hypotheses. For example, it seemed that it was beneficial for therapists to draw their patients' attention to the fixed period of the therapy and to its unavoidable conclusion after the specified number of weeks, even though this exposed them to their anger and disappointment. Attending to the time-frame could be therapeutic in itself, as patient and therapist share responsibility for using the time available to them. It was found that the "research framing" of the treatment (with its mechanical recording of sessions, its ongoing psychological measures, its regular supervision, and its firm regulation) far from being therapeutically damaging, as had been feared initially, was found to be mainly beneficial. One clinical report describes that it had been therapeutically valuable to have been helped to withstand pressure from a patient and his parent to extend the treatment beyond the stipulated period, because of the value of the example of boundary-setting for this family. Reports of the work with parents make it clear how essential this dimension of the IPP treatment was in encouraging parents to support their children's therapy. Reports of the systemic family therapy work describe the positive value to therapists of their model of "live supervision", and threw light on why improvement in these patients was on average more rapid than with the IPP patients. They showed how families' focus of attention was initially shifted away from the "problem adolescent" who had been presented as the one needing treatment to the larger family system in which his or her difficulties were located, leading to a sharing of emotional burdens placed on the "index patient", the depressed adolescent. Both the family therapists and child psychotherapists engaged in this study attached great importance to interactive and projective processes, both within the families to which the adolescents belonged and within the therapeutic situation, although within partially different theoretical frames (Trowell & Dowling, 2011).

THE IMPACT STUDY: improving mood with psychoanalytic psychotherapy and cognitive behavioural therapy

This successor to the Childhood Depression Study was the largest outcome study of its kind that has ever been undertaken. Its sample size was 470 cases, treated in three regions of England (London, East Anglia, and the North West). These cases were randomly assigned, almost equal numbers to each of three treatments. These, as described in the project design, were

» 28 once-weekly psychoanalytic psychotherapy sessions, with supportive parental work, designated as short-term psychoanalytic psychotherapy (STPP), with 7 sessions offered to parents
» cognitive behavioural therapy (CBT), 20 sessions over a 30-week period
» a brief psychosocial intervention (BPI), 12 sessions over a 20-week period

Manuals to ensure consistency of treatments were prepared for all three treatment modalities.

In effect, the outcomes measured the programmed interventions of three different professions: psychoanalytic child psychotherapists (with social work or similar support) clinical psychologists, and child and family psychiatrists. Again absent from the study was a "control group", with no treatment or placebo treatment. This option was once more ruled out for ethical reasons, and a "Treatment as Usual" option (in which a third of the sample would be treated within the NHS without any specialist intervention) was initially adopted as a substitute. This modality, however, evolved once the study had begun. It became a brief psychosocial intervention designed by psychiatrists, whose aim was to standardize high-quality psychiatric practice for depressed adolescents. It seems certain that the treatment provided in this arm of the study exceeded "Treatment as Usual" in quality and consistency. In effect, a third specialist arm of treatment was constituted, to be compared with the two modalities whose effectiveness the study was originally designed to measure. The absence of a genuine "control group" was methodologically a disadvantage, since it left unknown the comparative advantage of three in-effect specialist treatments over standard practice.

There are, however, compensating gains from the improvement of the mixed-mode model of care provided by psychiatrists, which may bring lasting clinical benefit, as this BPI model was manualized and can now be put to wider use. (CBT also followed a treatment manual.) As we have seen, the child psychotherapists had already decided to develop their own STPP model as a standard form of practice, re-writing and publishing their manual in book form and incorporating this method of treatment as a component element of their professional training.

Randomized controlled trials of this kind are primarily intended to investigate the comparative effectiveness of different treatments and thereby to influence decisions about their authorization (notably through NICE guidelines). However, it is striking that developments in clinical practice that took place in the context of the study are now being incorporated within professional practice and training, formalizing the inclusion of time-limited psychotherapy, which was previously practiced in some centres but not systematically presented as a child psychotherapy specialism.

A study of this kind postulates hypotheses at its outset, which it then tests. In this project, the initial hypotheses were that both STPP and CBT would be superior to BPI in their treatment outcomes. There was also a question of whether any superiority that STPP might show over CBT would justify its probably higher unit cost. Contrary to these hypotheses, the result of the study was that the three treatments achieved essentially similar positive results. STPP was not significantly more effective than CBT and was marginally more expensive to deliver. However, these differences in relative effectiveness and cost were slight. By far the most important finding was that each of these treatments was effective in reducing the symptoms of depression, both by the end of treatment and after the one-year follow-up. Although the framing of the project ensured competition and rivalry between the three treatment arms and their sponsoring professions, its findings gave each of them grounds for satisfaction. In the context of the general neglect and underfunding of mental health services, the IMPACT study provides grounds for support for each of these forms of treatment. (Its design and outcomes are reported in Goodyer et al., 2017.)

It was a valuable feature of IMPACT that it sought to measure not merely treatment, but also cost-effectiveness. Given the current pressure on mental health budgets and the difficulties in gaining sanction for psychoanalytic treatments, cost-effectiveness is a vital dimension of outcome research. What, however, ought to be taken into economic account is not only the cost of treatments, but also those borne by health services and society more broadly as a result of persisting mental illness. It has been shown that the long-term costs of persisting depression (leaving aside qualitative considerations of human well-being) are high.[1] Severe depression affects educational outcomes and the capacity to work, produce, and earn, and it also has later consequences for family formation and the intergenerational transmission of mental health problems. One needs a longitudinal study of a sample that includes those severely depressed in adolescence to establish what such long-term human and economic costs are. It seems likely that the long-term benefits of a remission of depression in adolescents (with so much of their lives still open to them) are large, and that the "opportunity costs" of not providing effective treatment are high.[2] For this reason the limiting of the measure of improvement in the sample to one year after completion of the treatment was unfortunate, although even this was a longer-term effect than is usually measured.

One striking feature of the study was the relatively low level of attendance at therapeutic sessions on the part of all of the sample, including those assigned to STPP: the mean attendance of STPP patients was 11 out of 28 planned sessions (39%), compared with 6 out of 12 (50%) for BPI, and 9 out of 20 (45%) for CBT. Trowell (2011) reports only "variable attendance", giving no figure, although it seems likely that a higher proportion of sessions were attended than in IMPACT, because of more intensive parent work and the younger age of the patients. The measured effectiveness of the treatments is also a little less: 74.3% of the CDS sample are without clinical symptoms at the end of treatment, against 68% of those in the IMPACT. The most remarkable finding of the Childhood Depression Study was that six months after the completion of the treatment, 100% of the sample were without clinical symptoms. The report of the IMPACT findings indicates a smaller post-treatment improvement and also warns that their post-treatment data is rather weak because of sample attrition.

There are different possible reasons for these. The smaller sample size of the Childhood Depression Study, where treatment was undertaken with a smaller number of patients in only three centres, instead of with a larger overall number distributed among 18 centres in the case of IMPACT, may have made it easier to deliver treatment to a higher standard. In the CDS, with only 35 cases in each treatment mode, divided between the Tavistock Clinic in London and in one centre each in Athens and Helsinki, it is known that therapists and parent workers were more highly selected to take part in the study than was possible with the 470 cases of IMPACT. Individual clinicians could also each see more cases in CDS than in the larger study, probably leading to more consistent work. On the other hand IMPACT may have come closer to normal clinical conditions in its service delivery.

A further possible explanation of the differences in the outcomes of the two studies lies in the mean ages of their sample populations. The average age of the IMPACT patients was 15.6 (ages 11–17), that of the Adolescent Depression study was 12 (ages 9–14). So far as attendance (or compliance) is concerned, the younger population will have been less independent of parents and other carers than the older adolescents, who were more free to make their own choices about attending therapy. It is also possible that parent work with younger adolescents is more effective than with those who are older, who are likely to be more emotionally separate from parents. It is also possible that depression is, in any case, more responsive to treatment in the younger age-group.

Randomized assignment to treatment modalities may itself depress outcomes in trials of this kind. If the relative suitability of patients for different modes of treatment were ascertained by their prior assessment, treatment success might be enhanced. It is possible—or indeed likely—that randomized allocation to a form of treatment, rather than an exercise of choice by patients, reduces their commitment and thus outcomes. This issue may well be particularly important in the context of mental heath treatments where engagement in and understanding of the treatment process may have a larger role than with physical treatments.

Positive advantages were found in treatments being undertaken in the context of a research study. There is often a better quality of organization and sometimes a greater staff commitment because of the research dimension. It seems that the visits and interviews by research staff to which patients were subject may have had an implicitly therapeutic function of their own. Some patients were reported as being unclear about the difference in roles of the therapists and researchers they met. Indeed a possible reason for the similarities of outcome of the different treatment modes are the elements that all of them have in common, in offering a relationship of interest and care to patients (whatever its particular therapeutic rationale) and perhaps also—from a psychoanalytic perspective—encouraging patients to reflect on and give a symbolic form to their experiences. Other researchers have shown that differences of theoretical orientation among psychotherapists have little bearing on the outcomes of their treatments.

The clinical records made available by these trials provide substantial opportunity for qualitative studies of the clinical process, with much larger numbers of patients with similar presenting problems and with more standardized and meticulous records of treatments than normally occur in the field. There is now the possibility, through detailed analysis of these records, to investigate the effects of differences in the samples, in family support, and in clinical practice, more than is usually feasible. Most qualitative analyses of child psychotherapy cases to date have been undertaken with very small samples, often as single-case studies, though with some ongoing comparison between them in such forms as clinical workshops. Progress has been made through methods of data analysis such as grounded theory and IPA in clarifying what happens in the course of a treatment. Usually this has depended on the discoveries of individual clinicians, and their supervisors, as they work through session material. It is possible that a different approach could be used with larger samples, through developing coding frames from particular cases that could then be "applied", to test hypotheses. While a more "industrial-scale" approach to data analysis might well lessen the possibility of new discoveries arising from individual cases, it could have a corresponding benefit in establishing the validity of specific hypotheses—for example, concerning the effects of frequency of attendance, of concurrent parent-work, or of interpretations that focus on negative feelings.

Parallel to the main trial, a qualitative study—IMPACT–My Experience (IMPACT–ME)—is exploring young people's experience of overcoming depression and of treatments in the IMPACT trial, and that of their parents. This is making use of data obtained from interviews (Midgley, Ansaldo, & Target, 2014; Midgley et al., 2015; Stapley, Midgley, & Target, 2015).

Advantage has been taken, in a doctoral study by Miriam Creaser (2015), of the co-existence of audio-transcripts of treatment sessions with written-up clinicians' session records, to compare each of these forms of data (or "inscription devices") with the other with a small sample of cases. It emerges that there were substantial differences between these two forms of record, more than the high level of accuracy conventionally attributed to clinical write-ups would have predicted.[3] In no straightforward way could the clinicians' written-up record be regarded as merely an abridged version of the literal transcript. Significant processes of selection were involved in what was described by the clinicians. Their accounts provided in essence a narrative of the transference relationship, omitting other topics recorded in the transcripts. They also captured phenomena, from their observation and self-reflection, which were not accessible from the transcript alone. It will be valuable to undertake further research into these different kinds of data. The belief sometimes expressed by analysts that an electronic record of a session can add nothing to their trained recollection can no longer be accepted.

The Tavistock Adult Depression Study (TADS)

This randomized control trial of psychoanalytic psychotherapy provided for severely depressed adult patients was the first of its kind and scale. A total of 129 patients were included in the study, selected from the 308 originally screened and the 235 interviewed as potential participants. The patients were suffering from high levels of depression of at least two years' duration, and a criterion for selection for the study was that they had been the subjects of at least two previously unsuccessful treatments. It was pointed out that a clinical method of once-weekly psychoanalytic psychotherapy has been developed for use within the public sector, but that it had been little researched.

The theory employed in LTPP assumes that, in patients with treatment-resistant depression, problems with psychosocial functioning impair help-seeking and illness-combating behaviours, and may also have an emotional impact upon health care/service providers in a way that affects the care they offer (Fonagy et al., 2015).

The justification for the 18 months of treatment provided (60 50-minute sessions) was the idea that in such a lengthy (compared with a shorter) treatment patients are gradually able to internalize a psychological capacity which enables them to relate to pathogenic personal experiences, memories, feelings, beliefs and relationships in a more reflective, yet also more active way (Taylor et al., 2012).

The sample was divided into two nearly equal groups of 67 and 62 and randomly assigned to long-term psychoanalytic psychotherapy (LTPP) and to a well-managed form of Treatment as Usual (TAU): this was psychiatric care involving different treatments as indicated by patients' needs. The psychoanalytic psychotherapy was provided by qualified and experienced clinicians at the Tavistock and Portman NHS Foundation Trust. It seems to have been the case that the quality and consistency of psychoanalytic therapy provided was high, more so than might be expected to be feasible in many contemporary services.

The trial revealed a substantial superiority of the psychoanalytic psychotherapy (LTPP) over treatment as usual (TAU), but it is notable that this superiority became manifest only by the end of the two-year follow-up period, after the end of the treatment. At the end of the 18 months of treatment itself, the outcomes of the two treatments were little different. The eventual post-follow-up states represented a significant improvement in the well-being of the patients treated, but nevertheless fell short of a complete remission or "cure". This, however, was unsurprising, considering the chronic and long-standing nature of the depressive illness being treated. The movement was generally from severe to moderate depression, which, with patients with this diagnosis, was accounted a success. The significance of the fact that improvement persisted through to the end of the follow-up period with LTPP, but not with TAU, may be that these patients had acquired a greater resource for reflecting on and managing their depression, through their experience of psychoanalytic psychotherapy. (The research findings are summarized in Fonagy et al., 2015 and in Taylor et al., 2012.)

The study demonstrates the effectiveness of psychoanalytic psychotherapy compared with "treatment as usual", but it did not compare it with an alternative specialist treatment, such as CBT. (In the Adolescent Depression Study, the situation was reversed: CBT was a treatment arm, but there was no TAU control group.) This study measured the health economic costs attributable to these patients in the 12 months prior to treatment, showing them to be substantial

(McCrone et al., 2017). Lost work and unpaid care formed the largest element of these costs). The research did not measure any change in these costs subsequent to treatment.

The principal published report of the study to date is concerned almost exclusively with demonstrating the measured results of the trial, and it contains a great deal of condensed technical information concerning diagnostic measures and statistical procedures. There is little information available at this point concerning the conduct and experience of the psychoanalytic psychotherapy and the treatment-as-usual modes, although from a psychoanalytic and psychiatric point of view these are of great interest. Presentations of case material have revealed interesting and moving descriptions of patients and their own and their therapists' experience of their treatment. As with the other trials reported above, the existence of such a large number of transcripts of audio-recorded clinical treatments represents a valuable resource for subsequent qualitative analysis of the treatment process that is being undertaken. Research-based psychological measures undertaken during the study—a source of data distinct and separate from the clinical record—has revealed differences between anaclitic and introjective kinds of depression, a psychoanalytic conceptualization also described in the *STPP Manual* (Rost, Luyten, & Fonagy, 2018).

The articulation and cross-referencing of "quantitative" and "qualitative" findings can be difficult to achieve. The researchers responsible for testing and measurement procedures may be non-expert in the understanding of clinical processes, and the clinicians may be non-expert in diagnostic and assessment measures. However, it would be desirable to bring about further creative dialogue between these different modes of understanding.

These studies have demonstrated that psychoanalytic therapies can be made the object of randomized controlled trials like other therapeutic interventions. Such trials need not infringe the conditions necessary for psychoanalytic psychotherapy, although there are some differences compared with conventional treatments (for example, random patient assignment, regular contact of patients with researchers, assessment, follow-ups, audio-recording of sessions). In the TADS study it was found that patients experienced the involvement of researchers and their regular contact with them not as an imposition or interference, but as an additional supportive resource for them.

Of the greatest significance is that all three of these trials reported positive outcomes for psychoanalytic treatments, using research methods that meet contemporary scientific standards. Since psychoanalysis, by comparison with other therapies such as CBT and drug-treatments, has often been described as lacking an "evidence base", this is an important development. The research engagement of psychoanalysts and child psychotherapists has been of benefit in itself, since they have seemed at times to be averse to the scientific scrutiny of their work. The fact that psychoanalytic psychotherapies produced outcomes at least equal to those obtained from other treatments should serve to qualify them for recognition as acceptable forms of treatment.[4]

Some critical reflections

Outcome studies of these kinds have limitations. The mean outcomes of treatments of a large patient sample, even if positive, may leave unanswered questions about the differential success or failure of treatments, concerning who benefited most and who least. The problem is that criteria of statistical validity that can be achieved with an entire sample may not be attainable for its smaller subsets. It may be that lesser standards of proof should be tolerated in the investigation of such differences, which may be those of most relevance to clinical practice.

A limitation of these studies lies in the fact that each of them has investigated, for reasons of valid research design, just one specific clinical pathology: severe depression. In a system that relies on current diagnostic criteria, logical inferences cannot be made from the findings from the treatment of one defined psychopathology to those with other diagnoses. In principle one might expect to see systematic studies of the outcome of treatments of the entire range of mental illnesses. In reality, such studies are unlikely to take place, for reasons of expense and priority. There is a vast discrepancy between the resources made available for research into mental illnesses and physical illnesses (such as cancer).

The diagnostic criteria used in psychiatry and mental health are, in any case, a much blunter instrument than many of those employed in physical medicine. Psychoanalytic understandings of mental illnesses are, in any case, divergent from the symptom-based methods that dominate psychiatry. The existence of "co-morbidity" (multiple disorders) in many mental health patients in itself indicates the inadequacy of standard diagnostic criteria. Psychoanalytic understandings focus on unconscious relationships to primary emotional objects, with symptoms such as severe depression and anxiety as their expression. The fact that clinicians working with these perspectives have achieved positive outcomes with patients in one symptom category (severe depression) may lead one to anticipate comparable success with others (such as anxieties) whose origin also lies, in their view, in a disturbed internal world. Small-scale studies and even methods of routine clinical audit can be means of evaluating and refining clinical judgements. Although such methods do not achieve the "gold standard" of randomized double-blind outcome trials, they can nevertheless add to the kinds of knowledge that are most useful in clinical practice.

Notes

1. "In the United Kingdom, the prevalence of major depressive disorder is estimated to be between 5% and 10% of people seen in primary care settings and 10% to 14% of medical inpatients. . . . Between 10% and 15% of older people have symptoms of depression" (NICE, 2014, p. 1).

2. A reason for giving high priority to child and adolescent mental health services is that such patients often still have significant support available to them (from families, schools, and colleges, for example), and that their early mental health difficulties may not yet have caused irrevocable damage to their life-chances. This is perhaps in contrast to the situation of many seriously ill adult mental health patients.

3. This assumption has been challenged, for example by Donald Spence (2000, 2002, 2007).

4. At the time of writing IMPACT had received more favourable recognition from the NICE guidelines procedures than has TADS.

CHAPTER FOURTEEN

Observational research methods

I n recent decades there has been much growth in learning and teaching practices that make use of psychoanalytic observational methods. The first of these was "psychoanalytic infant observation", initially developed as a practice at the Tavistock Clinic by Esther Bick in 1949. A two-year experience of weekly infant observation has been the prerequisite of clinical training in psychoanalytic child and adolescent psychotherapy in Britain since then.[1] It has also been adopted in a one-year form as part of the training of psychoanalysts in the British Psychoanalytical Society, and in other professional trainings, notably in social work (Le Riche & Tanner, 1998; Tanner, 1999; Trowell & Miles, 1991). "Infant observation" has in fact become an international movement in its own right, with regular conferences organized by two different quasi-federations, one largely Anglophone and the other largely Francophone. *The International Journal of Infant Observation* is now in its twenty-first year of publication, and several book-length volumes of papers on this field of work have been published (Briggs, 2002; Hingley-Jones, Parkinson, & Allain, 2017; Miller, Rustin, Rustin, & Shuttleworth, 1989; Reid, 1997; Sternberg, 2005; Thomson-Salo, 2014).

At the Tavistock, young child observation (of children aged 2–5, beyond infancy) is undertaken alongside infant observation; it also been the subject of significant publication (Adamo & Rustin, 2014). Infant and young child observation are normally practised and studied within courses that introduce psychoanalytic perspectives. For some students these are a prerequisite of a subsequent clinical psychoanalytic training, but for others the purpose is to enhance their understanding and capability in different kinds of professional work—for example, with children and families if they are social workers, teachers, or nurses.

A further development of this method has taken place within these occupations, most substantially in social work. This naturalistic observational method has been found to throw light on many contexts in which relationships of care, learning, and development are central. Classroom interactions (Price, 2005), therapeutic communities, the care of the elderly, hospital neo-natal care, and day-nurseries are examples of such settings. The journal *Infant Observation* is a source of articles on much of this work.

The methods of infant and young child observation have been further developed to enhance learning where observers are active participants and not merely passive observers in a work-setting. This adapted method is usually termed "work discussion"—psychoanalytic work discussion would describe it better. This method, also devised at the Tavistock, involves the presentation in supervised seminars of issues of psychosocial significance arising from experiences in work settings. These are not wholly "observational" in their nature, as is the case with infant and young child observation, since participants are expected to be involved in active roles of some kind, and their experiences in such work are part of the field of study. Sometimes work discussion may come close to a form of clinical supervision, where participants are presenting therapeutic work, but its main purpose is to facilitate reflection on varieties of non-clinical roles and relationships. Examples of this work are presented in M. E. Rustin and Bradley (2008) and the first international conference on "Work Discussion" took place in Vienna in June 2016. (Papers from the conference were published in *Infant Observation*, 1918, Vol. 21, Nos. 1–2.)

The method of infant observation has been further developed by Robert Hinshelwood and Wilhelm Skogstad in *Observing Organisations* (2000) for the study of organizational settings in the field of health care. Their chosen method followed the infant observation protocols, with observers visiting to observe an institutional setting for an hour per week for approximately 12 weeks, at a regular time, and attending a supervised seminar to discuss their experiences. The initial aim of this work was to support the training of psychiatrists, as a means of deepening understanding of the context in which mental illness was treated, and in *Observing Organisations* contributors describe the considerable impact of the experience on them. Hinshelwood and Skogstad recognized that their method could be seen as a form of research into the institutions observed. Although from a research point of view the protocol of only 12 one-hour visits to an institution and reliance on passive observation as the primary source of data had its limitations, nevertheless the published papers captured the often troubling climate of relationships in settings of mental health care.

These practices were first intended for professional development rather than being programmes of research. However, they always depended on offering students first-hand experience of learning and have often given rise to new understandings of the contexts in which observations were made. Discovering connections between psychoanalytic concepts and theories and the experiences to which they give additional meaning has always been central to this work. The belief has been that psychoanalytic understanding depends on learning from emotional experience, as well as from psychoanalytic ideas. An element of observation, including reflection on one's own states of mind, is a central element of all psychoanalytically informed practice. For these educational purposes, psychoanalytic observation is defined as a specific form of learning. But once developed, these capacities are called upon to enhance many kinds of working practice and become part of a larger totality of skills.

One can, for example, note the central importance of observational capabilities in the development of organizational consultancy within the Tavistock tradition, based on psychoanalytic and sociosystemic principles. Consultancy work in many kinds of institutions has involved the close observation of human interactions, with sensitivity to unconscious dynamics as one of its key resources. Many significant publications report this work (Huffington, Halton, Armstrong, & Pooley, 2004; Obholzer & Roberts, 1994). A recent collection, *Social Defences against Anxiety: Explorations in Paradigm* (Armstrong & Rustin, 2015) revisited Isobel Menzies' famous 1960 paper on the nursing system of a hospital, examining how much of its argument needed to be revised in the light of changes that had taken place during the 55 years since its publication. Practices derived from the method of work discussion were described by several contributors as relevant responses to the occupational anxieties they investigated.

As, over many years, reports of infant and young child observations and of experiences in work settings were discussed, substantive discoveries were being made. These concerned, for example, the experience of infants and young children within families, hospital settings, and day care, and the complexities of relationships within institutions. The enhancement of capacities through training in observational methods can itself lead to changes in the institutions being observed. Thus even the primary training function of infant observation and its adjuncts has made a contribution to knowledge. A recent collection of papers, *Observation in Health and Social Care* (Hingley-Jones, Parkinson, & Allain, 2017) describes several work-settings in which observational practices have made a difference.

Understandings were accumulating for some time before it was recognized that infant observation and its cognate activity amounted to a field of research in its own right. This was in the context of the larger debate about research methods in psychoanalysis, which has been discussed in earlier chapters. What was proposed in 1989 as a potential field of infant observation research could, in just over 20 years, become the subject of a survey of what had by now been achieved (Urwin & Sternberg, 2012).[2]

The development of this field has not been without its arguments. One issue was whether psychoanalytic research can be successfully undertaken in settings other than those of clinical practice. The orthodox psychoanalytic view is that while infant observation is a valuable pre-clinical element in psychoanalytic training, it can add little or nothing to the knowledge base of psychoanalysis. The siting of infant observation as a very early psychoanalytic experience for trainees gives some circumstantial support to this point of view, since most of those who undertake observations usually begin with little psychoanalytic knowledge. How, then, could it be expected that most infant and young child observers would contribute to research in this field?

A theoretical argument has been advanced to the effect that observational studies have no role in the generation of psychoanalytic knowledge. According to this, the transference relationship between analyst and analysand is the principal mode of access to the unconscious mind. Infant mental life is best understood through the traces it leaves in unconscious states of mind of adults or children, which can be accessed in clinical practice, through the evidence of dreams, free associations, play (in the case of children), and through the understanding of the phenomena of the transference and countertransference. It is through psychoanalytic interpretations and from an understanding of patients' responses to these that the truth of conjectures about unconscious mental states of infantile origin is ascertained. This argument asserts that transference-based practice is the only solid ground on which psychoanalytic theories can be built.

The most influential advocate of this view has been André Green, although the object of his insistence on the irrelevance of observational studies to psychoanalysis was not the Tavistock infant observational method, but the laboratory, protocol-based forms of infant observation practiced by developmental researchers such as Daniel Stern (1985) and Colwyn Trevarthen (2010; Trevarthen & Aitken, 2001).[3] In a public debate (Sandler, Sandler, & Davies, 2000), which took place between advocates of structured observational methods and Green's psychoanalytic purism, the receptive and unstructured form of infant observation developed by Bick was largely disregarded. It seems that when Green later became aware of the naturalistic "psychoanalytic" approach to infant observation from the traditions founded by Esther Bick, his own antipathy to it lessened.[4]

More recently, there has been a further critique of the view that infant observational methods can be a source of psychoanalytic discovery, by Steven Groarke (2008, 2010) a psychoanalyst with considerable experience of teaching infant observation. He has been critical of the view that infant observation can be a potential source of psychoanalytic knowledge. He holds that its value consists in its experience of learning in an emotionally significant situation, rather than as a source of information framed in conceptual terms. This position depends in part on a broader approach to experiences of "being" (which he believes should have primacy) rather than of "knowing", which is set out in the philosophical writings of Gadamer, but also on the view—a distinction that he shares with André Green—that the development of knowledge in psychoanalysis depends on the testing of analytic conjectures about unconscious states of mind through interpretation, feasible in the analytic situation but not in that of infant observation. Rustin, in his replies to these criticisms, agreed that indeed the main purpose of infant observational work lay in the development of the sensibilities of observers (M. J. Rustin, 2011a, 2011b). However, he defended the view that infant observational methods were contributing new knowledge to the psychoanalytic field.

There are implicitly theoretical as well as methodological issues at stake in this argument. Melanie Klein's and, subsequently, Bion's and Winnicott's interests in the earliest relationships between mother and baby were the basis for the interest in what can be directly observed of their interactions. Klein's belief that the infant has a relation to its object from birth makes the nature and perception of the object (notably the breast) from a baby's point view of great significance. The intensity of the emotions of the baby towards mother that Klein had described (e.g., the extremities of cannibalistic and invasive attack on mother's body, as well as the intensities of love) encouraged attention to what one might observe of these states, if one looked. But most crucial was the idea of the relationship between "container and contained" as the essence of the maternal function. Bion's insight was that it was through this process of "containment" (the mother's mental function in processing and modulating the states of mind of her infant) that the baby's mind was formed. Bion proposed that the oscillation between disintegrated and more focused states of mind could be observed in psychotic patients within the consulting room. He suggested that what he had observed in that setting could be understood as analogous to the mental experiences of infants, especially if these were in relationships with mothers or carers where no adequate containing function had been present. It is to be noted that Esther Bick's (1964, 1968) early infant observation work, and her investigation through this of experiences of somatic and psychological anxiety in infants, was taking place in close parallel with Bion's theoretical conjectures. It seems likely that these gifted psychoanalysts influenced each other's thinking.

This focus on the first months of life was a significant departure from Freud's—and, indeed, Anna Freud's—view of development, which gave its primary attention to its post-infancy phases. According to their view, it is only with the emergence of the classical Oedipus complex and the repression of oedipal desires that the unconscious mind emerges as a distinct entity.[5] The primary narcissism asserted by Freud as the first phase of development, is, from this perspective, almost a state of innocence. There is no innocence, however, in Klein's phase of infancy, in which babies are subject almost from the start of life to emotional storms of love, hate, and terror in relation to their object. Whether one can describe these earliest states of mind as "unconscious" is uncertain, in so far as "unconsciousness" depends for its meaning on its contrast with the conscious. It seems to be the case that the unconscious, in its intense and alternately loving and hating forms, is all of mental life, until a mental apparatus and a self-reflective capacity emerges, and a distinction between what is conscious and what is not then gains its relevance.

The idea that understanding of these early states of mind might be obtained through the practice of infant observation was supported by a closely related theoretical development, which also initially took place within the Klein–Bion tradition, though it became later incorporated into the psychoanalytic mainstream. This was the idea of the countertransference as a source of understanding. Countertransference states of mind were evoked in the analyst, it was held, through the effects of projective identification—that is, the evacuative or communicative ways in which unbearable aspects of a mind were lodged in the mind of its object. This was held by Bion to be both a phenomenon of infant–mother relationships and of the transference and countertransference states that arise within psychoanalysis. It is because of the phenomena of the transference and countertransference that infant observation constitutes such a valuable space for learning about unconscious mental life. It is through the unconscious transmission of baby's states of mind and feeling, in particular to mother, that observers can gain access to the intense states of mind that pervade the relationships of mother and baby. (There are often also wider family relationships—for example, between parents and with siblings—to be taken into account.) Such states of feeling may also be communicated to the seminar group in which the observer is working. These may include strong emotions of ambivalence—for example, identification with a supposedly neglected baby, sympathy for an over-stressed mother, jealousy of the maternal–baby couple—which may be unconsciously distributed among group members. Differences of view and feeling expressed within a seminar may reflect the conflicted aspects of the observer's own response to the family she is observing.

It is in large part through the immersion of observers in the emotional force-field of the infant observation that access is given to the mental life of infants, and also of the parents whose role in the earliest months is to live in a sympathetic or symbiotic relationship to them. Those who disbelieve that much can be learned of psychoanalytic interest from infant observation contrast the supposedly "external" witnessing of mother–baby behaviours in the observational hour with the access to unconscious states gained in the psychoanalytic clinical setting. But the feelings evoked in infant observation are far from merely "external". It is the resonances between mother's and baby's states of mind, and the states of mind of observers, that explain why infant observation is such a powerful way of learning about the unconscious, and thus about early mental life.

It is only in the last 10 or so years that the potential of infant observation as a method of psychoanalytic research has become fully recognized (Rustin, 2006; Urwin & Sternberg, 2012). The practice of research involves a move from the observation of what is happening in a particular family towards a more generalized recognition of kinds or patterns of development. This move from the individual to the typical is similar to the ways in which new understandings emerge in clinical psychoanalytic practice. There, particular "cases" or unconscious processes come to be recognized as instances of distinct conceptual kinds. It is through these cumulative understandings that the lexicon of psychoanalytic ideas has developed.

The most influential psychoanalytic discovery to have been made through the use of infant observation came very early on, in the work of its pioneer, Esther Bick. Her paper on the "Second Skin" (1968) identified a pattern of development in infants that took place when maternal containment had been, as she conjectured, insufficient. She saw that in this circumstance infants could evolve a form of "self-containment" that was simultaneously both somatic and psychological. The anxiety experienced in their early life by such insufficiently held or contained infants was about "falling to pieces", of being unable to develop a boundary around themselves that would protect them sufficiently from excessive external and internal stimuli. "Second-skin" infants were seen to have created an abnormally rigid psychological and bodily carapace to hold themselves together where parental figures had been unable to provide sufficient containment for them. The everyday activities of the parenting of infants—soothing, holding, feeding, cleaning, keeping warm, etc.—are about managing excesses of bodily and psychological stimuli that would otherwise overwhelm infants. Bick brought together in her work both an acute observational sensitivity and a complex and subtle grasp of psychoanalytic ideas, and it was through these capabilities that she was able to identify, in the young children she described, a distinct developmental pattern. Bick's paper is an example of the way in which, in psychoanalysis as in other fields, even a small number of well-understood "cases" can make additions to knowledge of lasting value and influence.

The character-adaptation, in infants and young children, which Bick characterized as the "second-skin" formation, has become a valuable insight in the context of young child observation, in understanding the responses of certain children to the stresses of separation involved in day nursery care. Donald Meltzer's paper "A One-Year-Old Goes to Nursery" (2007) described one such child coping with painful separation from parental care by excessive self-reliance and insensitivity to his contact with other children, and by a tendency to repeatedly bump into them and knock them aside, as if they could barely be recognized as having feelings of their own.

Stephen Briggs' doctoral research project, published as *Growth and Risk in Infancy* (1997), made use of data gathered from observations of infants deemed by referrers at the outset to be at some developmental risk. This study was unusual in employing a comparative method, with five observed cases. Its outcome was the development of a typology of container–contained relationship, which drew on the ideas of Wilfred Bion and Gianna Williams. Its classifications, using a topographical idea of shapes, were of three kinds of containing relationship: concave (receptive), convex (intrusive), and flat (unresponsive). Briggs mapped the patterns of relationship that he observed between mothers and infants against these more abstract models of containment. While the "kinds" he identified provide valuable concepts, the "fit" between the particular qualities of each observation and these classifications was unavoidably imperfect. Briggs described how the transference–countertransference relationships between himself and the observed families contributed to his understanding of them. This was a complicated experience. Sometimes his anxieties brought him into touch with a mother's neediness and distress, but in another instance a family seemed to be showing him that any worries that he (and perhaps others from the professional world to which be belonged) might have, had little justification. His was, after all, a study of families where an infant was believed to be at possible risk.

Briggs' study was unusual in bringing together a focus that arose from its researcher's field of social work, with an infant observational method whose primary attention is usually to "normal" patterns of development. This was a valuable conjunction of approaches, bringing the exploratory and non-judgmental approach of the infant observational approach to bear on situations that can sometimes give rise to concern. For the most part, where infant observations have been undertaken for educational and developmental purposes, it has been usual to avoid the selection of families where there were believed to be risks. The concern has been to avoid exposing observers to situations that might call for a clinical response, which they would not be qualified to provide. Whereas therapeutic practice with children and families has necessarily been concerned with experiences of difficulty, the main focus of psychoanalytic observational studies has been on less troubled areas of the developmental spectrum.

However, it has become recognized in recent years that observational approaches have value in both the understanding and alleviation, of problems with relationships in the early years. On the one hand, it was appreciated that skills in infant and young child observation could be valuable for professionals who work in settings where such problems are being addressed. Examples of these are mother–baby clinics, or neo-natal units, or children's centres. Observational capabilities, already learned in the pre-clinical phase of training of child psychotherapists, are a valuable part of a therapist's skills. Infant observation, young child observation, and work discussion methods are valuable for the professional development of those who work in these settings.

Some discoveries have arisen from this work. For example, Pamela Sorensen's observations of babies being cared for in a neo-natal unit led her to reflect on their frequent exposure to excessive shocks and stimuli, unmediated (through the circumstances of incubator care) by close parental attention. Her paper "Observations of Transition Facilitating Behavior" (2000) identified the needs of such infants for a caring environment that would, as far as possible, take account of their vulnerability to the sudden impacts of light, noise, heat, and cold, which, in the busy settings of hospitals, could be traumatic to infants. This paper and Didier Houzel's (1999) work together contribute to a new psychoanalytic understanding of the psychosomatic conditions favourable to early development.

A further development has arisen from awareness of the possible meaning of observing and being observed not only for observers as a form of learning, but also for mothers and babies who being observed. A crucial idea is that the difficulties that mothers might experience in their function of "containment" might be related to the absence of a "container" within them. It was recognized that mothers who experience such difficulties may often have had poor experiences of being parented themselves and may, in addition, now lack support from partners or others to whom they are close.[6] The issue, then, was, could infant observation itself provide a kind of supplementary containment for such mothers and their infants, and if so, how?

From very early on in the development of infant observation, it became recognized that the observer's presence was often emotionally significant to mothers, even though observers were enjoined to establish and maintain their relationships with their families at a fairly low level of intensity and to avoid intrusive interventions in their lives. Observers found that any absences on their part could cause distress to the mothers they observed and that their dependable interest in mother and baby was often a support to them. Looking after infants is an exhausting, sometimes stressful experience, and mothers are often left alone in this role for many hours. Thus an observer's weekly visits can become a valued moment in mother's week, even though this may not have been her expectation when they were first arranged. In a related way, the end of a two-year observation can be experienced by both mother and observer as a painful separation. In agreeing to the observation of their baby and themselves, mothers are asked to "give" something, to enable an observer to learn about the development of a child, and are offered nothing in return. Nevertheless, it has come to be realized that an observer's presence over two years or a year can be a helpful one to mothers. One of the reasons why it has been possible to extend the practice of infant observation, with good conscience on the part of the educators and with few mishaps over a long period of time, is that it has indeed been found by most families to be an experience that they have been, on the whole, pleased to have, despite the sacrifice of privacy that it has meant for them. Some of the work of observation seminars is to reflect on these aspects of an observation.

Thus it was that, while infant observation normally had no therapeutic purpose, the emotional significance of observation for the families came to be recognized. From this emerged the idea that perhaps the significance of an observer's presence for mothers and their infants could be given a therapeutic purpose, as a non-intrusive intervention offered to mothers who were finding serious difficulty in establishing a relationship between themselves and their infants. Valuable work, initially in France and then in the United Kingdom, has taken place in recent years to develop a practice of "therapeutic infant observation" (Delion, 2000; Gretton, 2006; Houzel, 1999; Wakelyn, 2011; Wattillon-Naveau, 1999). This has involved some changes in the usual "educational" guidelines for infant observations. One is the need for "therapeutic observers" to be already to be experienced in infant observation, and preferably also to have been trained as psychotherapists. A second is the necessity for supervision of such observation to be more intensive and frequent than in educational settings. And a third is the recognition that a "therapeutic" observer will usually be more active in the family setting than is usual in infant observations.

What has emerged from reports of this work is that there can be benefits from this intervention as a consequence of an observer's reliable and containing presence for the mother and baby. Mothers in difficulty with their babies may feel isolated, ashamed, persecuted, or frightened, both of their own states of mind and of the harm they fear they may do to their babies, as well as of interventions from officialdom in the outside world. Crucial in this situation is an observer's capacity to remain calm with mother and baby, to respond sensitively to the baby's needs when necessary, and to avoid being seen as an agent of surveillance and potential sanction. What may differentiate a therapeutic observer's method of support for mothers from that of other care professionals is her capacity to tolerate painful states of feeling and to refrain from excessive "action". The observer's supervision, or supervision group, needs to provide her with the containment she also needs, as further absorber of stresses within the mother–baby couple. The understanding of the container–contained relationship, which has been crucial to the development of the infant observation method from its beginnings, is the key to its value as a therapeutic resource.

No doubt, a psychotherapist undertaking this work will have insights that seem to invite being offered as interpretations. Sometimes a supervisor will offer her interpretations to the therapeutic observer, to assist her in keeping track of what is going on in the family and in her own mind. But while sometimes "interpretations" of a discreet kind may be offered by "therapeutic observers", therapeutic observation is not psychotherapy. Useful interpretations offered in this situation are more likely to help mother to "see" her baby more clearly, as not the same as her frightening or inconsolable "baby in phantasy", than to be focused on herself. An idea of "infant-centred interpretations" may be relevant to the therapeutic observation. It seems likely that the benefits of these observations will depend considerably on the baby's own desire for life and its capacity to find those capacities in his mother that he needs, with the help of the observer.

One outcome of reflections on the potential therapeutic value of observation is an enhancement of understanding of the value it might have in the training of those who work with families and young children, such as nursery teachers and health visitors. Its value lies not only in the more sensitive understanding of them that this can encourage, but also in a fuller recognition of what they can themselves contribute through the quality of their own attention. From training in observation, professionals and practitioners may learn that sometimes they can do more by doing less, since their own presence and understanding can be a form of action in itself.

There are now several case studies that show how much this approach can achieve. As with most psychoanalytic research, it is from the comparison and accumulation of such cases that substantial new areas of knowledge arise. Further study of this practice is needed. One hopes that this is a form of intervention that can prevent some of the catastrophes that can follow breakdowns in mother–baby relationships.[7]

Infant observation as a form of research is now fairly well developed. Its literature describes its intellectual history, theoretical foundations, and methodological principles, as well as beginning to map its substantive findings in various areas. This field begins to follow the pattern of development of psychoanalytic clinical research, in which one finds continuing appraisals of the knowledge generated by each of the component traditions of psychoanalysis in overview texts, dictionaries, and anthologies. In this way, clinical psychoanalytic research—and still to a small degree, infant observational research—has developed many of the attributes and practices of a "normal science", within its own paradigm. Young child observation and work discussion are at an earlier stage in this developmental trajectory.

Observational and clinical research methods

The methods of data collection and data analysis that have been evolved in the practice of clinical research in psychoanalysis need little modification for use in psychoanalytic observational research or "work discussion". Because the primary interest in each of these fields is to investigate unconscious mental processes and interactions and to identity their different kinds, case-study methods (whether single or multiple) are those best adapted to discover relevant data. The perspectives set out in earlier chapters as most relevant to clinically based study are equally significant in these observational research fields. For example, it is desirable to pay regard to dimensions of both meaning and cause, to look for explanation in terms of part–whole relations as well as in terms of correlations of variables, and to see the relevance of conceptions of complexity and systemic self-organization (M. J. Rustin, 2002). These are as relevant to understanding the development of infants and young children, and their relations to their environments, as to the understanding of clinical patients and the transference–countertransference relationships of the therapeutic setting. The interactions and relations found to exist in work settings and their unconscious dimensions lend themselves to analysis in similar ways. So far as data analysis is concerned, the coding procedures of grounded theory and interpretative phenomenological analysis are as applicable to the data sets of infant observation, young child observation, and work discussion reports as they are to the clinical records of psychoanalytic cases. There is a similar "fit" between the implicit "coding" or theme-finding procedures of the normal supervision of psychoanalytic observational studies for learning purposes and grounded theory and IPA methods. (One of the first single-case studies of an infant observation undertaken for a doctoral thesis, by Wendy Shallcross, 2015, demonstrates the value of grounded-theory analysis.)

Clinical research in psychoanalysis has developed so successfully because it has been located in an established professional practice, driven, in essence, by the mental health needs of its clients. It has always been a form of "learning by doing", developing its infrastructure of supporting theories and techniques as its practice required. This is why it has been able to evolve a distinctive kind of "clinical empiricism" as its primary source of knowledge, even during the period when it was largely excluded from the organization, accreditation, and funding of formal academic research.

Observational psychoanalytic studies do not have the substantial heuristic advantage that arises from the use of interpretation in clinical research, although the development of therapeutic observation brings it closer to the clinical domain. Furthermore, as we have said, whereas the most important contributions to psychoanalytic knowledge have tended to come from experienced psychoanalysts, most infant observers are newcomers to the field. These factors suggest that the development of observational psychoanalytic knowledge may depend on the organization of specific programmes of research—for example, for research degrees and on designed research projects—more than has been the case for clinical research. This is always likely to be the case for areas of psychoanalytic knowledge that are not supported by a substantial field of professional practice. We will later consider these issues in connection with the broader social and cultural applications of psychoanalysis.

Notes

1. Sternberg (2005) has described its crucial role in these trainings.

2. Valuable reflections on the methodological issues involved in this work are to be found in Price and Cooper (2012) and Cooper (2017).

3. In fact, the convergences of understanding between naturalistic infant observation and laboratory-based studies are of great interest and value. Music (2016) reviews these fields of research.

4. In the debate referred to, Stern pointed out that he was himself a psychoanalyst and was committed to psychoanalysis. However, it appears that, from his perspective, it is only at a later, post-infancy stage of development that the unconscious emerges as an identifiable element of the mind. It is thus only at this point that psychoanalytic ideas become practically relevant.

5. Anna Freud's disagreement with Klein, at the time of the Controversial Discussions, about whether, in therapeutic work with young children, it was appropriate to interpret their unconscious phantasies, is related to this issue. The strengthening of ego function, which Anna Freud recommended as the main task of therapy with very young children, can be seen to have as its concomitant the facilitation of a necessary process of repression, which only then gives rise to the possibility and necessity of psychoanalytic interpretation. Klein's view was different from this: that, even in the analysis of very young children, the interpretation of unconscious phantasies was appropriate.

6. This idea offers an explanation of how difficulties in the care of infants may be passed on between generations of parents and children.

7. The research project "Identities in process: Becoming Bangladeshi, African Caribbean and White Mothers", funded by the Economic and Social Research Council (ESRC), made use of both observation in the subjects' families (Urwin, 2007) and the "Free Association Narrative Interview" (Hollway, 2015, Hollway & Jefferson, 2012). Focusing infant observational research on issues of maternal identity was illuminating. (This is further discussed in chapter 15.)

CHAPTER FIFTEEN

Socio-psychoanalytic research

F reud always believed that the science of psychoanalysis could contribute to the understanding of virtually all aspects of human life, not only to what could be learned about individuals from its practice in the clinic. "As a 'depth psychology', a theory of the mental unconscious, it can become indispensable to all the sciences which are concerned with the evolution of human civilization, and its major institutions such as art, religion and the social order" (Freud, 1926e, p. 248). He himself wrote several major texts on psychoanalytic aspects of the social, including *Totem and Taboo* (1912–13), *Group Psychology and the Analysis of the Ego* (1921c), *The Future of an Illusion* (1927c), *Civilization and Its Discontents* (1930a), and *Moses and Monotheism* (1939a), and his example has been followed throughout the history of the field by many other psychoanalysts and writers influenced by psychoanalysis. Among the many instances one can cite of powerful and influential work of this kind are those by Adorno (1978), Fanon (1952), Mitscherlich & Mitscherlich (1975), Mitchell (1974), Marcuse (1955, 1958), and Žižek (1990, 1993).

In the understanding of individual psychopathologies, the interpretative assumption is that there is something "abnormal" and "irrational" that needs explanation. To understand such conditions, psychoanalysis competes with (or complements) the theories and methods of psychiatry, clinical psychology, and neuroscience. However, these disciplines are compelled by the nature of neurosis and insanity to recognize that the phenomena they are concerned with are different from "normal" states of mind and are therefore difficult to explain in the ways by which we make sense of conventional patterns of behaviour. "Mental illness" is characterized by its "strangeness" and by the discomfort it causes for those who find themselves in close contact with it. It is, almost by definition, a condition whose sufferers are in violation of the shared norms of human interaction and who, for this reason, have long been excluded from it, by placement in asylums, or by medication designed to contain mental abnormalities (Goffman, 1969; Scheff, 1999; Spillius, 1993). The different professional disciplines that seek to treat mental illness—psychiatry, clinical psychology, neuroscience, and psychoanalysis—all have to take account of an element of the irrational and the incomprehensible: the ways in which its sufferers do not experience the world as non–sufferers do. Psychoanalysts' understanding of these conditions is distinct from those of other clinical professions, but they have nonetheless influenced them, as one can see most clearly from the categories in the *DSM–5* (APA, 2013).

Psychoanalysis has gained an entry into the field of social explanation for the most part where irrationalities in society have become highly disturbing and difficult to overlook. Economists' explanations of behaviour as the outcomes of rational self-interest, anthropologists' by reference to the shaping effects of cultures, and those of sociologists who make use of both interest- and norm-based models are believed by their disciplines to be sufficient to understand their fields of phenomena. Although some of the founding figures of sociology, such as Max Weber and Emile Durkheim, gave great importance to phenomena that could be said to have an unconscious dimension (for example, Weber's idea of charismatic authority, and Durkheim's of the "collective conscience"), later sociologists have mostly not seen a need to explore these ideas in specifically psychoanalytic terms (M. J. Rustin, 2016a). The central paradigms of these major social sciences have found no place for the idea of the dynamic unconscious. It is only where explanations based on the solid ground of social interests and values have seemed inadequate to explain extremes of behaviour, or what Žižek has referred to as "excess", that psychoanalytic explanation has gained a place in social scientific debate.

Freud's *Civilization and Its Discontents* (1930a) and the work of Theodore Adorno (1951) were early instances of such psychoanalytic interventions into the understanding of the social. Freud's *Group Psychology and the Analysis of the Ego* (1921c) and *Civilization and Its Discontents* were uncannily prophetic and responsive to their historical moment. Their recognition of the evil potential of mass behaviour drew on the earlier writings by Gustav Le Bon (1895) and Wilfred Trotter

(1916) about the behaviour of masses and crowds. Freud's description of the unconscious dynamics of the relations between leaders and followers and the mutual projections of emotions between them anticipated what would happen in Germany with the Nazis' capture of power. Freud surely saw the roots of this in the resentments and hatreds being enacted in the period between 1918 and 1933.

Members of the Frankfurt School, in exile in the United States, sought to understand the nature of Nazism as both a political and a psychological phenomenon. Adorno's essay "Freudian Theory and the Pattern of Fascist Propaganda" (1951) brought together an interrogation of the arguments of Freud's *Group Psychology and the Analysis of the Ego* (1921c) with an analysis of the psychological techniques deployed by the Nazis to win and enforce control over their followers. One of its central arguments is that the emergence of a society of disoriented masses whose ties with others and with traditional beliefs had been disrupted created the space and for a relationship to leaders who would satisfy their unconscious needs. It was the capacity of the Nazi leadership, and in particular Hitler, "to turn their own unconscious outwards" and thereby to enable their followers to identify unconsciously with them that gave them such power. In an analysis that has resonances with the recent politics of the United States, Adorno argued that the mindlessness and repetitiveness of the Nazi messages paradoxically contributed to their power.

There was an element of self-deception in the popular adherence to Nazi doctrines, which could survive their evident absurdity. Once caught up in this scale of delusion (e.g., about Hitler's omniscience, the inevitability of victory, and the demonic capacities of the Jews) to withdraw belief in the leader would risk psychological collapse. The appearance in recent political turbulence in United States politics of "alternative facts" suggests some parts of that society are not far from this condition.[1] Adorno pointed out that the dual nature of Hitler, as both a superman and entirely ordinary, was the consequence of his role in unconscious fantasy as a projection of the ego ideal of members of the disoriented and massified population.

Two other major intellectual interventions after the Second World War offered understandings of the Nazi catastrophe that were explicitly or implicitly psychoanalytic. Although Hannah Arendt repudiated psychoanalytic explanation (perhaps because of what she saw as its undue focus on individual psychopathology), her *Origins of Totalitarianism* (1951) is implicitly psychoanalytic in the terms in which it describes totalitarian societies (M. J. Rustin, 2016b). The psychoanalytic affinities of Arendt's arguments are easier to recognize in the light of the later development of psychoanalysis as a theory of object relations. Arendt describes the dehumanization and demonization of the enemies of Nazism and its project to eliminate these from the earth. The mechanisms of paranoid-schizoid states of mind described by Klein and the extreme forms of splitting of good and bad to which they give rise, and her emphasis on innate hatred and destructiveness as an element in human nature, have a clear correspondence with the hate-filled Nazi programme of elimination characterized by Arendt.

The Mitscherlichs' *The Inability to Mourn* (1975) offered an analysis of the unconscious effects of this historic catastrophe 30 years later. It described the disavowal in post-war West Germany of the memories of the suffering that had been inflicted by the Nazi regime on other peoples and had been suffered by the German people in the course of the Second World War, in the destruction of its armies and its cities. They argued that the "German Economic Miracle", which had been so celebrated in the post-war years, could best be understood as a "manic defence" against the experience of loss and guilt, denying both. The publication of this book coincided with a larger awakening of memory and sensibility among Germans, especially those of a new generation, represented by Willy Brandt's public acts of repentance for the atrocities of the war and in the works of novelists and film-makers who were now able to explore this history. (Violent acts of terrorism directed against the elites held to be responsible for what had happened were another reaction to the recent past.) It was remarkable that the Mitscherlichs' psychoanalytically framed intervention was so widely discussed in Germany, their book becoming a best-seller. It appears to have had a therapeutic function in that society, in making possible an understanding of a repressed and split-off past.

I have argued in this book that the principal context for the development of psychoanalytic theories since Freud has been the clinical consulting room. This is because it has been able to offer some of the attributes of a scientific laboratory for the study of the phenomena of the unconscious within controlled and replicable conditions. This has been a context in which hypotheses, emerging and framed as "puzzles" within the central psychoanalytic paradigm, could be explored and tested through the comparative study of clinical cases. Although their methods of investigation mostly did not follow the protocols of academic science (including psychology), clinical researchers have often been rigorous and precise in their use of ideas and in their analysis of clinical data. Their work has led to the cumulative development and ordered "speciation" of psychoanalytic theories and clinical techniques, within several of its constitutive subparadigms. There have been productive adaptations of clinical methods of psychoanalytic research within associated fields of practice, such as infant and young child observation and the observation of institutions. The adoption of systematic methods of qualitative data analysis, from the fields of sociology and psychology, have recently made it possible to develop more transparent and accountable descriptions of both clinical and observational psychoanalytic research than occurred in the years when psychoanalysis was more remote from the academy and its disciplines.

A considerable volume of high-quality psychoanalytic research has taken place in these contexts, over a long period. For this reason it is feasible to describe the methods appropriate to such research and to set out templates for investigations that researchers can follow.

However, these relatively closed and controlled settings are unlike the conditions in which the psychoanalytic investigations of larger-scale social phenomena have to be undertaken. The rules that psychoanalysis has developed for research within its secluded rooms cannot be followed when it is practised "outdoors", where there is the risk of "wild analysis" and where it is difficult to distinguish valid interpretation from mere speculation. But if different "rules" have perforce had to be adopted for such un-boundaried research, what are they? Can they be set down as guidelines for productive research? It seems that few answers have been offered to these methodological questions in the psychoanalytic literature. Socio-psychoanalytic researchers have offered some brilliant understandings of happenings in different societies and have persuasively deployed psychoanalytic concepts and theories, often taken from classical sources such as Freud's writings, in doing so. But what they seem to have had little to say about are their actual methods of research.[2]

Socio-psychoanalytic research methods in practice

There are similarities between psychoanalytic investigations in the clinic and in the larger society. In both contexts, the phenomena that are the objects of inquiry are unconscious and resistant to recognition. Almost by definition, a psychoanalytic discovery about an aspect of social life will assert the existence of something unexpected, distinct from and often challenging to the self-understandings of subjects. Sometimes, the insights it offers will be resisted or attacked. It is, of course, difficult to formulate rules and procedures for studying phenomena that most would prefer not to recognize. Indeed, the validity of psychoanalysis as a field of knowledge has often been disputed because of antipathy towards the very idea of the unconscious.

The difficulties posed by resistance to interpretation are often overcome in clinical practice because the deviations of individuals from the pathways of predictable normality or rationality are usually of concern to those closely related to them, if not to the individuals themselves. The clinical practice of psychoanalysis was designed to enable such abnormal conditions to be investigated. But in the wider society, who is in a position to conduct such investigations? Because there is often no place within a society from which challenges to common-sense beliefs can be made, such investigations may be interpreted as attacks on received ideas.

For example, psychoanalytic investigations of racism and anti-Semitism have defined these phenomena in ways that are unwelcome to those who are racists or anti-Semites. For the anti-Semite, it is Jews and their attributes that are the problem, not the doctrines of anti-Semitism. For the racist, racial inferiority is a fact of nature, and racist beliefs need no explanation in terms of unconscious mechanisms of projection. If one holds that the subordination of females by males in society is the natural condition, determined by the inferiority of women, the idea that it is not "natural" but, rather, the unconscious outcome of specific social arrangements is likely to be unwelcome.

Feminist psychoanalysts such as Mitchell (1974), Dinnerstein (1976), and Chodorow (1978) argued from their different perspectives, that gender identities and their inequalities were "produced" as the "oedipal" effects of specific family forms and could be changed if these unconscious processes were understood. These ideas challenged patriarchal ideas and conventional ideas of family norms.

Sometimes the psychoanalytic interpretation of social phenomena has had an explicit political purpose – the psychoanalyst as social critic. For example, in characterizing Fascist propaganda as a skilful manipulation of unconscious resentments and hatreds, Adorno described a kind of social madness; in doing this, he intended to warn against its recurrence. When Hannah Arendt (1951) described Nazism as embodying a phantasy in which a "race" defined as non-human should be entirely eliminated, she was arguing against totalitarian mentalities. Marcuse's (1955, 1964) analysis of the transition from a producer-driven capitalism based on "surplus repression" to a consumption-driven society in which the gratification of desires was encouraged was not a celebration of consumer freedom, but as a warning against its effects. Marcuse characterized the state of "liberated" consumer society as one of "repressive desublimation", no closer to authentic relationships between human beings than its repressed "industrial" predecessor.

A fourth impressive example of socio-psychoanalytic analysis is Norbert Elias's (2000) historical account of the dependence of "civilization" on the inhibition—or repression—of appetites and impulses, through the widespread inculcation of "manners", beginning within court elites and spreading downwards through the social hierarchy. As Zigmunt Bauman (1979) pointed out, Elias's history of civilization was a working-through in historical terms of the thesis of Freud's *Civilization and Its Discontents*, in which Freud had argued that the repression and sublimation of instinctual desires was essential if "civilization" (i.e. ordered, law-bound society) was to be attained. Elias's historicized version of Freud's argument was positive in its view of social development. It was so respectful of the civilized nature of Western society that it seems hardly to amount to social criticism at all. Yet Elias' view of evolving European "civilization" is more politically committed than it might appear, since it was counterposed to two contemporary antitheses. One of these was the Nazism from which Elias was an exile, and the other the revolutionary Marxism of the social scientist exiles from the Frankfurt School of Social Research (Elias was from the same German city, but not the same Institute) whose members did not share his belief in a benign process of social evolution.

The differences of view between Marcuse and Elias with regard to the nature and consequences of Freudian repression, and those between the revolutionary and reformist psychoanalytic contributors to feminist debates, show that socio-psychoanalytic research is like research in other human sciences in providing evidence that can sustain different political perspectives. Its aim should not be to reinforce particular political viewpoints or merely provide intellectual weapons in their support but, rather, to throw light on what is unrecognized in social situations, even where this calls into question accepted beliefs.

A further point of similarity between the clinical and social objects of psychoanalytic study lies in the fact that both need to be researched and understood as "cases". Cases are bounded singular entities that embody complex relations between their "internal" elements and with these and their external environment. Psychoanalytic clinical study moves between engagement with the unique attributes of a patient and the transference–countertransference interactions of a therapy, and a search to locate conceptual categories to give meaning to these particulars. Socio-psychoanalytic phenomena need to be identifiable as particular, complex entities if their systematic study of them is to be feasible, difficult as this may be in the un-laboratory-like settings of societies.

Questions of scale

The argument has been made earlier that clinical practice and psychoanalytic infant observation in families provide relatively constant "settings" in which unconscious mental phenomena can be studied. The consistency of these settings makes it possible to identify similarities and differences and to recognize "kinds" of phenomena. The common requirement of scientific study is to hold most variables constant, so that changes in specific variables can be traced. Clinical and observational sessions can be compared with one another via their transcripts or recordings. An infant observation research literature has thus emerged in recent decades, giving a means of understanding early emotional development complementary to the inferences derived from its reliving in the transference relationship between analysts and patients.

The study of group relations pioneered by Wilfred Bion and described in his *Experiences in Groups* (1961) has established another context for the psychoanalytic study of social phenomena. This has given rise to substantial practices of group psychotherapy and the study of "group relations" in conferences designed to constitute a "laboratory" for this. Bion's original ideas have been elaborated and extended through this work. However, its principal aims have been educative and formative for participants, rather than being oriented towards research. More is said about the central ideas of Bion's "basic assumption" paradigm below.

Organizations and institutions constitute a further context, mid-way in scale between the clinical encounter and the study of wider social processes. Organizations such as corporations and their divisions or public bureaucracies and institutions such as schools and hospitals manifest greater similarities of structure and process than do the large complex societies in which they are located. They are constituted through boundaries that make it possible to differentiate between processes internal and external to them and to identify transactions that take place between the inside and the outside. There are practical and material interests in understanding organizations and their dynamics, and an activity/profession of organizational consultancy (with a distinct psychoanalytic subspecialism) has evolved to develop this field of knowledge. The Tavistock Institute of Human Relations in Britain and social scientists such as Kurt Lewin in the United States were among its pioneers. Psychoanalytic and social systemic perspectives were linked in a somewhat uneasy interaction in the most creative periods of this work between 1950 and 1980 (Trist & Murray, 1993a, 1993b, 1993c). A substantial practice of psychoanalytic organizational consultancy has developed over recent decades, with its own association (https://www.ispso.org) and publications.

However, the earlier aspiration to bring about changes in organizational structures and processes through the transformative potential of psychoanalytic and systemic ideas has become reduced in scope. The reassertion of hierarchical, market-dominated organizational models from the 1980s has limited the space for the more dialogic, democratic, consensual approaches of the earlier psychosocial researchers, such as those at the Tavistock. The necessities of market survival have obliged organizational consultants to address the needs of individual development and occupational survival of their clients, through such methods as executive coaching. What was once a research programme that offered to transform major organizations through its psychosocial insights has become more limited in its aims. This is evident in the contrast between the ambitious research publications of the earlier era (Trist & Murray, 1993a, 1993b, 1993c) and those of more recent times.

Nevertheless, a significant practice of psychoanalytic organizational analysis and consultancy has continued, and I discuss some of the themes of its work later in this chapter.

Problems of evidence and method

There is therefore no standard method for studying the unconscious in the wider society, as there can be in more "closed" settings where "variables" and observations are easier to control.

Sometimes a psychoanalytic concept is powerful enough to bring recognition of something hitherto unconscious, repressed, or split off. Freud's "infantile sexuality" was of this kind. Others are "borderline states of mind", the "manic defence" of the German economic miracle, and the "death instinct" and desire for destruction, which, Hanna Segal believed, were unconscious motivations of the nuclear arms race. It is when explanation in terms of unconscious forces brings to light a cause that was previously unrecognized that a new understanding is achieved. It is the presence of the unexpected in a psychoanalytic insight that may indicate a new discovery.

Socio-psychoanalytic explanation has been productive where there has been awareness of a substantial unconscious "excess" within a social situation. Psychoanalytic ways of thinking have won a place in the social sciences mainly when this has been the case, but they have gained little traction in social scientific practice, where irrationalities are less obvious or disturbing.

One specific context in which a psychoanalytic approach showed its relevance was the case, in 2000, of Victoria Climbié, where social and medical services had failed to prevent the killing, by the child's aunt and her partner who were caring for her, of a child who was known by them to be at risk. Margaret Rustin, in her paper on the official report on this failure (M. E. Rustin, 2005), examined how it was that public authorities failed to act on the knowledge that they had in their possession. She made reference in her discussion to the concept of "borderline states of mind" and its dissociation from emotional reality. She drew on John Steiner's idea of "turning a blind eye", developed in his analysis of Sophocles' play *King Oedipus* (Steiner, 1993b). Although this account was based on the analysis of a single case, it had a broader significance, since there were several other cases of children's deaths in circumstances of failures of professional oversight. The Grenfell Fire disaster of 2017 was the outcome of a similar disregard by authorities of information about serious risks that had been, in some sense, known to them.

The element of "excess" in these cases lies in the discrepancy between what is known to participants and their apparent incapacity to act on that knowledge. Žižek (1990, 1993) has described many instances of such "excess" in social practices, sometimes with a delight in paradox that is unsettling to conventional thinking. He suggested, for example, that some prohibitions whose ostensible aim was to suppress indulgence in harmful substances (drugs, tobacco, or alcohol) were unconsciously motivated by resentment of the "theft of enjoyment" by those being subjected to correction. He noted a similar dynamic, in the former Yugoslavia, in the categorizations by each other of the people of Balkan nations. He saw a kind of "geography in the mind", in which the undesirable attributes of irresponsibility and fecklessness were located in fantasy in a nation further south, rationality and civilization supposedly having their origins in the cultures of northern Europe. A resentment of others' pleasures motivates this world view, while hatred can provide a form of "jouissance" in itself. While Žižek's model of the emotional geography of the Balkans is no doubt an exaggeration, if not parody, of the truth, it nevertheless has application to many forms of ethnic hostility that have involved spatial projections of intolerable emotions. Freud argued that jokes gave pleasure because of the release and expression of forbidden desires that they permitted their hearers. The pleasures gained from Žižek's writing are of this kind: he practises as well as theorizes the vicissitudes of jouissance.

In each of the instances of writing I have referred to, psychoanalytic ideas whose original discovery lay in clinical practice or in the sphere of "pure" psychoanalytic theory were a precondition for the interpretation of social phenomena. Concepts of repression, of mourning and manic defence, of the "law of the father" (Lacan), of "borderline" and paranoid-schizoid states of mind, and of projection and projective identification were among those crucial to such interpretations.

It has usually been the case that the pressure to explain social phenomena psychoanalytically has come from the disturbing presence and effects of the phenomena themselves. The mental states of patients and disturbing conditions in society place demands on interpreters to find ideas that give them meaning. Psychoanalytic theories have a generative capacity of their own, additional to those stimulated into existence by clinical phenomena. This has led to extensions of their explanatory scope, by deduction or analogy in the clinical and social spheres. For example, the sub-paradigm in psychoanalytic child psychotherapy, which is made up of the theory and practice of work with severely deprived children (Boston & Szur, 1983), has led to its differentiation into more specialized subfields—for example, into the kinds of damage arising from subjection to emotional or physical neglect, violence, or sexual abuse or the problems arising in the remedial settings of adoption or fostering. The discovery that the phenomena of "narcissistic personality organizations" were to be found not only in clinical consulting room but also in wider social milieus came through seeing this concept's theoretical implications, as well as from the awareness of the increasing impact on society of narcissistic states of mind (M. J. Rustin, 2017a; M. E. Rustin & Rustin, 2010).

An idea that has seen its original scope of application extended is that of social defences against unconscious anxiety, which was first put forward by Elliott Jaques (1955) and Isabel Menzies (1960). This has its origin in Melanie Klein's theory of paranoid-schizoid and depressive anxieties and was found illuminating by Jaques and Menzies (later Menzies Lyth) in their work as organizational consultants at the Tavistock Institute of Human Relations. For Jaques, the original context of application was industrial relations in a manufacturing company. For Menzies, it was the nursing system in a general hospital. In her study she observed discrepancies between the stated aims of nurse training and its outcomes. She observed that nurse trainees were dissatisfied, became ill, or failed to complete their training in unexpectedly large numbers. This raised serious questions for Menzies and for the hospital matron who had commissioned her study. She contrasted the idea of caring for patients as whole persons with the hospital's routines, in which the emotional content of nursing work was denied and repressed. She saw that there was little human contact between nurses and their patients, who were depersonalized and referred to by their illness or bed number rather than by name. She noted the intolerance of the young nurses' distress. It was this gap between the actual and the expected and desirable that led her to seek explanations in terms of unconscious processes. Her central argument was that the dysfunctional organization of nurse training could be explained as an unconscious social defence against the anxieties engendered in the trainee nurses by their proximity to the damaged bodies and sufferings of their patients.

Menzies Lyth (1989) later found this idea to have relevance to other contexts of care, such as day nurseries where the anxieties of care-workers were, as we would now say, insufficiently "contained", and in which the emotional needs of those being cared for went unnoticed. Researchers whom she supervised (Bain & Barnett, 1986) saw staff engaged in social conversation while in another room nursery children were left in a distressed state. This idea has since been further extended, through the conjunction of the social systemic concept of an institution's "primary task" (Miller & Rice, 1967), with the idea of unconscious social defences against anxiety. A recent collection of essays (Armstrong & Rustin, 2015) explored the hypothesis that different occupations might be dominated by distinct "primary tasks", and that these might each give rise to a specific form of anxiety and defence against it. This volume outlined the idea that occupations such as social work, day nursery care, the work of head-teachers, and hedge fund managers in the financial sector might each have their specific primary tasks, anxieties, and defences against them. This provides an agenda for further research, whose advantage may be that its fields are sufficiently circumscribed to allow a consistent method of study and an accumulation of knowledge.

Wilfred Bion (1961) had seen the relevance of his theory of "basic assumptions"—states of shared nonconscious phantasy that emerged in his work with small study groups—to larger social institutions. Thus, he believed the unconscious state of mind of "dependency" to have a central place in the social relations of churches; that of "fight–flight" to be prominent in military organization; and fantasies of "pairing" to be associated with messianic hopes, including those associated with sexual romance. These ideas have remained powerful resources in the practice of group relations. Bion's basic assumptions (and the rational "work group" whose functioning is liable to be threatened by them[3]) are a kind of unconscious defence against anxiety, capable of undermining or subverting the functioning of organizations.

Olya Khaleelee (2010) insightfully observed the operations of the "basic assumption" of dependency to the threatened culture of the welfare state in the 1980s. In the epoch of Thatcherism, the idea of a "dependency culture" was attacked by governments, and reforms brought an enforced change in many institutions from the basic assumption of "dependency" to one of "fight–flight", in which individuals had to defend themselves in a system now dominated by market relations and a newly proclaimed "enterprise culture". Khaleelee observed that this transition was proving traumatic for some of those who had been most committed to the values of collectivism and welfare,[4] and that this was making adaptation to this new environment difficult. This work demonstrated how Bion's "basic assumptions" model could be a valuable resource for socio-psychoanalytic analysis.

One can initiate the practice of psychoanalytic social explanation from either end of a chain that links psychoanalytic theories to the experience of unconscious processes. Starting at the theoretical end of this chain, one can imagine a research programme that looked for social instantiations of ideas drawn from the lexicon of psychoanalytic ideas. Its question might be, to what social phenomena might key psychoanalytic concepts find a fruitful application? Such concepts might include repression, paranoid-schizoid and depressive anxieties, container–contained relations, pathological personality organizations, borderline states of mind, gang and group mentalities, mourning, and melancholia.

One can see from the examples given earlier that "fundamental" psychoanalytic concepts of this kind have been essential to the understanding of certain social phenomena. But in reality, such discoveries have rarely been by deduction from theoretical first principles. More often, stimuli to investigation have come from the social phenomena themselves. Valuable socio-psychoanalytic discoveries have mostly come through the practice of "learning from experience" in the social sphere.

Research practices

What research methods are serviceable for the psychoanalytic study of social phenomena? Can there be an equivalent "laboratory" for their study? Although there probably cannot be, methods can nevertheless be identified to frame investigations of this kind. One of these arises from the practice of psychoanalytic consultancy. Organizations and institutions are entities that are bounded and stable to the extent that they can be studied as "cases". The studies by Menzies and Jaques referred to above are early examples of learning through consultancy. The role of the psychoanalytic consultant has an active, quasi-therapeutic aspect, in that the validity of insights is tested in a process like that of clinical interpretation. Psychoanalytic consultancy is a kind of action research, usually on a small scale. Validation arises not from subjects' explicit assent to insights offered by the consultant, but from evidence that interpretations have given rise to thought and change. The essays contained in Obholzer and Roberts (1994), and in Huffington, et al. (2004) give examples of socio-psychoanalytic insights learned and tested through consultancy.

A second research method is the adaptation of psychoanalytic infant observation to the observation of institutions, which has been set out by Hinshelwood and Skogstad (2000). In this work, priority was given to the consistency of the method and settings of observation, and to maintaining a detached stance by abstaining from interpretation or practical involvement. The institutional observations they reported took place, however, over a time-span of only three months. It seems likely that more could be learned from more sustained observations and through the eliciting of information by more active means than passive observation. The opportunity to reflect on reported observations within a supervisory group is likely also to be valuable in unconscious processes—for example, through studying countertransference responses in observers. A detailed, literal record of what is observed—its "thick description", in Geertz's (1973) terms—is essential especially when the purpose is to identify processes that are "beneath the surface" but influence conscious mental life and behaviour.

A third practice that may be serviceable for psychoanalytic social research is that of psychoanalytic work discussion (M. E. Rustin & Bradley, 2008). This, like infant observation and young child observation, is a method designed for the purpose of teaching and learning, although research findings have emerged from it. Participants in work discussion meet as a seminar group (usually weekly), and members report in turn on an aspect of their work experience that has emotional significance. Topics described may, for example, be the anxieties of clients, relationships among working colleagues, or the impact of external events, such as an institutional inspection or reorganization. Reflection on such experiences with a supervisor and seminar group may elucidate unconscious dynamics present in a work situation.

It is unlikely that those undertaking work discussions as part of their education will initially be able to function as researchers. However, it has sometimes been possible for those leading work discussion seminars to draw conclusions from what is reported which add to the understanding of institutions. Some of the essays published in M. E. Rustin & Bradley (2008) provide examples of this. These include descriptions of the tension between "gang" and "group" mentalities that characterizes the experience of Mexican street children in Gianna Williams' essay and the report by a hospital nurse of the difference that could be made to a child patient's experience of painful treatment by a nurse's contact with her fears.

Papers published in *Social Defences against Anxiety* (Armstrong & Rustin, 2015) showed that work discussion could both clarify the nature and causes of anxieties and also be an effective way of managing and containing them. Emil Jackson's report of his work discussion seminar with the teachers of adolescents in schools is an example. This seminar enabled anxieties aroused in teachers by their exposure to the sexuality of their students to be acknowledged, rather than hidden in fear and shame. Recognition of these anxieties made them easier for teachers to cope with them. In these case studies discoveries were made about the unconscious social processes. Even without their being tested in formal investigations, such discoveries may be found through practitioner experience to be significant. Psychoanalytic ideas have often been diffused in such lateral, rhizomatic ways through the experience of practitioners, rather than through the hierarchical modes of transmission more common in academic science. It may thus be feasible to deploy the method of psychoanalytic work discussion for the purpose of research.

A fourth means of undertaking socio-psychoanalytic investigations is through forms of interviewing designed to reveal individuals' unconscious preoccupations and beliefs, and the formation of identities through social experiences. The Biographical Narrative Interview Method (BNIM) (Chamberlayne, Rustin, & Wengraf, 2002) is of value in this regard, as is the Free Association Narrative Interview (FANI) (Hollway & Jefferson, 2012), and substantial studies in the field of Oral and Life History (Bertaux, 1981; Chamberlayne, Bornat, & Wengraf, 2000; Merridale, 2000, 2005; Thompson, 1978). Crucial to both is the insistence that subjects are given freedom to shape their own autobiographical narratives, following an initial prompting question to focus the subject's attention on what is of most relevance to the researcher. This approach is different from standard interview protocols, "structured" or "semi-structured", which ask subjects to answer questions previously devised by researchers. In the BNIM, a second interview allows interviewers to take up elements present in the subject's original narrative. The aim is to ensure that the narrative remains authored by the subject and is not unduly influenced by the researcher's frame of reference.

These methods have similarities to the value accorded by analysts to the "free association" of patients. Interview narratives may reveal unconscious patterns and compulsions. These may well require "decoding" by researchers in their analysis of the data. There is a multidimensional protocol for this process in BNIM, which involves differentiating between subjects' "told" narratives and their "lived lives" in their actual chronological sequence, as this can be discerned from the narrative and also the discrimination, at a micro-level, of different forms of narration and what these may signify, in terms of a narrative's tendency to rationalize, idealize, or truthfully account for a subject's experience.

Sometimes a transference–countertransference relationship can be perceived in this interview process, as subjects respond to the unusual receptivity of their interviewer. This is again somewhat reminiscent of the "blank screen" offered by the psychoanalyst, encouraging the transference projections of patients and enabling these to be understood as communications.

It might be thought that the primary orientation of this method is towards the individual subject and her psychological state, but this need not be so. Subjects' narratives often bring into view the social world through which their identities have developed. It thus becomes possible to recognize the presence both of the individual within the social, and of the social within the individual. The idea that the individual is unavoidably a product of society, and that society is continually being produced and reproduced by individuals, is fundamental to this methodological perspective, even though mainstream sociology and psychology separate the individual and the social. The recent emergence of the "hybrid" field of psychosocial studies attempts to repair this damaging split in the metatheory of the human sciences.

The Free Association Narrative Method (FANI) has been developed specifically to focus on unconscious aspects of its subjects' social experiences. A research project using this method was undertaken in the context of widespread public anxieties about crime (Hollway & Jefferson, 2012). The researchers learned that the anxieties that gave rise to reported fears of crime were more often displaced effects of underlying unconscious states of anxiety in subjects than a concomitant of the actual the incidence of crime in their locality.

This was similar to the findings of psychoanalytic research into catastrophic social events such as major accidents (Garland, 2002). There it was found that serious mental harm arising from such traumas was most often related to underlying personal vulnerabilities, in the absence of which victims will often recover without lasting psychological injury. These findings have a bearing on the reparative measures best adopted when such disasters occur.

A subsequent study by Hollway (2015), Urwin (2007), and colleagues made use both of the FANI interview method and of psychoanalytic infant observation, to study the states of mind of young mothers in a deprived district of London. This revealed that the main vulnerability of mothers in an Asian community was the outcome of their separation from their own mothers, where the latter had remained in the mothers' Asian country of origin. In their culture, grandparents traditionally give a great deal of support to their daughters when they have children. It was found that the extent of family support available to these young mothers, compared with indigenous white working-class mothers from the same district, was the most significant difference between them. This research has relevance for family support services. Inferences about social relations were again able to be drawn from a study whose research methods focused on individual subjects.

While these are fine examples of research, this field is less advanced, in its accumulation of knowledge and in its forms of investigation, than the clinical research programme of psychoanalysis. A great deal of work still needs to be done to establish a generative paradigm of socio-psychoanalytic research.

Notes

1. It is too much to say that supporters of Brexit would be faced with psychological collapse if they recognized that their vote in the Referendum was, in the light of the facts that have subsequently emerged, mistaken. However, it does seem to be the case that once a stand has been taken on mainly "emotional" grounds (with positive feelings assigned to the British or English nation and negative feelings towards "Europe", or the reverse), rational, evidence-based arguments may count for little.

2. But see Clarke and Hoggett (2009) and the book series *Studies in the Psychosocial* edited by Redman, Frosh, and Hollway (for volumes in this series, visit: https://www.palgrave.com/gp/series/14464). Stamenova & Hinshelwood (forthcoming) throws considerable new light on these questions.

3. David Armstrong (2005) has argued that Bion's followers have tended to neglect his belief in the usual capacity of the work group to survive its unconscious undermining by "basic assumption" states of mind.

4. At a "Psychoanalysis and the Public Sphere" conference in the 1980s, interpretation by Khaleelee of a reluctance to recognize the presence of this persisting "basic assumption" in left-wing responses to Thatcherite reforms led to fury in the audience, such that the speaker felt obliged to withdraw from the conference.

CHAPTER SIXTEEN

Psychoanalytic cultural methods

This chapter discusses issues of method in the psychoanalytic interpretation of literature and art, primarily from the perspective of the British object-relations tradition, recognizing in the first instance the enormous presence and influence of psychoanalysis in many fields of culture.[1] Some genres of fine art, such as surrealism, have been explicit in their interest and borrowings from psychoanalysis. Many eminent literary and art critics have absorbed psychoanalytic thinking into their work. William Empson (1935), Lionel Trilling (1951), Adrian Stokes (Sayers, 2015; Stokes & Williams, 2014), Harold Bloom (1973), Stanley Cavell (1987) and the philosopher Richard Wollheim (1993b) are among them. An influential approach to film studies (Metz, 1974) has been influenced by the psychoanalytic ideas of Lacan, but film has also been studied from an object-relations perspective (Sabbadini, 2003, 2014). Freud himself and many successor psychoanalysts have written insightfully about literature and art—for example, Ernest Jones (1949), Ella Freeman Sharpe (1950), Hanna Segal (1952), Ronald Britton (1998a), John Steiner (1993a), Ignes Sodré (2014), Gregorio Kohon (2014), Meg Harris Williams and Margot Waddell (1991) and Thomas Ogden (Ogden & Ogden, 2013). Freud believed that great writers such as Sophocles and Shakespeare, to whom his writings make many references, anticipated the discoveries of psychoanalysis, and that psychoanalysts needed to learn from their work.

A large industry, that of advertising, so central to modern consumer culture, has exploited the understanding of unconscious wishes and desires for its own purposes. (One of its pioneers was Edward Bernays, Freud's nephew). In so far as culture can be understood as the sphere of symbolic representation, then psychoanalysis constitutes a culture or subculture in itself, as well as providing a way of understanding forms of cultural practice other than its own.

"Culture" is a slippery term, with many overlapping meanings, extending all the way from the idea of the cultural as a dimension of virtually every aspect of human experience to the idea of culture as a specialized sphere of symbolic production (Williams, 1961). In this chapter I am focusing on the artefacts of cultural production, principally drawn from literature and drama, and my psychoanalytic frame of reference is mainly that of the British object-relations tradition.

There is a significant question to be asked. Is the psychoanalytic study of culture and the methods of research that it deploys similar to or different from the psychoanalytic study of other phenomena or forms of life? Can one identify methods that those who wish to think psychoanalytically about cultural artefacts have used or should use? It has been argued above that such methods have been developed for psychoanalytic research in the consulting room, in observing families and young children, and in the study of social institutions. Are there methods analogous to these kinds of work that can shape the study of cultural practices and the artefacts—poems, plays, films, novels, buildings, paintings, sculptures—which they create?

The unconscious as the object of psychoanalytic cultural study

I have suggested that the distinctive objects of most kinds of psychoanalytic study are unconscious phenomena, which, almost by definition, are non-transparent, and indeed whose recognition is resisted by their subjects, whether these be individuals. institutions, or societies. The purpose—it is often a practical or therapeutic one—of such study is to bring the unconscious within the domain of consciousness. Psychoanalysts bring to this work a distinctive capability and techniques by which unconscious phenomena can be recognized. The consulting room and the relations of the transference and countertransference are their primary means of understanding.

Do the objects of culture to which psychoanalysts give their attention have such hidden attributes? Do these artefacts, or their creators, have an "unconscious" dimension that psychoanalysts are in a privileged position to understand? Do the analysts know something that authors and writers don't know? Or is the relationship between analysts and artists and their work of a different kind, not like that of analyst and patient? And if it is different, as I believe it is for what reasons and in what ways might this be?

The difference lies in the fact that artists are themselves creators of understanding, with the ability to understand and describe the phenomena of unconscious mental life as great and often greater than those of psychoanalysts. Freud fully understood this. On his 70th birthday, when greeted as the "discoverer of the unconscious", Freud corrected the speaker and disclaimed the title: "The poets and philosophers before me discovered the unconscious", he said. "What I discovered was the scientific method by which the unconscious could be studied" (Trilling, 1951). It follows that artists and imaginative writers should not primarily be seen as "objects" for psychoanalytic investigation, in which deciphering their unconscious minds is the main purpose. Instead, they should be seen by analysts not as quasi-patients on a virtual couch but, rather, as primary researchers into the mind, like themselves. But artists and writers make use of quite different forms of inquiry and representation from those used by analysts.

Nonetheless, one psychoanalytic approach to culture has taken as its focus the "psychoanalytic study of the artist", in which his personality and its formation is explored, sometimes bringing together what is known about the artist's life and what can be inferred from his work. Freud's (1910c, 1914b) studies of Leonardo da Vinci and Michelangelo had this character and have remained of great interest. Psychoanalysts have asked what qualities in writers and artists make good creative work possible and have suggested that a particular kind of attention to conflicts in the artist's inner world is a major element of this (Segal, 1952). There are sometimes evident connections between the passions and states of mind that writers explore in their work and the issues important to them in their lives. Some great imaginative writing is explicitly autobiographical—Wordsworth's great poem, *The Prelude*, and Byron's *Childe Harold's Pilgrimage*, are examples. Many novels interweave autobiographical and fictional elements.[2] Often psychoanalytic critics come close to equating the states of mind explored and expressed in poetry to the states of mind of the poets themselves. For example, Ronald Britton (1998a) interpreted Blake's writings as articulations of a certain kind of fundamentalism and antipathy to some aspects of reality. A poet such as Keats has often been written about as the embodiment of qualities admired by psychoanalysts. The phrase most quoted in this connection, "negative capability", came from Keats' critical reflections in a letter on the qualities needed in an authentic poet.[3]

It is to be expected that psychoanalysts will be attentive to connections between the personality and formation of the artist or writer and his or her work. Notwithstanding theories in vogue at one time about the "death of the author" (Barthes, 1977), which saw authors as cogs in the wheels of complex textual machines, most works of art and literature are produced by individual artists. (The performance arts, including cinema, have a more social mode of production.) Authors' life-experiences will often be closely connected with the content of what they produce. But links between artists' biographies and their creative output are far from simple. Psychoanalytic criticism can give too much attention to the biography of artists and too little to their works. Freud (1910) admitted that he had little competence in regard to issues of artistic form and technique. There is a risk of "psychoanalytic reductionism" and of a failure to recognize works of art as independent objects with their own specific qualities, if they are mainly interpreted as symptomatic expressions of the internal conflicts of their authors' minds.

It is most productive for psychoanalytic interpreters and critics to explore the meanings and qualities of works of art in themselves, as representations of states of mind whose significance extends far beyond the psychologies of their authors. Shakespeare's plays provide powerful reasons for adopting this broader perspective. The range of experience represented in his plays far exceeds what can be convincingly attributed to his actual life-experiences, about which, in any case, rather little is known. (For example, there are few letters by or about Shakespeare, few descriptions of him, and no directly autobiographical writing by him.) His plays imagine and give seeming reality to the experiences of people of many kinds. It is this exceptional capacity to identify with others, to imagine the different settings of their lives, and to find symbolic forms to explore the complexity of their beings, which distinguishes his work. If psychoanalytic interpreters are going to have anything enlightening to say about Shakespeare, it is to his works and not his life that their main attention must be given. But from this necessity, some general implications follow regarding the methods of interpretation of works of art that psychoanalysts should adopt.

One can illustrate this by reference to some of the states of mind that are given meaning and explanation in Shakespearean drama.[4] For example, *Othello* is an exploration of states of mind of extreme jealousy and of the processes of projective identification by which one mind can invade, capture, and destroy the mind of another (Rusbridger, 2013; Sodré, 2014). In the opening speech of *Richard III*, Richard of

Gloucester reveals to the audience that he is going to dissimulate and murder his way to power, in a spirit of envy for what others possess, and he does not. He describes his miserable and unloved infancy, as a misshapen child, which has brought him to this state of mind, anticipating the insights of psychoanalysis into what can happen when infants are deprived of love. One of Shakespeare's attributes of genius is that he could make fully articulate and conscious, in image-rich speeches such as those of Richard III, Hamlet, Lear, Othello, and Macbeth, complicated inner states of mind that are normally hidden and unrecognized even by those to whom they belong. One of the dramatic functions of the device of the soliloquy is to signify that what are being revealed are private or "internal" states of mind, which cannot be shared with others. We might say that these are states of mind that are normally repressed or split off. Shakespeare thus developed a means of representing the "inner world" of characters centuries, of course, before the idea of an inner world existed as a scientific concept. Exploration of such intimate and complex states of mind is most often undertaken in poetry, a form of writing and reception that belongs to a "private" sphere. Shakespeare gave his dramatic characters the capabilities of poets, in their form and depth of expression. What a utopian conception of human potentiality this was!

What is exceptional about Richard II and Richard III, and Macbeth and Lady Macbeth (who divide the burden of the terrible knowledge of their thoughts, desires and actions between them) or Hamlet, or King Lear is the extraordinary amount they know about themselves, or come to know through the course of the action of the plays. Plainly not all of Shakespeare's major characters have this degree of self-knowledge. Part of the dramatic effect and meaning of *Coriolanus* lies in its hero being shown to understand himself so little, and to suffer his tragic fate because of this. But, of course, his author understood Coriolanus, his weaknesses of character, and the familial and political origins of these all too well.

What Shakespeare achieved in his work was an imaginative identification with experiences of life that were far from his own. Similar in this respect are the works of the ancient Greek tragedians, Aeschylus, Sophocles, and Euripides, about whose lives and personalities we also know little. The character formations imagined in their plays became decisive contributions to the understanding of human nature and have shaped our vocabularies of character and feeling more deeply than the findings of scientific psychology. The formulations of the Greek tragedies have also been suggestive and informative in the development of psychoanalysis—for example, in what Freud was able to learn from

Sophocles' tragedy of Oedipus, and in later reflections by John Steiner (1993b) on the three Oedipus plays.

The creation of an imaginative space that lies between the author and his or her audience is characteristic of most significant art. One can think of artists as having a distinctive capacity to find and occupy a "third position", in Ronald Britton's (1998a) terms, from which creations of their imagination are able to have their own independent being. The distinction drawn by Coleridge (1817, chaps. 4 and 13) between fancy and imagination or in psychoanalytic terms between shallow wish-fulfilment, in inferior work, and the realization of truths in greater work (Segal, 1952), is related to this element of "thirdness". To achieve this, artists and writers need to be able to reflect on their own work, from the perspectives of the potential spectator and that of their own "internal spectator", which enables them to adjust their own work in order to achieve the standard they aim for. Writers and painters have to ask themselves, does this or that passage "work" as it should do? This is another kind of "thirdness".

Writers sometimes refer to their characters acquiring a life of their own, as if in the act of writing characters become agents in making their own story. When Joseph Conrad writes about the captains and fellow-officers of merchant ships, we might imagine that he has been in these places in these men's shoes (as he had been), but we know that these are not merely memories of actual people he had known. Captain MacWhirr, of *Typhoon*, or the hero of the *Shadow Line* taking up his first command, are "as if" persons who exist in an imagined, created space and time, whose relationship to reality is a refracted and complex one. Fictional characters like these are not versions or surrogates of the author, nor are they disguised descriptions of real persons, although actual observations may have contributed to their characterization. Indeed, such "borrowings" from real life are often significant in fictional works. In the Preface to his novel *Victory: An Island Tale* (1902), Conrad referred to encounters with the real individuals who had been starting-points for his characters.

Relations between writers and their characters and their representations of them are different from those that analysts have with their patients, and their descriptions in case reports. The subjects of the latter descriptions are real people, in their actual relationships with their analysts, from the perspective of their unconscious mental life. Even though descriptions of patients are usually incomplete, nevertheless their aim must be to convey as much of the truth about them as is possible. Readers of over-theoretical descriptions of cases may ask "Where is the patient?" believing that something is missing if there is no description of a recognizable person against which to test the relevance of concepts.

What, then, do psychoanalysts—and those who think in a psychoanalytic way—do when they try to understand and write about works
of art and literature? If artists need to have an implicit understanding
of unconscious phenomena to represent them, what can psychoanalysts add through their interpretations of such works? Is their belief
that they can discover something "unconscious" of which an author
was unaware? Is an alternative to focusing on authors' minds to reflect
instead on the inner worlds of their fictional characters? Some psychoanalytic writing about literature does just this, often in insightful ways.
But before we consider what this can contribute to the understanding of
works of culture, some preliminary reflections may be useful.

Psychoanalytic interpretation as a genre of cultural criticism

Clearly the function of criticism is to broaden or deepen the understanding of readers or audiences of what they read or view. At one stage such
a task was thought of as a work of mere explication or clarification,
from within a perspective whose implicit assumptions did not need to
be made explicit, still less set out in theoretical terms. T. S. Eliot's (1923)
definition of criticism as "The elucidation of works of art and the correction of taste" was exemplary, in its time, of this view. But from the 1960s
onwards the pressure of social and political divisions on many fields
of cultural practice—differences of social class, gender, race and ideology, for example—challenged these assumptions. Major revaluations of
established cultural canons were proposed, from such orientations as
those of feminism, Marxism, "queer theory", anti-colonialism, and the
"relativist" positions represented in post-structuralism. Cultures, and
thus the societies of which they were a part, were now being made and
re-made not just through the practices of "creative" writers and artists,
but also by an influential new stratum of cultural critics and theorists,
located mostly in a vastly expanded university system. They sought (in
contest with one another) to define the theoretical terms in which cultural work was to be understood and assigned value. At some points it
seemed that cultural theorists were assigning more importance to their
own work than to that of the artists and writers whom they were osten-
sibly seeking to interpret.

    A question then arises: if psychoanalytic writing about literature,
visual art, and other cultural artefacts is one among many varieties of cultural criticism, what new kind of understanding does it offer? One should
note, in fact, that its practice in Britain long preceded the "paradigm shift"
in the field of critical theory that I have described above. Psychoanalytic
literature and art critics in Britain have, on the whole, shared the evaluations

of the established culture concerning the most admired kinds of art and literature, and rarely sought to challenge these. Their contribution was mainly to offer a new dimension to the understanding of already canonical works by discovering in them additional levels of "unconscious" meaning. The established tradition of literary criticism, after its "professionalization" in the 1930s, defined emotional depth, the exploration of moral qualities and complexities, and textual precision as its central criteria of value. Psychoanalytic approaches similarly esteemed these qualities in cultural works, as they did in their own clinical practices. They found their approach relevant to some works of popular as well as "high culture" (Bainbridge, Ward, & Yates, 2013; Bainbridge & Yates, 2014; Bell, 1999; MacRury & Rustin, 2014; Richards, 1994), and in relation to cinema (Sabbadini, 2003, 2014) responding to a more "democratic" tendency in mainstream cultural analysis. For these reasons, British psychoanalytic criticism, within the object-relations traditions, has remained somewhat aloof from most contemporary controversies in cultural theory (for example, regarding class, gender, colonialism, and race) on which Lacanian ideas have had a much greater influence (M. J. Rustin, 2017b). Its orientation towards imaginative and "creative" practices—for example, in the educational sphere—is only partially a challenge to the dominant culture.

Within this context, how does one decide what psychoanalytic interpretation can add to the understanding of works of art? The point of departure within this tradition should be Freud's own observation, quoted above, that "The poets and philosophers before me discovered the unconscious. What I discovered was the scientific method by which the unconscious could be studied." Thus, the question is what is the discovery concerning unconscious mental life, which a writer has made in a specific work? Can this discovery be assigned a meaning within the conceptual (or scientific) framework of ideas that psychoanalysts find useful? What should be crucial in the psychoanalytic understanding of art is the *artist's* understandings and their impact on their audiences, not the psychoanalyst's concepts, seeking their realization or confirmation in a work of art or literature. Bion's aphorism, "eschew memory and desire", intended as advice for the analyst in the consulting room, is relevant *a fortiori* to analysts in their response to art.

The experience of "excess"

How is it to be decided if there is a discovery or insight in a work that calls for such psychoanalytic interpretation? How is this to be recognized, since there may be little direct correspondence between the writer's representation of such an insight and the psychoanalyst's? It is rare indeed that fictional writers provide conceptual signposts for psychoanalysts—their modes of understanding are usually quite different. The evidence that there is an "unconscious" dimension in a work that justifies its explanation lies, rather, in the presence of a kind of "excess", in a term of Žižek's (and before him Lacan's), which was discussed in chapter 15—that is to say, in a response by the reader or viewer to a work, or an aspect of it, which seems in some unexpected way to be powerful and inexplicable. It is this excess that may denote the presence and of an unconscious dimension.

In work that Margaret Rustin and I have done (M. E. Rustin & Rustin, 2001, 2002), an element of unexpectedly intense response has been, for us, an essential stimulus to psychoanalytic reflection. For example, in regard to E. B. White's 1952 story for children, *Charlotte's Web*, the issue was to understand, why should we be moved by the life-giving actions and eventual death of a spider? Or, in writing about *Macbeth*, why should we feel such a sense of loss when Lady Macbeth and Macbeth each die, when they have been so monstrous in their actions? Or, writing about the Harry Potter novels, why should we attach such significance to the fact that three of the characters (Harry, Voldemort, and Snape), each involved in the stories' central struggle between the forces of love and hatred, should all have had childhoods in which they were deprived of affection? Or, why do we believe that the adventure of the goldfish who wants to be a human child, and who changes her name from Brunhilde, her father's name for her, to Ponyo (the title of Miyazaki's animation film), is a metaphor for something deeper than a story about a fish (M. E. Rustin & Rustin, 2012)? One of several areas of interest of the revived *Doctor Who* series on British television (2005 to present) is the complexity of the relationships between the Doctor(s) and his/her companions, in which oedipal issues lie beneath the surface (MacRury & Rustin, 2014). In the case of Shakespeare's *Romeo and Juliet*, the specific experience engendered by the play to which we responded was the headlong rush of its action, which repeatedly denied to its characters space and time to think about what was happening to them (M. J. Rustin, 1991b).

Our belief has been that the writers and directors in question have all grasped, in the scenarios that they have imagined, significant unconscious aspects of mental life. Their narratives have brought these implicit meanings home to audiences in powerful ways. Our aim has been to explore these emotional effects within the conceptual framework of psychoanalysis.

Thus we suggested that Charlotte the spider is experienced by child readers as a mother whose labour and sacrifices make the survival of her child possible, enabling him to outlive her. Here the metaphorical child is a piglet, Wilbur, whom she has taken under her protection. The writer draws his child readers into a transference relationship with these characters.

The reason audiences mourn the deaths of the Macbeths is because of their recognition of their love for each other and their dependence on each other for their psychic survival, even though they wholly fail to sustain this. *Macbeth* is thus the tragedy of a marriage that has ended in disaster. Shakespeare understood all this, at a time when the idea of a companionate marriage between quasi-equal partners had barely emerged in his culture (M. E. Rustin & Rustin, 2002).

The idea that human personalities are inherently divided between impulses to love and to hate, and that the balance between these depends on the qualities of parental care (by whoever takes this role) lies at the centre of J. K. Rowling's *Harry Potter* stories. Part of the emotional power of Miyazaki's film *Ponyo* can be understood if we recognize in it a metaphor for a child's adoption, the bringing together of a child who wants to be in a family and who experiences a rebirth when she sees this prospect, with a family ready to receive her.

In the case of *Romeo and Juliet*, the idea that best helped to explain the catastrophic flow of events of the play and their tragic outcome was Bion's theory of thinking and the conditions of emotional containment that this depends on (M. J. Rustin, 1991b). The play demonstrates how these conditions come to be lacking, in its representations of family structures, social conflict, and fragile political authority. It is a quite a step between what Shakespeare represented through the particulars of his play and the post-Kleinian theory of thinking that can illuminate its action, although their essential understandings are congruent with one another.

Thus we discover as psychoanalytic interpreters of fictional works that particular stories can be seen to be instances of more generic "kinds" of life-journeys. Just as, in Freud's view, jokes can pleasurably convey meaning (through the release of forbidden desires), so fictional narratives may be effective because their deeper or unconscious meanings are conveyed by inviting identification with characters who seem remote from everyday life. One can describe in psychoanalytic terms what is unconsciously at issue in such works. However, the primary understandings are those of their authors, not of their interpreters. It is, indeed, the power of works of art that inspires the desire to understand them more fully.

Psychoanalytic interpretations of novels or plays are sometimes criticized for falsely equating fictional with real persons, attributing unconscious motivations to them rather as analysts might reflect on their patients. But actors and directors often imagine "back-stories" for characters as a means of understanding them. Shakespeare has Richard III tell his own back-story, which is later angrily filled out by his mother, the Duchess of York (*Richard III*, IV, iv, 165–175). Of course there are risks of going beyond the evidence of the text in such interpretations, but in doing so one may be merely setting out what an author has already deeply understood.

Classic examples of psychoanalytic interpretation of literature and drama

Many exceptional works of psychoanalytic interpretation of imaginative works are consistent with the approach set out above. Freud's (1900a, pp. 261–264) seminal interpretation of King Oedipus was like this. He saw in Sophocles' play manifestations of unconscious desires that he made central to psychoanalysis. He also saw in Oedipus's heroic will to understand the reasons for the disaster that had taken place in his kingdom a metaphor for what psychoanalysts have to do if they are to understand the unconscious.

John Steiner (1993b) had a different insight into King Oedipus and into the two companion Theban plays. For all Oedipus's determination to solve the puzzle that had been set for him by the disastrous state of the city he ruled and by the Sphinx, Steiner noted that Oedipus and those around him had failed to see facts that were right before their eyes. Oedipus silenced the prophet who brought them to his attention, because of his anxiety about what he might learn if he listened to him. (The Greek tragedians, and later Shakespeare, well understood the hatred that can be directed towards bearers of unwanted knowledge.) At this time Steiner was writing about narcissistic personality organi-zations and their "borderline" states of mind, arising from his clinical work with patients. He saw the tragedy as the outcome of Oedipus's refusal to know—a defence against anxiety, which he termed "turning a blind eye". In writing about *Oedipus at Colonus* (a play whose action follows that of *Oedipus Rex* but preceded it in Sophocles' writing), Steiner extended his view of Oedipus's narcissism, noting Oedipus's complacency in his sanctified exile. It seems that the dramatist and the psychoanalyst share an understanding of a phenomenon, though each in their own ways.

What are the connections between these two forms of knowledge? There are instances, such as those given above, where psychoanalysts' reflections on imaginative writing have stimulated the development of their own theoretical ideas. Such are the ideas of the Oedipus complex in the first case and the borderline defence of "turning a blind eye" in the second. There can be parallels between the experiences of literature and the clinical consulting room. They are each contexts for understanding states of mind and feeling. Aristotle, in his *Poetics,* argued that the actions (and characters) of tragedy could represent a universal kind of truth, even though a play represents a particular situation, in one place and time. ("Poetry, therefore, is a more philosophical and a higher thing than history: for poetry tends to express the universal, history the particular.")

There are many instances where psychoanalytic interpretation has both enhanced understanding of a work of literature and shown the explanatory power of psychoanalytic ideas, but where no new development of psychoanalytic theories is involved. An interpretation of Shakespeare's *Richard III* can illustrate this. Richard of Gloucester seems to be an ideal-typical representation of the personality organization characterized by Herbert Rosenfeld (1971, 1987) as destructive narcissism. Shakespeare understood how envy and hatred can be the central motivating forces of a character. The implications of this character formation, and its imagined origins, are elaborated as the play proceeds. This reading of the play, like the experience of thinking about a patient in analysis, can deepen for the analyst their understanding of an idea that draws on its formulation in psychoanalytic writing.

Through such interpretations, psychoanalytic ideas can be broadened in their scope of application and illustrated in ways that enhance our understanding of them. Sometimes this leads to their further development. Hanna Segal (1974, 1984), for example, provided powerful readings of a number of fictional works, including—Conrad's *The Shadow Line* (1917), and Golding's *The Spire* (1964). In the first, she described Conrad's hero as undergoing what Elliot Jaques had characterized as a "mid-life crisis" and added to the texture of the concept in doing so. In the second, she elaborated the meaning of the Kleinian ideas of manic defence and denial and extended its scope of application.

One of the affinities between psychoanalysis and some imaginative literature lies in a shared awareness of the multidimensional capabilities of language. Psychoanalysts approach the communications of patients (for example, dreams and free associations, and play in the case of children) with an attentive eye to their implicit and metaphorical meanings. For Freud, the sources of this complexity lay in repression. Repressed desires and unconscious anxieties may be recognized and expressed or may be communicated only indirectly—for example, through condensations and displacements of meaning that correspond to the linguistic figures of metaphor and metonymy. There are other aspects of the self—states of envy, jealousy, guilt, shame, and anxiety, for example—which are often denied and disavowed, but which nevertheless find elliptical or concealed expression. These are the implicit meanings that analysts seek to understand and sometimes interpret to patients.

Poetry is distinctively characterized by the compressed and multidimensional quality of its use of language. Terry Eagleton (2008) put this well when he described the affinity between semiological understandings of poetic language and the less theorized assumptions of advocates of "close reading", from a more empirical tradition.[5] He has argued that the main reason for a psychoanalytic perspective being relevant to literature is its understanding of the psychological. Novels have a kind of complexity different from that of poetry, which is expressed through narrative and character, as well as imagery.

Meg Harris Williams and Margot Waddell (1991) have argued for the congruence between poetic and psychoanalytic conceptions of the mind and its development, providing illuminating readings of certain works of literature—for example, the plays of Shakespeare, the poetry of Keats, and the novels of George Eliot—to illustrate their view. The affinity between many forms of art and literature and the psychoanalytic tradition has its origin in their rejection of a narrowly rationalistic view of the mind and their insistence on the centrality of emotional and imaginative life. This conception was forcefully articulated within the Romantic tradition, at a point when a rationalistic and scientific world view was becoming the most powerful organizer of Western culture. Its continuing influence explains some of the convergence between psychoanalytic ways of thinking and the conceptions of culture to which it has most affinity.

Non-literary cultural forms

Understanding of the unconscious is represented in forms of art other than literature. Richard Rusbridger (2008, 2013) in his writings about two operas, Mozart's *Don Giovanni*, and Verdi's *Otello*, and Francis Grier in papers on Verdi's *Rigoletto* (Grier, 2011) and *La Traviata* (Grier, 2014), have shown how this could be achieved through musical expression. Rusbridger has shown that the psychological mechanisms of projective identification through which Iago is able to colonize and pervert the mind of Othello is represented not only through language and gesture (as is accomplished in Shakespeare's play), but also by the transfer in the composition of musical themes and tropes from one character and his voice to another, thus enabling the non-verbal experience of the music to bear some of its emotional meaning. His paper on *Don Giovanni* (2008) develops parallel insights. Rusbridger and Grier are unusual in being fully attuned to the registers of both psychoanalysis and music. They can thus show how much unconscious understanding Mozart and Verdi were able to convey through the music as well as the words of their operas.

Powerful psychoanalytic interpretations have been offered of the visual arts also. Adrian Stokes (Stokes & Williams, 2014) proposed a psychoanalytic way of understanding the spatial and textural properties of architectural forms, suggesting that contrasts between inside and outside, the rough and the smooth, and the shaping and modulation of physical openings reflected architects' understanding of infantile anxieties about containment and exposure and created symbolic resolutions of these. He saw a link between built forms and the primary human relationship to mother's body, in which he was influenced by Klein's theory of early development. He believed that the experience of architecture was illuminated by this perspective. John Summerson's descriptions, in *Heavenly Mansions* (1963), of the multiple iteration of forms of maternal containment in the traditional designs of churches, with their repeated representation at different scales (we might say as fractals) of symbolic shelter and enclosure ("aedicules"), was a similar kind of insight. Jenifer Wakelyn's (2000) fine essay on still-life painting established a link between this genre of art and the infants' early perceptual experience of objects in space, seen in psychoanalytic terms.

The appeal of the varieties of slapstick comedy can also be understood in relation to the experiences of young children, as they manage the excitements and anxieties of their own bodies in their environment. Buster Keaton's blank face surely functions as a screen on which viewers can project their identification with him, as he performs with virtuosity his defiance of the threats that the force of gravity and physical objects pose to his survival. Although for very young children the boundaries between the conscious and the unconscious minds have barely been set, it is to the unconscious child-in-the adult that these images communicate when they are seen by grown-up audiences.

The argument here is that the point of departure for psychoanalytic interpretation of works of art should be the recognition of what their authors have discovered implicitly about unconscious mental life. This "psychoanalytic" recognition may initially be an apprehension in feeling. The closest possible attention to the detail of what an artist or writer has produced is the prerequisite for psychoanalytic interpretation, just as close attention to a patient is the prerequisite for interpretation in the consulting room.

However, "close reading" and deep emotional responsiveness to a text or artwork may be insufficient to make significant connections between works of art and psychoanalytic understanding. It is usually necessary to recognize not only what unconscious meaning an artist has represented, but also through what techniques, and within what conventions of expression this has been achieved. Originality in a work often involves departures from established conventions within its genre. In order to understand the qualities of a work, one needs to understand the "kind" to which it belongs and the expectations that audiences will have brought to it. Critical understanding requires attention to context.

Such "contexts"—the field within which works of art or literature are produced—are of emotional and indeed unconscious significance to arts and writers. Harold Bloom's *Anxiety of Influence* (1973) asserted this when he argued that major poets in the Western tradition were often engaged in oedipal struggles with their forerunners. He enables us to see that the primary object-relations of artists and writers are not confined to the parental figures of their early lives. Rather, as artists and writers form a commitment to their vocation, they often develop relations to the significant creative figures of their artistic field.

One kind of "reduction" to which the psychoanalytic interpretation of art is susceptible assumes that the primary "objects" of symbolic representation lie in the earlier relationships of artists to their inner world, arising from their experiences of infancy. Since it is normal in psychoanalytic practice to seek to find the infant in the older child or adult, why would it not follow that in the study of works of art one would also be looking for the traces of the infantile self? Sometimes this has been a fruitful approach. It has been important to the psychoanalytic study of art from when Freud's essay on Leonardo da Vinci put forward hypotheses about Leonardo's childhood and its influence on his work. Hanna Segal's theory of art also focuses on such primary object-relations. Some great works of literature are themselves representations of the primary developmental experiences that psychoanalysis has set out to theorize and describe. Wordsworth's *The Prelude* is such an example. Primary relational anxieties arising in later phases of the life-cycle are central issues in other plays of Shakespeare: the Macbeths' desperation about succession and King Lear's and Prospero's responses to ageing and their unavoidable displacement by the young are examples.

Artists and their objects

This psychoanalytic conception of the functions of art and literature has sometimes been unduly partial in its approach. It can fail to recognize that the "objects" to which artists and writers become attached and which become their "internal objects" are not only inner-world residues of the familial objects of their earliest years, but may have been adopted in later life from the fields of art in which they have chosen to work. Such "objects" may be forerunner artists with whom they identify positively or negatively, as Harold Bloom argued. They may be the actual forms and processes of art work, its genres, conventions, and techniques. The idea that artists may have an "internal" relation to the objects of their work implies that there is a psychodynamic aspect to questions of how artists are formed and influenced by the example of their forerunners and contemporaries. Such "influences" have some of the attributes of transferences and identifications, both conscious and unconscious.

Such attachments and rejections have been explored and represented in works of art themselves, and in artists' own reflective writings. For example, Eduard Manet wrote about the impact on him of the paintings of Velasquez, which he had seen in Madrid. Some of his own portraits transpose Velasquez's ways of seeing and celebrating noble human qualities from the Spanish court of the seventeenth century to the more democratic Paris of the nineteenth century. The dignified attributes of subjects painted at court are transposed to street people. Bob Dylan's early "Song to Woody" expresses, both in musical form and in words, a homage to Woody Guthrie, his folksinger forerunner. The song describes a visit to Guthrie when he was nearing the end of his life, and Dylan expresses in it what will become his lifelong identification with him. Truffaut's early film, *Les Quatres-Cent Coups*, portrays through his child hero Truffaut's own estrangement from his family and the beginnings of his attachment to cinema (we see him and his boyhood friend sneaking into the picture house) as his substitute "family". His later film, *La Nuit Américaine*, in which Truffaut plays the part of a director making a film, is both a joyous celebration of the cinema to which Truffaut was devoted as the central commitment of his life and the continued emotional troubles of the Antoine Doinel character who was, in several pictures, an apparent surrogate for Truffaut himself.[6] There are different kinds of "internal object" that psychoanalytic interpreters may find represented and explored in works of art.

In working as clinicians, psychoanalysts can depend primarily on the ideas and techniques that have been evolved within their own field, to understand and help their patients. In attempting to interpret works of culture they have, in addition, to give their close attention to another "field": that of the form of art or literature to which they are responding. This is a difficult double task. It is perhaps because of this complexity that there has been so little accumulation of "findings", or "codification of methods", in this field, compared with what has been achieved in the clinical field of psychoanalysis.

Questions of method

What, then, can be proposed, by way of methods of research, for the psychoanalytic interpretation of cultural artefacts? The initial question to be asked is, what intention did an artist or writer have in creating a particular work? (Wollheim, 1968, 1987) The meaning of a work of art depends in the first instance on its creator's own understanding of it, on the particular interpretation of the world of experience—such as of persons, objects, senses, or feelings—which he or she desires to represent. There is a tendency in psychoanalytic writing about art or literature to overlook the specific intentions of artists and writers and the techniques and conventions employed by them, and instead regard their representations of reality as if they were unmediated reality itself.

Artists can represent "reality" only through the mediation of signifying procedures—words on a page or marks on a canvas—and the conventions that shape these: for example, "realism" in the novel or drama, "perspective" or "impressionism" in painting. Such signifying procedures may be concealed or disavowed by the writers and artists who employ them, with the effect of enabling their works to be seen as descriptions or pictures of reality itself—the world as it is, or as we actually see it—rather than as what is always an artist's interpretation of it. The power of such representations can be to structure the world so that it is seen and experienced as imaginative writers and artists see them. Thus an effect of those kinds of "modernist" literature, by writers such as Proust, Joyce, James, or Woolf, that explored and represented complex states of individual consciousness (in ways that now seem convergent with psychoanalytic ways of thinking) was to enable readers to recognize and develop these psychological capabilities in themselves. Artists and writers thus both represent and re-make the world. Life does imitate art, often.

Serious challenges to an established world-view involve drawing attention to the conventions of representation by which it has been previously "normalized". This may be achieved by "shock" artistic effects—challenges to realism in literature, naturalism in literature, and tonality in music in the early twentieth century were achieved through the impact of works that defied these conventions. But they do this also by explicitly contesting cultural rules and conventions themselves, through critical arguments that make visible their latent functions, and to replace them with new regulatory principles. Although there has long been a specialist vocation of literary and cultural critic (which may have begun with Aristotle and Plato), creative writers and artists have often been the most influential writers of reflective criticism, defining new frameworks and artistic "paradigms" through which their own works can be understood.

Psychoanalytic interpreters of art and literature are necessarily reflecting on works that are themselves representations of experience, shaped by an artist's purposes and technical resources. They are thus engaged in "double mediations": interpretations of what are already interpretations of experience. It might seem surprising, given this multi-layered complexity, that psychoanalysts can offer a distinctive and insightful kind of understanding of works of art and literature at all, Yet nevertheless they have done this. How has this happened?

We have referred to correspondences perceived by psychoanalysts between the understandings that artists have achieved in their repre-sentations of particulars (images, narratives, the actions of drama, for example), and the more universal or typifying formulations of psycho-analytic concepts and theories. Freud's statement that artists had first discovered the unconscious, but that psychoanalysis had developed a scientific method for understanding it, captures this distinction.

A complex passage of ideas and sensibilities has also taken place in the reverse direction, not through psychoanalysts' interpretation of works of art, but through writers' and artists' engagements with psychoanalytic ideas and sensibilities and the assimilation of these in their work. Thus not only have psychoanalysts been influenced by the creative arts, but the arts and literature have been influenced by psy-choanalysis, sometimes through artists' personal experience of analysis, but more widely through the influence of psychoanalysis on the cultures that psychoanalysts and cultural producers both inhabit. How writers and artists can productively assimilate psychoanalytic ways of thinking is an issue for them, not for psychoanalysts. The boldest and most self-conscious of such conjunctions was that of the Surrealists, whose work was in part a project to shock its publics into an awareness of the uncon-scious and its depths and paradoxes. More pervasive convergences have taken place through the presence of psychoanalysis in the cultures that artists and psychoanalysts shared. Specific influences are often difficult to trace, and it may be that the more obvious and literal such influences are, the less is their significance. Actual fictional representations of psy-choanalysts in films or novels are not the most profound evidence of the presence of psychoanalytic ways of thinking in our culture.

Thus the primary methodological lesson to be learned in regard to the relations between psychoanalysis as one field of understanding and literature and the arts as another is that the greatest need, if productive work is to be done, is to respect the specificities and autonomy of each of them. What I hope to have shown, however, is that the psychoanalytic interpretation of works of art and culture can bring illuminating insights to both fields. This is one of the ways in which Freud's hope that psychoanalytic understanding would encompass the whole field of human life—or at least a central dimension of it—can be best realized.

Notes

1. It should be noted that in recent decades the largest psychoanalytic influence on academic literary and cultural studies has come from the Lacanian tradition. However, this is not the subject of this chapter.

2. Examples are Joyce's *Portrait of the Artist as a Young Man* (1916), Fitzgerald's *Tender Is the Night* (1934), Baldwin's *Go Tell It on the Mountain* (1953), Kerouac's *On the Road* (1957), and Plath's *The Bell Jar* (1963), but also novels by Dickens, Charlotte Bronte, Tolstoy, and many others.

3. "Several things dovetailed in my mind, & at once it struck me, what quality went to form a Man of Achievement especially in Literature & which Shakespeare possessed so enormously—I mean *Negative Capability*, that is when a man is capable of being in uncertainties, Mysteries, doubts, without any irritable reaching after fact & reason . . ." (Keats, 1817).

4. Freud (1916d) provides some examples of psychoanalytic character analysis.

5. "The poetic text for Lotman is thus a 'system of systems', a relation of relations. It is the most complex form of discourse imaginable, condensing together several systems each of which contains its own tensions, parallelisms, repetitions and oppositions, and each of which is continually modifying all of the others. A poem, in fact, can only be re-read, not read, since some of its structures can only be perceived retrospectively. Poetry activates the *full* body of the signifier, presses the word to work to its utmost under the intense pressure of surrounding words, and so to release its richest potential" (Eagleton, 2008, p. 102; see also Eagleton, 2006).

6. In an interview about the film, one of the actresses, Natalie Baye, said that the film director whose part Truffaut plays in the film is scarcely different from the actual Truffaut who is directing the film. Cinema was his real passion, she says. In *La Nuit Americaine*, life and art come close to one another. The fictional director narrates his experiences on the set in voice-overs, and at one exhilarating moment of filming we hear "Cinema is king."

REFERENCES

Abram, M. H. (1953). *The Mirror and the Lamp: Romantic Theory and the Critical Tradition*. Oxford: Oxford University Press.

Adamo, S., & Rustin, M. E. (Eds.) (2014). *Young Child Observation: A Development in the Theory and Method of Young Child Observation*. London: Karnac.

Adorno, T. (1951). Freudian theory and the pattern of Fascist propaganda. In: A. Arato & E. Gebhardt (Eds.), *The Essential Frankfurt School Reader* (pp. 118–137). Oxford: Blackwell, 1978.

Akobeng, A. K. (2005). Understanding randomised controlled trials. *British Medical Journal Archives of Diseases in Childhood, 90* (8). Available at: http://adc.bmj.com/content/90/8/840

Anderson, J. (2006). Well-suited partners: Psychoanalytic research and grounded theory. *Journal of Child Psychotherapy, 32* (3): 329–348.

APA (2013). *Diagnostic and Statistical Manual of Mental Disorders, Fifth Edition (DSM-5)*. Washington, DC: American Psychiatric Association.

Archer, M. (2003). *Structure, Agency and the Internal Conversation*. Cambridge: Cambridge University Press.

Arendt, H. (1951). *The Origins of Totalitarianism*. New York: Schocken Books.

Armstrong, D. (2005). *Organization in the Mind: Psychoanalysis, Group Relations and Organizational Consultancy*. London: Karnac.

Armstrong, D., & Rustin, M. J. (2015). *Social Defences against Anxiety: Explorations in a Paradigm*. London: Karnac.

Atran, S. (1990). *Cognitive Foundations of Natural History: Towards an Anthropology of Science*. Cambridge: Cambridge University Press.

Bacon, F. (1620). *The New Organon*. Cambridge: Cambridge University Press, 2008.

Bain, A., & Barnett, L. (1986). *The Design of a Day-Care System in a Nursery Setting for Children Under Five*. Occasional Paper 8. London: Tavistock Institute of Human Relations.

Bainbridge, C., Ward, I., & Yates, C. (2013). *Television and Psychoanalysis*. London: Routledge.

Bainbridge, C., & Yates, C. (2014). *Media and the Inner World: Psycho-Cultural Approaches to Emotion, Media and Popular Culture*. London: AIAA.

Baldwin, J. (1953). *Go Tell It on the Mountain*. London: Penguin, 2001.

Barnes, B., Bloor, D., & Henry, J. (1996). *Scientific Knowledge: A Sociological Analysis*. Chicago, IL: University of Chicago Press.

Barthes, R. (1977). Death of the author. In: *Image, Music Text*. London: Fontana.

Bateson, G. (1972). *Steps Towards an Ecology of Mind*. San Francisco, CA: Chandler Publishing.

Bauman, Z. (1979). The phenomenon of Norbert Elias. *Sociology, 13* (1 January).

Bell, D. (1999). The singing detective: A place in mind. In: D. Bell (Ed.), *Psychoanalysis and Culture: A Kleinian Perspective*. London: Karnac.

Bentinck van Schoonheten, A. (2016). *Karl Abraham: Life and Work, a Biography*. London: Karnac.

Bernstein, B. (1975). *Class Codes and Control, Vol. 3: Towards a Theory of Educational Transmissions*. London: Routledge & Kegan Paul.

Bertaux, D. (Ed.) (1981). *Biography and Society: The Life History Approach in the Social Sciences*. London: Sage.

Bhaskar, R. (1975). *A Realist Theory of Science*. London: Verso, 1997.

Bick, E. (1964). Notes on infant observation in psychoanalytic training. *International Journal of Psychoanalysis, 45*: 558–566.

Bick, E. (1968). The experience of the skin in early object relations, *International Journal of Psychoanalysis, 49*: 484–486.

Bion, W. R. (1957). Differentiation of the psychotic from the non-psychotic. *International Journal of Psychoanalysis, 38*: 206–275.

Bion, W. R. (1961). *Experiences in Groups*. London: Heinemann.

Bion, W. R. (1962). *Learning from Experience*. London: Heinemann.

Bion, W. R. (1967a). Notes on memory and desire. *Psychoanalytic Forum, 2*: 271–280. Reprinted in E. B. Spillius (Ed.), *Melanie Klein Today, Vol 2: Mainly Practice* (pp. 17–21). London: Routledge, 1988.

Bion, W. R. (1967b). *Second Thoughts*. London: Heinemann.

Bion, W. R. (1970). *Attention and Interpretation. A Scientific Approach to Insight in Psycho-Analysis and Groups*. London: Heinemann.

Bion, W. R. (1980). *Bion in New York and São Paulo*. Strath Tay: Clunie Press.

Black, M. (1962). *Models and Metaphors*. Ithaca, NY: Cornell University Press.

Bloom, H. (1973). *The Anxiety of Influence: A Theory of Poetry*. Oxford: Oxford University Press.

Bloor, D. (1976). *Knowledge and Social Imagery*. Chicago, IL: University of Chicago Press.

Bollas, C. (1995). *Cracking Up: The Work of Unconscious Experience*. London: Routledge.

Boston, M., & Szur, R. (Eds.) (1983). *Psychotherapy with Severely Deprived Children*. London: Routledge.

Bourdieu, P. (1984). *Distinction: A Social Critique of the Judgement of Taste*. London: Routledge.

Bowlby, J. (1952). *Maternal Care and Mental Health*. Geneva: World Health Organization.

Bowlby, J., Robertson, J., & Rosenbluth, D. (1952). A two-year-old goes to hospital. *Psychoanalytic Study of the Child, 7* (1): 82–94.

Briggs, A. (Ed.) (2002). *Surviving Space: Papers on Infant Observation*. London: Karnac.

Briggs, S. (1997). *Growth and Risk in Infancy*. London: Jessica Kingsley.

Britton, R. (1989). The missing link: Parental sexuality in the Oedipus complex. In: R. Britton, M. Feldman, & E. O'Shaughnessy, *The Oedipus Complex Today: Clinical Implications*. London: Karnac.

Britton, R. (1998a). *Belief and Imagination*. London: Routledge.

Britton, R. (1998b). Subjectivity, objectivity and triangular space. In: *Belief and Imagination* (pp. 41–58). London: Routledge.

Britton, R., & Steiner, J. (1994). Interpretation: Selected fact or overvalued idea? *International Journal of Psychoanalysis, 75* (5–6): 1069–1078.

Bryant, A., & Charmaz, C. (Eds.) (2007). *The Sage Handbook of Grounded Theory*. London: Sage.

Byrne, D. (1998). *Complexity Theory and the Social Sciences: An Introduction*. London: Routledge.

Byrne, D., & Ragin, C. C. (Eds.) (2012). *Handbook of Case Study Research*. London: Sage.

Capra, F. (1997). *The Web of Life*. London: Flamingo.

Carlberg, G. (2007). Laughter opens the door: Turning points in child psychotherapy. *Journal of Child Psychotherapy, 23* (3): 331–349.

Cavell, S. (1987). *Disowning Knowledge in Six Plays of Shakespeare*. Cambridge: Cambridge University Press.

Chamberlayne, P., Rustin M. J., & Wengraf, T. (Eds.) (2002). *Biography and Social Exclusion in Europe*. Bristol: Policy Press.

Chamberlayne, P., Bornat, J., & Wengraf, T. (Eds.) (2000). *The Turn to Biographical Methods in Social Sciences*. London: Routledge.

Charmaz, K. (2006). *Constructing Grounded Theory*. London: Sage.

Chodorow, N. (1978). *The Reproduction of Mothering*. Berkeley, CA: University of California Press.

Cioffi, F. (1970). Freud and the idea of a pseudo-science. In: F. Borger & F. Cioffi (Eds.), *Explanation in the Behavioural Sciences*. London: Cambridge University Press.

Cioffi, F. (1998). *Freud and the Question of Pseudoscience*. London: Open Court.

Cipriani, A., Zhou, X., Del Giovne, C., Hetrik, S., Qin, B., Whittington, C., et al. (2016). Comparative efficacy and tolerability of antidepressants for major depressive disorder in children and adolescents: A network meta-analysis. *The Lancet, 388* (10047): 881–890.

Clarke, S., & Hoggett, P. (2009). *Researching beneath the Surface: Psycho-Social Research Methods in Practice*. London: Karnac.

Coleridge, S. T. (1817). *Biographia Literaria*. London: Everyman's Library, 1975.

Conrad, J. (1915). *Victory: An Island Tale*. London: Everyman's Library Classics, 1998.

Conrad, J. (1917). *The Shadow Line*. London: J. M. Dent.

Cooper, A. (2017). Soft eyes: Observation as research. In: H. Hingley-Jones, C. Parkinson, & L. Allain (Eds.), *Observation in Health and Social Care: Applications for Learning Research and Practice with Children and Adults* (pp. 177–200). London: Jessica Kingsley.

Cooper, A., & Lousada, J. (2005). *Borderline Welfare: Feeling and Fear of Feeling in the Modern Welfare State*. London: Karnac.

Creaser, M. (2015). *A Comparison of Audio Recordings and Therapists' Process Notes in Child and Adolescent Psychoanalytic Psychotherapy*. Doctoral dissertation, UEL/Tavistock Clinic, London. Available at: http://repository.tavistockandportman.ac.uk/1353/1/Creaser%20-%20A%20 Comparison.pdf

Cregeen, S., Hughes, C., Midgley, N., Rhode, M., & Rustin, M. (2017). *Short-Term Psychoanalytic Psychotherapy for Adolescents with Depression: A Treatment Manual*. London: Karnac.

Crews, F. (1997). *The Memory Wars: Freud's Legacy in Dispute*. London: Granta Books.

Crews, F. (2017). *Freud: The Making of an Illusion*. London: Profile Books.

Damasio, A. (2000). *The Feeling of What Happens*. London: Heinemann.

Darwin, C. (1859). *On the Origin of Species*. Oxford: Oxford University Press, 2008.

Davidson, D. (1963). Actions, reasons and causes. In: *Actions and Events*. Oxford: Oxford University Press, 1980.

Dawkins, R. (1976). *The Selfish Gene*. Oxford: Oxford University Press.

Deleuze, G., & Guattari, F. (1980). *Capitalism and Schizophrenia, Vol. 2: A Thousand Plateaus*. London: Continuum, 1987.

Delion, P. (2000). The application of Esther Bick's method to the observation of babies at risk of autism. *Infant Observation*, 3 (3): 84–90.

Denzin, N. K. (1970). *The Research Act: A Theoretical Introduction to Sociological Methods*. Chicago, IL: Aldine.

Dicks, H. V. (1970). *Fifty Years of the Tavistock Clinic*. London: Routledge & Kegan Paul.

Dinnerstein, D. (1976). *The Mermaid and the Minotaur*. New York: Harper & Row.

Eagleton, T. (2006). *How to Read a Poem*. Oxford: Wiley-Blackwell.

Eagleton, T. (2008). *Literary Theory: An Introduction* (2nd ed.). Oxford: Wiley-Blackwell.

Eagleton, T. (2014). *How to Read Literature*. New Haven, CT: Yale University Press.

Eco, U., & Sebeok, T. A. (Eds.) (1988). *The Sign of Three: Dupin, Holmes, Peirce*. Bloomington, IN: Indiana University Press.

Edelman, G. (1992). *Bright Air, Brilliant Fire: On the Matter of the Mind*. London: Penguin.

Elias, N. (1991). *The Society of Individuals*. London: Continuum.

Elias, N. (2000). *The Civilising Process* (revised ed.). Oxford: Blackwell.

Eliot, T. S. (1923). The function of criticism. In: *Selected Essays*. London: Faber & Faber, 1999.

Empson, W. (1935). *Seven Versions of Pastoral*. London: Penguin.

Eysenck, H. (1973). *The Uses and Abuses of Psychology*. London: Pelican.

Eysenck, H. (2002). *The Decline and Fall of the Freudian Empire*. Piscataway, NJ: Transaction Books.

Fanon, F. (1952). *Black Skin, White Masks*. London: MacGibbon & Kee.

Ffytche, M. (2011). *The Foundations of the Unconscious: Schelling, Freud and the Birth of the Modern Psyche*. Cambridge: Cambridge University Press.

Fitzgerald, S. (1934). *Tender Is the Night*. London: Penguin, 2001.

Fonagy, P. (1993). The research agenda: The vital need for empirical research in child psychotherapy. *Journal of Child Psychotherapy*, 29 (2): 129–136.

Fonagy, P. (2001). *Attachment Theory and Psychoanalysis*. London: Karnac.

Fonagy, P. (2003). Psychoanalysis today. *World Psychiatry*, 2 (2): 73–80.

Fonagy, P., & Moran, G. (1993). Selecting single case research designs for clinicians. In N. E. Miller, L. Luborsky, J. P. Barber, & J. P. Docherty (Eds.), *Psychodynamic Treatment Research: A Handbook for Clinical Practice* (pp. 62–95). New York: Basic Books.

Fonagy, P., Rost, F., Carlyle, J., McPherson, S., Thomas, R., Fearon, P., et al. (2015). Pragmatic randomized controlled trial of long-term psychoanalytic psychotherapy for treatment-resistant depression: The Tavistock Adult Depression Study (TADS). *World Psychiatry*, 14: 312–321.

Fonagy, P., & Target, M. (1994). The efficacy of psychoanalysis for children with disruptive disorders. *Journal of the American Academy of Child & Adolescent Psychiatry*, 33 (1): 45–55. Available at: http://hewittlab.sites.olt.ubc.ca/files/2015/08/Fonagy1994.pdf

Fonagy, P., & Target, M. (2002). *Psychoanalytic Theories: Perspectives from Developmental Psychopathology*. London: Whurr.

Forrester, J. (1997). *Dispatches from the Freud Wars*. Cambridge, MA: Harvard University Press.

Foucault, M., & Rabinow, P. (1991). *Foucault's Reader: An Introduction to Foucault's Thought*. London: Penguin.

Freud, S. (1895d). *Studies on Hysteria. Standard Edition, 2*.

Freud, S. (1900a). *The Interpretation of Dreams. Standard Edition, 4/5*.

Freud, S. (1901b). *The Psychopathology of Everyday Life. Standard Edition, 6*.

Freud, S. (1905c). *Jokes and Their Relation to the Unconscious. Standard Edition, 8*.

Freud, S. (1905e). Fragments of an analysis of a case of hysteria. *Standard Edition, 7*: 1–122.

Freud, S. (1909b). Analysis of a phobia in a five-year-old boy. *Standard Edition, 10*: 1–150.

Freud, S. (1909d). Notes upon a case of obsessional neurosis. *Standard Edition, 10*: 151–318.

Freud, S. (1910c). *Leonardo da Vinci and a Memory of His Childhood. Standard Edition, 11*.

Freud, S. (1911c). Psycho-analytic notes on an autobiographical account of a case of paranoia. *Standard Edition, 22*.

Freud, S. (1912–13). *Totem and Taboo. Standard Edition, 13*.

Freud, S. (1914b). The Moses of Michelangelo. *Standard Edition, 13*.

Freud, S. (1916d). Some character-types met with in psycho-analytic work. *Standard Edition, 14*.

Freud, S. (1918b). From the history of an infantile neurosis. *Standard Edition, 17*.

Freud, S. (1921c). *Group Psychology and the Analysis of the Ego. Standard Edition, 18*.

Freud, S. (1926e). *The Question of Lay Analysis. Standard Edition, 20*.

Freud, S. (1927c). *The Future of an Illusion. Standard Edition, 21*.

Freud, S. (1930a). *Civilization and Its Discontents. Standard Edition, 21*.

Freud, S. (1939a). *Moses and Monotheism. Standard Edition, 23*.

Galatzer-Levy, R. M. (1995). Psychoanalysis and dynamical systems theory: Prediction and self similarity. *Journal of the American Psychoanalytic Association, 43*: 1085–1113.

Galatzer-Levy, R. M. (2005). Chaotic possibilities: Towards a new model of development. *International Journal of Psychoanalysis, 85* (2): 419–441.

Galatzer-Levy, R. M. (2009). Finding your way through chaos, fractals, and other exotic mathematical objects: A guide for the perplexed. *Journal of the American Psychoanalytic Association, 57* (5): 1227–1249.

Galison, P., & Stump, D. J. (Eds.) (1996). *The Disunity of Science*. Stanford, CA: Stanford University Press.

Gallie, W. B. (1952). *Peirce and Pragmatism*. Harmondsworth: Pelican.

Garland, C. (Ed.) (2002). *Understanding Trauma: A Psychoanalytic Approach.* London: Karnac.

Geertz, C. (1973). *The Interpretation of Cultures.* New York: Basic Books.

Geertz, C. (1983). *Local Knowledge: Further Essays in Interpretive Anthropology.* New York: Basic Books.

Gellner, E. (1975). *The Legitimation of Belief.* Cambridge: Cambridge University Press.

Gellner, E. (1985). *The Psychoanalytic Movement: The Cunning of Unreason.* London: Paladin.

Gellner, E. (1994). *Plough, Sword and Book: The Structure of Human History.* London: Collins Harvill.

Gellner, E. (1995). Freud's social contract. In: *Anthropology and Politics* (pp. 62–93). Oxford: Blackwell.

Giddens, A. (1979). *Central Problems in Social Theory.* Basingstoke: Macmillan.

Giddens, A, (1984). *The Constitution of Society.* Cambridge: Polity Press.

Gilmore, K. (2000). A psychoanalytic perspective on attention-deficit/hyperactivity disorder. *Journal of the American Psychoanalytic Association, 48* (4): 1259–1293.

Glaser, B., & Strauss, A. (1967). *The Discovery of Grounded Theory.* London: Weidenfeld & Nicolson.

Goethe, J. W. (1790). *The Metamorphosis of Plants.* Cambridge, MA: MIT Press, 2009.

Goffman, E. (1969). The insanity of place. *Psychiatry, 32*: 357–387.

Golding, W. (1964). *The Spire.* London: Faber & Faber.

Gomm, R., Hammersley, M., & Foster, P. (Eds.) (2000). *Case Study Method.* London: Sage.

Goodyer, I. M., Reynolds, S., Barrett, B., Byford, S., Dubicka, B., Hill, J., et al. (2017). Cognitive behavioural therapy and short-term psychoanalytical psychotherapy versus a brief psychosocial intervention in adolescents with unipolar major depressive disorder (IMPACT): A multicentre, pragmatic, observer-blind, randomised controlled superiority trial. *The Lancet, 4* (2): 109–119.

Gould, S. G. (2007). *Punctuated Equilibrium.* Cambridge, MA: Harvard University Press.

Gretton, A. (2006). An account of a year's work with a mother and her 18-month-old son. *Infant Observation, 9* (1): 21–34.

Grier, F. (2011). Thoughts on *Rigoletto. International Journal of Psychoanalysis, 92*: 1541–1559.

Grier, F. (2014). *La Traviata* and Oedipus, *International Journal of Psychoanalysis, 96*: 389–410.

Groarke, S. (2008). Psychoanalytic infant observation: A critical assessment. *European Journal of Psychotherapy and Counselling, 10* (4): 299–321.

Groarke, S. (2010). Making contact. *Infant Observation*, *13* (2): 209–222.

Grünbaum, A. (1974). *The Foundations of Psychoanalysis: A Philosophical Critique*. Berkeley, CA: University of California Press.

Grünbaum, A. (1993). *Validation in the Clinical Theory of Psychoanalysis*. Madison, CT: International Universities Press.

Hacking, I. (1983). *Representing and Intervening*. Cambridge: Cambridge University Press.

Hacking, I. (1999). *The Social Construction of What?* Cambridge, MA: Harvard University Press.

Harré, R. (1979). *Social Being*. Oxford: Blackwell.

Harré, R. (1981). *Great Scientific Experiments*. Oxford: Oxford University Press.

Harré, R. (1986). *Varieties of Realism: A Rationale for the Natural Sciences*. Oxford: Blackwell.

Harré, R., & Madden, E. H. (1975). *Causal Powers: A Theory of Natural Necessity*. Oxford: Blackwell.

Harris Williams, M., & Waddell, M. (1991). *The Chamber of Maiden Thought*. London: Routledge.

Harvard Law School (2018). *The Case Studies*. http://casestudies.law.harvard.edu

Heimann, P. (1950). On counter-transference, *International Journal of Psychoanalysis*, *31* (1/2): 81–84. Reprinted in: *About Children and Children-No-Longer. Collected Papers 1942–80*, ed. M. Tonnesman. London: Tavistock/Routledge, 1986.

Henriques, J., & Morley, D. (Eds.) (2017). *Stuart Hall: Conversations, Projects and Legacies*. London: Goldsmiths Press.

Henry, G. (1974). Doubly deprived. *Journal of Child Psychotherapy*, *3* (4): 15–28.

Hill, C. (1961). Protestantism and the rise of capitalism. In: F. J. Fisher (Ed.), *Essays in the Social and Economic History of Tudor and Stuart England* (pp. 15–49). Cambridge: Cambridge University Press.

Hill, C. (1991). *Change and Continuity in Pre-Revolutionary England*. Princeton, NJ: Yale University Press.

Hingley-Jones, H. Parkinson, C., & Allain L. (Eds.). (2017). *Observation in Health and Social Care: Applications for Learning Research and Practice with Children and Adults*. London: Jessica Kingsley.

Hinshelwood, R. D. (1989). *A Dictionary of Kleinian Thought*. London: Free Association Books.

Hinshelwood, R. D. (2013). *Research on the Couch: Single-Case Studies, Subjectivity and Scientific Knowledge*. London: Routledge.

Hinshelwood, R. D., & Skogstad, W. (2000). *Observing Organisations: Anxiety, Defence and Culture in Health Care*. London: Routledge.

Hoggart, R. (1967). *The Uses of Literacy*. London: Chatto & Windus.

Hollway, J. (2015). *Knowing Mothers: Researching Maternal Identity Change.* Basingstoke: Palgrave Macmillan.

Hollway, W., & Jefferson, T. (2012). *Doing Qualitative Research Differently* (2nd ed.). London: Sage.

Holmes, J. (2014). *John Bowlby and Attachment Theory.* London: Routledge.

Hopkins, J. (2004). Conscience and conflict: Darwin, Freud and the origins of human aggression. In: D. Evans & P. Cruse (Eds.), *Emotions, Evolution and Rationality* (pp. 225–248). Oxford: Oxford University Press.

Houzel, D. (1999). A therapeutic application of infant observation in child psychiatry. *Infant Observation*, 2 (3): 42–53.

Huffington, C., Halton, W., Armstrong D., & Pooley, J. (Eds.) (2004). *Working Beneath the Surface: The Emotional Life of Contemporary Organizations.* London: Karnac.

Hughes, J. (2004). *From Obstacle to Ally: The Evolution of Psychoanalytic Practice.* London: Brunner-Routledge.

Hume, D. (1739). *Treatise on Human Nature.* London: Penguin, 1985.

Hume, D. (1777). *Enquiry Concerning Human Understanding.* Oxford: Oxford University Press, 1963.

Jaques, E. (1955). Social systems as a defence against persecutory and depressive anxiety. In: M. Klein, P. Hermann, & R. E. Money-Kyrle (Eds.), *New Directions in Psychoanalysis* (pp. 478–498). London: Tavistock Publications.

Jones, E. (1949). *Hamlet and Oedipus.* New York: W. W. Norton, 1976.

Joseph, B. (1985). Transference: The total situation. *International Journal of Psychoanalysis*, 66: 447–454. Reprinted in: *Psychic Equilibrium and Psychic Change: Selected Papers of Betty Joseph.* London: Routledge/Institute of Psychoanalysis, 1989.

Joseph, B. (1989). *Psychic Equilibrium and Psychic Change: Selected Papers of Betty Joseph.* London: Routledge/Institute of Psychoanalysis.

Joyce, J. (1916). *Portrait of the Artist as a Young Man.* London: Penguin, 2000.

Kauffman, S. (1995). *At Home in the Universe: The Search for Laws of Complexity.* London: Viking.

Keat, R., & Urry, J. (1975). *Social Theory as Science.* London: Routledge.

Keats, J. (1817). *Letter to George and Thomas Keats, 22 December.* https://ebooks.adelaide.edu.au/k/keats/john/letters/letter24.html

Keegan, J. (1976). *The Face of Battle.* London: Bodley Head, 2014.

Kerouac, J. (1957). *On the Road.* London: Penguin, 2000.

Khaleelee, O. (2010). From autonomy to dependency? *British Journal of Psychotherapy*, 26 (2): 213–218.

King, P., & Steiner, R. (1991). *The Freud–Klein Controversies 1941–45.* London: Routledge/Institute of Psychoanalysis.

Klein, M. (1961). *Narrative of a Child Analysis.* London: Vintage Classics, 1998.

Knorr-Cetina, K. (1999). *Epistemic Cultures: How the Sciences Make Knowledge*. Cambridge, MA: Harvard University Press.

Kohon, G. (2014). *Reflections on the Aesthetic Experience: Psychoanalysis and the Uncanny*. London: Routledge.

Kuhn, T. S. (1962). *The Structure of Scientific Revolutions*. Chicago, IL: Chicago University Press.

Kuhn, T. S. (1970). Reflections on my critics. In: I. Lakatos & A. Musgrave (Eds.), *Criticism and the Growth of Knowledge* (pp. 231–278). Cambridge: Cambridge University Press.

Kuhn, T. S. (1977). Logic of discovery or psychology of research. In: *The Essential Tension: Selected Studies in Scientific Tradition and Change* (pp. 266–292). Chicago, IL: University of Chicago Press.

Kuhn, T. S. (1996). Postscript (1969). In: *The Structure of Scientific Revolutions* (3rd ed.). Chicago, IL: University of Chicago Press.

Kuhn, T. S. (2000). The road since *Structure. The Road Since Structure: Philosophical Essays 1970–1993* (pp. 90–104). Chicago, IL: University of Chicago Press.

Labinger, J., & Collins, H. (Eds.) (2001). *The One Culture: A Conversation about Science*. Chicago, IL: University of Chicago Press.

Lakatos, I. (1970). Falsification and the methodology of scientific research programmes. In: I. Lakatos and A. Musgrave, *Criticism and the Growth of Knowledge*. Cambridge: Cambridge University Press.

Lakoff, G., & Johnson, M. (1980). *Metaphors We Live By*. Chicago, IL: University of Chicago Press.

Lange, K. W., Reichl, S., Lange, K. M., Tucha, L., & Tucha, O. (2010). The history of attention deficit hyperactivity disorder. *ADHD Attention Deficit and Hyperactivity Disorders*, 2 (4): 241–255.

Langer, S. (1942). *Philosophy in a New Key: A Study in the Symbolism of Reason, Rite and Art*. Cambridge, MA: Harvard University Press.

Langer, S. (1953). *Feeling and Form*. London: Routledge.

Laplanche, J., & Pontalis, J.-B. (1967). *The Language of Psychoanalysis*. London: Hogarth Press, 1988.

Latour, B. (1983). Give me a laboratory and I will raise the world. In K. Knorr-Cetina & M. Mulkay (Eds.), *Science Observed*. London: Sage.

Latour, B. (1987). *Science in Action*. Cambridge, MA: Harvard University Press.

Latour, B. (1988). *The Pasteurisation of France*. Cambridge, MA: Harvard University Press.

Latour, B. (1993). *We Have Never Been Modern*. Hemel Hempstead: Harvester Wheatsheaf.

Latour, B., & Woolgar, S. (1979). *Laboratory Life: The Construction of Scientific Facts*. London: Sage.

Layard, R., & Clarke, D. (2015). *Thrive: The Power of Psychological Therapy*. London: Penguin.

Le Bon, G. (1895). *The Crowd: A Study of the Popular Mind*. www.gutenberg. org/ebooks/445

Lecourt, D. (1975). *Marxism and Epistemology: Bachelard, Canguilhem, Foucault*. London: New Left Books.

Le Riche, P., & Tanner, K. (1998). *Observation and Its Application to Social Work*. London: Jessica Kingsley.

Locke, K. (2007). Rational control and irrational free-play: Dual-thinking modes as necessary tension in grounded theorising. In: A. Bryant & C. Charmaz (Eds.), *The Sage Handbook of Grounded Theory* (pp. 565–579). London: Sage.

Luria, A. R. (1972). *The Man with a Shattered World*. London: Penguin.

Lush, D. (2011). Clinical facts, turning points and complexity theory. *Journal of Child Psychotherapy, 37* (1): 31–51.

MacRury, I., & Rustin, M. J. (2014). *The Inner World of Doctor Who*. London: Karnac.

Mahoney, M., & Moes, A. (1997). Complexity and psychotherapy: Promising dialogues and practical issues. In: P. Perna & F. Masterpasqua (Eds.), *The Psychological Meaning of Chaos: Translating Theory into Practice* (pp. 177–198). Washington, DC: American Psychological Association.

Malinowski, B. (1927). *Sex and Repression in Savage Society*. London: Routledge, 2003.

Mandelbrot, B. (1983). *The Fractal Geometry of Nature* (revised ed.). New York: W. H. Freeman.

Marcuse, H. (1955). *Eros and Civilization*. Boston, MA: Beacon Press.

Marcuse, H. (1958). *Soviet Marxism: A Critical Analysis*. New York: Columbia University Press.

Marcuse, H. (1964). *One-Dimensional Man*. London: Routledge & Kegan Paul.

Marmot, M. (2016). *The Health Gap: Challenge of an Unequal World*. London: Bloomsbury.

Masson, D. (1984). *The Assault on Truth: Freud's Suppression of the Seduction Theory*. London: Faber & Faber.

McCrone, P., Rost, F., Koeser, L., Koutoufa, I., Stephanou, S., Knapp, M., et al. (2017). The economic cost of treatment-resistant depression in patients referred to a specialist service. *Journal of Mental Health* (23 December): 1–7 [Epub ahead of print].

McDougall, J. (1986). *Theatres of the Mind: Illusion and Truth on the Psychoanalytic Stage*. London: Free Association Books.

McDougall, J. (1988). *Dialogue With Sammy: A Psychoanalytic Contribution to the Understanding of Child Psychosis*. London: Free Association Books.

McDougall, J. (1989). *Dialogues with Sammy*. London: Free Association Books.

Mead, M. (1928). *Coming of Age in Samoa*. London: Penguin, 2001.

Medawar, P. (1972). *The Hope of Progress: A Scientist Looks at Problems in Philosophy, Literature and Science*. London: Methuen.

Meltzer, D. (1967). *The Psycho-Analytical Process*. London: Heinemann.

Meltzer, D. (2007). A one-year-old goes to nursery: A parable of confusing times, *Journal of Child Psychotherapy, 10* (1): 89–104.

Meltzer, D. (1984). *Dream Life: A Re-Examination of the Psycho-Analytical Theory and Technique*. London: Karnac, 2009.

Menzies, I. E. P. (1960). The functioning of a social system as a defence against anxiety: A report on the nursing service of a general hospital. *Human Relations, 13*: 95–121.

Menzies Lyth, I. (1989). Day-care of children under five: An action research study. In: *The Dynamics of the Social* (pp. 215–247). London: Free Association Books.

Merridale, C. (2000). *Night of Stone: Death and Memory in Russia*. London: Granta.

Merridale, C. (2005). *Ivan's War*. London: Faber.

Merridale, C. (2016). *Lenin on the Train*. London: Allen Lane.

Merton, R. K. (1968). Sociological theories of the middle range. In: *Social Theory and Social Structure* (revised ed., pp. 39–72). New York: Free Press.

Metz, C. (1974). *Film Language: Semiotics of the Cinema*. Oxford: Oxford University Press.

Midgley, N. (2004). Sailing between Scylla and Charybdis: Incorporating qualitative approaches into child psychotherapy research. *Journal of Child Psychotherapy, 30* (1): 89–111.

Midgley, N. (2006). The inseparable bond between cure and research: Clinical case study as a method of psychoanalytic inquiry. *Journal of Child Psychotherapy, 32* (2): 122–147.

Midgley, N., Anderson, J., Grainger, E., Nesic-Vukovic, T., & Urwin, C. (2009). *Child Psychotherapy and Research*. London: Routledge.

Midgley, N., Ansaldo, F., & Target, M. (2014). The meaningful assessment of therapy outcomes: Incorporating a qualitative study into a randomized controlled trial evaluating the treatment of adolescent depression. *Psychotherapy, 51* (1): 128–137.

Midgley, N., Parkinson, S., Holmes, J., Stapley, E., Eatough, V., & Target, M. (2015). Beyond a diagnosis: The experience of depression among clinically-referred adolescents. *Journal of Adolescence, 44*: 269–279.

Mill, J. S. (1843). *A System of Logic: Ratiocinative and Inductive*. Cambridge: Cambridge University Press, 2011.

Miller, E. J., & Rice, A. K. (1967). *Systems of Organisation: The Control of Task and Sentient Boundaries*. London: Tavistock Publications.

Miller, L., Rustin M. E., Rustin M. J., & Shuttleworth, J. (Eds.) (1989). *Closely Observed Infants*. London: Duckworth.

Miller, M. (1999). Chaos, complexity and psychoanalysis, *Psychoanalytic Psychology*, *16* (3): 355–379.

Mills, C. W. (1959). *The Sociological Imagination*. London: Penguin, 1970.

Mitchell, J. (1974). *Psychoanalysis and Feminism*. London: Allen Lane.

Mitchell, M. (2009). *Complexity: A Guided Tour*. Oxford: Oxford University Press.

Mitscherlich, A., & Mitscherlich, M. (1975). *The Inability to Mourn: Principles of Collective Behaviour*. New York: Grove Press.

Money-Kyrle, R. (1968). Cognitive development. *International Journal of Psychoanalysis*, *49*: 691–698.

Money-Kyrle, R. (1971). The aim of psychoanalysis. *International Journal of Psychoanalysis*, *52*: 103–106.

Moran, G. S., & Fonagy, P. (1987). Psychoanalysis and diabetic control: A single-case study. *British Journal of Medical Psychology*, *60* (4): 357–372.

Moran, M. H. (1991). Chaos theory and psychoanalysis: The fluidistic nature of the mind. *International Review of Psycho-Analysis*, *18* (2): 211–221.

Music, G. (2016). *Nurturing Natures: Attachment and Children's Emotional, Sociocultural and Brain Development* (2nd ed.). London: Routledge.

NICE (2014). *Single Technological Appraisal: Vortioxetine for Treating Major Depressive Disorder. Final Scope*. https://www.nice.org.uk/guidance/ta367/documents/major-depressive-disorder-vortioxetine-id583-final-scope2

Obholzer, A., & Roberts, V. Z. (Eds.) (1994). *The Unconscious at Work*. London: Routledge.

Ogden, B. H., & Ogden, T. H. (2013). *The Analyst's Ear and the Critic's Eye*. London: Routledge.

O'Shaughnessy, E. (1981). A commemorative essay on W. R. Bion's theory of thinking. *Journal of Child Psychotherapy*, *7* (2): 181–189.

O'Shaughnessy, E. (1994). What is a clinical fact? *International Journal of Psychoanalysis*, *75* (5/6): 939–948.

Panksepp, J. (1998). *Affective Neuroscience: The Foundations of Human and Animal Emotions*. New York: Oxford University Press.

Parsons, T. (1951). *The Social System*. London: Routledge & Kegan Paul.

Pavord, A. (2005). *The Naming of Names: The Search for Order in the World of Plants*. London: Bloomsbury.

Perna, P. (1997). Reflections on the therapeutic system as seen from the science of chaos and complexity. In: P. Perna & F. Masterpasqua (Eds.), *The Psychological Meaning of Chaos: Translating Theory into Practice* (pp. 253–271). Washington, DC: American Psychological Association.

Perna, P., & Masterpasqua, F. (1997). The history, meaning and implications of chaos and complexity. In: P. Perna & F. Masterpasqua (Eds.), *The Psychological Meaning of Chaos: Translating Theory into Practice* (pp. 1–19). Washington, DC: American Psychological Association.

Phillips, A. (2007). After Strachey. *London Review of Books, 29* (19): 36–38.

Plath, S. (1963). *The Bell Jar*. London: Faber, 2005.

Poincaré, J. H. (1908). *Science and Method*. New York: Dover, 1952.

Popper, K. R. (1934). *The Logic of Scientific Discovery*. London: Hutchinson, 1959.

Popper, K. R. (1945). *The Open Society and Its Enemies, Vols. 1 & 2*. London: Routledge & Kegan Paul.

Popper, K. R. (1957). *The Poverty of Historicism*. London: Routledge.

Popper, K. R. (1963). *Conjectures and Refutations* (pp. 35–65). London: Routledge & Kegan Paul.

Price, H. S. (2005). Lutfa, a "slow" learner: Understanding school literacy learning in its social and emotional context. *Infant Observation, 8* (1): 45–58.

Price, H. S., & Cooper, A. M. (2012). The baby in mind: The practical and clinical relevance of debates about the epistemological status of the observed baby. In: C. Urwin & J. Sternberg, *Infant Observation and Research: Emotional Processes in Everyday Lives*. London: Routledge.

Prigogine, I. (1996). *The End of Certainty*. New York: Free Press.

Prigogine, I., & Stengers, I. (1984). *Order out of Chaos*. New York: Bantam.

Quinodoz, J.-M. (1994). Clinical facts or psychoanalytic clinical facts. *International Journal of Psychoanalysis, 75* (5/6): 963–976.

Quinodoz, J.-M. (1997). Transitions in psychic structures in the light of deterministic chaos theory. *International Journal of Psychoanalysis, 78*: 699–718.

Ragin, C. C., & Becker, H. S. (Eds.) (2010). *What Is a Case? Exploring the Foundations of Social Enquiry* (11th ed.). Cambridge: Cambridge University Press.

Reicherz, J. (2007). Abduction: The logic of discovery in grounded theory. In A. Bryant & C. Charmaz (Eds.) *The Sage Handbook of Grounded Theory* (pp. 214–228). London: Sage.

Reid, S. (Ed.) (1997). *Developments in Infant Observation: The Tavistock Model*. London: Routledge.

Rey, H. (1994). *Universals of Psychoanalysis in the Treatment of Psychotic and Borderline States*. London: Free Associations Books.

Richards, B. (1994). *Disciplines of Delight*. London: Free Association Books.

Robertson, J. (1952). *A Two-Year-Old Goes to Hospital: A Scientific Film*. London: Concord Media.

Robertson, J. (1958). *Young Children in Hospitals*. New York: Basic Books.

Rose, N. (1999). *Governing the Soul, Second Edition*. London: Free Association Books.

Rosenfeld, H. (1971). A clinical approach to the psychoanalytic theory of the life and death instincts: An investigation into the aggressive aspects of narcissism, *International Journal of Psychoanalysis, 52*: 169–178.

Rosenfeld, H. (1971). A clinical approach to the psychoanalytic theory of the life and death instincts: an investigation into the aggressive aspects of narcissism, *International Journal of Psychoanalysis*, *52*: 169–178.

Rosenfeld, H. (1987). Destructive narcissism and the death instinct. In: *Impasse and Interpretation* (chapter 6). London: Tavistock Publications.

Rost, F., Luyten, P., & Fonagy, P. (2018). The anaclitic-introjective depression assessment: Development and preliminary validity of an observer-rated measure. *Clinical Psychology & Psychotherapy, 25* (2): 195–209.

Ruelle, D. (1991). *Chance and Chaos*. Harmondsworth: Penguin.

Runciman, W. G. (2009). *The Theory of Cultural and Social Selection*. Cambridge: Cambridge University Press.

Rusbridger, R. (2008). The internal world of Don Giovanni. *International Journal of Psychoanalysis, 89* (1): 181–194.

Rusbridger, R. (2013). Projective identification in *Othello* and Verdi's *Otello*. *International Journal of Psychoanalysis, 94*: 33–47.

Rustin, M. E. (1991). The strengths of a practitioner's workshop as a new model in clinical research. In: R. Szur & S. Miller (Eds.), *Extending Horizons: Psychoanalytic Psychotherapy with Children, Adolescents, and Families*. London: Karnac.

Rustin, M. E. (1999). Multiple families in mind. *Clinical Child Psychology and Psychiatry, 4* (1): 51–62.

Rustin, M. E. (2004). What follows family breakdown? Assessing children who have experienced deprivation, trauma and multiple loss. In: M. E. Rustin & E. Quagliata (Eds.), *Assessment in Child Psychotherapy* (pp. 74–94). London: Karnac..

Rustin, M. E. (2005). Conceptual analysis of critical moments in Victoria Climbié's life. *Child and Family Social Work, 10*: 11–19.

Rustin, M. E. (2006). Where do I belong? In: J. Kenrick, C. Lindsey, & L. Tollemache (Eds.), *Creating New Families: New Approaches to Fostering, Adoption and Kinship Care* (pp. 107–126). London: Karnac.

Rustin, M. E., & Bradley, J. (Eds.) (2008). *Work Discussion*. London: Karnac.

Rustin, M. E., & Quagliata, E. (2004). *Assessment in Child Psychotherapy*. London: Karnac.

Rustin, M. E., & Rustin, M. J. (2001). *Narratives of Love and Loss: Studies in Modern Children's Fiction* (2nd ed.). London: Karnac.

Rustin, M. E., & Rustin, M. J. (2002). *Mirror to Nature: Drama, Psychoanalysis and Society*. London: Karnac.

Rustin, M. E., & Rustin, M. J. (2010). States of narcissism. In: E. McGinley & A. Varchevker (Eds.), *Mourning, Depression and Narcissism throughout the Life Cycle*. London: Karnac.

Rustin, M. E., & Rustin, M. J. (2012). Fantasy and reality in Miyazaki's animated world. *Psychoanalysis, Culture and Society, 17* (2): 169–186.

Rustin, M. E., & Rustin, M. J. (2017). *Reading Klein*. London: Routledge.

Rustin, M. E., & Rustin, M. J. (Eds.) (forthcoming). *New Discoveries in Child Psychotherapy: Findings from Qualitative Research*. London: Routledge.

Rustin, M. J. (1991a). Psychoanalysis, philosophical realism, and the new sociology of science: In: *The Good Society and the Inner World*. London: Verso.

Rustin, M. J. (1991b). Thinking in *Romeo and Juliet*. In: *The Good Society and the Inner World*. London: Verso.

Rustin, M. J. (2001). Give me a consulting room . . . The generation of psychoanalytic knowledge. In: *Reason and Unreason: Psychoanalysis, Science, Politics*. London: Continuum Books.

Rustin, M. J. (2002). Looking in the right place: Complexity theory, psychoanalysis and infant observation. *Infant Observation, 5* (1): 122–144.

Rustin, M. J. (2006). Infant observation research: What have we learned so far? *Infant Observation, 9* (1): 35–52.

Rustin, M. J. (2011a). In defence of infant observational research. *European Journal of Psychotherapy and Counselling, 13* (2): 153–168.

Rustin, M. J. (2011b). Infant observation and research: A reply to Steven Groarke. *International Journal of Infant Observation, 14* (2): 179–190.

Rustin, M. J. (2014). *Research on the Couch: Single-Case Studies, Subjectivity and Scientific Knowledge* by R. Hinshelwood [Book Review]. *Journal of Child Psychotherapy, 40* (1): 118–126.

Rustin, M. J. (2016a). Sociology and psychoanalysis. In: A. Elliott & J. Prager (Eds.), *The Routledge Handbook of Psychoanalysis in the Social Sciences and Humanities* (pp. 259–277). London: Routledge.

Rustin, M. J. (2016b). The totalitarian unconscious. In: M. Ffytche & D. Pick (Eds.), *Psychoanalysis in the Age of Totalitarianism* (pp. 221–238). London: Routledge.

Rustin, M. J. (2017a). Narcissism and melancholia from the psychoanalytical perspective of object relations. In: B. Sheils & J. Walsh (Eds.), *Narcissism, Melancholia and the Subject of Community* (pp. 41–63). London: Palgrave Macmillan.

Rustin, M. J. (2017b). Psychoanalysis and cultural studies in Britain. *Psychoanalysis Culture and Society, 22* (3): 243–261.

Sabbadini, A. (2003). *The Couch and the Silver Screen: Psychoanalytic Reflections on European Cinema*. London: Routledge.

Sabbadini, A. (2014). *Moving Images*. London: Routledge.

Sacks, O. (1985). *The Man Who Mistook His Wife for a Hat*. London: Picador.

Sandler J. (1988). *Projection, Identification, Projective Identification*. London: Routledge.

Sandler, J., Sandler, A.-M., & Davies, R. (Eds.) (2000). *Clinical and Observational Psychoanalytic Research: Roots of a Controversy*. London: Karnac.

Saussure, F. de (1916). *Course in General Linguistics*. London: Bloomsbury, 2013.

Sayers, J. (2015). *Art, Psychoanalysis, and Adrian Stokes: A Biography*. London: Karnac.

Scheff, T. J. (1997). *Emotions, the Social Bond and Human Reality: Part–Whole Analysis*. Cambridge: Cambridge University Press.

Scheff, T. J. (1999). *Being Mentally Ill: A Sociological Study* (3rd ed.). London: Routledge.

Schore, A. (1994). *Affect Regulation and the Origin of the Self*. London: Routledge, 2015.

Segal, H. (1952). A psychoanalytical approach to aesthetics. *International Journal of Psychoanalysis*, 33: 196–207.

Segal, H. (1974). Delusion and artistic creativity: Some reflexions on reading "The Spire" by William Golding. *International Review of Psycho-Analysis*, 1: 135–141.

Segal, H. (1984). Joseph Conrad and the mid-life crisis. *International Review of Psycho-Analysis*, 11: 3–9.

Seligman, S. (2005). Dynamic systems theories as a metaframework for psychoanalysis. *Psychoanalytic Dialogues*, 15 (2): 285–319.

Shallcross, W. (2015). *What Can Be Learned from a Single Case of Infant Observation*. Doctoral dissertation, Tavistock and Portman NHS Foundation Trust, London. Available at: http://repository.tavistockand portman.ac.uk/1123/1/Shallcross%20-%20Infant%20Observation%20 thesis.pdf

Shapin, S., & Shaffer, S. (1985). *Leviathan and the Air Pump: Hobbes, Boyle and the Experimental Life*. Princeton, NJ: Princeton University Press.

Sharpe, E. F. (1950). *Collected Papers on Psychoanalysis*. London: Hogarth Press.

Shaw, M., & Smith, G. D. (2008). *The Grim Reaper's Road Map: An Atlas of Mortality in Britain*. Bristol: Policy Press.

Shigeru, I. (1999). Psychotherapy and chaos theory: The metaphoric relationship between psychodynamic therapy and chaos theory. *Psychotherapy: Theory, Research, Practice, Training*, 36 (3): 274–286.

Shulman, G. (2010). The damaged object: A "strange attractor" in the dynamical system of the mind. *Journal of Child Psychotherapy*, 36 (3): 259–288.

Smith, A. (1759). *The Theory of Moral Sentiments*. London: Penguin, 2009.

Smith, J., Flowers, P., & Larkin, M. (2009). *Interpretive Phenomenological Analysis*. London: Sage.

Smith, J. A., Harré, R., & Van Langenhove, L. (1995). Idiography and the case study. In: *Rethinking Psychology*. London: Sage.

Sodré, I. (2014). *Imaginary Existences: A Psychoanalytic Exploration of Phantasy, Fiction, Dreams and Daydreams*. London: Routledge.

Solms, M. (2015). *The Feeling Brain: Selected Papers on Neuropsychoanalysis*. London: Routledge.

Sorensen, P. (2000). Observations of transition facilitating behavior: Developmental and theoretical implications. *International Journal of Infant Observation and Its Applications, 3* (2): 46–54.

Spence, D. P. (1982). *Narrative Truth and Historical Truth: Meaning and Interpretation in Psychoanalysis.* New York: W. W. Norton.

Spence, D. P. (1993). Traditional case studies and prescriptions for improving them. In: N. E. Miller, L. Luborsky, J. P. Barber, & J. P. Docherty (Eds.), *Psychodynamic Treatment Research.* New York: Basic Books.

Spence, D. P. (1994). The special nature of clinical facts. *International Journal of Psychoanalysis, 75* (5/6): 915–926.

Spence, D. P. (1998). Rainforest or mud field? *International Journal of Psychoanalysis, 79:* 643–647.

Spence, D. P. (2000). Remembrance of things past. *Journal of Clinical Psychoanalysis, 9* (1): 149–162.

Spence, D. P. (2002). The virtual case report. *Psychoanalytic Quarterly, 71:* 679–698.

Spence, D. P. (2007). Perils and pitfalls of memory-based reporting: How case histories can become more evidenced-based. *Psychoanalytic Inquiry, 27* (5): 602–616.

Spillius, E. (1976). Hospital and society. *British Journal of Medical Psychology, 49:* 97–140.

Spillius, E. (1993). Asylum and society. In: E. Trist & H. Murray (Eds.), *The Social Engagement of Social Science, Vol. 1: The Socio-Psychological Perspective* (pp. 586–612). Philadelphia, PA: University of Pennsylvania Press.

Spillius, E. B. (2007). Varieties of envious experience. In: *Encounters with Melanie Klein: Selected Papers of Elizabeth Spillius* (pp. 140–162). London: Routledge.

Spillius, E. B., Milton, J., Garvey, P., Couve, C., & Steiner, D. (Eds.) (2011). *The New Dictionary of Kleinian Thought.* London: Routledge.

Spinoza, B. (1677). *Ethics.* London: Dent, 1959.

Spruiell, P. V. (1993). Deterministic chaos and the sciences of complexity: Psychoanalysis in the midst of a general scientific revolution. *Journal of the American Psychoanalytic Association, 41* (1): 3–44.

Stake, E. (1994). Case studies. In N. S. Denzin & Y. S. Lincoln (Eds.), *Handbook of Qualitative Research* (chapter 14). London: Sage.

Stamenova, K., & Hinshelwood, R. D. (Eds.) (forthcoming). *Methods of Research into the Unconscious: Applying Psychoanalytic Ideas to Social Science.* London: Routledge.

Stanford Encyclopedia of Philosophy (2002). *Ludwig Wittgenstein.* https://plato.stanford.edu/entries/wittgenstein

Stanford Encyclopedia of Philosophy (2011). *Thomas Kuhn.* https://plato.stanford.edu/entries/thomas-kuhn

Stanford Encyclopedia of Philosophy (2014). *Donald Davidson*. https://plato.stanford.edu/entries/davidson

Stanford Encyclopedia of Philosophy (2017). *Abduction (with Supplement: Peirce on Abduction)*. https://plato.stanford.edu/entries/abduction

Stanford Graduate School of Business (2018). *Case Study Library*. http://www.laaf.org/case-library

Stapley, E., Midgley, N., & Target, M. (2015). The experience of being the parent of an adolescent with a diagnosis of depression. *Journal of Child and Family Studies, 25* (2): 618–630.

Steiner, J. (1993a). *Psychic Retreats: Pathological Organizations in Psychotic, Neurotic and Borderline Patients*. London: Routledge.

Steiner, J. (1993b). Two types of pathological organisation in *Oedipus the King* and *Oedipus at Colonus*. In: *Psychic Retreats: Pathological Organizations in Psychotic, Neurotic and Borderline Patients*. London: Routledge.

Steiner, R. (1994). "The Tower of Babel" or "after Babel" in contemporary psychoanalysis. *International Journal of Psychoanalysis, 75* (5/6): 883–902.

Stern, D. N. (1985). *The Interpersonal World of the Infant*. London: Karnac.

Sternberg, J. (2005). *Infant Observation at the Heart of Training*. London: Karnac.

Stokes, A., & Williams, M. H. (2014). *Art and Analysis: An Adrian Stokes Reader*. London: Karnac.

Stove, D. (1982). *Popper and After: Four Modern Irrationalists*. Oxford: Pergamon Press.

Strachey, J. (1934). The nature of the therapeutic action of psycho-analysis, *International Journal of Psychoanalysis, 15*: 127–159.

Strübing, S. (2007). Research as pragmatic problem-solving: The pragmatist roots of empirically grounded theorising. In: A. Bryant, & C. Charmaz (Eds.), *The Sage Handbook of Grounded Theory* (pp. 580–602). London: Sage.

Summerson, J. (1963). *Heavenly Mansions*. New York: W. W. Norton.

Szasz, T. (1961). *The Myth of Mental Illness*. New York: Harper & Row.

Taylor, D., Carlyle, J., McPherson, S., Rost, F., Thomas, R., & Fonagy, P. (2012). Tavistock Adult Depression Study (TADS): A randomised controlled trial of psychoanalytic psychotherapy for treatment-resistant/treatment-refractory forms of depression. *BMC Psychiatry, 12* (1): 60.

Tanner, K. (1999). Observation: A counter culture offensive. Observation's contribution to the development of reflective social work practice. *Infant Observation, 2* (2): 12–32.

Tawney, R. H. (1926). *Religion and the Rise of Capitalism*. London: John Murray. Available at: https://archive.org/details/in.ernet.dli.2015.275610

Thompson, P. (1978). *The Voices of the Past: Oral History*. Oxford: Oxford University Press.

Thomson-Salo, F. (2014). *Infant Observation: Creating Transformative Relationships*. London: Routledge.

Toulmin, D. (2001). *Return to Reason*. Cambridge, MA: Harvard University Press.

Toulmin, S. (1972). *Human Understanding*. Princeton, NJ: Princeton University Press.

Trevarthen, C. (2010). Communication and cooperation in early infancy: A description of primary intersubjectivity. In: M. Bullowa (Ed.), *Before Speech: The Beginning of Interpersonal Communication* (pp. 321–349). Cambridge: Cambridge University Press.

Trevarthen, C., & Aitken, K. J. (2001). Intersubjectivity: Research, theory, and clinical applications. *Journal of Child Psychology and Psychiatry*, 42 (1): 3–48.

Trilling, L. (1951). Freud and literature. In: *The Liberal Imagination* (pp. 34–57). London: Mercury Books, 1961.

Trist, E., & Murray, H. (Eds.) (1993a). *The Social Engagement of Social Science, Vol. 1: The Socio-Psychological Perspective*. Philadelphia, PA: University of Pennsylvania Press.

Trist, E., & Murray, H. (Eds.) (1993b). *The Social Engagement of Social Science, Vol. 2: The Socio-Technical Perspective*. Philadelphia, PA: University of Pennsylvania Press.

Trist, E., & Murray, H. (Eds.) (1993c). *The Social Engagement of Social Science, Vol. 3: The Socio-Ecological Perspective*. Philadelphia, PA: University of Pennsylvania Press.

Trotsky, L. (1932). *The History of the Russian Revolution*. London: Pathfinder Press, 1980.

Trotter, W. (1916). *The Instinct of the Herd in Peace and War*. London: Legacy Books, 2010.

Trowell, J. (2011). *Childhood Depression: A Place for Psychotherapy* (pp. 241–253). London: Karnac.

Trowell, J., & Dowling, A. (2011). Reflections and thoughts: Learning from the study. In: J. Trowell (Ed.), *Childhood Depression: A Place for Psychotherapy* (pp. 241–253). London: Karnac.

Trowell, J., & Miles, G. (1991). The contribution of observation training to professional development in social work. *Journal of Social Work Practice*, 5 (1): 51–60.

Tuckett, D. (1993). Some thoughts on the presentation and discussion of the clinical material of psychoanalysis. *International Journal of Psychoanalysis*, 74 (6): 1175–1189.

Tuckett, D. (1994a). The conceptualisation and communication of clinical facts in psychoanalysis: Foreword. *International Journal of Psychoanalysis*, 75 (5/6): 865–870. P866.

Tuckett, D. (1994b). Developing a grounded hypothesis to understand clinical process: The role of conceptualization in validation. *International Journal of Psychoanalysis*, 75 (5/6): 1159–1180.

Tuckett, D. (Ed.) (2008). *Psychoanalysis Comparable and Incomparable: The Evolution of a Method to Describe and Compare Psychoanalytic Approaches.* London: Routledge.

Turner, V. V. (1974). *Dramas, Fields and Metaphors: Symbolic Action in Human Society.* Ithaca, NY: Cornell University Press.

Urry, J. (2003). *Global Complexity.* Cambridge: Polity Press.

Urwin, C. (Ed.) (2007). Becoming a mother: Changing identities. Infant observation in a research project. *Infant Observation, 10* (3): 231–338 [Special Issue].

Urwin, C., & Sternberg, J. (Eds.) (2012). *Infant Observation and Research: Emotional Process in Everyday Lives.* London: Routledge.

Verhulst, F. (1999). Psychoanalysis and chaos theory, *International Journal of Psychoanalysis, 80* (3): 623–625.

Waddell, M. (1999). *Inside Lives.* London: Karnac.

Wakelyn, J. (2000). On looking at still life painting. *Soundings, 15* (Summer).

Wakelyn, J. (2011). Therapeutic observation of an infant in foster care. *Journal of Child Psychotherapy, 37* (3): 280–310.

Walby, S. (2009). *Globalization and Inequalities: Complexity and Contested Modernities.* London: Sage.

Waldrop, M. M. (1992). *Complexity: The Emerging Science at the Edge of Order and Chaos.* New York: Simon & Schuster.

Wallerstein, R. S. (1988). One psychoanalysis or many? *International Journal of Psychoanalysis, 69*: 5–21.

Wallerstein, R. S. (2005). Will psychoanalytic pluralism be the enduring state of our discipline? *International Journal of Psychoanalysis, 86*: 623–626.

Wallerstein, R. S., & Fonagy, P. (1999). Psychoanalytic research and the IPA: History, present status and future potential. *International Journal of Psychoanalysis, 80* (1): 91–110.

Wallerstein, R. S., & Sampson, H. (1971). Issues in research in the psychoanalytic process. *International Journal of Psychoanalysis, 52*: 11–50.

Wattillon-Naveau, A. (1999). The contribution of baby observation to the technique of baby-infant psychotherapy. *Infant Observation, 3* (1): 24–32.

Weber, M. (1930). *The Protestant Ethic and the Spirit of Capitalism.* London: Allen & Unwin.

Weber, M. (1949). *The Methodology of the Social Sciences.* Glencoe, IL: Free Press.

Wesseley, S. (2001). Randomised controlled trials: The gold standard. In: C. Mace, S. Moore, & B. Roberts (Eds.), *Evidence in the Psychological Therapies: A Critical Guide for Practitioners* (pp. 46–60). London: Brunner-Routledge.

White, E. B. (1952). *Charlotte's Web.* London: Penguin, 2014.

WHO (2016). *ICD–10: International Classification of Diseases and Related Health Problems.* Geneva: World Health Organization. Available at: www.who.int/classifications/icd/icdonlineversions/en

Wilkinson, R. G., & Pickett, K. E. (2009). *The Spirit Level: Why More Equal Societies Almost Always Do Better*. London: Allen Lane.

Will, D. (1980). Psychoanalysis as a human science. *British Journal of Medical Psychology*, 53: 201–211.

Will, D. (1986). Psychoanalysis and the new philosophy of science. *International Review of Psycho-Analysis*, 13: 163–173.

Williams, R. (1961). *The Long Revolution*. London: Chatto & Windus.

Williams, R. (1977). Structures of feeling. In: *Marxism and Literature* (pp. 128–135). Oxford: Oxford University Press.

Winnicott, D. W. (1978). *The Piggle: An Account of the Psychoanalytic Treatment of a Little Girl*. London: Penguin, 1991.

Wittgenstein, L. (1953). *Philosophical Investigations*. Oxford: Blackwell.

Wollheim, R. (1968). *Art and Its Objects*. London: Harper & Row.

Wollheim, R. (1987). *Painting as an Art*. London: Thames & Hudson.

Wollheim, R. (1993a). Desire, belief and Dr Grünbaum's Freud. In: *The Mind and Its Depths*. Cambridge, MA: Harvard University Press.

Wollheim, R. (1993b). *The Mind and Its Depths*. Cambridge, MA: Harvard University Press.

Žižek, S. (1990). East Europe's Republics of Gilead. *New Left Review, 183* (Sept.–Oct.): 50–62.

Žižek, S. (1993). Enjoy your nation as yourself. In: *Tarrying with the Negative: Kant, Hegel and the Critique of Ideology* (pp. 200–238). Durham, NC: Duke University Press.

INDEX

Tavistock Adult Depression Study
(TADS) 10, 133, 232, 234, 236
Tavistock and Portman NHS
Foundation Trust 224, 233
Tavistock Clinic 43, 81, 92, 151, 230, 237
Tavistock Institute of Human
Relations 81, 116, 117, 258, 261
Tawney, R. H. 76
Taylor, D. 233
theft of enjoyment 260
theoretical conjecture 9, 50
theoretical entities 54
theoretical sampling 161, 162
theoretical systems, as disciplines 22
theory(ies), general vs. middle-range
145, 159
theory families 54
theory of special relativity 106
therapeutic infant observation 247
therapeutic purpose, of
psychoanalysis 49
thermodynamics, laws of 84, 127
third position 90, 273
Thompson, P. 265
Thomson-Salo, F. 237
tides, ebb and flow of, and phases of
moon, constant conjunction
of 52
tipping point 127
Tolstoy, L. 286
topographical model of mind 61
totalitarian mentalities 256
totalitarian societies 253
Toulmin, D. 93
Toulmin, S. 25, 28
and competitive evolution of
disciplines 22–24
and Kuhn 22–24
toxicity 58
transference(s) (passim)
gathering of 83
as observational research tool
240, 242
role in generation of psychoanalytic
knowledge 240
theory of 69
transference-based interpretation 223

transference–countertransference
interactions/relationship of
psychoanalytic practice 38,
257, 265
access to unconscious structures of
mind in 82
clinical facts located in 8, 138, 156
communications in 69
conscious and unconscious
meanings and intentions in
5, 170
in observational research 245
strange attractors in 134
understanding of clinical patients
in 249
transference–countertransference
phenomena 39, 69, 140, 178
transference interpretation 105
transference phenomena, unconscious
39
transference projections 266
transference relationship 6, 27, 28, 66,
68, 83, 143, 144, 149, 152, 158,
232, 240, 258, 277
transference situation, total 170
as object of investigation 38
transference theory 68
transitional phenomena 221
transitional space 221
transmission, rhizomatic 43
Treatment as Usual (TAU) 228, 233
treatment equivalence 102
Trevarthen, C. 241
Trilling, L. 25, 268, 270
Trist, E. 81, 122, 258, 259
Trotsky, L. 129
Trotter, W. 252
Trowell, J. 224, 227, 230, 237
Truffaut, F. 283, 286
Tucha, L. 59
Tucha, O. 59
Tuckett, D. 8, 137, 139, 154, 174, 176
tuning variable 134
Turner, V. V. 64
turning a blind eye 109, 260, 278
turning point(s) 128, 135, 153
Tustin, F. 221

unconscious anxiety, social defences
    against 261
unconscious communication 68
unconscious mind, theory of 88
unconscious phantasy(ies) 26, 58, 68,
    121, 138
  effect of 39
unconscious phenomena 2, 25, 107,
    140, 269, 274
unconscious, the 55, 145
  as actant 43
  discovery of, by artists, poets, and
      philosophers 270, 275, 285
  Freud's discoveries about 25
  as object of psychoanalytic cultural
      study 269–274
  royal road to 27
  science of 4
Urry, J. 4, 129, 158
Urwin, C. 173, 240, 243, 250, 266

Van Langenhove, L. 41, 95
Velasquez, D. 283
Verdi, G. 280, 281
Verhulst, F. 136
virus(es) 88, 112
  biological 37, 53
  computer 37, 53

Waddell, M. 268, 280
Wakelyn, J. 247, 281
Walby, S. 129
Waldrop, M. M. 136
Wallace, W. 86
Wallerstein, R. S. 76, 137, 139, 154
Ward, I. 275

Wattillon-Naveau, A. 247
wave optics 17
Weber, M. 63, 64, 71, 252
Wengraf, T. 265
Wesseley, S. 101
White, E. B. 276
WHO *see* World Health Organization
wild analysis 255
Wilkinson, R. G. 219
Will, D. 59
Williams, G. 244, 264
Williams, M. H. 268, 280, 281
Williams, R. 75, 269
Winnicott, D. W. 27, 110, 173,
    221, 241
Wittgenstein, L. 23, 71, 74
Wolf Man (Freud) 100
Wollheim, R. 28, 72, 268, 284
Woolf, V. 284
Woolgar, S. 31, 84, 106
Wordsworth, W. 118, 270, 282
work discussion(s) 10, 239, 248, 24
  methods, as research tool 245
  psychoanalytic 238, 264, 265
work group 262
World Health Organization (WHO)
    6, 79

X-ray crystallography 88

Yates, C. 275
young child observation 254, 264
  as observational research tool 237,
      238, 239, 244, 245, 248, 249

Žižek, S. 251, 252, 260, 276

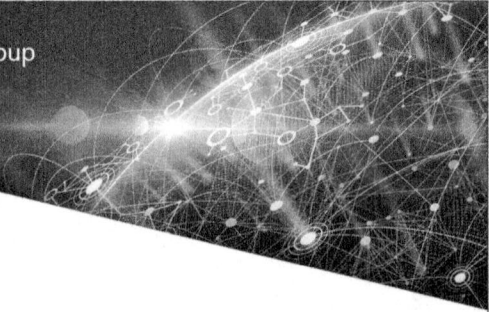

Printed in Dunstable, United Kingdom

64752085R00194